Study Guide to Accompan
Anderson, Sweeney, and Willi...

AN INTRODUCTION TO
MANAGEMENT SCIENCE

QUANTITATIVE APPROACHES TO DECISION MAKING

Second Edition

Prepared by

John A. Lawrence, Jr.
Barry Alan Pasternack
California State University
Fullerton, California

WEST PUBLISHING COMPANY
St. Paul   New York   Los Angeles   San Francisco

HOW TO USE THIS STUDY GUIDE

The Study Guide for An Introduction to Management Science is a useful supplement for reinforcing and expanding the ideas and techniques of the text. It is not simply a programmed text, a review booklet, or a collection of problems. Rather, all these concepts, as well as others, are incorporated into the study guide. Its goal is to not only help reinforce the concepts introduced in the text, but also allow for further development of the models, the recognition of new applications, and model limitations.

Each chapter of the study guide corresponds to the same chapter in the text and consists of five parts: (1) the "key concepts" of the chapter; (2) the chapter "review"; (3) the chapter "glossary"; (4) the chapter "check list"; and (5) an extensive "problem" section. All notation and approaches to the quantitative techniques in the study guide coincide with those of the text, making cross reference and use easy. All problems in the study guide, however, are different from those in the text. This provides you the opportunity to draw on a wide variety of problems and to gauge the importance of the subject matter in a broader spectrum of business situations.

The "key concepts" section consists of statements of the central ideas and themes of the chapter. It is broad in description but capsulizes the thrust of the chapter. It is intended to answer the question, "What should be learned from this chapter?"

The "review" section outlines the chapter. Emphasis is placed on the assumptions, descriptions, and solution techniques of the models presented in the chapter. Algorithms and approaches are summarized for easy reference (however they are not developed as this is the function of the text itself). The review section is divided into two to four subsections with each subsection summarizing the correspondingly numbered key concept. Occasionally, some of the ideas of the text are expanded slightly. In short, the review section provides a concise synopsis of the chapter material without giving a detailed analysis of derivations.

The "glossary" section lists alphabetically the nomenclature which is introduced for the first time in the chapter. These words and phrases are part of the vocabulary of management science and should be mastered for a clear understanding of the material. Some of the definitions are stated differently in the study guide than in the text, although, of course, they do not vary in meaning. Page numbers giving the first appearance of the word or phrase in the text are provided for quick reference.

The chapter "check list" is a concise list of the techniques to be learned in each chapter. Each topic is presented with a reference to the section in which the topic is discussed. A small space is also provided so that you may write, in your own words, a brief description of the topic. This is intended to provide an excellent outline and review of the major points in the chapter. As the pages of the study guide are perforated, you may wish to remove these pages for studying or reference use during open book examinations.

The purpose of the "problem" section is to aid, solidify, and challenge your understanding of the material. This section is designed so that you are gradually given more independence in the problem solution by first observing a problem worked in full, then performing the required operations in an outlined problem, and finally solving problems without the benefit of any aids. The first problem of each chapter is always worked in full to illustrate an approach and show the necessary calculations. Several other problems in the chapter are also worked in full at various points in the section, usually where new major concepts are introduced. Following many completely worked problems are problems whose solutions are outlined. This means the approach is outlined, but you must carry through with the calculations that are demanded in the outline. Answers to the various parts of the outlined problems are given as the problem is worked as a check. Finally, about two-thirds of the problems in the section are given without any hints or aids. Below each of these problems space is provided in which to work out the solution. Answers to selected problems are provided in the back of the study guide for your use; however, the actual solution procedure is not given. Problems worked in full are preceded by a "W", those outlined are preceded by an "O", and those with answers in the back of the text are preceded by an "*".

The study guide and text are designed to complement each other. To effectively use this study guide we recommend that you first read the material in the text. The study guide will serve to highlight the important concepts introduced in the text and give additional examples of the analyses and procedures covered.

Before beginning the problems in each chapter of the study guide or the text we advocate a reading of the "review section" for that chapter. This should serve as a concise summary of the information contained in that chapter and aid in placing the material in its proper perspective. The problems worked in full or outlined should next be reviewed to familiarize yourself with the solution procedure. Once this is completed you should find yourself ready to solve the remaining problems contained in the "problem section".

CONTENTS

1 INTRODUCTION

KEY CONCEPTS

1. Definition and value of management
   science in decision making
2. General quantitative analysis approach
   to decision making

REVIEW

1. Management Science

Management science is a term given to a general approach to decision making which is based on the scientific method of problem solving.
Although there exists no common definition of management science, it can
be thought of as the art of mathematical modeling of decision problems and
the science of developing solution techniques for these mathematical
models. Several reasons for a management science approach to decision
making include: (1) the problem may be too complex to be handled any other
way; (2) quantitative justification may be required (by stockholders,
government agencies, etc.); (3) the problem may be a new one with no past
experience upon which to make a logical decision; (4) the problem may be a
recurring one, and the same quantitative procedure may be used repetitively
for decision making with only changes in the input data.

There are several advantages to mathematical modeling: (1) it
helps to deal with a problem in its entirety; (2) it enables the manager
to view a problem concisely and determine what data is relevant; (3) it
may help reveal cause-effect relationships which are not immediately
apparent; and most importantly, (4) hopefully, a mathematical model can be
solved so that a solution can be recommended. One disadvantage is that
mathematical models are only idealizations of real-life. Many assumptions

1

are made, and estimates and "guesstimates" are usually employed within the model. Hence a solution to the model is precisely that--a solution to a model. Care must be exercised in implementing the conclusions of the model in the real situation.

2. Quantitative Approach to Decision Making

A general five-step quantitative approach to decision making can be stated.

Step one is problem definition. Here, a need for a management science approach is recognized. The problem must be precisely and concisely defined. A "problem" can mean: (1) a new situation for which a course of action has not been determined; (2) an area which has not performed as anticipated for which corrective action may be indicated; or (3) simply a re-evaluation of current policy to see if improvement can be made.

Step two is model development. In this step the parameters or uncontrollable inputs of the problem must be recognized, the decision variables or controllable inputs specified, and the objective and constraints expressed quantitavely. If any of the uncontrollable inputs of the model are subject to variation, the model is called a stochastic model; otherwise the model is referred to as a deterministic model. Mathematical models are built by "translating" verbal statements into mathematical expressions involving the decision variables of the problem. For instance, consider a company which has a contract calling for 1,000 units per day and has two plants which can produce 700 and 800 per 24 hour day respectively. Then if we let x be the number of hours per day the first plant is operational, y be the number of hours per day the second plant is operational, we would write, "the number of units produced at the first plant plus the number of units produced at the second plant is at least 1,000" as:

$$700 \left(\frac{x}{24}\right) + 800 \left(\frac{y}{24}\right) \geq 1,000.$$

Step three is the data gathering step where the data concerning the uncontrollable inputs is sought. This is usually very time consuming. Some data may be readily available, but other data must be obtained by accounting reports, extensive statistical studies, or even by "best guess" or approximations.

Step four is the model solution step where the "best" feasible solution (one satisfying all of the stated constraints) is generated. If the solution appears highly illogical or proves not to be as accurate as desired, modifications to the model are made. It could be that even the general form of the model is changed, and the problem solved again.

After the model appears to give satisfactory results, a report must be generated to convey the model's solutions. This report should contain a statement of the problem, the assumptions made, and an indication of the general approach to problem solution. Of course a concise summary of a recommendation based on the model's results should be stated. The report should be written in such a way that it is easily understood by the decision maker.

Often extremely accurate but very complex mathematical models can be developed for certain problems. However, due to their complexity, techniques may not be available for easily solving the model. Additionally the cost involved in modeling the intricacies may outweigh any benefit derived from it. Also data upon which the model is predicated may be rough at best. Hence sometimes from both a cost-effective and mathematical point of view, it is beneficial to develop and solve less accurate but simpler models than highly complex ones.

GLOSSARY

ANALOG MODEL - While physical in form, a model that does not have a physical appearance similar to the real object or situation it represents. (6)

CONSTRAINTS - Restrictions or limitations imposed on the problem situation. (8)

CONTROLLABLE INPUT - The decision alternatives or inputs that can be specified by the decision maker. (9)

DETERMINISTIC MODEL - A model where all uncontrollable inputs are known and cannot vary. (9)

FEASIBLE SOLUTION - A decision alternative or solution that satisfies all constraints. (12)

ICONIC MODEL - Physical replica or representation of a real object. (6)

INFEASIBLE SOLUTION - A decision alternative or solution that violates one or more constraints. (11)

MATHEMATICAL MODEL - Mathematical symbols and expressions used to represent a real situation. (6)

OBJECTIVE FUNCTION - A mathematical expression used to identify the objective of a problem situation. (8)

STOCHASTIC MODEL - A model where at least one uncontrollable input is uncertain and subject to variation. (10)

UNCONTROLLABLE INPUT - The environmental factors or inputs that cannot be specified by the decision maker. (9)

Chapter 1 Check List

W 1) Consider a department store which must make weekly shipments of a certain product from two different warehouses to four branch stores.

    a) How could management science be used to solve this problem?

    b) What would be the uncontrollable inputs for which data must be gathered?

    c) What would be the decision variables of the mathematical model? The objective function? The constraints?

    d) Is the model stochastic or deterministic?

    e) Can you suggest assumptions that could be made to simplify the model?

SOLUTION:

    a) Management science can provide a systematic, quantitative approach for determining a minimum cost shipment from the warehouse to the stores.

    b) Fixed costs and variables shipping costs; the demand each week at each store; the supply each week at each warehouse.

    c) Decision variables – how much to ship from each warehouse to each store; objective function – minimize total shipping costs; constraints – meet the demand at the stores without exceeding supplies at the warehouses.

    d) Stochastic – weekly demands fluctuate as do weekly supplies; transportation costs could vary depending on the amount shipped, the other goods sent with this shipment, the time of year, etc.

    e) Make the model deterministic by assuming fixed shipping costs per item, demand is constant at each store each week, and the weekly supplies in the warehouses are also constant.

2) Consider a company which is about to introduce three new items. Each
    of the items is made from two different compounds. The company figures
    it can sell all the items it can make if it sells them at current
    market value.

    a) How could management science be used to solve this problem?

    b) What would be the uncontrollable inputs for which data must be
        gathered?

    c) What would be the decision variables of the mathematical model?

    d) Is the model stochastic or deterministic?

    e) Can you suggest assumptions that could be made to simplify the
        model?

* 3) Zizzle Company is a new small local company that is about to manufacture Zizzle briefcases in three styles. The company wants to
determine how to use its resources most efficiently to get the product
mix that will maximize its profits. One manager has advocated hiring
an outside consulting firm to analyze sales potentials and customer
preferences. He also suggests doing a complete time and motion study
of the production process and analyzing the potential for acquiring
additional manpower and material resources. In short he is suggesting
an extremely accurate but complex study. A second manager suggests a
simplified model using "best guesses", rough approximations and simplifying assumptions as a starting point. The data for this model can be
obtained in a short period of time, and the model can be solved
"in house" at a fraction of the cost of the more complex model. Which
manager's advice would you follow?

4) Suppose the Zizzle Company of problem 3 is a large national conglom-
erate which plans to market tens of thousands of the briefcases. Which
manager's advice would you follow in this case?

* 5) List the five steps in quantitative decision making and discuss the possible problems that could occur at each step.

W 6) Phontose Company has determined that the price it can charge for its new phone answering machine with deluxe controls depends on the quantity produced. Based on supply and demand considerations, for each 1,000 produced per month the price must be reduced $2. Currently Phontose is producing 5,000 per month and selling them at $155. It has facilities for producing 15,000 per month. Because of commitments, Phontose will not decrease its production.

    a) Write a mathematical model which will give the selling price of telephone answering machines, P, based on the number produced per month, x.

    b) Write a mathematical model in terms of P and x which gives the total revenue, R, based on the number of telephone answering machines produced in a month.

    c) Rewrite the mathematical model in (b) for the total revenue in terms of x only.

(Continued)

d) If the objective is to maximize the total revenue, write a complete mathematical model of the problem taking the production limit into account.

SOLUTION:

a) Since selling price is decreased $2 per 1,000 produced, we can conclude that if 0 were sold the price would be (5 x 2) = $10 greater than the current selling price of $155, i.e. 165.

Now P = 165 − $2 (number of thousands produced)

$$= 165 - 2 \left(\frac{x}{1,000}\right)$$

$$= 165 - .002x.$$

b) R = (price per item) x (number of items produced)
    = Px

c) Substitute from part (a) for P:

R = Px
   = (165 − .002x)x =
   $$= 165x - .002x^2$$

d) Verbally, maximize revenue subject to

1) amount produced is less than or equal to 15,000.
2) amount produced is greater than or equal to 5,000.

Thus the mathematical model is:

MAX $165x - .002x^2$

s.t.   x $\leq$ 15,000

        x $\geq$ 5,000

0 7) Bank Guard Company provides security service for banks and savings and loan companies during business hours. The number of guards supplied is a function of the average number of people in the facility. If L = the average number of people in the facility and one guard is provided for an average of 25 customers develop a mathematical model for N, the number of guards required by a bank. If the cost per guard is C_G per hour develop a mathematical model for C, the daily cost of guard service (based on an 8 hour day).

(Continued)

Outline of Solution:

$$\text{Number of guards required} = \frac{\text{Average number people in facility}}{25 \text{ people per guard}}$$

Daily cost = (Cost per guard per hour) x 8 (Hours per day) x (Number of guards required)

Answer: $C = .32C_G L$

8) For problem 7, suppose the cost of night guard service is C_N, develop a mathematical model for the total cost of security for a 24 hour day. What is the total security cost if C_G = $10/hour, C_N = $100 per night and L = 50 people? Discuss your model if L = 65 people.

* 9) Three crude oils are to be blended into two grades of gasoline: regular and premium. The cost of the crude oils are C_1, C_2, and C_3 per gallon respectively, and the selling price for regular is S_R, and for premium is S_P. There are restrictions on the percentage of each crude oil that can be blended into regular and premium mixtures.

a) Given the above problem, as a manager, what are the uncontrollable inputs of this problem? What are the controllable inputs (decision variables)?

b) Develop a mathematical model for the profit function for this problem.

10) a) For problem 9, develop mathematical models for the following two constraints:

   i) The amount of crude oil 1 used in regular must not exceed 10% of the total gasoline mixture of regular.

   ii) The amount of crude oil 3 used in premium must be at least 50% of the total gasoline mixture of premium.

b) If S_R = .65, S_P = .70, C_1 = .50, C_2 = .52, C_3 = .55 and if the daily availability of the crude oils are 1,000, 2,000, and 500 gallons respectively, develop a mathematical model that will maximize daily profit subject to the supply constraints and the constraints of part (a) of this example.

2 LINEAR PROGRAMMING: THE GRAPHICAL METHOD

1. Definition and introduction of linear programs

2. Graphical solution procedure for linear programs in two variables

3. Mathematical terminology and concepts for solving linear programs in more than two variables (the procedure to be presented in the next chapter)

REVIEW

1. Linear Programs

A _linear program_ is a mathematical model which seeks to maximize or minimize a linear _objective function_ (such as profit or cost) subject to linear inequalities or equalities called _constraints_. Mathematically this means that in the objective function and in each constraint, each variable appears in a separate term multiplied by a constant (which could be 0) and is raised to the first power. Conceptually this means that if we are considering manufacturing product Y which nets a profit of $5 per pound, that if two pounds are manufactured the profit contribution is $10, and if 2,000 pounds are manufactured the profit contribution is $10,000. Thus the profit is $5 per pound regardless of the amount of product Y produced. Similarly if 3/4 pound of copper and 1/4 pound of iron go into making one pound of product Y, then if two pounds of product Y are produced, 1½ pounds of copper and ½ pound of iron will be used, and if 2,000 pounds of product Y are produced, then 1,500 pounds of copper and 500 pounds of iron will be used. Again the 3/4 pound of copper and 1/4 pound of iron per pound of product Y do not vary with the amount of product Y produced.

Additionally, the variables are assumed to be non-negative and can take on a continuous range of values. This means for example they can not be restricted to whole numbers only.

2. Graphical Method

A linear program in two variables can be solved graphically by the following procedure:

1) Graph each constraint

   Do this by graphing each constraint as a straight line equation. One side is the "less than" side, the other the "greater than" side. To determine which side is which take any point on one side (such as (0,0)) and plug in its values for x_1 and x_2 to see if it gives a number which is less than or greater than the right hand side value of the constraint. The intersection of all constraints is the feasible solution region.

2) Assign an arbitrary value to the objective function and graph this straight line equation.

3) Move this line parallel to itself (so that the value of the objective function increases for a maximization problem or decreases for a minimization problem) until the last point of the feasible region is touched.

4) Determine the optimal solution by solving the two equations in two unknowns which determine this point.

5) Substitute these values back into the objective function to determine the optimal value of the objective function.

Note that if a linear program has an optimal solution, it will occur at an extreme point. If the objective function is parallel to one of the constraints, it can happen that the last points touched are the entire line segment of this constraint. In this case, all points on this line segment, including the two extreme points, are optimal solutions.

3. Equation Solving and Standard Form

One way to solve several simultaneous linear equations in several unknowns is by elementary row operations consisting of:

1) Multiplying an equation by a non-zero constant;

2) Adding a multiple of one equation to another equation.

The solution to the equations does not change as a result of performing elementary row operations. The objective of row operations in solving equations is to transform the equations so that for each equation there appears a variable multiplied by +1 in this equation, and the same variable is multiplied by zero in every other equation.

In linear programming problems with several variables it is necessary to work with equations, not inequalities. To transform a "less than or equal to" constraint into an equality it is necessary to add a variable called a <u>slack variable</u>. To transform a "greater than or equal to" constraint into an equality it is necessary to subtract a variable called a <u>surplus variable</u>. Both slack and surplus variables are also non-negative. A linear program in which all the constraints have been transformed into equations and whose variables are all non-negative is said to be in <u>standard form</u>.

CONSTRAINT - An equation or inequality which limits the values the decision variables can assume.   (22)

DECISION VARIABLES - The variables of a problem which can be assigned values by the decision maker.   (24)

ELEMENTARY ROW OPERATIONS - A procedure for finding the solution to a system of simultaneous linear equations.   (57)

EXTREME POINT - A corner point of the feasible region of the constraints of a linear programming problem.   (42)

FEASIBLE REGION - The set of all possible feasible solutions.   (34)

FEASIBLE SOLUTION - A solution that satisfies all the constraints of the problem including the non-negativity constraints.   (25)

LINEAR EQUATIONS OR FUNCTIONS - Mathematical expressions in which each term is of the form of a constant times a variable raised to the first power (plus a constant).   (28)

LINEAR PROGRAM - A mathematical model which seeks to maximize or minimize a linear objective function subject to linear constraints in non-negative variables.   (27)

MATHEMATICAL MODEL - A representation of a problem by mathematical expressions.   (27)

NON-NEGATIVITY CONSTRAINTS - Constraints which allow the decision variables to assume only positive or zero values.   (27)

OBJECTIVE FUNCTION - A mathematical function that is to be maximized or minimized.   (24)

OPTIMAL SOLUTION - The feasible solution which gives the best value of the objective function.   (25)

REDUNDANT CONSTRAINT - A constraint which when removed does not alter the feasible region.   (41)

SIMULTANEOUS LINEAR EQUATIONS - A system of linear equations each of which must be satisfied by the same values of the variables.   (57)

SLACK VARIABLE - A variable added to the left hand side of a "less than or equal to" constraint to transform it into an equation.   (53)

SOLUTION - Any set of values for the decision variables.   (25)

STANDARD FORM - A linear program in which all the constraints are
equalities and all the variables are restricted to be non-negative.
(52)

SURPLUS VARIABLE - A variable subtracted from the left hand side of a
"greater than or equal to" constraint to transform it into an
equation.   (55)

Chapter 2 Check List

W 1) Given the following linear program:

$$\text{MAX} \quad 5x_1 + 2x_2$$

$$\text{s.t.} \quad x_1 + x_2 \leq 5$$

$$x_1 + 2x_2 \leq 8$$

$$x_1, x_2 \geq 0$$

a) Solve graphically for the optimal solution to the linear program.

b) Suppose the last constraint were $x_1 + 2x_2 \leq b$, where b is some positive constant. For what values of b is this constraint a redundant constraint?

SOLUTION:

a) (1) Graph the equation $x_1 + x_2 = 5$.

When $x_1 = 0$, $x_2 = 5$.

When $x_2 = 0$, $x_1 = 5$.

Draw the line between these points. (0,0) is on. the "less than" side. Graph the line $x_1 + 2x_2 = 8$.

Draw the line between these points. (0,0) is on the "less than" side.

(2) Set $5x_1 + 2x_2 = 10$ (say)

When $x_1 = 0$, $x_2 = 5$.

When $x_2 = 0$, $x_1 = 2$.

Draw the line between these points.

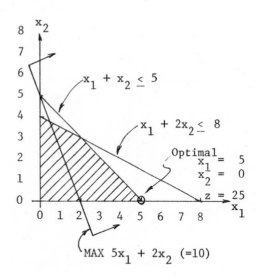

(3) Move the objective function line parallel to itself until it touches the last point of the feasible region (the intersection of the x_1 axis and the first constraint.

(4) Solve for the optimal solution. $x_1 + x_2 = 5$ and $x_2 = 0$ gives $x_1 = 5$, $x_2 = 0$ as the optimal solution.

(5) Substitute these values into objective function: $z = 5(5) + 2(0) = 25$ for the optimal value of the objective function.

b) Note that changing b moves this line parallel to itself. The constraint set will change as b changes until it just touches the set formed by the x_1-axis, the x_2-axis, and the constraint $x_1 + x_2 \leq 5$. This occurs at $x_1 = 0$, $x_2 = 5$. Substituting, this gives $b = x_1 + 2x_2 = (0) + 2(5) = 10$. For $b \geq 10$, the feasible region is formed by the x_1-axis, the x_2-axis, and $x_1 + x_2 \leq 5$.

W 2) Given the following linear program:

$$\text{MAX} \quad 4x_1 + 5x_2$$

$$\text{s.t.} \quad x_1 + 3x_2 \leq 22$$

$$-x_1 + x_2 \leq 4$$

$$x_2 \leq 6$$

$$2x_1 - 5x_2 \leq 0$$

$$x_1, x_2 \geq 0$$

a) Solve the problem by the graphical method.

b) What would be the optimal solution if the second constraint were $-x_1 + x_2 = 4$?

c) What would be the optimal solution if the first constraint were $x_1 + 3x_2 \geq 22$?

SOLUTION: (See the graph following step (5))

a) (1) Graph $x_1 + 3x_2 = 22$. When $x_1 = 0$, $x_2 = 7\ 1/3$; when $x_2 = 4$, $x_1 = 10$. Draw the line. (0,0) is on the "less than" side.

Graph the line $-x_1 + x_2 = 4$. When $x_1 = 0$, $x_2 = 4$; when $x_2 = 6$, $x_1 = 2$. Draw the line. $(0,0)$ is on the "less than" side.

Graph the line $x_2 = 6$. This is a horizontal line with $x_2 = 6$. $(0,0)$ is on the "less than" side.

Graph the line $2x_1 - 5x_2 = 0$. When $x_1 = 0$, $x_2 = 0$. When $x_1 = 5$, $x_2 = 2$. Draw the line. $(1,1)$ is on the "less than" side.

(2) Set $4x_1 + 5x_2 = 20$(say). Graph this line. When $x_1 = 0$, $x_2 = 4$; when $x_2 = 0$, $x_1 = 5$. Draw the line.

(3) Move the objective function line parallel to itself until the last point of the feasible region is touched. This is at the intersection of the first and fourth constraints.

(4) Solve for the optimal solution (by elementary row operations): The point is on the following two lines:

$$x_1 + 3x_2 = 22$$
$$2x_1 - 5x_2 = 0$$

There is already a $+1$ multiplying x_1 in first constraint. We want to eliminate x_1 from second constraint. Subtract from the second constraint 2 times the first constraint (leave the first constraint alone). Result:

$$x_1 + 3x_2 = 22$$
$$-11x_2 = -44$$

Now divide the second constraint by -11. This will give $+1$ multiplying x_2 in this constraint. To eliminate x_2 from first constraint, multiply the <u>new</u> constraint by 3 and subtract from first constraint. Result:

$$x_1 = 10$$
$$x_2 = 4$$

(5) Substitute these values into the objective function:
$z = 4(10) + 5(4) = 60$. This is the optimal value of the
objective function.

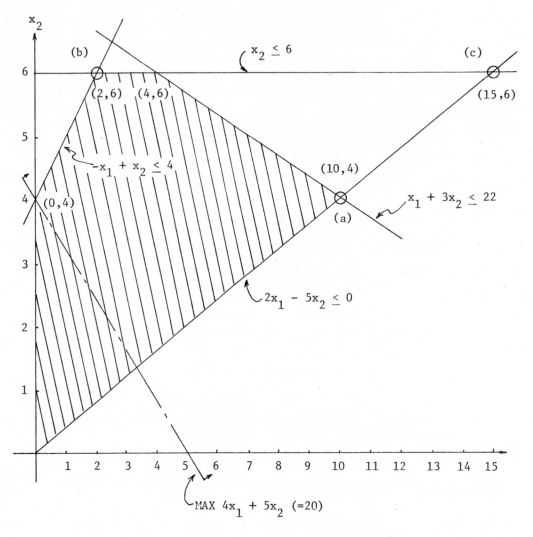

b) The feasible region is simply the line segment of $-x_1 + x_2 = 4$
between $(0,4)$ and $(2,6)$. Observe that $(2,6)$ gives the optimal
solution.

c) The feasible region is now the triangular section between $(4,6)$,
$(15,6)$ and $(10,4)$. Observe $(15,6)$ gives the optimal solution.

0 3) Solve graphically for the optimal solution to the following linear program:

$$\text{MIN} \quad 5x_1 + 2x_2$$

$$\text{s.t.} \quad 2x_1 + 5x_2 \geq 10$$

$$4x_1 - x_2 \geq 12$$

$$x_1 + x_2 \geq 4$$

$$x_1, \, x_2 \geq 0$$

Outline of Solution:

(1) Graph $2x_1 + 5x_2 = 10$. Which side is the "greater than" side?

Graph $4x_1 - x_2 = 12$. Which side is the "greater than" side?

Graph $x_1 + x_2 = 4$. Which side is the "greater than" side?

(2) Graph $5x_1 + 2x_2 = 10$ (say).

(3) Move this line parallel to itself (toward smaller values of objective function) until the last point of the feasible region is touched.

(4) Which lines intersect at this point? Solve the two equations in two unknowns.

(5) Substitute your solution into the objective function to find the optimal value.

Answer: $x_1 = 16/5$; $x_2 = 4/5$; $z = 88/5$

O 4) Given the following linear program:

$$\text{MAX} \quad 4x_1 + 2x_2$$

$$\text{s.t.} \quad x_1 \quad \leq \quad 4$$

$$3x_1 + 8x_2 \leq 24$$

$$2x_1 + x_2 \geq 6$$

$$x_1, x_2 \geq 0$$

a) Solve the problem graphically.

b) What would be the optimal solution(s) if the objective function were MIN $4x_1 + 2x_2$?

Outline of Solution:

a) (1.) Graph x_1 = 4 (a vertical line). Which side is the "less than" side?

Graph $3x_1 + 8x_2$ = 24. Which side is the "less than" side?

Graph $2x_1 + x_2$ = 6. Which side is the "greater than" side?

(2) Graph $4x_1$ to $2x_2$ = 16 (say).

(3) Move this line parallel to itself increasing the value of the objective function until the last point of the feasible region is touched.

(4) Which lines intersect at this point? Solve the two equations in two unknowns.

(5) Substitute your solution into the objective function to find the optimal value of the objective function.

b) Now move the objective function line in the other direction until it touches the last points of the feasible region. This will be an entire line segment. Solve for the extreme points of the line segment by solving two equations in two unknowns for each point. The answer is that the optimal solution can be either extreme point or any point on the line segment in between.

Answers:

a) $x_1 = 4$; $x_2 = 3/2$; $z = 19$.

b) The optimal solution occurs at the following extreme points:
$x_1 = 3$; $x_2 = 0$; and $x_1 = 24/13$, $x_2 = 30/13$; and also at all
points between these two points on the line segment: $2x_1 + x_2 = 6$.

* 5) Solve graphically for the optimal solution to the following linear
program:

$$MAX \quad 8x_1 + 10x_2$$

$$s.t. \quad x_1 + 4x_2 \leq 12$$

$$3x_1 + 2x_2 \leq 12$$

$$2x_1 + x_2 \leq 8$$

$$x_1, x_2 \geq 0$$

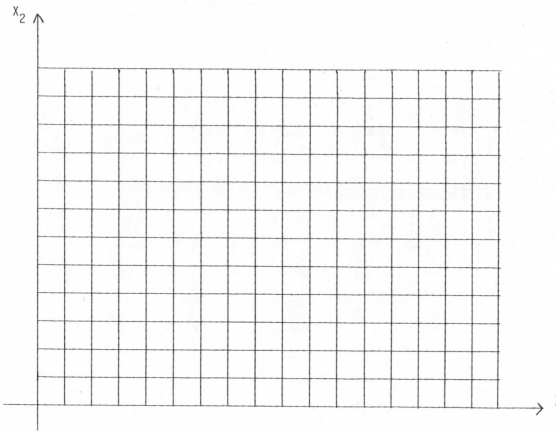

6) Given the following linear program:

$$\text{MAX} \quad 4x_1 + x_2$$

$$\text{s.t.} \quad 2x_1 + 3x_2 \leq 12$$

$$x_1 + 2x_2 \leq 4$$

$$3x_1 + 2x_2 \leq 12$$

$$x_1, \, x_2 \geq 0$$

a) Solve the linear program by the graphical method. Identify any redundant constraints.

b) Repeat part a) given that the objective function is a MINIMIZATION and all constraints are "greater than or equal to".

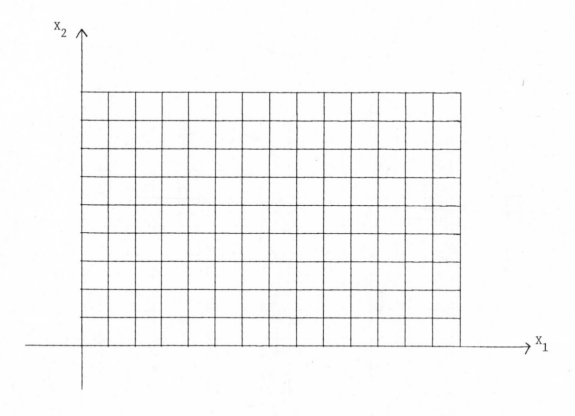

7) Given the following constraint set for a linear program:

$$7x_1 + 2x_2 \le 14$$

$$x_1 + 4x_2 \le 10$$

$$3x_1 + 7x_2 \le 21$$

$$x_1, x_2 \ge 0$$

a) Suppose Shifty Consulting Service told you the optimal solution to a linear program with this constraint set was $x_1 = 1$, $x_2 = 3$. How do you know Shifty is wrong?

b) Suppose Shifty Consulting Service told you the optimal solution to a linear program with this constraint set was $x_1 = 1$, $x_2 = 2$. How do you know Shifty is wrong?

c) What is the optimal solution if the objective function is MAX $x_1 + 2x_2$?

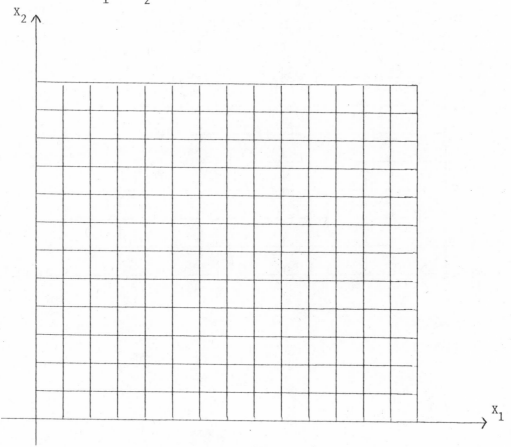

* 8) Consider the following constraint set for a linear programming problem:

$$x_1 \le 5$$
$$3x_1 + 2x_2 \le 18$$
$$x_1 + x_2 \le 7$$
$$x_1, x_2 \ge 0$$

a) Identify all extreme points of the feasible region.

b) For each extreme point, construct an objective function so that extreme point is the only optimal solution for the problem.

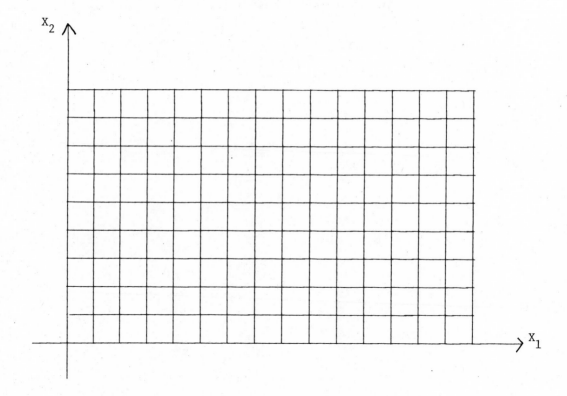

9) Given the following linear program:

$$\text{MAX} \quad 2x_1 - x_2$$

$$\text{s.t.} \quad 3x_1 + 4x_2 \leq 12$$

$$-x_1 + x_2 \leq 0$$

$$x_1 + 5x_2 \leq 5$$

$$x_1, x_2 \geq 0$$

a) Solve the problem by the graphical method.

b) Suppose the constraint $x_2 \leq 2$ were added. How would this affect the optimal solution?

c) Suppose the constraint $x_2 \geq 2$ were added. How would this affect the optimal solution?

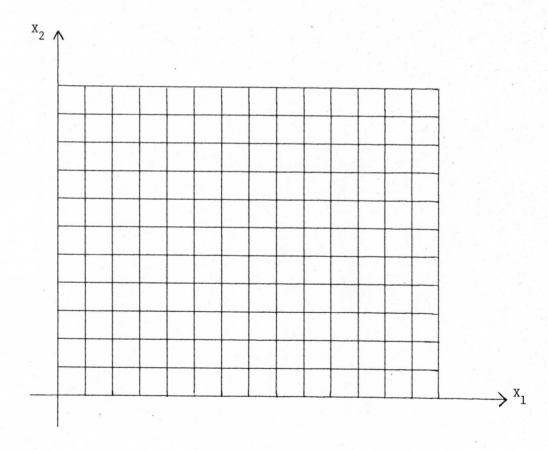

W 10) Write the original problem of exercise 2) is standard form. What is the optimal solution, including the optimal values for the slack and/or surplus variables?

SOLUTION:

$$\text{MAX} \quad 4x_1 + 5x_2$$

$$
\begin{array}{lrcl}
\text{s.t.} & x_1 + 3x_2 + s_1 & = & 22 \\
& -x_1 + x_2 + s_2 & = & 4 \\
& x_2 + s_3 & = & 6 \\
& 2x_1 - 5x_2 + s_4 & = & 0 \\
\end{array}
$$

$$x_1, \ x_2, \ s_1, \ s_2, \ s_3, \ s_4 \geq 0$$

This is done by adding a slack variable to every "less than or equal to constraint. If there had been a "greater than or equal to" constraint a surplus variable would have been subtracted. The optimal solution found for exercise 2 was $x_1 = 10$, $x_2 = 4$. Substituting these values into the above equations we see that the optimal values for the slack variables are the values required to maintain the equality when $x_1 = 10$, $x_2 = 4$, i.e. $s_1 = 0$, $s_2 = 10$, $s_3 = 2$, $s_4 = 0$.

* 11) Consider the following linear program:

$$\text{MIN}\quad 3x_1 + x_2$$

$$\text{s.t.}\quad x_1 + x_2 \geq 40$$

$$2x_1 + 4x_2 \geq 60$$

$$x_2 \leq 12$$

$$x_1,\ x_2 \geq 0$$

a) Write the problem in standard form.

b) Solve this problem graphically giving the optimal values of all
    variables including the slack and surplus variables.

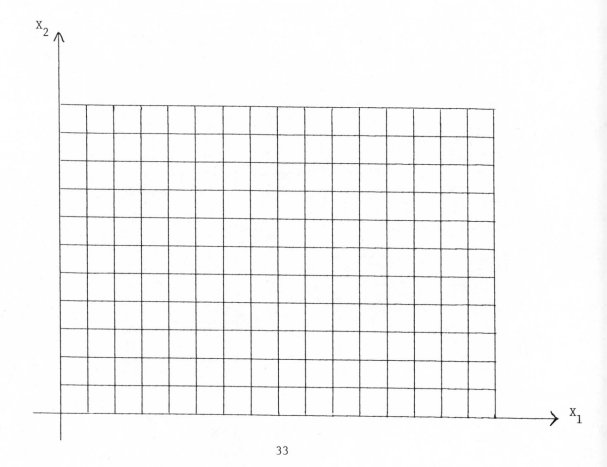

12) Consider the following linear program:

$$\text{MAX} \quad 60x_1 + 43x_2$$

$$\text{s.t.} \quad x_1 + 3x_2 \geq 9$$

$$6x_1 - 2x_2 = 12$$

$$x_1 + 2x_2 \leq 10$$

$$x_1, \, x_2 \geq 0$$

a) Write the problem in standard form.

b) What is the feasible region for the problem?

c) Show that regardless of the objective function the optimal solution will occur at one of two points. Solve for these points and then determine which one maximizes the objectives function.

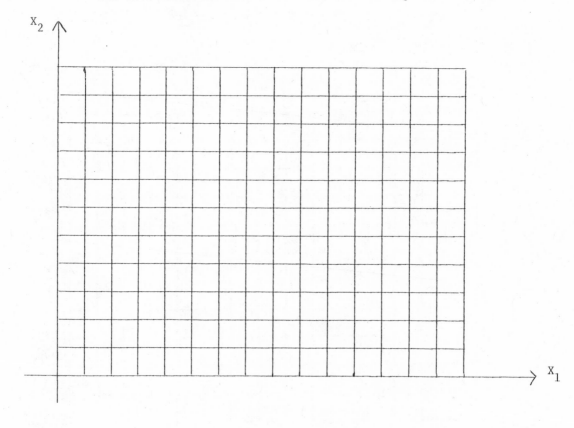

W 13) As the manager of the TV division of a major company you must decide the daily production schedule of television sets. Basically two types of sets are produced: black and white and color. Profit on black and white sets is $20 per set while the profit on a color set is $50 per set. Because the company still wants to offer low price models, at least 25% of the sets must be black and white. Now each set must pass through two phases of production: the manufacturing and the packaging of the set. There are 40 man-hours available daily in the manufacturing phase, 16 man-hours available in the packaging phase. Each black and white set requires .2 hours to manufacture whereas each color set requires .4 hours to manufacture. Packaging requires .1 hours per set for either model. What daily production schedule do you recommend? Discuss the applicability of modeling this problem as a linear program.

SOLUTION:

DEFINE DECISION VARIABLES:

x_1 = # black and white sets produced daily

x_2 = # color sets produced daily

DEFINE OBJECTIVE:

MAX Daily Profit =
MAX (Profit per B & W set)(# B & W sets produced daily)
  + (Profit per color set)(# color sets produced daily) =
MAX $20x_1 + 50x_2$

LIST CONSTRAINTS:

(MANUFACTURING PHASE) Total manufacturing hours used daily ≤ 40
  (Man. hours per B & W set)(# B & W sets produced daily)
  + (Man. hours per color set)(# color sets produced daily) ≤ 40

$.2\ x_1 + .4\ x_2 \leq 40$

(PACKAGING PHASE) Total packaging hours used daily ≤ 16
  (Pack. hours per B & W set)(# B & W sets produced daily)
  + (Pack. hours per color set)(# color sets produced daily) ≤ 16

$.1\ x_1 + .1\ x_2 \leq 16$

(MIN. B & W SETS) # B & W sets produced daily ≥ .25 (Total sets produced daily)
  # B & W sets produced daily ≥ .25 (# B & W sets produced daily + # color sets produced daily)

$x_1 \geq .25\ (x_1 + x_2)$ or $.75\ x_1 - .25\ x_2 \geq 0$

35

Summarizing: MAX $20x_1 + 50x_2$

$$\text{s.t. } .2x_1 + .4x_2 \leq 40$$

$$.1x_1 + .1x_2 \leq 16$$

$$.75x_1 - .25x_2 \geq 0$$

$$x_1, \ x_2 \geq 0$$

Solving graphically we find x_1 = 28 4/7, and x_2 = 85 5/7, for an optimal daily profit of $4,857.14. Ordinarily linear programming should not be used if the variables are restricted to be integers. But since this is a daily production schedule, the 4/7 of a B & W TV and the 5/7 of a color TV will simply be the first pieces worked on the next day. If this were a one-time operation, linear programming would not give the exact optimal answer.

O 14) A federal contract for production of two crucial parts for a new missile system will be awarded to NUPARTS provided that the government's equal opportunity program requiring that at least 1/3 of the employees be women is met. The two parts are a simple switch and a container that will couch the explosive. Under union contract each person must work on both devices regardless of sex; however, the company's policy is to have women work six hours per day on the non-hazardous switches, and only two hours per day on the hazardous containers. Men work four hours per day on each part. Because of this work differential, men are paid $100 per day, women $80 per day. If 4,000 switches and 1,000 containers are required per day and if each container takes one man-hour to produce and each switch 1/2 man-hours to produce, what should be the hiring policy of NUPARTS to minimize its daily cost in salaries.

Outline of Solution:

Variables: x_1 = # men hired, x_2 = # women hired

Objective Function: MIN total daily cost in salaries

Constraints: Total switches made by men + switches made by women
$\geq$ 4,000 (daily)
Total containers made by men + container made by women
$\geq$ 1,000 (daily)
Total # female employees $\geq$ 1/3 (total male employees + female employees)

Answer: # men = 125; # women = 250, minimum daily salary cost = $32,500.

15) Monthly scheduling of production of two kinds of desks, standard and deluxe is required by the DESKO Company. The profit per desk, the wood required, the production time and the finishing time per desk are summarized in the following table along with the availability of the resources:

	Wood (Linear Feet)	Prod. Time (Man-Hours)	Finishing Time (Man-Hours)	Profit
Standard	25	1	.3	$30
Deluxe	40	1	1.2	$70
Monthly Avail.	12,000	400	300	

What monthly production schedule maximizes profits and what is the maximum profit?

* 16) As an accountant/analyst for the WEBUILD Construction Company you must decide how to supply the company with the heavy equipment machines (bulldozers, steamshovels, etc.) that it needs for the coming year. The average purchase price of a new machine is $40,000 per machine and on the average the salvage value per machine after a year is $20,000. WEBUILD can also lease used machines for $8,000 per year (paid in advance). WEBUILD has $1,000,000 available in its budget to lease or purchase machines. The part of the $1,000,000 not used on the acquisition of the machines will be invested at 8%. There are 60 projects requiring four machines each throughout the year. Because of the reliability of the new machines, it is figured each new machine would be available for eight projects, whereas each leased machine would be available for five. How many machines should be leased and purchased in order to minimize the total annual cost to WEBUILD?

17) As a financial consultant to a real estate investment group you must suggest how the group should invest its current funds of $1,000,000. There are basically two kinds of investments available: houses and apartments. Currently inflation is making the home investment attractive as returns seem to be on the order of 20% yearly. However, the return on apartment investment is still a healthy 10%. These figures are after taxes, interest on loans, etc. Because of the uncertainty in the housing market, the group wishes to put no more than $400,000 in homes. The bank you will be dealing with for loans requires 25% down on homes, but only 10% down on apartments. However, the bank will loan at most $7,000,000 to the group. If the policy of the investment group is to liquidate after one year, what is your recommendation for the allocation of the funds?

* 18) As the manager of the advertising division of a large bottling company, you must decide how much money to allocate for new product advertising and for continuing advertising over the coming year. The advertising budget is $10,000,000. Because the company wants to push its new products at least 1/2 of the advertising budget is to be allocated on new products. Also to maintain a firm place in the traditional market, at least $2,000,000 is to be spent on this line. The company figures that each dollar spent on traditional drinks will translate into 100 bottles sold, whereas each dollar spent on new products will result in only 50 bottles sold (because of the harder sell needed for a new product). Additionally, to attract customers the company has lowered the profit margin on new products to 2¢ per bottle compared to 4¢ per bottle for traditional sellers. How should you allocate the money to maximize the profits if the company wants to sell at least 750 million bottles of soda?

19) A businessman is considering opening a small specialized trucking firm. To make the firm profitable, it is estimated that it must have a daily trucking capacity of at least 84,000 cu. feet. Two types of trucks are appropriate for the specialized operation. The first is a 2,400 cu. ft. model costing $18,000. It will use only one driver. The second is a 6,000 cu. ft. model costing $45,000. It will use a driver plus two helpers. There are 41 potential driver/helpers available and there are facilities for at most 40 trucks. What is the minimum cost outlay to meet the objectives? What would your recommendation be if the businessman

a) wanted to use only one kind of truck?

b) wanted to use the minimum number of trucks?

c) wanted to have an equal number of each kind of truck,

while still maintaining the minimum cost outlay?

* 20) A toy company which produces stuffed toy animals has geared up for the Christmas rush by hiring temporary workers giving it a total production crew of 400 workers. The company makes three sizes of stuffed animals. The profit per toy, the production time and the material used per toy is summarized in the table below.

SIZE	PROFIT	PROD. TIME (HRS.)	MATERIAL (LBS.)
Small	$1	.05	.4
Medium	$3	.10	1.0
Large	$6	.15	2.0

Daily shipments of up to 20,000 pounds of material are available. If the "productive" work day of an average worker is six hours and the company wishes to distribute exactly as many small toys as medium and large toys combined, how many of each should be produced daily.

(HINT: One of the constraints is an equality. From this, one of the variables can be rewritten in terms of the other two. This in turn reduces the problem to a problem in two variables which can be solved graphically.)

21) Given the following constraints to a mathematical model:

a) $\quad \sqrt{x_1} \leq 4$

b) $\quad \sqrt{x_1} + x_2 \leq \sqrt{3x_1} + 2x_2 + 3$

c) $\quad \dfrac{x_1}{x_1 + x_2} \leq .3$

Explain why each of these constraints as it stands is not a constraint in a linear program. Show how each could be transformed into an appropriate linear constraint.

22) Given the following two equations:

$$4x_1 + 3x_2 = 27$$

$$x_1 + 2x_2 = 8$$

a) Solve the two equations for x_1 and x_2 using elementary row operations.

Suppose the left hand side of the first constraint had a term of $+x_3$ and the second constraint had a term of $+2x_3$.

b) Using the same elementary row operations as in a), transform the two equations into the form:

$$x_1 \qquad + c_1 x_3 = b_1$$

$$x_2 + c_2 x_3 = b_2$$

Note that the solution to a) is a solution to these new equations when $x_3 = 0$.

c) Transform the two equations in three unknowns into the form:

$$x_1 + c_1 x_2 \qquad = b_1$$

$$c_2 x_2 + x_3 = b_2$$

Do this by elementary row operations on:

    i)   the original system of equations
    ii) your answer to part b)

Show that they give the same system of equations. What is a solution to these two equations in three unknowns when $x_2 = 0$?

3 LINEAR PROGRAMMING: THE SIMPLEX METHOD

KEY CONCEPTS

1. Tableau form representation of a linear programming problem

2. The Simplex Method for solving linear programs in tableau form

3. The use of artificial variables to transform any standard form into tableau form

REVIEW

1. Tableau Form

A linear programming problem is said to be in tableau form if all constraints are equations with the right hand side (RHS) greater than or equal to zero, and for each equation there appears a variable with coefficient +1 in that equation and that variable appears with coefficient 0 in every other equation. The variable that appears with coefficient +1 in a particular equation and 0 in the other equations is called the basic variable associated with that equation. All variables which are not basic variables are called non-basic variables.

In general, when there are more variables than equations, there are an infinite number of solutions to the system of equations. But even though there are an infinite number of solutions, it is sometimes difficult to determine even one solution. The value of the tableau form is that an easy solution can be found by setting the non-basic variables to zero and the basic variables to the corresponding (RHS) value. This is called a basic feasible solution. Basic feasible solutions correspond to extreme points of the feasible solution region. The following is an example of tableau form:

$$x_2 + 3x_3 \quad - 2x_5 \qquad = 7$$

$$4x_3 + x_4 + 3x_5 \qquad = 8$$

$$x_1 \quad - 2x_3 \quad + 2x_5 \qquad = 16$$

$$4x_5 + x_6 = 10$$

The basic variables for the four equations are x_2, x_4, x_1, and x_6 respectively and the basic feasible solution is $x_1 = 16$, $x_2 = 7$, $x_3 = 0$, $x_4 = 8$, $x_5 = 0$, $x_6 = 10$.

A linear program in tableau form can be written in a <u>tableau</u>. A tableau is basically a tabular representation of the coefficients of the equations with some fringe information:

(1) Above the table of equation coefficients is written the objective function coefficients. These represent the direct per unit increase in the objective function for each variable neglecting the effect of the constraints.

(2) To the left of the table is written the corresponding basic variable for each equation and its objective function coefficient.

(3) At the bottom are two rows: The z_j row which represents the decrease in the value of the objective function per unit increase in x_j due to the effect of the constraints. It is obtained by multiplying each column coefficient by the objective function coefficient of the corresponding basic variable for that equation and summing them. Doing this for the RHS gives the current value of the objective function. The last row is the marginal profit row or net evaluation row ($c_j - z_j$) gotten by subtracting z_j from c_j for each column. The complete tableau for the above example with an objective function of MAX $3x_1 + 3x_2 + 10x_3 + x_4 + 5x_5 + x_6$ is:

Basis	c_j	x_1	x_2	x_3	x_4	x_5	x_6	
		3	3	10	1	5	1	
x_2	3	0	1	3	0	-2	0	7
x_4	1	0	0	4	1	3	0	8
x_1	3	1	0	-2	0	2	0	16
x_6	1	0	0	0	0	4	1	10
z_j		3	3	7	1	7	1	87
$c_j - z_j$		0	0	3	0	-2	0	

2. The Simplex Method

The **simplex method** is an _iterative_ procedure for solving linear
programs in tableau form. The simplex method generates new basic feasible
solutions that give a larger value (or at least the same value) of the
objective function by generating new tableau forms for the system of
equations. When no further improvement can be made the optimal solution
has been attained.

Basically the simplex method is a three-step procedure:

(1) Find the most positive $c_j - z_j$. This is the entering or PIVOT
column. If there are none, STOP; the optimal solution has
been attained.

(2) For _positive_ elements in the pivot column find the ratio of
the (RHS element)/(PIVOT column element). The minimum ratio
determines the leaving or pivot row. (The intersection of
the pivot row and pivot column is called the pivot element.)

(3) Generate the next tableau by:

(i) Divide the pivot row by the pivot element.
(ii) For all other rows, multiply the new row generated in
(i) by the corresponding element in the pivot column and
subtract it from the current row.

Complete the "fringes" of the tableau and go to (1).

In the simplex method, Step 1 determines the variable giving the highest per unit increase in the value of the objective function; Step 2 determines which variable goes to zero first as this variable is increased; Step 3 generates a new tableau with the variable in Step 1 replacing the variable in Step 2 in the basis.

The above procedure is for a maximization problem. For a minimization problem we can either: (1) multiply the objective function by −1 and maximize; OR (2) change Step 1 to find the most negative $c_j - z_j$ and stop if there are none.

3. Artificial Variables

When a problem is written in standard form it usually does not correspond to tableau form although some equations may have a variable with coefficient of +1 in that equation and coefficient 0 in the other equations. For those equations that do not, simply add an artificial variable to that equation and assign it an objective function coefficient of −M, where M is thought of as an extremely large number near infinity. Then proceed with the simplex method. Because of the large negative contribution (−M) per unit of each artificial variable, if the problem has an optimal solution, it will occur with the artificial variables equal 0.

Note that once an artificial variable becomes non-basic it may be dropped, since it has to be zero in any feasible solution.

ARTIFICIAL VARIABLE – A variable added to an equation that does not have a corresponding basic variable to generate an initial tableau form. (108)

BASIC FEASIBLE SOLUTION – A basic solution whose components are all non-negative (this corresponds to an extreme point). (75)

BASIC SOLUTION – A solution obtained by setting (n – m) variables to zero and solving the remaining m equations in m variables uniquely. (75)

BASIC VARIABLE – A variable whose coefficient in one row is +1 and whose coefficient in all other rows is 0. (75)

BASIS – The ordered set of basic variables. (84)

CURRENT SOLUTION – Solution obtained by setting the non-basic variables in a simplex tableau to zero and basic variables of the tableau to the RHS. (88)

ITERATION – One complete cycle of steps in a solution procedure (such as the simplex method). (87)

NET EVALUATION ROW – The $c_j - z_j$ row which gives the marginal profit for each variable in the linear program. (85)

NON-BASIC VARIABLE – A variable whose column coefficients do not form a unit column. (75)

PIVOT COLUMN – The column associated with the entering variable in the simplex method (determined by the most positive $c_j - z_j$). (88)

PIVOT ELEMENT – The element in the PIVOT column that is also in the PIVOT row (89)

PIVOT ROW – The row corresponding to the leaving variable in the simplex method (determined by the ratio test). (91)

SIMPLEX METHOD – An iterative procedure for solving linear programs that generates successively better basic feasible solutions. (74)

SIMPLEX TABLEAU – A table that keeps track of the coefficients of the variables of the equations as well as "fringe" information concerning contributions to the objective function. (79)

TABLEAU FORM - Standard form with the following characteristics: (1) the right hand side is greater than or equal to zero; (2) for each constraint there is a variable which appears with coefficient +1 in that constraint and zero in all others. (78)

UNIT COLUMN - A column in a tableau consisting of a "+1" in one row and "0" in every other row. (82)

z_j ROW - Row in a simplex tableau gotten by multiplying each element in a column by the c_j of the corresponding basic variable in that row and summing. (This gives the unit decrease in the objective function due to the constraints per unit increase in the corresponding variable.) (84)

W 1) Given the problem in section 1 of the review section:

    a) Explain the meaning of each number in the tableau.

    b) Note x_3 will be the entering variable. Explain why the ratio test is only done on positive elements in the x_3 column.

    c) Use the simplex method to solve for the optimal solution for this problem.

SOLUTION:

    a) The tableau was:

		x_1	x_2	x_3	x_4	x_5	x_6	
Basis	c_j	3	3	10	1	5	1	
x_2	3	0	1	3	0	-2	0	7
x_4	1	0	0	4	1	3	0	8
x_1	3	1	0	-2	0	2	0	16
x_6	1	0	0	0	0	4	1	10
	z_j	3	3	7	1	7	1	87
	$c_j - z_j$	0	0	3	0	-2	0	

The c_j row gives the objective function coefficient of all variables. This can be considered as the "marginal revenue" contribution to profit. The c_j column gives the c_j's for the basic variables.

The numbers inside the box are the coefficients of the variables of the current set of constraints which have been obtained by row operations from the original set of constraints.

The right column not only gives the RHS of the constraints in current form, but also the values of the corresponding basic variables when the non-basic variables have been set to 0.

The z_j row gives a "marginal cost" or decrease in profit due to an increase of one more unit of the corresponding column variable.

The RHS element of the z_j row, (87) gives the current value of the objective function when the basic variables equal the RHS and the non-basic variables equal zero.

The $c_j - z_j$ row gives the marginal profit (= marginal revenue -marginal cost) or the net increase in the value of objective function per unit of the corresponding variable.

b) Keeping x_5 at zero value, the constraints reduce to:

$$x_2 + 3x_3 = 7 \qquad \text{or} \qquad x_2 = 7 - 3x_3 \qquad\qquad (1)$$

$$4x_3 + x_4 = 8 \qquad \text{or} \qquad x_4 = 8 - 4x_3 \qquad\qquad (2)$$

$$x_1 - 2x_3 = 16 \qquad \text{or} \qquad x_1 = 16 + 2x_3 \qquad\qquad (3)$$

$$0x_3 + x_6 = 10 \qquad \text{or} \qquad x_6 = 10 + 0x_3 \qquad\qquad (4)$$

Note by increasing x_3 only x_2 and x_4 decrease. From (1) $x_3 \leq 7/3$ else $x_2 < 0$, and from (2) $x_3 \leq 2$ else $x_4 < 0$. Thus x_3 will be increased to $8/4 = 2$.

c) Since x_3 has most positive $c_j - z_j$ it is the entering variable; since $8/4$ gives the minimizing ratio, x_4 is the leaving variable and 4 is the pivot element.

- (i)   Divide the second row by 4. (Put this row into new tableau first.)
- (ii) Then

   - a) multiply the new row in (i) by 3 and subtract from first row to get a zero in the third column.
   - b) multiply the new row in (i) by -2 and subtract from third row to get a zero in column 3.
   - c) leave fourth row alone since it already has a zero in column 3.

Then fill in the "fringes" of the tableau to get:

53

Basis	c_j	x_1	x_2	x_3	x_4	x_5	x_6	
		3	3	10	1	5	1	
x_2	3	0	1	0	-3/4	-17/4	0	1
x_3	10	0	0	1	1/4	3/4	0	2
x_1	3	1	0	0	1/2	7/2	0	20
x_6	1	0	0	0	0	4	1	10
z_j		3	3	10	7/4	37/4	1	93
$c_j - z_j$		0	0	0	-3/4	-17/4	0	

Since all $c_j - z_j \leq 0$, this is the optimal tableau. Thus the optimal solution is: $x_1 = 20$, $x_2 = 1$, $x_3 = 2$, $x_4 = 0$, $x_5 = 0$, $x_6 = 10$, $z = 93$.

0 2) Solve the following problem by simplex method.

$$\text{MAX} \quad 2x_1 + 3x_2 - x_3$$

$$\text{s.t.} \quad 3x_1 + 6x_2 \quad \leq 30$$

$$4x_1 + 2x_2 + x_3 \leq 20$$

$$x_2 + x_3 \leq 10$$

$$x_j \geq 0 \quad j = 1,2,3$$

Outline of Solution:

    (i)   Write the problem in standard form by adding slack variables to all constraints. Note that this is also tableau form.

    (ii) Form a simplex tableau. Note the original basis is s_1, s_2, s_3

    (iii) Iteration 1 (a) pivot column is x_2
                               (b) pivot row is first row
                               (c) 6 is pivot element

Iteration 2: (a) pivot column is x_1

(b) pivot row is second row

(c) pivot element is 3

Iteration 3: The tableau is

Basis	c_j	x_1	x_2	x_3	s_1	s_2	s_3	
		2	3	-1	0	0	0	
x_2	3	0	1	-1/6	2/9	-1/6	0	10/3
x_1	2	1	0	1/3	-1/9	1/3	0	10/3
s_3	0	0	0	7/6	-2/9	1/6	1	20/3
	z_j	2	3	1/6	4/9	1/6	0	50/3
	c_j-z_j	0	0	-7/6	-4/9	-1/6	0	

and is optimal. Optimal solution $x_1 = 10/3$, $x_2 = 10/3$, $x_3 = 0$, $s_1 = 0$, $s_2 = 0$, $s_3 = 20/3$, $z = 50/3$.

* 3) Given the following linear program:

$$\text{MAX} \quad 3x_1 + 4x_2 + 2x_3$$

$$\text{s.t.} \quad x_1 + x_2 + x_3 \leq 50$$

$$2x_1 + 3x_2 - x_3 \leq 30$$

$$x_j \geq 0 \quad j = 1,2,3$$

a) Write the problem in standard form.

b) Is the resulting standard form also tableau form? Explain.

c) Solve the problem by the simplex method.

4) Solve the following problem by the simplex method.

$$\text{MIN} \quad -2x_1 + 3x_2 - 4x_3$$

$$\text{s.t.} \quad 3x_1 + 4x_2 - x_3 \leq 12$$

$$2x_1 + 2x_2 + 3x_3 \leq 18$$

$$x_j \geq 0 \quad j = 1,2,3$$

* 5) Consider the following linear program.

$$\text{MIN} \quad 2x_1 - 3x_2 - 4x_3$$

$$\text{s.t.} \quad x_1 + 2x_2 + x_3 \geq 5$$

$$3x_2 + 2x_3 \leq 12$$

$$x_j \geq 0 \quad j = 1,2,3$$

a) Write the problem in standard form. Is this also tableau form?

b) Solve the problem by the simplex method.

6) Consider the following tableau at a particular stage of the simplex method.

Basis	c_j	x_1	x_2	x_3	s_1	s_2	s_3	
		4	2	-1	0	0	0	
	0	1	-1	6	0	1		10
	0	0	4	2	1	1		20
	1	0	0	-3	0	1		30
z_j								
c_j-z_j								

a) Complete the tableau.

b) What is the current basic solution?

c) What would be the effect on the objective function in each of the following cases?

   (i) x_3 were increased by 1
   (ii) x_3 were increased by 3
   (iii) s_1 were increased by 1.5
   (iv) s_3 were increased by 2

d) What is the entering variable? Write the equations corresponding to the above tableau keeping all non-basic variables except the entering variable equal to zero. Justify why we only do the ratio test on positive numbers of the pivot column.

e) Explain why the entering variable could not be increased to 10 at this iteration.

f) To what value will the entering variable increase?

g) By how much will the objective function be improved in the next tableau? Using your equations in (d), what will be the value of the other current basic variables in the next tableau.

* 7) Consider the following linear program.

$$\text{MAX} \quad 4x_1 + 3x_2$$

$$\text{s.t.} \quad x_1 \quad\quad \leq 6$$

$$2x_1 + 3x_2 \leq 18$$

$$-x_1 + x_2 \leq 4$$

$$x_j \geq 0$$

a) Solve the problem graphically.

b) Solve the problem by the simplex method and show what point on the graph corresponds to each simplex tableau.

c) In doing (b), you chose the entering variable by choosing the one with the most positive $c_j - z_j$. Why?

d) Why would choosing any variable with a positive $c_j - z_j$ also be a valid way of selecting the entering variable?

e) There are two positive $(c_j - z_j)$'s at the first iteration. Solve the problem by the simplex method again, but this time choosing the other variable with a positive $c_j - z_j$ at the first iteration. Show what points these new simplex tableaus correspond to on the graph. Comment.

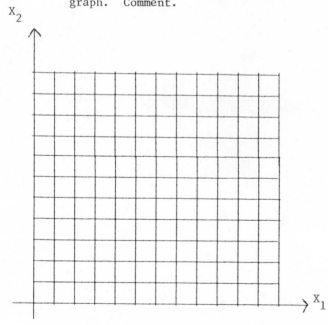

X_2

X_1

8) Consider the following linear program.

$$\text{MAX} \quad 2x_1 + 5x_2$$

$$\text{s.t.} \quad x_1 + x_2 \le 10$$

$$- x_1 + x_2 \le 6$$

$$x_1 + 2x_2 \le 16$$

$$x_1, x_2 \ge 0$$

a) Solve the problem graphically.

b) Solve the problem by the simplex method.

c) Your answer to (b) should have $s_1 > 0$. From your graphical solution in (a) explain why you would expect this?

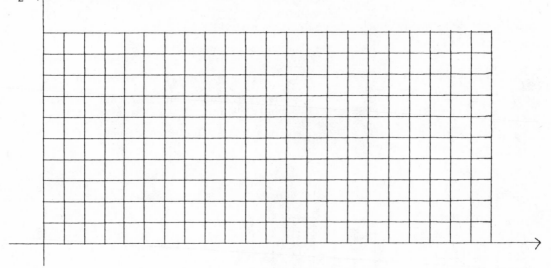

9) The following is a linear programming formulation of a mathematical model:

$$\text{MAX} \quad 5x_1 + 6x_2 + 3x_3 + x_4$$

$$\text{s.t.} \quad 7x_1 + 2x_2 + 4x_3 + 3x_4 \leq 500$$

$$4x_1 + x_2 + 2x_3 + x_4 \leq 750$$

$$2x_1 + 3x_2 + x_3 + 2x_4 \leq 200$$

$$x_j \geq 0 \quad j = 1,2,3,4$$

The optimal tableau is

Basis	c_j	x_1	x_2	x_3	x_4	s_1	s_2	s_3	
		5	6	3	1	0	0	0	
x_3	3	1.7	0	1	.5	.3	0	$-$ .2	110
s_2	0	.5	0	0	$-$ .5	$-$.5	1	0	500
x_2	6	.1	1	0	.5	$-$.1	0	.4	30
z_j		5.7	6	3	4.5	.3	0	1.8	510
$c_j - z_j$		$-$ .7	0	0	-3.5	$-$.3	0	-1.8	

a) What is the optimal solution including the optimal value of the objective function?

b) The second constraint said we had at most 750 tons of steel available. How much steel was used?

c) Write the original problem in standard form. Show that $x_1 = 0$, $x_2 = 10$, $x_3 = 10$, $x_4 = 10$, $s_1 = 410$, $s_2 = 710$, $s_3 = 140$ is feasible for the original problem. Why must this necessarily satisfy the constraints as written in the final tableau? Show that it does.

W 10) Given the following linear program

$$\text{MAX} \quad 2x_1 + 3x_2 + 4x_3$$

$$\text{s.t.} \quad x_1 + x_2 + x_3 \leq 30$$

$$2x_1 + x_2 + 3x_3 \geq 60$$

$$x_1 - x_2 + 2x_3 = 20$$

$$x_j \geq 0 \quad j = 1,2,3$$

a) Write the problem in standard form. Explain why this is <u>not</u> tableau form.

b) Add artificial variables to get the first tableau form and amend the objective function appropriately.

c) Solve the problem by the simplex method.

d) What change to the above procedure would you make if the objective function were a minimization instead of a maximization.
(DO NOT RESOLVE)

<u>SOLUTION</u>:

a) $$\text{MAX} \quad 2x_1 + 3x_2 + 4x_3$$

$$\text{s.t.} \quad x_1 + x_2 + x_3 + s_1 \qquad\quad = 30$$

$$2x_1 + x_2 + 3x_3 \qquad - s_2 = 60$$

$$x_1 - x_2 + 2x_3 \qquad\qquad = 20$$

$$x_j \geq 0 \quad j = 1,2,3,$$

$$s_j \geq 0 \quad j = 1,2$$

This is not tableau form because the second and third constraints have no variables with +1's in those constraints only and zeroes elsewhere.

b) Add an artificial variable (a_1) to row 2, and an artificial variable (a_2) to row 3. Give them objective function coefficients on $-M$ to form the following tableau.

Basis	c_j	x_1	x_2	x_3	s_1	s_2	a_1	a_2	
		2	3	4	0	0	-M	-M	
s_1	0	1	1	1	1	0	0	0	30
a_1	-M	2	1	3	0	-1	1	0	60
← a_2	-M	1	-1	[2]	0	0	0	1	20
	z_j	-3M	0	-5M	0	M	-M	-M	-80M
	$c_j - z_j$	3M+2	3	5M+4	0	-M	0	0	

Since a_2 is an artificial variable and will be non-basic, we can drop its column.

c)   Iteration #2

Basis	c_j	x_1	x_2	x_3	s_1	s_2	a_1	
		2	3	4	0	0	-M	
s_1	0	½	3/2	0	1	0	0	20
← a_1	-M	½	[5/2]	0	0	-1	1	30
x_3	4	½	-1/2	1	0	0	0	10
	z_j	-½M+2	-(5/2)M-2	4	0	M	-M	-30M+40
	$c_j - z_j$	½M	(5/2)M+5	0	0	-M	0	

Since a_1 is an artificial variable and will be non-basic we can drop its column.

63

Iteration #3

Basis	c_j	x_1 2	x_2 3	x_3 4	s_1 0	s_2 0	
← s_1	0	1/5	0	0	1	$\overline{3/5}$	11
x_2	3	1/5	1	0	0	-2/5	6
x_3	4	3/5	0	1	0	-1/5	13
z_j		3	3	4	0	-2	70
$c_j - z_j$		-1	0	0	0	2 ↑	

Iteration #4

Basis	c_j	x_1 2	x_2 3	x_3 4	s_1 0	s_2 0	
s_2	0	1/3	0	0	5/3	1	55/3
x_2	3	1/3	1	0	2/3	0	40/3
x_3	4	2/3	0	1	1/3	0	50/3
z_j		11/3	3	4	10/3	0	320/3
$c_j - z_j$		-5/3	0	0	-10/3	0	

Thus optimal solution is $x_1 = 0$, $x_2 = 40/3$, $x_3 = 50/3$, $s_1 = 0$, $s_2 = 55/3$, $s_3 = 0$, $z = 320/3$.

d) The coefficients of the artificial variables in the objective function would be +M instead of -M.

O 11) Given the following linear program.

$$\text{MAX} \quad 3x_1 - x_2 + 2x_3$$

$$\text{s.t.} \quad x_1 + 2x_2 + x_3 = 14$$

$$2x_1 + 3x_2 \quad \leq 18$$

$$x_1 \quad \geq 6$$

$$x_j \geq 0 \quad j = 1,2,3$$

a) Write the problem in standard form.

b) Add the _fewest_ number of artificial variables to get the initial tableau form.

c) Solve the problem by the simplex method.

Outline of Solution:

a) Add slack variable to second constraint, surplus variable to third constraint.

b) Since x_3 can be a basic variable as well as s_1, only one artificial variable need be added to the third constraint.

c) Iteration 1: a) x_1 is entering variable
   b) a_1 is leaving variable (drop its column)
   c) pivot element is 1

   Iteration 2: a) s_2 is entering variable
   b) s_1 is leaving variable
   c) pivot element is 2

Iteration 3: Optimal tableau

		x_1	x_2	x_3	s_1	s_2	
Basis	c_j	3	-1	2	0	0	
x_3	2	0	1/2	1	$-\frac{1}{2}$	0	5
s_2	0	0	3/2	0	$\frac{1}{2}$	1	3
x_1	3	1	3/2	0	$\frac{1}{2}$	0	9
	z_j	3	11/2	2	$\frac{1}{2}$	0	37
	$c_j - z_j$	0	-13/2	0	$-\frac{1}{2}$	0	

Optimal solution $x_1 = 9$, $x_2 = 0$, $x_3 = 5$, $s_1 = 0$, $s_2 = 3$, $z = 37$.

* 12) Solve the following linear program by the simplex method.

$$\text{MAX} \quad x_1 + 2x_2 - 3x_3$$

$$\text{s.t.} \quad x_1 \qquad\qquad\qquad \geq 5$$

$$2x_1 + 3x_2 + 4x_3 \leq 24$$

$$3x_1 + 2x_2 + x_3 = 18$$

$$x_j \geq 0 \quad j = 1,2,3$$

13) Consider the following linear program.

$$\text{MIN} \quad 2x_1 + 3x_2 + 8x_3$$

$$\text{s.t.} \quad 4x_1 + 2x_2 + x_3 \geq 15$$

$$2x_1 + x_2 + 6x_3 \geq 30$$

$$x_j \geq 0 \quad j = 1,2,3$$

a) Write the problem in standard form.

b) Why can you not multiply the equations in (a) by −1 to get tableau form?

c) Solve the problem by the simplex method.

14) Consider the following linear program.

$$\text{MAX} \quad 6x_1 + 10x_2$$

$$\text{s.t.} \quad x_1 \qquad \geq 4$$

$$x_2 \leq 6$$

$$3x_1 + 2x_2 = 18$$

$$x_1, x_2 \geq 0$$

a) Solve the problem graphically.

b) Solve the problem by the simplex method and show the corresponding point on the graph associated with each tableau. When does the first feasible solution occur? Is it optimal?

W 15) Now Products has developed a new air conditioning system which it plans to market in a few months. The primary channel for the product will be independent distributors. However, the product will also be distributed by a large department store chain and a discount store chain.

Because of differing distribution and promotional costs, the profit realized by Now Products varies with the distributor. The table below summarizes pertinent data for the problem.

	Actual Profit Per Unit Sold	Estimated Advertising Cost Per Unit Sold	Estimated Sales Force Effort Per Unit Sold
Independents	$100	$10	2 Hours
Department Store	$ 85	$ 8	3 Hours
Discount Store	$ 70	$15	2 Hours

Now Products has a weekly advertising budget of $5000 as well as 20 salesman (at 40 hours per week) available to promote the product. Facilities are such that Now Products can realize a production contractual capacity of at most 500 units per week. Additionally, arrangements with the discount store require that they receive at least 20% of all units produced. Now Products wishes to know how to market this product in terms of weekly distribution to each of the distributors.

SOLUTION:

Let x_1 = # air-conditioning units sold to independents weekly.

x_2 = # air-conditioning units sold to department store weekly.

x_3 = # air-conditioning units sold to discount store weekly.

MAX $100x_1 + 85x_2 + 70x_3$

s.t. $10x_1 + 8x_2 + 15x_3 \leq 5000$ (adv. budget)

$\quad\quad 2x_1 + 3x_2 + 2x_3 \leq 800$ (salesman hours)

$\quad\quad x_1 + x_2 + x_3 \leq 500$ (capacity)

$\quad\quad .2x_1 + .2x_2 - .8x_3 \leq 0$ *(contract)

$\quad\quad x_j \geq 0 \; j = 1,2,3$

*obtained from $x_3 \geq .2 (x_1 + x_2 + x_3)$ or

$\quad\quad -.2x_1 - .2x_2 + .8x_3 \geq 0$ or

$\quad\quad .2x_1 + .2x_2 - .8x_3 \leq 0$

Problem in standard form:

MAX $100x_1 + 85x_2 + 70x_3$

s.t. $10x_1 + 8x_2 + 15x_3 + s_1 = 5000$

$\quad\quad 2x_1 + 3x_2 + 2x_3 + s_2 = 800$

$\quad\quad x_1 + x_2 + x_3 + s_3 = 500$

$\quad\quad .2x_1 + .2x_2 - .8x_3 + s_4 = 0$

$\quad\quad x_j \geq 0 \; j = 1,2,3 \quad s_j \geq 0 \quad j = 1,2,3,4$

Iteration 1

Basis	c_j	x_1	x_2	x_3	s_1	s_2	s_3	s_4	
		100	85	70	0	0	0	0	
s_1	0	10	8	15	1	0	0	0	5000
s_2	0	2	3	2	0	1	0	0	800
s_3	0	1	1	1	0	0	1	0	500
s_4	0	$\boxed{.2}$	.2	-.8	0	0	0	1	0
z_j		0	0	0	0	0	0	0	0
c_j-z_j		100	85	70	0	0	0	0	

Iteration 2

Basis	c_j	x_1	x_2	x_3	s_1	s_2	s_3	s_4	
		100	85	70	0	0	0	0	
s_1	0	0	-2	55	1	0	0	-50	5000
s_2	0	0	1	$\boxed{10}$	0	1	0	-10	800
s_3	0	0	0	5	0	0	1	-5	500
x_1	100	1	1	-4	0	0	0	5	0
z_j		100	100	-400	0	0	0	500	0
c_j-z_j		0	-15	470	0	0	0	-500	

Iteration 3

Basis	c_j	x_1	x_2	x_3	s_1	s_2	s_3	s_4	
		100	85	70	0	0	0	0	
s_1	0	0	-7.5	0	1	-5.5	0	5	600
x_3	70	0	.1	1	0	.1	0	-1	80
s_3	0	0	-.5	0	0	-.5	1	0	100
x_1	100	1	1.4	0	0	.4	0	1	320
z_j		100	147	70	0	47	0	30	37,600
c_j-z_j		0	-62	0	0	-47	0	-30	

Thus, the optimal solution is: sell 320 air-conditioned to independents weekly, 80 to the discount store for optimal weekly profit of $37,600.

* 16) Suppose we own a company which is going into the solar energy field. There are three types of systems that can be produced:

System	Profit
Cheap	$1 (thousand)
Moderate	$3 (thousand)
Expensive	$5 (thousand)

Demand for the expensive model will be at most five per week, while we could sell as many of the others as we could produce. There are two scarce resources used in the production of each system. The quantities used by each system are:

System	Material A (tons)	Material B (tons)
Cheap	1	1
Moderate	2	3
Expensive	4	3

We get 100 tons of Material A and 90 tons of Material B delivered to us each week.

What production rate of each system do you recommend?

17) Small TV, Inc. has facilities for making three kinds of television
     sets: standard, deluxe, and a remote control model. The televisions
     essentially go through two processes: assembly and packaging. There
     are 30 hours available weekly for assembly and 24 hours available
     weekly for packaging. The hours required and the profits for each of
     the three sets are summarized below:

	Assembly	Packaging	Profit
Standard	2	2	$30
Deluxe	1	4	$20
Remote Control	2	3	$40

What is your recommendation to Small TV for average weekly production
and what weekly profits should Small TV expect from your recommendation?

* 18) Shibley Car Painting Company is expanding to a new facility. Shibley basically gives two kinds of paint jobs: deluxe and standard. The car painters union has defined three categories of workers and has negotiated a weekly rate and salary for each category. The table below summarizes the weekly maximum number of each type of paint jobs to be performed each week by job category.

Category	Deluxe Jobs Per Week	Standard Jobs Per Week	Weekly Salary
Apprentice	1	2	$130
Painter	2	3	$200
Expert	3	5	$300

If no more than 20% of the workers can be apprentices, and if Shibley is willing to take at least 30 standard jobs and 15 deluxe jobs per week, how many of each category of employee should be hired in order to minimize the total weekly outlay in salaries.

19) A rush order has just been received by COMGEN for 120 large generators, 40 to be delivered to each of three Air Force installations near
San Francisco, Los Angeles and Seattle. COMGEN wishes to ship these
generators at minimum cost from its warehouses in Denver and Phoenix.
Denver has 70 units in stock, Phoenix 60. If the table below gives
the unit shipping cost in hundreds of dollars, what shipping pattern
should be used and what total cost should COMGEN expect?

		To		
		SF	LA	SEATTLE
From	Denver	2	3	2
	Phoenix	2	1	5

20) As a consultant to an investment group, you wish to advise your clients on selecting a proper portfolio. Together they have $500,000 to invest.

	ANNUAL RETURN
Low risk stocks	7%
High risk stocks	11%
Bonds	8%
Savings Account	5%

It is desired to always have at least $100,000 of liquid investments which can be tapped at any time (including the first year). Bonds have a five year maturity date and stocks will be kept for at least one year to assure the advantage of capital gains. It is also desired to have $200,000 available for future investments at the end of a year. Being a fairly conservative group, they wish to have no more than one-fourth of the money in stocks in high risk stocks, and they wish to have at least as much in bonds as in stocks. What diversification do you recommend and what annual return should the investment group expect?

* 21) The Accounting Department requires information on the number of employees the DENSAM Company will be hiring for its new restaurant located across the street from a famous university. The restaurant will operate from 7:00 a.m. to 11:00 p.m.. It has broken down its requirements into four hour periods.

	Employees Required
7:00 a.m. – 11:00 a.m.	12
11:00 a.m. – 3:00 p.m.	20
3:00 p.m. – 7:00 p.m.	18
7:00 p.m. – 11:00 p.m.	22

Staffing is to be done by hiring personnel for eight hour shifts commencing at 7:00 a.m., 11:00 a.m., and 3:00 p.m. Additionally there are enough students who wish to work the before and after school eight-hour shift which includes the 7:00 p.m. – 11:00 p.m. and 7:00 a.m. – 11:00 a.m. periods. What is the minimum number of personnel the Accounting Department should expect to handle?

22) A radio company has contracts to meet minimum production levels for each of its three models: (1) the hand held transistor, (2) table model, and (3) deluxe stereo model. Each model goes through two processes before completion: manufacturing and packaging. The following table gives the minimum contract requirements and the times in each process for each model as well as the profit per model and total hours available each week for each process.

	Manufacturing (Hrs/Unit)	Packaging (Hrs/Unit)	Profit ($/Unit)	Contract Required
Transistor	.25	.09	8	100
Table	.30	.12	15	150
Stereo	.40	.25	25	80
TOTAL AVAILABLE	150	60		

a) What production schedule should be followed to realize maximum profits? (HINT: This can be formulated in two constraints by defining variables to take into account the minimum required.)

b) Explain briefly how your formulation above would change if we could realize a profit of $2 for each unused packaging hour by reassigning workers elsewhere. (DO NOT RESOLVE)

4 LINEAR PROGRAMMING: OTHER TOPICS

KEY CONCEPTS

1. Recognition, both graphically and in the
    simplex tableau, of the following cases:
    (i) <u>infeasibility</u>, (ii) <u>unboundedness</u>,
    (iii) <u>alternate optimal solutions</u>

2. Definition of <u>degeneracy</u> and its treat-
    ment in the simplex method

3. Sensitivity analysis of objective func-
    tion, right hand side, and matrix
    coefficients of a linear program

4. Formulation, use, and properties of
    <u>duality</u> in linear programming

REVIEW

1. Special Terminations in Linear Programming

In both the graphical solution procedure and the simplex method,
cases can arise in which there is not a unique optimal solution to the
linear program. These cases are (i) no feasible solution for the constraints of a linear program--<u>infeasibility</u>, (ii) the objective function
can be increased without bound over the feasible solution region (decreased
without bound for a minimization problem)--<u>unboundedness</u>, (iii) the objective function can be maximized (or minimized) at more than one point of the
feasible solution region--<u>alternate optimal solutions</u>.

Infeasibility occurs when the constraints of the problem are
inconsistent; that is, not all the constraints can be satisfied simultaneously. In the graphical method infeasibility is easily noted when all constraints are graphed and there are no points to form a feasible solution
region. In the simplex method, infeasibility is detected when an "optimal"

tableau has been reached and an artificial variable is basic at positive value.

Unboundedness is a condition which can only exist theoretically. In no instance in real life could an unbounded (infinite) profit be made or an unbounded (unlimited negative) cost be incurred. Should this condition occur, the problem has been misformulated usually by the omission of some constraints. Unboundedness is observed graphically when the feasible region extends to infinity in some direction and the objective function line can be moved parallel without limit to successively better values. In the simplex method, unboundedness is detected in a maximization problem, if any $c_j - z_j > 0$, and all the values in the pivot column are less than or equal to zero.

Alternate optimal solutions can arise in linear programming problems. They can be important because of "secondary" considerations that may be appealing to the decision maker such as making the greatest or fewest variety of products that combine to give the maximum profit. Graphically we have seen alternate optimal solutions occur when a constraint of the feasible region is parallel to the objective function and this entire line segment is the last set of points touched by the objective function line. Note that if more than one point is optimal, there are an infinite number of optimal points. In the simplex method, the condition for alternate optimal solutions is that at optimality (i.e. all $c_j - z_j \leq 0$) there exists some $c_j - z_j = 0$ for a non-basic variable. If a pivot operation is done on this variable, a new optimal basic feasible solution is obtained.

2.   Degeneracy in Linear Programming

Degeneracy in linear programming is when a basic variable takes on a value of zero (i.e. a zero in the RHS of the constraints of the tableau). This can occur initially two ways: (i) during formulation (such as $x_1 \leq x_2$ or $x_1 - x_2 \leq 0$) or (ii) during the simplex method when a tie occurs for the minimum value in the ratio test.

In general, there are no computational difficulties when degeneracy occurs. If a tie for the ratio test occurs, select the pivot row by an arbitrary method such as the upper row of those determining the tie. In subsequent iterations, treat the zero on the RHS as any other number. Thus if its corresponding pivot column element is non-positive, it does not figure in the ratio test. If the pivot column element is positive, the ratio is zero, and hence will be the winner of the ratio test.

In a degenerate problem it is theoretically possible for the same set of tableaus to be generated over and over again without improving the value of the objective function or reaching an optimal solution. However, in practice, such cycling has rarely been found to occur.

3. Sensitivity Analyses

Sensitivity (post-optimality) analysis is the study of the effect on the optimal solution when the coefficients of the problem change. It is important because of the ever-changing real life environment. Other uses include helping to decide the precision necessary for estimates of the coefficients and determining the value to place on additional units of the resources.

The idea of sensitivity analysis is to calculate the limits of changes in the coefficients of the problem that will not change the optimal basis. Hence, changes in this range allow determination of the optimal solution without resolving the problem from scratch.

Sensitivity analysis covers all three data inputs of linear programming: (i) the cost coefficients (c_j); (ii) the RHS elements (b_i); and, (iii) the matrix (a_{ij}) coefficients. Analysis of each is summarized below.

Changes to the k-th cost coefficient, c_k

    (i)   Change c_k to $c_k + \Delta c_k$ in the "c_j row" of the tableau (and in the "c_j column" if basic).

   (ii)   If x_k is a basic variable, recalculate the entire "z_j row" in terms of Δc_k.

  (iii)   Recalculate the entire "$c_j - z_j$ row" in terms of Δc_k.

  (iv)   Determine the range of values for Δc_k that will keep all entries in the "$c_j - z_j$ row" less than or equal to zero (greater than or equal to zero for a MINIMIZATION problem).

   (v)   Add these limits for Δc_k to c_k to determine the range in values of c_k that will keep the solution optimal. (This is called finding the range of optimality for basic variables or the range of insignificance for non-basic variables.)

Changes to the i-th RHS element, b_i

    (i)   In the original problem change b_i to $b_i + \Delta b_i$.

   (ii)   Choose column k corresponding to the slack or artifical variable which was the basic variable in the original tableau. Obtain the new RHS values by adding (RHS of optimal tableau) + Δb_i (k-th column of optimal tableau).

(iii)   Determine the range of values for Δb_i that will keep all entries in the RHS column greater than or equal to zero.

(iv)   Add these limits for Δb_i to b_i to determine the range of values of b_i that will keep the solution feasible. (This is called finding the range of feasibility for b_i).

Note that changing the availability of the resources (b_i) changes the value of the objective function. The negative of the $c_j - z_j$ values (hence, the z_j values) of the slack variables are the values placed on obtaining an additonal unit of the corresponding constraint resource. These are called the shadow prices of the resources.

Changes to a_{ij}

Changing the coefficients in the constraints is mathematically complex for the simplex method. However, qualitatively the following statements can be made: (1) Changing the a_{ij} of a non-basic variable will have no effect unless the change is large enough, (2) Increasing the a_{ij} of a positive basic variable in a less than or equal to constraint will decrease the value of the objective function, whereas decreasing its value will increase the value of the objective function. The converse is true for "greater than or equal to" constraints.

4.   Duality

Associated with every linear program (called the primal) there exists a strongly related linear program known as the dual. It is convenient to think of the primal linear program in canonical form, that is as a maximization problem with constraints of the "<" form and having non-negative variables. Then the dual is a minimization problem with constraints of the ">" form also having non-negative variables. There is one variable in the dual for each constraint in the primal, and one constraint in the dual for each variable in the primal. The coefficients of the i-th constraint in the dual are the corresponding coefficients of the i-th variable in the primal. The RHS values of the dual are the objective function coefficents of the primal, and the objective function coefficients of the dual are the RHS values of the primal. Hence given the following primal problem,

$$\text{MAX} \quad 2x_1 + 3x_2 + 4x_3$$

$$\text{s.t.} \ 5x_1 + 6x_2 + 7x_3 \le 8$$

$$9x_1 + 10x_2 + 11x_3 \le 12$$

$$x_j \ge 0 \quad j = 1,2,3$$

the dual would be

$$\text{MIN} \quad 8u_1 + 12u_2$$

$$\text{s.t.} \quad 5u_1 + 9u_2 \geq 2$$

$$6u_1 + 10u_2 \geq 3$$

$$7u_1 + 11u_2 \geq 4$$

$$u_1, \ u_2 \geq 0$$

An interpretation of a primal problem is to find the amount of each product to produce to maximize profit without using more resources than are available. The corresponding interpretation of the dual problem would be to find a set of prices for the resources which minimize the total value of the resources. The constraints of dual require the total value of the resources necessary to produce a unit of each product to exceed or equal the unit profit of the product. Thus the dual variables play the same role (and in fact are) the shadow prices of the resources.

There are many primal-dual relationships including the following. The optimal value of the objective function of the primal is the optimal value of the objective function of the dual. When the primal is solved, the negative of the $c_j - z_j$ values (hence the z_j values) of the slack variables give the optimal value of the dual variables. And, if the dual problem is converted to a MAXIMIZATION problem, the negative of the $c_j - z_j$ values of the surplus variables are the optimal values of the primal variables (they would be the positive values if the problem were solved without first converting to a maximization problem). Thus if one solves the primal problem, the dual is also solved and vice versa. This is important because it is generally mathematically easier and computationally more efficient to solve the problem which has fewer constraints.

GLOSSARY

ALTERNATE OPTIMAL SOLUTIONS - When a linear program has more than one optimal solution.   (143)

CANONICAL FORM - For a maximization problem one with all "less than or equal to" constraints with non-negative variables; for a minimization problem one with all "greater than or equal to" constraints with non-negative variables.   (168)

DEGENERATE SOLUTION - A basic feasible solution in which at least one of the basic variables (hence a RHS element) equals zero.   (146)

Δa_{ij}, Δb_i, Δc_j - The amount of change in constraint coefficient a_{ij}, in RHS element b_i, or cost coefficient c_j respectively.   (150)

DUAL LINEAR PROGRAM - An associated linear program to a primal problem with n variables and m constraints; the dual has m variables and n constraints; the c_j's of the dual are the b_i's of the primal and vice versa, and the a_{ij}'s of the primal are the a_{ji}'s of the dual.   (168)

PRIMAL LINEAR PROGRAM - The original formulation of a linear program.   (168)

RANGE OF FEASIBILITY - Range of a b_i value that will not change the variables that make up the optimal basis.   (161)

RANGE OF INSIGNIFICANCE - Range of a c_j value of a non-basic variable that will not alter the optimal solution to a linear program.   (151)

RANGE OF OPTIMALITY - Range of a c_j value of a basic variable that will not change the value of the basic variables in the optimal solution to a linear program.   (154)

SHADOW PRICE - The value of one additional unit of a resource associated with a linear programming constraint .   (159)

UNBOUNDED SOLUTION - When the value of the objective function of a maximization (minimization) problem can be increased (decreased) without bound over the feasible region.   (140)

Chapter 4 Check List

W 1) a) Show graphically why the following two linear programs do not have optimal solutions and <u>explain the difference between the two</u>.

(i) MAX $2x_1 + 6x_2$
s.t. $4x_1 + 3x_2 \leq 12$
$2x_1 + x_2 \geq 8$
$x_1, x_2 \geq 0$

(ii) MAX $3x_1 + 4x_2$
s.t. $x_1 + x_2 \geq 5$
$3x_1 + x_2 \geq 8$
$x_1, x_2 \geq 0$

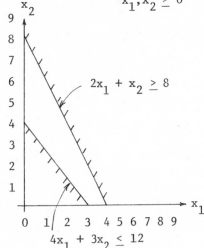

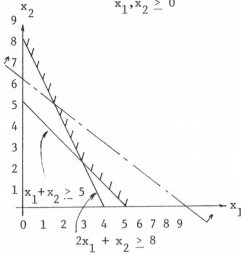

b) At a given iteration a tableau for the first problem is given on the left, and for the second problem on the right. Explain why each tableau shows the corresponding problem has no optimal solution.

Basis	c_j	x_1 2	x_2 6	s_1 0	s_2 0	a_1 -M	
x_1	2	1	3/4	1/4	0	0	3
a_1	-M	0	-1/2	-1/2	-1	1	2
z_j	2	3/2+ 1/2M	1/2+ 1/2M	M	-M	6-2M
c_j-z_j	0	9/2- 1/2M	-1/2- 1/2M	-M	0	

Basis	c_j	x_1 3	x_2 4	s_1 0	s_2 0	
s_2	0	0	1	-2	1	2
x_1	3	1	1	-1	0	5
z_j	3	3	-3	0	15	
c_j-z_j	0	1	3	0		

a) See graph. Note that (i) has no feasible solution region; hence, no optimal solution. Note that in (ii) the feasible solution region is unbounded and the objective function line can be increased without bound.

b) (i) is "optimal" and there is an artificial variable positive which means there is no feasible solution. In (ii) $c_3 - z_3 > 0$ but the pivot column is less than or equal to zero. Keeping x_2 at zero value the two equations reduce to:

$$-2s_1 + s_2 = 2 \text{ or } s_2 = 2 + 2s_1$$
$$\text{and} \quad - s_1 + x_1 = 5 \text{ or } x_1 = 5 + s_1$$

This means that as s_1 is increased neither s_2 nor x_1 tends to zero. Hence s_1 can be increased without bound and the objective function will increase 3 units for each unit s_1 is increased. Thus the problem is unbounded.

W 2) Given the following linear program

$$\begin{aligned}
\text{MAX} \quad & x_1 + 3x_2 \\
\text{s.t.} \quad & 3x_1 + 2x_2 \le 12 \\
& 2x_1 + 6x_2 \le 24 \\
& x_1, x_2 \ge 0
\end{aligned}$$

a) Solve this problem graphically and by the simplex method. Describe the set of all optimal solutions in both cases.

b) Give an optimal solution with $x_1 = 1$.

SOLUTION:

a) Graphically

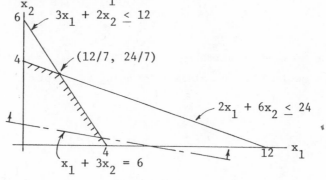

Optimal solution occurs at $(0, 4)$ and $(12/7, 24/7)$ and all points on the line between these points.

By the simplex method: Iteration 1

Basis	c_j	x_1	x_2	s_1	s_2	
		1	3	0	0	
s_1	0	3	2	1	0	12
s_2	0	2	$\boxed{6}$	0	1	24
z_j		0	0	0	0	0
$c_j - z_j$		1	3	0	0	

Iteration 2

Basis	c_j	x_1	x_2	s_1	s_2	
		1	3	0	0	
s_1	0	$\boxed{7/3}$	0	1	-1/3	4
x_2	3	1/3	1	0	1/6	4
z_j		1	3	0	1/2	12
$c_j - z_j$		0	0	0	-1/2	

The optimal solution is: $x_1 = 0$, $x_2 = 4$. However $c_1 - z_1 = 0$. Thus a new optimal basic solution by using x_1 is pivot column as follows:

Basis	c_j	x_1	x_2	s_1	s_2	
		1	3	0	0	
x_1	1	1	0	3/7	-1/7	12/7
x_2	3	0	1	-1/7	3/14	24/7
	z_j	1	3	0	1/2	12
	$c_j - z_j$	0	0	0	-1/2	

b) Note that the $c_1 - z_1 = 0$ implies the value of the objective function does not change for any increase in x_1. Referring to the tableau at iteration 2, keeping s_2 at zero value the equations reduce to

$$(7/3)x_1 + s_1 = 4 \text{ or } s_1 = 4 - (7/3)x_1$$
$$(1/3)x_1 + x_2 = 4 \text{ or } x_2 = 4 - (1/3)x_1$$

Thus when $x_1 = 1$, the $x_2 = 11/3$, $s_1 = 5/3$, $s_2 = 0$.

O 3) Given the following linear programming problem.

MIN $-2x_1 + 5x_2$

s.t. $x_1 - 3x_2 \geq 9$

$ax_1 + x_2 \leq 10$

$x_1, x_2 \geq 0$

a) Solve graphically when a takes on the following values.

     (i) $a = 1$

    (ii) $a = 2$

  (iii) $a = -2$

b) Without actually calculating them, characterize the "stopping tableau" for each of the above cases if the simplex method were used to solve the problem.

Outline of Solution:

a) Graph the first constraint

    (i)   Graph the second constraint as: $x_1 + x_2 \leq 10$
          Solve graphically for an optimal solution
          (Answer: $x_1 = 9/34$, $x_2 = 1/4$)

    (ii)   Graph the second constraint as: $2x_1 + x_2 \leq 10$
          Note there are no feasible solutions.

  (iii)   Graph the second constraint as: $-2x_1 + x_2 \leq 10$
          Note the objective function can be decreased without bound.

b)   (i)   All $c_j - z_j$ are? artificial variables are?

    (ii)   All $c_j - z_j$ are? artificial variables are?

  (iii)   Some $c_j - z_j$ are? the corresponding columns are?

Answers for (b) (i) ≥ 0, none positive (ii) ≥ 0, some artificial variables $= 0$ (iii) < 0; ≤ 0.

4) Show both graphically and by the simplex method that the following
   problem is infeasible.

$$\text{MAX} \quad 2x_1 + 5x_2$$

$$\text{s.t.} \quad 3x_1 + 4x_2 \geq 12$$

$$x_1 + x_2 \leq 2$$

$$x_1, x_2 \geq 0$$

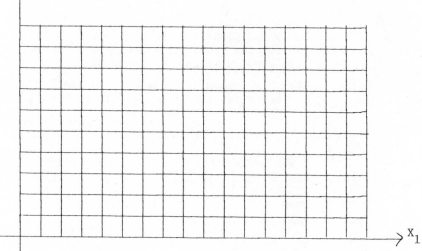

* 5) Given the following problem

$$\text{MAX} \quad 4x_1 + 6x_2$$

$$\text{s.t.} \quad x_1 - x_2 \geq 5$$

$$2x_1 + 3x_2 \leq 24$$

$$x_1, x_2 \geq 0$$

a) Solve this problem graphically.
b) Solve the problem by the simplex method.
c) Reason intuitively why the problem is unbounded if the coefficient of x_2 in the second constraint is -3 instead of 3.
d) Resolve the problem both graphically and by the simplex method with the change in (c) and verify the problem would then be unbounded.

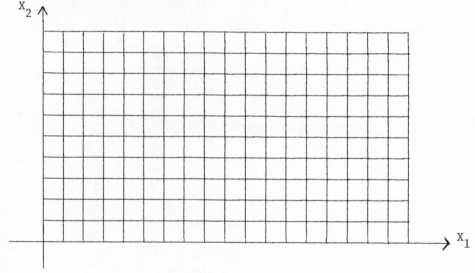

6) Solve the following linear program.

$$\text{MAX} \quad 4x_1 + x_2 + 3x_3$$

$$\text{s.t.} \quad x_1 - x_2 + x_3 \leq 10$$

$$2x_1 + x_2 + x_3 \geq 8$$

$$3x_1 - 2x_2 + 4x_3 \leq 24$$

$$x_j \geq 0 \quad j = 1,2,3$$

* 7) Solve the following problem by the simplex method.

$$\text{MAX} \quad 4x_1 + 5x_2 + x_3$$

$$\text{s.t.} \quad 3x_1 + 2x_2 + x_3 \geq 18$$

$$2x_1 + x_2 \leq 4$$

$$x_1 + x_2 - x_3 = 5$$

$$x_j \geq 0 \quad j = 1,2,3$$

8) Consider the following linear program.

$$\text{MAX } 6x_1 + 9x_2$$

$$\text{s.t. } x_1 + x_2 \geq 10$$

$$2x_1 + 3x_2 \leq 24$$

$$x_1, x_2 \geq 0$$

a) Solve the problem both graphically and by the simplex method.

b) Give all optimal basic feasible solutions and give the optimal value of the objective function.

c) Show that $x_1 = 11$, $x_2 = 2/3$ satisfies both constraints and gives the same optimal value of the objective function. Explain how this point could be generated both on the graph and in the tableau.

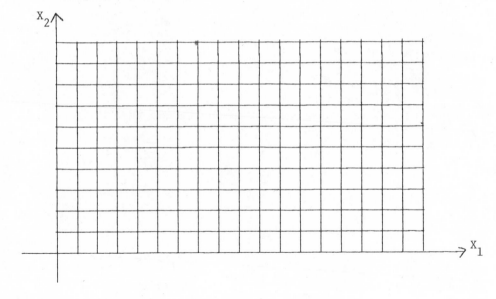

W 9) At some iteration of the simplex method the tableau is

Basis	c_j	x_1	x_2	x_3	s_1	s_2	s_3	
		4	1	3	0	0	0	
x_3	3	0	1	1	1	0	4	2
x_1	4	1	-2	0	1	0	2	5
s_2	0	0	3	0	1	1	-1	6
z_j		4	-5	3	4	0	20	26
c_j-z_j		0	6	0	-4	0	-20	

Solve for the optimal solution.

SOLUTION:

There is a tie in the ratio test $(2/1 = 2,\ 6/3 = 2)$. This means the next tableau will give a degenerate solution. Choose the first row arbitrarily as the pivot row.

Basis	c_j	x_1	x_2	x_3	s_1	s_2	s_3	
		4	1	3	0	0	0	
x_2	1	0	1	1	1	0	4	2
x_1	4	1	0	2	3	0	10	9
s_2	0	0	0	-3	-2	1	-13	0
z_j		4	1	9	13	0	44	38
c_j-z_j		0	0	-6	-13	0	-4	

This is optimal. Note that s_2 is basic but equals zero. Optimal Solution: $x_1 = 9$, $x_2 = 2$, $x_3 = 0$, $s_1 = 0$, $s_2 = 0$, $s_3 = 0$, $z = 38$.

O 10) At a given iteration the simplex tableau is:

Basis	c_j	x_1	x_2	x_3	x_4	s_1	s_2	s_3	
		4	5	1	10	0	0	0	
x_1	4	1	0	2	0	1	1	-1	2
x_1	5	0	1	5	0	2	4	-1	4
x_4	10	0	0	-5	1	-4	-2	3	2
z_j		4	5	-17	10	-26	4	21	48
$c_j - z_j$		0	0	18	0	26	-4	-21	

Do two iterations of the simplex method.

Outline of Solution:

Iteration 1: s_1 enters; tie between x_1 and x_2 for leaving variable – arbitrarily choose x_1 (degeneracy occurs).

Iteration 2: s_3 enters, x_2 leaves (note same point is generated, simply different basis).

Answer:

Basis	c_j	x_1	x_2	x_3	x_4	s_1	s_2	s_3	
		4	5	1	10	0	0	0	
s_1	0	-1	1	3	0	1	3	0	2
s_3	0	-2	1	1	0	0	2	1	0
x_4	10	2	1	4	1	0	4	0	10
z_j		20	10	40	10	0	40	0	100
$c_j - z_j$		-16	-5	-39	0	0	-40	0	

11) Given the following tableau.

Basis	c_j	x_1	x_2	x_3	s_1	s_2	s_3	
		5	10	15	0	0	0	
x_1	5	1	1	0	0	-1	3	4
s_1	0	0	K	0	1	2	2	0
x_3	15	0	-1	1	0	0	1	2
z_j		5	-10	15	0	-5	30	50
$c_j - z_j$		0	20	0	0	5	-30	

a) Suppose K = -2. Do one iteration of the simplex method.

b) Suppose K = +2. Do one iteration of the simplex method. What is the relationship between the basic feasible solution of the new tableau and the one above?

W 12) Consider the following optimal tableau where s_1, s_2, and s_3 were the slack variables added to the original problem.

Basis	c_j	x_1	x_2	x_3	x_4	s_1	s_2	s_3	
		5	25	4	10	0	0	0	
x_3	10	0	2	1	1	1	0	-1	50
x_1	5	1	3	-1	0	-1	0	4	80
s_2	0	0	4	2	0	4	1	1	100
z_j		5	35	5	10	5	0	10	900
$c_j - z_j$		0	-10	-1	0	-5	0	-10	

a) What is the range of insignificance of c_2 and what is the value of the objective function in this range?

b) What is the range of optimality of c_1 and what is the value of the objective function in this range?

c) How much would you be willing to pay for an extra unit of the first resource (for which s_1 is the corresponding slack variable)?

d) If you were offered another three units for $12, would you accept the offer?

SOLUTION:

a) Change c_2 to $c_2 + \Delta c_2$ in c_j row. Since X_2 is non basic no change will be made in the basic c_j column or the z_j row. Thus the only change in the $c_j - z_j$ row is $c_2 - z_2 = -10 + \Delta c_2$. Thus if $c_2 - z_2 \leq 0$, then $-\infty \leq \Delta c_2 \leq 10$. Let $c_2' = c_2 + \Delta c_2 = 25 + \Delta c_2$. Then from above the range of insignificance is $-\infty \leq c_2' \leq 35$ (= 25 + 10). The value of the objective function in this range is 900.

b) Change c_1 to $c_1 + \Delta c_1$ in the c_j row <u>AND</u> in the basic c_j column. Then the tableau reads:

Basis	c_j	x_1	x_2	x_3	x_4	s_1	s_2	s_3	
		$5+\Delta c_1$	25	4	10	0	0	0	
x_3	10	0	2	1	1	1	0	-1	50
x_1	$5+\Delta c_1$	1	3	-1	0	-1	0	4	80
s_2	0	0	4	2	0	4	1	1	100
z_j		$5+\Delta c_1$	$35+3\Delta c_1$	$5-\Delta c_1$	10	$5-\Delta c_1$	0	$10+4\Delta c_1$	$900 + 80\,\Delta c_1$
c_j-z_j		0	$-10-3\Delta c_1$	$-1+\Delta c_1$	0	$-5+\Delta c_1$	0	$-10-4\Delta c_1$	

For optimality,

$$-10 - 3\Delta c_1 \leq 0 \qquad \text{or} \qquad \Delta c_1 \geq -10/3$$

$$-1 + \Delta c_1 \leq 0 \qquad \text{or} \qquad \Delta c_1 \leq 1$$

$$-5 + \Delta c_1 \leq 0 \qquad \text{or} \qquad \Delta c_1 \leq 5$$

$$-10 - 4\Delta c_1 \leq 0 \qquad \text{or} \qquad \Delta c_1 \geq -5/2$$

Combining the above inequalities we have: $-5/2 \leq \Delta c_1 \leq 1$. If $c_1' = c_1 + \Delta c_1$, then $5/2 \leq c_1' \leq 6$ is the range of optimality. The optimal value of the objective function in this range is $900 + 80\,\Delta c_1$.

c) The value of an extra unit of the first resource is the effect the extra unit will have on the value of the objective function, or its shadow price. This is found in the z_j row and is +5.

d) Changing b_1 to b_1 to Δb_1 would result in the following RHS in the optimal tableau (note the coefficients of Δb_1 are from the s_1 column in the optimal tableau): $50 + \Delta b_1$; $80 - \Delta b_1$; $100 + 4\Delta b_1$. Since these values must be ≥ 0, then $-25 \leq b_1 \leq 80$. These values added to the original b_1 would give the range of feasibility.

101

O 13)   Given the following linear program

$$MAX \quad 2x_1 + x_2 + 3x_3$$

$$s.t. \quad x_1 + 4x_2 + 4x_3 \leq 20$$

$$4x_1 + 4x_2 + x_3 \leq 20$$

$$x_1, x_2 \geq 0$$

a)   Solve this linear program.

b)   Calculate the range of optimality (or insignificance) for each of the three variables.

c)   Suppose a profit could be made on the slack of the first constraint. What profit value on this slack would be sufficient to change the optimal solution?

d)   By how much would the optimal value of the objective function change for a unit increase in the RHS of the second constraint?

e)   Calculate the range of feasibility for b_2.

f)   Describe in words the effects on the value if the objective function of a_{21} were increased.

Outline of Solution:

a)   Solving the linear program we get $x_1 = 4$, $x_2 = 0$, $x_3 = 4$ for the optimal solution.

b)   (i)   Change c_1 to $c_1 + \Delta c_1$ in both the c_j row and basic c_j column and calculate the limits on Δc_1 that keep all $c_j - z_j \leq 0$.

   (ii)   Change c_2 to $c_2 + \Delta c_2$ in the c_j row only since x_2 is non-basic. Only $c_2 - z_2$ changes in the $c_j - z_j$ row. What are the limits on Δc_2 that keep $c_2 - z_2$ positive?

   (iii)   Repeat (i) for c_3 changing to $c_3 + \Delta c_3$.

c)   This is equivalent to finding the range of insignificance for c_4 (the objective function coefficient of s_1). Handle this the same way as (ii) above.

d) This is the shadow price (or z_j value) of s_2.

e) Add to the RHS values in the optimal tableau Δb_2 times the coefficients in the s_2 column of the optimal tableau. Find the values of Δb_2 that keeps the RHS ≥ 0 in the optimal tableau. Add the original b_2 (= 20) to these values to calculate range of feasibility.

f) Since increasing a_{21} means more of the second resource is used per unit of x_1 and since the amount of the resource is fixed at 20, what conclusion do you draw?

Answers:

a) optimal tableau

Basis	c_j	x_1	x_2	x_3	s_1	s_2	
		2	1	3	0	0	
x_3	3	0	4/5	1	4/15	-1/15	4
x_1	2	1	4/5	0	-1/15	4/15	4
z_j		2	4	3	2/3	1/3	20
$c_j - z_j$		0	-3	0	-2/3	-1/3	

b) $3/4 \leq c_1' \leq 12$; $-\infty \leq c_2' \leq 4$; $1/2 \leq c_3' \leq 8$

c) $c_4' \geq 2/3$

d) 1/3

e) $5 \leq b_2' \leq 80$

f) value decreases

103

* 14)   Consider the following linear program

$$\text{MAX} \quad 5x_1 + 2x_2 + 3x_3$$

$$\text{s.t.} \quad x_1 + x_2 + x_3 \le 10$$

$$2x_1 + 3x_2 + 4x_3 \le 24$$

$$x_j \ge 0 \quad j = 1,2,3$$

    a)   Solve the linear program.

    b)   Give the range of optimality or insignificance on all variables including slack variables.

    c)   If you were offered another unit of the first resource for $4 would you accept the offer?

    d)   If you were offered another three units of the first resource for $12 would you accept the offer?

15)   Suppose a range of optimality for c_1 is given by $a \le c_1' \le b$. Now suppose c_1 is changed to a number larger than b. How would you solve for the optimal solution with resolving the problem from scratch?

16) Given the following linear program.

$$\text{MAX} \quad 4x_1 + 3x_2$$

$$\text{s.t.} \quad x_1 \qquad \le \quad 8$$

$$2x_1 + 3x_2 \le 19$$

$$x_1 + x_2 \le 12$$

$$x_1, \; x_2 \ge 0$$

a) Solve the problem by the simplex method.
b) Calculate the range of optimality for c_1, c_2.
c) Suppose the first constraint were changed to $x_1 \le 9$. How much would this change be worth. (You do not have to solve the problem over again).
d) Calculate the range of feasibility for b_1.
e) Solve the problem graphically.
f) Show what happens graphically when Δc_2 is increased to its limit in the range of optimality.
g) Explain graphically why the shadow price of the first resource, b_1, is valid only for $b_1 \le 9.5$.

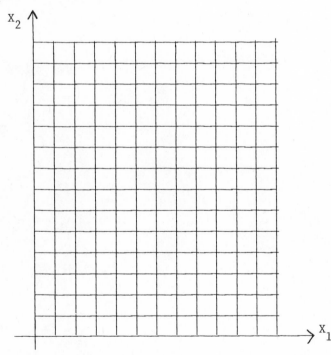

* 17) As owner of a chain of bakery shops, you are considering producing a
    new product called Breakfast Bars. Breakfast Bars is a mixture of
    three ingredients, we'll call them A, B, and C, which you wish to
    produce at minimum cost. To be able to be marketable, the following
    guidelines must be followed:

    (i)   At least 50% of the bar must be a combination of
           ingredients A and B.

    (ii)   No more than 30% of the bar can be ingredient A.

    (iii) At least as much ingredient B must be used as any
           other ingredient.

    If the cost per pound of the ingredients are 62¢ per pound of A, 54¢
    per pound of B, and 40¢ per pound of C, how much of each ingredient
    should go into a 8 ounce bar and what price would you charge to make
    a 50% profit? (Ignore manufacturing costs.)

18) Suppose the Asian Import Company (AIC) has 600 cubic feet of excess cargo space on its ships and has decided to import two new items: jade figurines and linen placemats. Each container of jade figurines is 4 cubic feet and will net a profit of $80. Each box of placemats is 2 cubic feet and will realize a profit of $60. AIC expects no more than 140 containers of jade figurines to be available per trip. Additionally, AIC wants to use no more than 480 man-hours for loading, unloading, storing, and processing the items through customs. The estimate is that a container requires 2 man-hours; however, because of special agricultural restrictions an extra 2 man-hours can be expected for the linen products.

a) How many containers of each product should be shipped?

b) What is the range of profit on jade containers for which this solution remains optimal?

c) What is the value of

   (i) an extra man-hour?

   (ii) an extra cubic foot of cargo space?

   (iii) an extra available jade container?

19) The SINK-FAST Company has a capability of making three kinds of sinks
    for distribution to hardware stores and building supply companies.
    Each sink is made from three components; A, B, and C which are in
    daily supply of 400 lbs., 200 lbs., and 300 lbs. respectively. The
    profit per sink and the amount of material needed for each sink are
    given in the following chart

	Profit	Mtl. A	Mtl. B	Mtl. C
Basic	$14	2	1	1
Standard	$30	8	1	0
Deluxe	$40	2	4	1

a) Solve for the optimal solution by the simplex method to show an
   optimal solution making two varieties of sinks.

b) Perhaps for ease of manufacturing SINK-FAST would like to concen-
   trate on making one kind of sink. Show there exists such an
   alternative optimal solution.

c) Perhaps for diversification, the SINK-FAST would like to manufacture all three kinds of sinks. Show there exists many
   (non-basic) optimal solutions producing all three sinks.

* 20) Given the following optimal tableau for a linear programming problem.

Basis	c_j	x_1	x_2	x_3	s_1	s_2	s_3	s_4	
		2	4	6	0	0	0	0	
s_3	0	0	0	2	4	-2	1	0	8
x_2	4	0	1	2	2	-1	0	0	6
x_1	2	1	0	-1	1	2	0	0	4
s_4	0	0	0	1	3	2	0	1	12
z_j		2	4	6	10	0	0	0	32
$c_j - z_j$		0	0	0	-10	0	0	0	

a) Give the optimal basic feasible solution associated with this tableau.

b) Give an optimal solution with x_3 replacing x_2 in the above basis.

c) Give an optimal solution with s_2 replacing x_1 in the tableau in part (a).

d) Are there any other optimal basic feasible solutions?

e) Using the three extreme points of (a), (b), (c), let us construct another solution by taking any weighted average of these points. Show why this solution will be: (i) feasible; (ii) optimal. (Such a weighted average is called a convex combination of extreme points.) Conclusion: A convex combination of optimal extreme points is optimal.

21) Consider the following linear programming tableau.

		x_1	x_2	x_3	s_1	s_2	s_3	
		5	2	1	0	0	0	
x_3	1	2	0	1	-6	1	0	8
x_2	2	1	1	0	4	0	0	4
s_3	0	4	0	0	3	-3	1	20
z_j		4	2	1	2	1	0	16
$c_j - z_j$		1	0	0	-2	-1	0	

a) Do one iteration of the simplex method by choosing the first row
as the pivot row. What new basic feasible solution did you get?
Does the new $c_j - z_j$ row indicate that it is optimal?

b) Repeat (a), but this time break the tie of the ratio test by
taking the second row as the pivot row. What new basic feasible
solution did you get? Does this new $c_j - z_j$ row indicate that it
is optimal?

c) Interpret the results of (a) and (b) by stating a conclusion
concerning optimality when degeneracy occurs.

* 22) Consider the following constraint set for a linear programming
problem:

$$2x_1 + x_2 \geq 4$$

$$x_1 + 2x_2 \geq 5$$

$$x_1 - 2x_2 \leq 1$$

$$x_1, x_2 \geq 0$$

a) Graph the constraints and note that they form an unbounded
feasible region.

b) Identify all extreme points.

c) Note that a linear program with an unbounded feasible region
may or may not have an optimal solution. Show this by imposing
the following objective functions on the problem:

    (i)   MAX $2x_1 - 5x_2$

    (ii)   MAX $2x_1 - 4x_2$

    (iii)   MAX $2x_1 - 3x_2$

Discuss the implications of each objective function.

23) A company that can make three kinds of tennis rackets denoted by x_1, x_2 and x_3 had decided to raise the price they charge for their rackets. Because of the sudden demand for all tennis products the increase in price is not expected to affect sales. The company has decided to raise the price on each kind by the <u>same</u> amount, Δ. However, if the price rises too much a large cost would be incurred for retooling and change in work schedules. The senior vice president has deferred to you the decision of the amount of the price rise. You have checked your computer program that generated the optimal weekly production schedule and the final tableau is given below. How much price rise per racket do you recommend and what will be the new optimal weekly profit?

Basis	c_j	x_1 10	x_2 26	x_3 60	s_1 0	s_2 0	s_3 0	
x_3	60	0	2	1	2	3	0	200
s_3	0	0	3	0	-6	4	1	500
x_1	10	1	-8	0	-6	-6	0	100
	z_j	10	40	60	60	120	0	13,000
	$c_j - z_j$	0	-14	0	-60	-120	0	

W 24) Given the following linear program.

$$\text{MAX}\quad 4x_1 + 3x_2$$

$$\text{s.t.}\quad x_1 + x_2 \leq 8$$

$$3x_1 + 2x_2 \leq 18$$

$$2x_1 + 5x_2 \leq 15$$

$$5x_1 - x_2 \leq 10$$

$$x_1,\; x_2 \geq 0$$

a) Write the dual linear program.
b) Solve the dual problem.
c) What is the optimal solution to the primal problem?
d) Verify this graphically.
e) Why would solving the dual problem by the simplex method be more convenient than solving the primal by the simplex method for this problem.

SOLUTION:

a) There are four variables and two constraints in the dual. The rows of the dual are formed from the columns of the primal.

DUAL   MIN $8u_1 + 18u_2 + 15u_3 + 10u_4$

$$\text{s.t.}\quad u_1 + 3u_2 + 2u_3 + 5u_4 \geq 4$$

$$u_1 + 2u_2 + 5u_3 - u_4 \geq 3$$

$$u_1,\; u_2 \geq 0$$

b) Change objective function to maximization to solve.

Basis	c_j	u_1 -8	u_2 -18	u_3 -15	u_4 -10	s_1 0	s_2 0	a_1 $-M$	a_2 $-M$	
a_1	$-M$	1	3	2	5	-1	0	1	0	4
a_2	$-M$	1	2	$\boxed{5}$	-1	0	-1	0	1	3
z_j		$-2M$	$-5M$	$-7M$	$-4M$	M	M	$-M$	$-M$	$-7M$
c_j-z_j		$2M-8$	$5M-18$	$7M-15$	$4M-10$	$-M$	$-M$	0	0	

Basis	c_j	u_1 -8	u_2 -18	u_3 -15	u_4 -10	s_1 0	s_2 0	a_1 $-M$	a_2 $-M$	
a_1	$-M$	$3/5$	$11/5$	0	$\boxed{27/5}$	-1	$2/5$	1	$-2/5$	$14/5$
u_3	-15	$1/5$	$2/5$	1	$-1/5$	0	$-1/5$	0	$1/5$	$3/5$
z_j		$-3M/5-3$	$-11M/5-4$	-15	$-27M/5+3$	M	$-2M/5+3$	$-M$	$-2M/5-3$	$-14M/5-9$
c_j-z_j		$3M/5-5$	$11M/5-14$	0	$27M/5-13$	$-M$	$2M/5-3$	0	$3M/5+3$	

Basis	c_j	u_1 -8	u_2 -18	u_3 -15	u_4 -10	s_1 0	s_2 0	a_1 $-M$	a_2 $-M$	
u_4	-10	$3/27$	$11/27$	0	1	$-5/27$	$2/27$	$5/27$	$-2/27$	$14/27$
u_3	-15	$6/27$	$13/27$	1	0	$-1/27$	$-5/27$	$1/27$	$5/27$	$19/27$
z_j		$-120/27$	$-305/27$	-15	-10	$65/27$	$55/27$	$-65/27$	$-55/27$	$-505/27$
c_j-z_j		$-96/27$	$-181/27$	0	0	$-65/27$	$-55/27$	$-M+65/27$	$-M+55/27$	

$u_1 = 0$, $u_2 = 0$, $u_3 = 19/27$, $u_4 = 14/27$ $z = 505/27$

c) $x_1 = -(c_j - z_j$ for $s_1) = 65/27$

$x_2 = -(c_j - z_j$ for $s_3) = 55/27$

114

d)

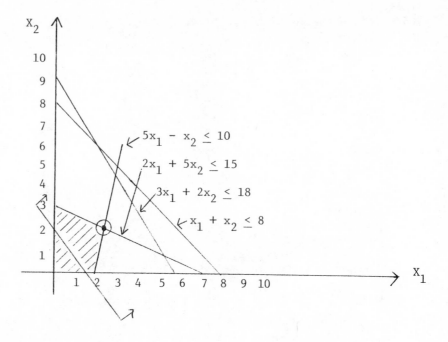

optimal point at intersection of

$$2x_1 + 5x_2 = 15$$

$$5x_1 - x_2 = 10$$

Solution $x_1 = 65/27$; $x_2 = 55/27$; $z = 505/27$.

e) There are fewer constraints and hence usually fewer iterations and fewer computations per iteration.

115

O 25) Given the following problem.

$$\text{MAX} \quad 2x_1 + x_2 + 3x_3$$

$$\text{s.t.} \quad x_1 + 2x_2 + 3x_3 \leq 15$$

$$3x_1 + 4x_2 + 6x_2 \geq 24$$

$$x_1 + x_2 + x_3 = 10$$

$$x_j \geq 0 \quad j = 1,2,3$$

a) Write the problem in canonical form.
b) Write the dual of the canonical primal.
c) Solve the primal.
d) What is the optimal solution for the dual.

Outline of Solution:

a) Constraint (1) is a "$\leq$" constraint; leave it alone.
Multiply constraint (2) by -1 to transform it into "$\leq$" form.
Rewrite constraint (3) as a "$\geq$" constraint and a "$\leq$" constraint
and multiply the "$\geq$" constraint by -1.

b) There are four dual variables, u_1, u_2, u_3' and u_3''. The objective function coefficients of the dual are the RHS coefficients of
the primal and the RHS coefficients of the dual are the objective function coefficients of the primal. The row coefficients
of the dual are the column coefficients of the primal.

c) Add four slack variables. Since two of the RHS are negative,
multiply by -1 and add two artificial variables. Then solve by
the simplex method.

d) The optimal solution for the dual is found as the negative of
the $c_j - z_j$ values of s_1, s_2, s_3 and s_4. Note $u_3 = u_3' - u_3''$.

Answers:

a)
$$\text{MAX} \quad 2x_1 + x_2 + 3x_3$$

$$\text{s.t.} \quad x_1 + 2x_2 + 3x_3 \leq 15$$

$$-3x_1 - 4x_2 - 6x_3 \leq -24$$

$$x_1 + x_2 + x_3 \leq 10$$

$$- x_1 - x_2 - x_3 \leq -10$$

$$x_j \geq 0 \quad j = 1,2,3$$

116

b) $\quad$ MIN $15u_1 - 24u_2 + 10u_3' - 10u_3''$

$\quad$ s.t. $\quad u_1 - 3u_2 + u_3' - u_3'' \geq 2$

$\qquad\qquad 2u_1 - 4u_2 + u_3' - u_3'' \geq 1$

$\qquad\qquad 3u_1 - 6u_2 + u_3' - u_3'' \geq 3$

$\qquad\qquad u_i \geq 0 \quad i = 1,2,3',3''$

c) The optimal tableau is

Basis	c_j	x_1	x_2	x_3	s_1	s_2	s_3	s_4	a_1	a_2	
		2	1	3	0	0	0	0	$-M$	$-M$	
x_3	3	0	1/2	1	1/2	0	$-1/2$	0	0	0	5/2
x_1	2	1	1/2	0	$-1/2$	0	3/2	0	0	0	15/2
s_4	0	0	0	0	0	0	1	1	0	-1	0
s_2	0	0	1/2	0	3/2	1	3/2	0	-1	0	27/2
z_j		2	5/2	3	1/2	0	3/2	0	0	0	45/2
$c_j - z_j$		0	$-3/2$	0	$-1/2$	0	$-3/2$	0	$-M$	$-M$	

Thus $x_1 = 15/2$, $x_2 = 0$, $x_3 = 5/2$, $z = 45/2$ is optimal.

d) $\quad u_1 = 1/2$, $u_2 = 0$, $u_3' = 3/2$, $u_3'' = 0$ (Thus $u_3 = 3/2$) $z = 45/2$.

117

* 26)   Given the following linear program

$$\text{MAX}\quad 10x_1 + 8x_2$$

$$\text{s.t.}\quad x_1 + 3x_2 \leq 15$$

$$4x_1 + x_2 \leq 16$$

$$x_1,\ x_2 \geq 0$$

a)   Formulate the dual.
b)   Solve both the primal and the dual graphically.
c)   Solve the primal by the simplex method and show that the optimal value of the dual variables are in fact those determined in (b).

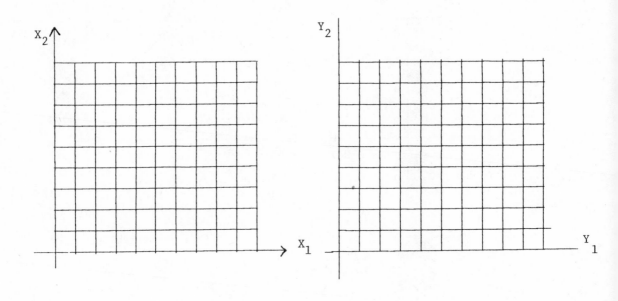

27) Given the following linear program

$$\text{MAX} \quad 3x_1 + 2x_2 - 3x_3$$

$$\text{s.t.} \quad x_1 + 3x_2 + 8x_3 \leq 56$$

$$2x_1 - x_2 - x_3 = 14$$

$$x_2 \geq 5$$

$$x_j \geq 0 \quad j = 1,2,3$$

a) Write the problem in canonical form.
b) Write the dual to the canonical primal.
c) Take the dual to the dual problem. Conclusion?

* 28)   Given the following linear program

$$\text{MAX} \quad 5x_1 + 2x_2 + 7x_3$$

$$\text{s.t.} \quad 2x_1 + 2x_2 + x_3 \le 15$$

$$x_1 - x_2 + x_3 \le 10$$

$$4x_1 + 3x_2 + x_3 \le 24$$

$$x_j \ge 0 \quad j = 1,2,3$$

a)   Formulate the dual.
b)   Solve the primal.
c)   What is the optimal solution for the dual?
d)   Show that this dual solution is feasible for the dual.
e)   Verify the optimal value of the objective function of the primal is the optimal value of the objective function for the dual.

29) Suppose in solving the primal it is found that the primal is unbounded. Recalling that the objective function of the dual is a minimization what does this indicate about the solution to the dual problem?

30) Consider problem #16 of Chapter 3.

    a)   Formulate the dual.
    b)   Solve the dual.
    c)   From the optimal dual tableau determine the optimal solution to the primal.
    d)   Interpret the meaning of each of the dual variables in this problem.

5 LINEAR PROGRAMMING: APPLICATIONS

REVIEW

1. Basic Linear Programming Models

There are an infinite variety of problems that may be formulated as linear programs. However specific names have been given to several types of linear programs with particular special structures that occur quite frequently. Four of the most common are product mix problems, diet problems, blending problems, and transportation problems. Although a particular problem could be formulated that has nothing to do with diets, for example, if the problem has the same structure as the diet problem it is classified as such.

A product mix problem has the following structure: (1) maximization objective function; (2) "less than or equal to" constraints; (3) nonnegative coefficients. It can be thought of as choosing the proper quantity of each product to produce to maximize profits while being restricted by scarce resources.

A diet problem has the following structure: (1) minimization objective function; (2) greater than or equal to constraints; (3) nonnegative coefficients. It can be thought of as choosing which foods to purchase to minimize total cost while still meeting nutritional requirements.

A blending problem is one in which the decision variables are defined to be the amount of some raw material (such as fiber) that is blended into some finished good (finished cloth). Hence the profit coefficients for these variables must take into account the selling price of the finished product and the cost of the raw material.

A transportation problem (see Chapter 7) deals with shipping goods from origins (i) to destinations (j). They have the following structure: (1) minimization objective function; (2) x_{ij} is the amount shipped from origin i to destination j; the constraints are: $\sum_j x_{ij} = s_i$ for all i and $\sum_i x_{ij} = d_j$ for all j. s_i and d_j are non-negative constants which can be thought of as supplies at the origins i, and demands at the destinations j respectively.

Linear programming has been successfully applied to the areas of finance, accounting, marketing, and management. In fact, recent surveys have determined that linear programming is the most used management science technique in business today.

Although on-the-job experience may be necessary to see specific uses of linear programs in a particular disciplines, observation and repetition are the key to developing the art of linear programming formulations.

2. Goal Programming

Often managers seek to achieve several goals which collectively are inconsistent. The problem then becomes one of meeting all of the goals "as closely as possible." Problems which have multiple objectives of this type rather than a traditional maximization or minimization objective are known as goal programming problems.

Goal programming problems are formulated as follows. A target or goal amount (a RHS value) is stated for each objective. Then equality constraints are formed by subtracting the eventual overachieved deviation, d_i^+, and adding the eventual underachieved deviation, d_i^-, from the objective. For example if it is desired that $3x_1 + 2x_2 = 120$ and $5x_1 + x_2 = 100$ then the corresponding goal programming constraints would be $3x_1 + 2x_2 - d_1^+ + d_1^- = 120$ and $5x_1 + x_2 - d_2^+ + d_2^- = 100$.

The objective is then to minimize a weighted sum of the derivations. In the above if it were 3 times as important that $3x_1 + 2x_2$ be at least 120 as it was for $5x_1 + x_2$ to be at most 100 the objective function would be MIN $0d_1^+ + 3d_1^- + d_2^+ + 0d_2^-$. Once the goals have been transformed into constraints and an appropriate objective function formulated, the simplex method is used to solve for the optimal solution in terms of meeting these goals.

Chapter 5 Check List

W 1) Frederick's Feed Company receives four raw grains from which it blends
its dry pet food. The pet food advertises that each 8 oz. serving
meets the minimum daily requirements for vitamins, protein, and iron.
The cost of each raw grain as well as the vitamin, protein, and iron
units per pound of each grain are summarized below.

Grain	Vitamin Units/lb	Protein Units/lb	Iron Units/lb	Cost/lb
1	9	2	0	.50
2	6	10	4	.70
3	8	0	15	.80
4	10	8	7	1.00

If the minimum daily requirement for vitamins is 3 units, protein
4 units, and iron 6 units, what blend of grains produces the required
pet food at minimum cost? FORMULATE ONLY.

SOLUTION:

Let x_j = #lbs. of grain j in one 8 oz. mixture of pet food.

OBJECTIVE: MIN (Total cost of producing 8 oz. mixture)
or MIN $.50x_1 + .70x_2 + .80x_3 + 1.00x_4$

CONSTRAINTS:

Amount of vitamins in mixture is at least 3
$9x_1 + 6x_2 + 8x_3 + 10x_4 \geq 3$

Amount of protein in mixture is at least 4
$2x_1 + 10x_2 + 8x_4 \geq 4$

Amount of iron in mixture is at least 6
$4x_2 + 15x_3 + 7x_4 \geq 6$

Total mixture = 8 oz. (= .5 lbs.)
$x_1 + x_2 + x_3 + x_4 = .5$

$x_j \geq 0 \quad j = 1,2,3,4$

2) Mineral Manufacturing (MM) produces four products from four raw
materials; iron, zinc, copper and silver. MM has access to 400 tons
of iron, 50 tons of zinc, 40 tons of copper, and one ton of silver
per week. The table below summarizes the amount of material needed
to make one unit of each of the four products and the profit per unit.

Product	Unit Profit	Iron (lbs)	Zinc (lbs)	Copper (lbs)	Silver (lbs)
V	$ 100	100	10	5	1
X	$ 200	60	0	10	.5
Y	$ 500	80	30	4	.5
Z	$1,500	0	2	0	2

a) What weekly production schedule should MM use? FORMULATE ONLY.

b) How would your formulation change if excess silver could be sold
for $160,000 per ton?

c) Suppose there were n products and m raw materials. If there were
b_i units of raw material i, and profit per unit of product j were
c_j, and each unit of product j required a_{ij} units of raw material
i, then generalize your formulation in (a).

127

* 3) Millard Construction is planning to build a planned community with the help of federal funds. These funds are to be distributed only if Millard meets federal standards for low cost housing. There are three types of units--houses, town-homes, and high rise condominiums. There are three styles of each of the houses and town-houses--low cost, standard, and deluxe. The high rise condominiums will only have standard and deluxe versions. The amount of total ground space (including allowances for parking and green belts) is given in the following table.

Ground Area (Sq. Ft.)

	Low Cost	Standard	Deluxe
Houses	1,800	2,200	3,000
Town-houses	740	1,600	2,230
Condominiums	X	1,000	1,500

The profit to Millard per unit is summarized in the following table.

Profit ($1,000's)

	Low Cost	Standard	Deluxe
Houses	5	12	25
Town-houses	4	10	18
Condominiums	X	9	16

Millard has 300,000 square feet for construction. To make the project "work", Millard wants houses and town-houses each to occupy between 25% and 40% of the total area while condominiums only need occupy 10% to 25% of the total area.

The federal government requires that at least 25% of the total units built in the complex be low cost units.

a) What mix of units should Millard build to maximize profits? FORMULATE ONLY.

b) Why will linear programming not be a technically correct formulation of this problem?

128

4) The SMM Company, which is manufacturing a new instant salad maker machine, has $500,000 to invest in advertising. The product is only going to be marketed in Dallas during its initial trial. The money is to be spent on an advertising "blitz" during one week in January and advertising is going to be limited to television. The company has three options available: day time advertising, evening news advertising (both the 6:00 and 11:00 news), and the Super Bowl. Even though the Super Bowl is a national telecast, the Dallas Cowboys will be playing in it, and hence, the viewing audience will be large in the Dallas area. A mixture of one minute TV spots is desired.

The table below gives pertinent data.

	Cost Per Minute	Estimated New Audience Reached With First Ad	Estimated New Audience Reached With Succeeding Ad
Day Time	$ 5,000	8,000	3,000
Evening News	$ 2,000	15,000	2,000
Super Bowl	$100,000	100,000	75,000

SMM has decided to take out at least one ad in each option. Further there are only two Super Bowl ads available, 10 day time spots, and 6 evening news spots available per day. If SMM wants to have at least five ads per day, but spend no more than $50,000 per day (except Super Bowl Sunday), how should the company advertise over the forthcoming week. FORMULATE ONLY.

W 5) At a certain school an instructor is evaluated on four criteria: (1) teaching; (2) research; (3) professional activities; and (4) committee work for the university. The Quantitative Analysis Department has a complicated formula for obtaining exact numerical scores (between 0 and 100) for each of the four criteria through student evaluations, evaluation of publications, participation at professional conferences, etc. Suppose this has been done and for a particular instructor the number scores of 82, 100, 65, and 78 were received for the four criteria respectively.

The instructor's overall rating is then decided by assigning weights to the four areas that meet the following guidelines.

(1) teaching plus research greater than or equal to 60%
(2) teaching greater than or equal to <u>any</u> other category
(3) research at least 20%
(4) professional activities at least 10%
(5) committee work at least 10%

Write a linear program that will solve for the maximum overall instructor rating.

<u>SOLUTION:</u>

Let x_j = the percentage assigned to area j

where j = 1 (teaching), 2 (research), 3 (professional activity), 4 (committee work)

NOTE: TOTAL PERCENTAGE = $x_1 + x_2 + x_3 + x_4$

<u>OBJECTIVE</u>

MAX (OVERALL RATING = WEIGHTED AVERAGE)

MAX $82x_1 + 100x_2 + 65x_1 + 78x_4$

CONSTRAINTS

(1) Teaching percentage + research percentage $\geq$ 60% (total percentage)
$x_1 + x_2 \geq .6 (x_1 + x_2 + x_3 + x_4)$ or
$.4x_1 + .4x_2 - .6x_3 - .6x_4 \geq 0$

(2) Teaching percentage $\geq$ research percentage
$x_1 \geq x_2$ or $x_1 - x_2 \geq 0$

Teaching percentage $\geq$ professional activity percentage
$x_1 \geq x_3$ or $x_1 - x_3 \geq 0$

130

Teaching percentage $\geq$ committee work percentage

$$x_1 \geq x_4 \quad \text{or} \quad x_1 - x_4 \geq 0$$

(3) Research percentage $\geq$ 20% (total percentage)

$$x_2 \geq .2 \, (x_1 + x_2 + x_3 + x_4) \quad \text{or}$$
$$-2x_1 + .8x_2 - .2x_3 - .2x_4 \geq 0$$

(4) Professional activity percentage $\geq$ 10% (total percentage)

$$x_3 \geq .1 \, (x_1 + x_2 + x_3 + x_4) \quad \text{or}$$
$$-.1x_1 - .1x_2 + .9x_3 - .1x_4 \geq 0$$

(5) Committee work percentage $\geq$ 10% (total percentage)

$$x_4 \geq .1 \, (x_1 + x_2 + x_3 + x_4) \quad \text{or}$$
$$-.1x_1 - .1x_2 - .1x_3 + .9x_4 \geq 0$$

(6) Total percentage = 100

$$x_1 + x_2 + x_3 + x_4 = 100$$
$$x_j \geq 0 \quad j = 1,2,3,4$$

(NOTE: By substituting 100 for $x_1 + x_2 + x_3 + x_4$ in constraints (1), (3), (4), and (5), we would have an equivalent and perhaps easier formulation. The above is illustrated as an aid for solving problem 6.)

* 6) Plaid Shirts Company makes four varieties of shirts: Collegiate, Traditional, European, and Funky. These shirts are each made from different combinations of three processed fabrics. Table I, below, shows the cost and weekly availability of the fabrics whereas Table II gives the selling price, total yards per shirt, the maximum and minimum fabric requirements, the demand, and minimum contract for each shirt style.

TABLE I

Fabric	Cost/Yd	Weekly Availability (Yds)
X	$2.50	4,000
Y	$3.25	2,000
Z	$4.00	3,000

TABLE II

Shirt	Total Yards of Fabric Needed Per Shirt	Fabric Requirements	Weekly Contracts	Weekly Demand	Selling Price
Collegiate	.90	At least 80% fabric X	500	600	$10.80
Traditional	1.00	At least 50% fabric X No more than 40% fabric Z	625	800	$ 8.00
European	.95	At least 50% fabric Y No more than 20% fabric Z	280	500	$15.20
Funky	1.2	At least 30% fabric Z	150	300	$12.00

What policy should Plaid Shirt Company use in manufacturing shirts in order to maximize its weekly profit? FORMULATE ONLY.

132

O 7) National Wing Company (NWC) is gearing up for the new B-48 contract.
Currently NWC has 100 workers equally qualified. Over the next three
months NWC has made the following commitments.

Month	Contract
1	20
2	24
3	30

Each worker can either be placed in production or can train new
recruits. A new recruit can be trained to be an apprentice in one
month. The next month he himself becomes a qualified worker (after two
months from start of training). Each trainer can train two recruits.
The production rate and salary per employee is estimated below.

Employees	Production Rate Wings/Month	Salary Per Month
Production	.6	$1,500
Trainer	.3	$1,800
Apprentice	.4	$1,100
Recruit	.05	$ 700

If after three months the company wishes to have no recruits or
apprentices, and to have at least 140 full time workers, how can NWC
accomplish this at minimum cost? FORMULATE ONLY.

Outline of Solution:

Problem Variables X_{1i} = # producing employees in month i

X_{2i} = # training employees in month i

X_{3i} = # apprentices in month i

X_{4i} = # recruits in month i

Objective: Min total cost over three months.

Constraints:

(Number of Wings produced by end of month i) $\geq$ (Sum of
Wing contract requirements)   (1-3)

(Number of producers + trainers in month i + 1)
= (Number of producers + trainers in month i)
+ (Number of apprentices in month i)   (4-5)

(Number of apprentices in month i + 1) = (Number of
recruits in month i)   (6-7)

(Number recruits in month i) $\leq$ 2 (Number of trainers
in month i)   (8-9)

(Number of producers + trainers in month 1) = 100   (10)

(Number of producers in month 4) = (Number of producers
in month 3) + (Number of apprentices in month 3) $\geq$ 140   (11)

(Why would there be no X_{31}, X_{23}, or X_{43}?)

Answer: Min $1500X_{11} + 1800X_{21} + 700X_{41} + 1500X_{12} + 1800X_{22} + 1100X_{32}$

$700X_{42} + 1500X_{13} + 1100X_{33}$

s.t. $.6X_{11} + .3X_{21} + .05X_{41} \geq 20$ (1)

$.6X_{11} + .3X_{21} + .05X_{41} + .6X_{12} + .3X_{22} + .4X_{32}$

$+ .05X_{42} \geq 44$ (2)

$.6X_{11} + .3X_{21} + .05X_{41} + .6X_{12} + .3X_{22} + .4X_{32}$

$+ .05X_{42} + .6X_{13} + .4X_{33} \geq 74$ (3)

$X_{12} + X_{22} = X_{11} + X_{21}$ (4)

$X_{13} = X_{12} + X_{22} + X_{32}$ (5)

$X_{32} = X_{41}$ (6)

$X_{33} = X_{42}$ (7)

$X_{41} \leq 2X_{21}$ (8)

$$X_{42} \leq 2X_{22} \tag{9}$$

$$X_{11} + X_{21} = 100 \tag{10}$$

$$X_{13} + X_{33} \geq 140 \tag{11}$$

$$X_{ij} \geq 0 \quad i = 1,2,3,4 \quad j = 1,2,3$$

8) Burt Wheeler is the manager of the manufacturing section of Wheeler Wheels, Inc. Wheeler has just accepted a contract calling for 1,000 standard wheels and 1,250 deluxe wheels in the first month and 800 standard and 1,500 deluxe wheels in the second month. The cost of producing standard wheels is $10 and deluxe wheels $16. Overtime rates are 50% higher. There are 1,000 hours of regular time and 500 hours of overtime available each month. The cost of storing either wheel from one month to the next is $2 per wheel. As manager, how should Burt schedule production over the next two months if it takes .5 hours to make a standard wheel and .6 hours to make a deluxe wheel. FORMULATE ONLY.

9) A small investment group wishes to maximize the value of its total assets one year hence and wishes to be totally liquid at that point. In any month the following transactions are possible: (1) invest in a 5¼% passbook savings account (= approximately .44% per month); (2) invest in 6 month certificates yielding 8% on an annual basis; (3) invest in 9 month certificates with annual yield of 9%; or (4) invest in 10% one-year certificates. If the group has $25,000 to invest and wishes to always have $5,000 available in a passbook account, how should the group invest their money over the next 12 months? FORMULATE ONLY.

O 10) Rosa Homes has five projects to subcontract. Three firms have submitted bids on the various contracts. To maintain good working
relationships with the firms, Rosa will award at least one contract
to each firm; however, no firm will be awarded more than two contracts. The chief accountant at Rosa has been given the task of
evaluating the bids and assigning the projects. The table below gives
the bids submitted in thousands.

<table>
<tr><td></td><td colspan="5">Project</td></tr>
<tr><td>Subcontractor</td><td>1</td><td>2</td><td>3</td><td>4</td><td>5</td></tr>
<tr><td>X</td><td>25</td><td>22</td><td>82</td><td>52</td><td>27</td></tr>
<tr><td>Y</td><td>20</td><td>18</td><td>75</td><td>44</td><td>28</td></tr>
<tr><td>Z</td><td>28</td><td>22</td><td>80</td><td>48</td><td>24</td></tr>
</table>

How should the contracts be awarded? FORMULATE ONLY.

Outline of Solution:

Let x_{ij} = # of project i's awarded to contractor j

$i = 1,2,3,4,5$ $j = 1(x), 2(y), 3(z)$

MIN (TOTAL PROJECT COSTS)

s.t. (1) For each project i,
the number of projects of type i awarded to all contractors = 1

(2) For each contractor j,
the total number of projects awarded ≥ 1
and the total number of projects awarded ≤ 2

137

Answer:

MIN $25000x_{11} + 20000x_{12} + 28000x_{13} + 22000x_{21} +$

$18000x_{22} + 22000x_{23} + 82000x_{31} + 75000x_{32} +$

$80000x_{33} + 52000x_{41} + 44000x_{42} + 48000x_{43} +$

$27000x_{51} + 28000x_{52} + 24000x_{53}$

s.t. $x_{11} + x_{12} + x_{13} = 1$

$x_{21} + x_{22} + x_{23} = 1$

$x_{31} + x_{32} + x_{33} = 1$

$x_{41} + x_{42} + x_{43} = 1$

$x_{51} + x_{52} + x_{53} = 1$

$x_{11} + x_{21} + x_{31} + x_{41} + x_{51} \geq 1$

$x_{11} + x_{21} + x_{31} + x_{41} + x_{51} \leq 2$

$x_{12} + x_{22} + x_{32} + x_{42} + x_{52} \geq 1$

$x_{12} + x_{22} + x_{32} + x_{42} + x_{52} \leq 2$

$x_{13} + x_{23} + x_{33} + x_{43} + x_{53} \geq 1$

$x_{13} + x_{23} + x_{33} + x_{43} + x_{53} \leq 2$

$x_{ij} \geq 0 \quad i = 1,\ldots,5; \quad j = 1,2,3$

11) An auto company with plants in Detroit, Louisville, and Oakland has contracts with dealers in Los Angeles, St. Louis and Washington giving these cities the "premiere rights" for the introduction of the new Zenith automobile on October 3. There are 1,500 cars stockpiled in Detroit, 1,200 in Louisville and 1,000 in Oakland. Each premiere city has been promised 900 Zenith automobiles. The table below gives the shipping cost per car between the various cities.

From/To	Los Angeles	St. Louis	Washington
Detroit	280	200	210
Louisville	300	180	170
Oakland	175	210	330

How should the company distribute the automobiles? FORMULATE ONLY.

* 12) Consider the following network as a series of pipes (arcs) leading from reservoir, s, through a series of intermediate pumping stations (nodes) which finally flow into city, t. The numbers on the arcs are the capacities of the pipes. Assume that water is restricted to flow from a lower numbered node to a higher numbered node, and then into t. Formulate a linear program which will give the maximum flow into t. Remember, the nodes are only pumping stations, thus what enters a node must leave that node. (HINT: Define X_{ij} as the flow from node i to node j along the arc between i and j.)

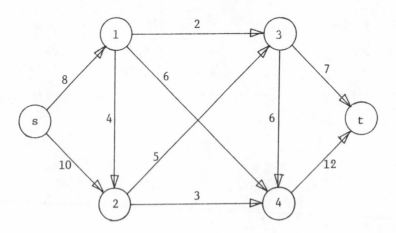

W 13) The campaign headquarters of Jerry Black, a candidate for the Board of
Supervisors has 100 volunteers. With one week to go in the election,
there are three major strategies remaining: media advertising,
door-to-door canvassing, and telephone campaigning. It is estimated
that each phone call will take approximately 4 minutes and each
door-to-door personal contact will take 7 minutes. These times
include time between contacts for breaks, transportation, dialing,
etc. Volunteers who work on advertising will not be able to handle
any other duties. Each ad will use the talents of three workers.

Volunteers are expected to work 12 hours per day during the final
seven days of the campaign. At a minimum Jerry Black feels he needs
30,000 phone contacts and 20,000 personal contacts and 3 advertisements during the final week. However he would like to see 50,000
phone contacts, 50,000 personal contacts and 5 advertisements developed
during this last week. If it is felt that advertising is twice as
important as personal contacts which in turn is twice as important as
phone contacts, how should the work be distributed during this final
week? FORMULATE ONLY.

SOLUTION:

Let x_1 = # workers doing phone work during the week

x_2 = # workers doing door-to-door canvassing during the week

x_3 = # workers preparing advertising during the week

GOALS:

(1) 50,000 phone contacts
(2) 50,000 personal contacts
(3) 5 advertisements

Now there are 7 days x (12 hours/day) x (60 minutes/hr.) =
5,040 minutes per worker.

Thus a phone worker could make $\dfrac{5,040}{4}$ = 1,260 phone calls during the
week.

Similarly a canvasser could contact $\dfrac{5,040}{7}$ = 720 contacts during the
week.

Thus the goals can be written as

$$1,260x_1 - d_1^+ + d_1^- = 50,000 \tag{1}$$
$$720x_2 - d_2^+ + d_2^- = 50,000 \tag{2}$$
$$1/3x_3 - d_3^+ + d_3^- = 5 \tag{3}$$

where d_i^+ is the number over the targeted figure on the RHS and d_i^- is
the number under the targeted figure on the RHS.

CONSTRAINTS:

    (1) At least 30,000 phone contacts
    (2) At least 20,000 personal contacts
    (3) At least 3 advertisements
    (4) There are 100 volunteers
    (5) Non-negativity of all variables

These can be written as

$$1{,}260x_1 \geq 30{,}000 \tag{1}$$

$$720x_2 \geq 20{,}000 \tag{2}$$

$$1/3x_3 \geq 3 \tag{3}$$

$$x_1 + x_2 + x_3 = 100 \tag{4}$$

$$x_1,\ x_2,\ x_3,\ d_1^+,\ d_1^-,\ d_2^+,\ d_2^-,\ d_3^+,\ d_3^- \geq 0 \tag{5}$$

OBJECTIVE FUNCTION:

It would not hurt Jerry Black if the goals were exceeded. However since the importance of the goals are in the ratio of 1:2:4, the objective function would be: MIN $d_1^- + 2d_2^- + 4d_3^-$. This function would be minimized subject to goals (1) – (3) and constraints (1) – (5).

142

* 14)   Consider the problem of United Electric (UE) Company which has
        facilities all over the United States. Currently UE has 150,000
        employees 5,000 of which are in management positions. The government
        contends that UE is delinquent in its Affirmative Action policies and
        will take action if UE does not rectify the situation. Although UE
        currently has 12,000 minority employees (8%) only 50 are in management
        positions (or 1% of the management positions). UE has submitted a
        plan to the federal government which expresses that UE has a target of
        20% minority employees by the end of the year. In negotiating with
        various minority groups, UE has promised that 10% of its management
        positions will be held by minorities by the end of the year.

        Attrition rates of all employees (both management and otherwise) is
        8% for non-minorities, 4% for minorities. Because of a good year, UE
        will create 6,000 new positions 200 of which will be management posi-
        tions. However, the mandate from the top is that it would be unwise
        from a community relations point of view if more than 2/3 of new
        employee hires be minorities, and if more than 2/3 of the promotions to
        management positions be minorities. Assume all management positions
        will be filled in-house and hence all hiring will be for non-management
        positions. Further, assume violations of the company mandate have
        equal weight with not meeting 10% of minority management positions.
        However, not meeting federal standards is considered three times more
        serious.

        FORMULATE as a goal program.
        (HINT: Let x_1 = new non-minority hires

                    x_2 = new minority hires

                    x_3 = number of non-minority management promotions

                    x_4 = number of minority management promotions).

15) In California in 1978, Proposition 13 passed. This seriously
curtailed the flow of property tax revenues to many local services.
Consider the plight of the city of San Angeles whose fire department
was funded totally out of property tax funds. For convenience let us
assume that there are three classifications of personnel. They are
listed below along with the 1977-78 staffing and average salaries
(including fringe benefits).

VARIABLE	CLASS	1977-78 PERSONNEL	AVERAGE SALARY
x_1	Administrators	5	$38,000
x_2	Firemen With $\geq$ 10 yrs. Experience	15	$32,000
x_3	Firemen With < 10 yrs. Experience	80	$20,000

Operating Expenses in 1977-78 amounted to $600,000. Another $330,000
was spent on new equipment, $210,000 on training programs and $100,000
on publicity (school trips, etc.). Other miscellaneous expenses
amounted to $90,000 so that the fire department operated on a budget of
$3,600,000.

With help from the state, San Angeles will suffer "only" a one-third
reduction in its budget. However, the 10% across the board pay
increase has been canceled.

The budget reduction has necessitated the following changes in policy.
There must be at least one administrator for every 20 firefighters
(currently there is one for every 19 firefighters). The city council
has decided to eliminate all publicity and has pared new equipment and
miscellaneous expenses by two-thirds. Operating expenses can only be
reduced by one-half. Training will be trimmed to $500 per fireman
(from the over $1,000 per fireman in the current budget). No new
personnel will be trained. There must be at least 75 firemen to carry
out a "skeleton" program for San Angeles.

The administration would like to have personnel position losses kept
to the one administrator and two firemen with more than 10 years
experience who are retiring and the five firemen with less than two
years experience who will leave for various reasons.

Because of seniority it is considered five times worse to fire a fire-
man with 10 years experience than one with less than 10 years
experience or an administrator. FORMULATE as a goal programming
problem.

6 THE ASSIGNMENT AND TRAVELING SALESMAN PROBLEM

KEY CONCEPTS

1. Description of the assignment problem

2. Hungarian method solution procedure for the assignment problem

3. The Traveling Salesman problem and the branch and bound solution procedure

REVIEW

1. Description

The assignment problem is an optimization problem which seeks to assign n workers to n jobs at minimum cost where there is a cost associated with each job for each worker. Each worker is to be assigned only one job and each job must be done. If there are fewer than n men (jobs) dummy workers (jobs) are added at zero cost so that the requirement of the same number of workers as jobs is met. If a worker is unable to do a particular job a large cost, M, is assigned to that worker-job combination.

Other problems which may fit the mathematical model of the assignment problem are: assigning machines to production runs, assigning salesmen to territories, assigning contracts to bidders, etc.

In some problems the decision maker wishes to find a maximum value assignment, such as assigning machines to production runs. To transform a maximization to a minimization problem an opportunity loss matrix can be constructed as follows: for each column, replace each element in the column by the difference between that element and the largest element in the column. These differences represent the amount lost by not assigning the best machine for each production run. Solving the problem of

minimizing the opportunity loss is equivalent to solving for the maximum
output; the numbers have simply been scaled.

2. Hungarian Method for Solving Assignment Problems

The Hungarian Method for solving minimization assignment problems
is basically a technique that systematically scales the problem so that
there is always some zero cost in each row and some zero cost in each
column. The process of scaling is called matrix reduction. When there
exists a complete zero cost assignment of workers to jobs, the problem is
solved.

The following is the Hungarian algorithm for solving assignment
problems:

STEP 0: (Initialization) There must be the same number of workers
as jobs and the problem must be a minimization problem. If
the problem is a maximization, convert it to an opportunity
loss problem and minimize.

STEP 1: For each row, subtract the minimum element in the row from
all elements in that row.

STEP 2: For each column, subtract the minimum element in the
column from all elements in that column.

STEP 3: Draw the minimum number of lines to cover all zeros. If
the minimum number of lines equals the number of workers
(or jobs) STOP--there exists a complete zero cost assignment.

STEP 4: If there are fewer lines than men, then determine the
minimum uncovered element and:

(1) subtract this number from all uncovered elements

(2) add this number to all elements covered by two lines

(3) leave elements covered by one line alone

THEN GO TO STEP 3.

Sometimes finding the minimum number of lines may not be obvious.
The following marking algorithm can be employed to find the minimum number
of lines to cover all zeroes at any iteration in the assignment algorithm
(see problem 1):

1. Consider in order each row and column for which an assignment
has not been made. For this row (column), if there remains
exactly one zero (not counting zeroes in columns (rows) previously assigned), make this zero element the assignment.

146

2. Repeat STEP 1 until (a) no more assignments can be made or (b) all the remaining rows and columns have two or more zeroes. If (a) go to STEP 3, this is a maximum assignment; if (b), by trial and error, make an arbitrary assignment and go to STEP 1.

3. Put a check mark by all rows that do not have assignments.

4. For each checked row, check all columns that have zeroes in them.

5. For each checked column, check all rows with assignments in them.

6. Repeat STEPS 4 and 5 until no more checks can be made.

7. The minimum number of lines can be obtained by drawing lines through unchecked rows and checked columns.

A mathematical model of the assignment problem can be developed as follows. Let x_{ij} = # of workers of type i doing job j. Since there is only one worker of type i (for each i), only one job of type j (for each j), and we want to minimize the total cost, the mathematical model would be:

$$\text{MIN} \quad \sum_i \sum_j c_{ij} \, x_{ij}$$

$$\text{s.t.} \quad \sum_j x_{ij} = 1 \quad \text{(for each i)}$$

$$\sum_i x_{ij} = 1 \quad \text{(for each j)}$$

$$x_{ij} \geq 0 \quad \begin{array}{l} i = 1,\ldots,n \\ j = 1,\ldots,n \end{array}$$

This is a linear program. Note the problem is additionally constrained by the fact that x_{ij} can only be assigned or not assigned (i.e. zero or one) for all i and j. This makes the problem a 0 - 1 integer linear program. However, if the above linear program is solved, it will be found that all extreme points have x_{ij} = 0 or 1 for all i and j. Hence the optimal solution to the linear program (an extreme point) satisfies the additional 0 - 1 constraints and is optimal for the assignment problem.

Thus using the simplex method to solve the above linear program provides an alternate way to solve the assignment problem.

3. The Traveling Salesman Problem

A problem that seeks to find a tour of minimum distance between n
nodes (cities) and return to the node of origin without visiting any other
node twice is known as a traveling salesman problem. It can be thought of as
dealing with a salesman who starts in city 1 is to visit n - 1 other
cities and returns to city 1 using the minimum mileage to complete the trip.

One method of solving the traveling salesman problem is to view it
as an assignment problem. Here the cost matrix is an n x n matrix with
the ij-th entry being the distance from city i to city j. (Note: traveling
from a city to itself is not allowed and this is given a cost of M). However, the problem is more constrained than the usual assignment problem.
This is because assignments from one city to the next are unacceptable if the
latter city has appeared previously in the tour and not all cities have been
visited. For example in a 4 x 4 problem an assignment of city 1 to city 3,
city 2 to city 4, city 3 to city 1 and city 4 to city 2 would be acceptable
for an assignment problem, however it is unacceptable for a traveling salesman problem. The sequences 1-3-1 and 2-4-2 are called unacceptable subtours.

A branch and bound procedure may be used to solve this problem. The
idea of this approach is that some or all of the constraints that forbid
subtours are relaxed (not considered) and the problem is solved as an
assignment problem. If these relaxed constraints are satisfied without
considering them then a solution has been found. If not, a previously
relaxed constraint is added and the procedure is repeated. This continues
until a solution has been found.

The branch and bound algorithm utilizes a branch and bound tree to
aid in the analysis. This consists of nodes and arcs. The nodes represent
trial solutions. If the node does not represent a tour, arcs may be created
from the node representing unacceptable routes for the above trial solution
(node).

The following is a summary of the branch and bound solution procedure
for the traveling salesman problem utilizing the assignment algorithm.

STEP 1: Arbitrarily choose a complete tour (such as 1-2-3-4-1 in a
4 city problem) and calculate its total distance. (This
provides an initial upper bound to the solution.)

STEP 2: Solve the problem as an assignment problem and put the value
of the solution in a node. (This is a lower bound on any
solution obtained by branching from this node. A lower
bound for this entire problem is the smallest node value for
which branching has not been completed.) If the assignment
problem is infeasible, no further branching is possible from
this node - GO TO STEP 4.

148

STEP 3: If the solution in STEP 2 is a tour:

    (1) There is no further branching from this node.

    (2) If the value of this solution (node) is less than the upper bound, change the upper bound to this value.

    (3) If no further branching is possible, STOP, otherwise perform STEP 4 on the minimum value node for which branching is possible.

STEP 4: If the solution is not a tour, select the <u>minimum</u> value node for which branching is possible.

    (1) If the node value is not smaller than the upper bound for the entire problem, STOP. The optimal solution is the tour that gives the upper bound when the procedure is stopped.

    (2) Form two branches from this node, by selecting any sub-tour (of the form a-b-c-...-z-a.) and make the a-b assignment unacceptable for one branch and the z-a assignment unacceptable for the other. Select one arbitrarily and put an M in this position in the assignment matrix. GO TO STEP 2.

ASSIGNMENT PROBLEM - A problem to assign n workers to n jobs at minimum cost. (252)

BRANCH AND BOUND - A solution procedure used for many problems, including the traveling salesman problem, which involves solving "relaxed" problems until the entire problem has been solved. (270)

DUMMY COLUMN - An extra column of zeroes added to an assignment problem when the number of columns is less than the number of rows. (259)

DUMMY ROW - An extra row of zeroes added to an assignment problem when the number of rows is less than the number of columns. (259)

HUNGARIAN METHOD - An algorithmic solution procedure for solving assignment problems. (254)

LOWER BOUND - The smallest possible value that can be attained in a problem. (272)

MATRIX REDUCTION - The scaling process in the Hungarian Method which reduces the matrix systematically until zero-valued assignment can be made. (255)

NODE - A possible branching point on a branch and bound tree. (276)

OPPORTUNITY LOSS MATRIX - A matrix used when the problem is a maximization problem; is is generated by subtracting each element in a column from the maximum element in that column. (262)

RELAXED CONSTRAINT - A constraint which is ignored while solving a problem. (272)

SUBTOUR - A sequence of some but not all nodes beginning and ending with the same node; each node in the sequence is visited only once. (276)

TRAVELING SALESMAN PROBLEM - A problem which seeks to find a tour of minimum cost between all nodes of the problem. (269)

TOUR - A sequence of nodes beginning and ending with the same node that does include all nodes. (269)

UPPER BOUND - The highest possible value that can be attained in a problem; it corresponds to a feasible solution in a traveling salesman problem. (271)

Chapter 6 Check List

W 1) A contractor pays his subcontractors a fixed fee plus mileage for work performed. On a given day the contractor is faced with three electrical jobs associated with various projects. He has four electrical subcontractors which are located at various places throughout the area. Given below are the distances between the subcontractors and the projects.

		Project		
		A	B	C
	Westside	50	36	16
	Federated	28	30	18
Subcontractors	Goliath	35	32	20
	Universal	25	25	14

How should the subcontractors be assigned to minimize the total mileage charges?

SOLUTION:

(We illustrate the marking algorithm in this solution procedure.) Is problem a minimization? Yes. Are there the same number of rows as columns? No. Add a dummy column to get

	A	B	C	Dummy
W	50	36	16	0
F	28	30	18	0
G	35	32	20	0
U	25	25	14	0

Iteration 1

STEP 1) Subtracting minimum number in each row gives back the same matrix.

STEP 2) Subtracting the minimum number in each column gives the matrix below.

STEP 3) Draw the minimum number of lines to cover all zeroes. (1-2)* the minimum lines can be gotten by the marking algorithm. W has only one zero (D) make this assignment. F and G have no zeroes

*The numbers in parenthesis correspond to the steps of the line covering algorithm.

152

remaining. Skip them. U has three zeroes remaining. Skip it.
Consider the columns. A has only one zero (U). Make this assign-
ment. No more assignments can be made. (3) Check F and G. (4)
Check D. (5) Check W. (6) Stop. (7) Draw lines through D and U.

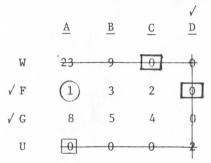

STEP 4) Minimum uncovered number is 2. Subtract 2 from all uncovered
numbers; add 2 to all twice covered numbers to get the matrix
below--go to STEP 3.

Iteration 2

STEP 3) Draw the minimum number of lines to cover all zeroes. (1-2) W has
two zeroes. Skip it. F has one zero (D), make this assignment. G
has no zeroes remaining. Skip it. U has three zeroes. Skip it.
A has three zeroes. Skip it. A has one zero (U); make this
assignment. B has no zeroes left. C has one zero left (W); make
this assignment. No more assignments can be made. (3) Check G.
(4) Check D. (5) Check F. (6) Stop. (7) Draw lines through W, U,
and D.

STEP 4) Minimum uncovered element is 1. Subtract 1 from all uncovered
elements; add 1 to all twice covered elements to get matrix below
--go to STEP 3.

153

STEP 3) Drawing the minimum number of lines to cover all zeroes would give 4 lines. Hence a solution can be gotten. By the marking algorithm (1-2) W has one zero (C). F has two zeroes, Skip it. G has one zero (D); make this assignment. U has two zeroes, skip it. B has one zero (U); make this assignment. Go back to F. There is one zero left (A). Make this assignment. This is a complete assignment.

	A	B	C	D
W	23	9	[0]	1
F	[0]	2	1	0
G	7	4	3	[0]
U	0	[0]	0	3

Assignment	Distance
Westside – Project C	16
Federated – Project A	28
Goliath – Unassigned	0
Universal – Project B	25
Total	69

154

O 2)   There are four operations through which a product must go and four
       machines available. With the exception of the six year old machine
       which cannot do operation C, each machine is capable of performing any
       of the four operations although at various speeds. Because of the
       high start-up costs of retooling, each machine is to be utilized for
       only one operation. The time in minutes to do each operation on each
       machine is listed below. How should the machines be assigned?

	A	B	C	D
New machine	8	6	10	15
2 year old machine	11	10	12	20
4 year old machine	12	12	12	22
6 year old machine	18	20	X	25

Outline of Solution:

   It is a minimization problem. There are the same number of workers as
   jobs. The cost of job C on six year machine is M.

   1)   Subtract the minimum number in each row. (Subtracting from M
        leaves M.)

   2)   Subtract the minimum number in each column.

   3)   Draw the minimum number of lines to cover all zeroes (3 lines).

   4)   Find minimum covered element (minimum element = 1). Subtract this
        from all uncovered elements. Add this to twice covered elements.
        Go to STEP 3.

   5)   Draw the minimum number of lines to cover all zeroes. (Since the
        minimum number of lines is four, make a complete assignment.)

   Answer:

        New machine – B   = 6
        2 year old machine – A = 11
        4 year old machine – C = 12
        6 year old machine – D = 25

                   Total 54 minutes

155

3) The three top accounting teams in the Top Notch Accounting Firm are to be assigned to the three biggest accounts in the firm. The estimated time in days to handle the accounts are given below

ACCOUNT

	Billows, Inc.	Pillows, Inc.	Willows, Inc.
Leimbach	10	12	15
Mednick	12	16	19
Yost	15	18	22

a) List all possible Team-Account combinations and choose the best.

b) Solve the problem by the Hungarian Method.

* 4) Tangerine County has four projects which are to be awarded to individual firms. There are five firms competing and because the government is sensitive to charges of conflict of interest, it will award at most one contract to each bidder.

a) The table below gives bids submitted in $100's.

Projects	Fitzpatrick Company	Mitchell Brothers	Wallace & Son	Holmes Const.	Quillstone Const.
Rebuild Playground	12	10	18	20	15
Build Roads	100	88	120	72	100
Construct New Office Building	180	140	150	130	170
Modernize County Courthouse	45	60	75	50	70

How should the contracts be awarded at minimum taxpayer expense?

b) After obtaining the optimal solution suppose Holmes Const. finds it cannot accomplish the road building project in a reasonable amount of time. Thus, Holmes has to be eliminated for consideration of this project. Using your last tableau as a starting point obtain the new optimal solution. (HINT: What is the only change in the last tableau?)

5) On–Time Airlines has just added five new routes on its schedules requiring five new pilots. The pilots have been given a request sheet and asked to list the routes in order from 1 to 5 they would like to fly. Based on the request sheets submitted below, give three ways On–Time could assign routes to pilots to maximize their overall happiness.

ROUTES

Pilot	Hawaii	Seattle	Las Vegas	New Orleans	Tampa
Capt. Flynn	1	2	3	4	5
Capt. Kidd	1	4	5	3	2
Capt. Marsh	1	2	4	3	5
Capt. Ook	3	5	1	2	4
Capt. York	3	5	2	4	1

W 6) As plant manager for a sporting goods manufacturing company you are in charge of assigning the manufacture of four new aluminum products to four different divisions. Because of varying expertise and workloads, the different departments can produce the new products at various rates. If only one new product is to be produced by each department and the daily output rates are given in the table below, which department should manufacture which product to maximize total daily product output?

NEW PRODUCT

Division	Bats	Tennis Rackets	Golf Clubs	Racquetball Rackets
1	100	60	120	80
2	100	80	140	100
3	110	75	150	120
4	85	50	100	75

SOLUTION:

Is this a minimization problem? No. Change to Opportunity Loss Matrix by subtracting each number in column 1 from 110, each number in column 2 from 80, each number in column 3 from 150, and each number in column 4 from 120 to get:

	B	TR	GC	RR
1	10	20	30	40
2	10	0	10	20
3	0	5	0	0
4	25	30	50	45

159

	B	TR	GC	RR
1	0	10	20	30
2	10	0	10	20
3	0	5	0	0
4	0	5	25	20

STEP 2) Subtracting the minimum number in each column leaves the matrix the same.

STEP 3) Cover all zeroes with minimum number of lines.

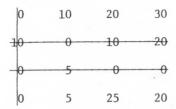

STEP 4) The minimum Uncovered Element = 5. Subtract 5 from every uncovered element. Add 5 to every twice covered element to get the matrix below. Go to STEP 3.

STEP 3) Cover the zeroes with the minimum number of lines.

	B	TR	GC	RR
1	0	5	15	25
2	15	0	10	20
3	5	5	0	0
4	0	0	20	15

STEP 4) The minimum uncovered element = 10. Subtract 10 from every uncovered element. Add 10 to every twice covered element to get the matrix below. Go to STEP 3.

STEP 3) Cover the zeroes with the minimum number of lines.

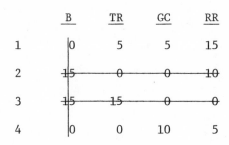

	B	TR	GC	RR
1	0	5	5	15
2	15	0	0	10
3	15	15	0	0
4	0	0	10	5

Since four lines are required there exists a complete assignment

Division	Product	Number
1	Bats	100
2	Golf Clubs	140
3	Racquetball Rackets	120
4	Tennis Rackets	50
	Total Products =	410

0 7) For the problem in exercise 6, suppose the company can sell all bats at a $2 profit, tennis rackets at a $6 profit, golf clubs at a $3 profit, and racquetball rackets at a $4 profit. What would be the optimal assignment policy?

Outline of Solution:

Convert the matrix to a profit matrix by multiplying the columns by 2, 6, 3, and 4 respectively. Convert the profit matrix to an Opportunity Loss Matrix by subtracting each element in a column from the maximum in that column. Solve by the assignment algorithm.

Optimal Solution:

Division	Product	Number	Profit
1	Golf Clubs	120	$ 360
2	Tennis Rackets	80	$ 480
3	Racquetball Rackets	120	$ 480
4	Bats	85	$ 170
		Total Profit	$1,490

8) A brush company wishes to send four new salesman into new suburban areas. Based on computerized tests which take into account certain personality traits of the salesman, ethnic make-up of the suburban areas, etc., the following is the best-guess as to the number of daily sales each salesman can expect in each area. How should the salesmen be assigned?

SUBURBS

	North	East	South	West
Barry	32	28	20	22
Dave	30	35	25	28
John	20	22	23	29
Tom	30	28	22	30

* 9) In the airline assignment problem number 5, the model did not take into account the degree of difference between the choices made by the pilots. In other words, perhaps Captain Flynn slightly prefers the Hawaii route over the Seattle route but Captain Marsh desperately wants the Hawaii route, and only lists Seattle as a distant second choice. Now consider giving the pilot a card listing the routes and tell the pilot he has 100 points he can distribute among the routes. Given the following submitted sheets, how should On-Time make its assigments?

	H	S	LV	NO	T
Cpt. F	50	25	15	10	0
Cpt. K	60	5	5	10	20
Cpt. M	100	0	0	0	0
Cpt. O	20	15	25	20	20
Cpt. Y	20	0	30	5	45

* 10) You are called in as a consultant to a city planning commission which
is trying to select three sites from among five submitted for new
fire stations. The city's goal is to minimize total response time
between the sites and its area of primary responsibility. No site is
to have more than one primary area of responsibility. The projected
response time in minutes between each proposed site and the three
areas to be covered are given below. Which three sites should be
selected and what should be the primary responsibility for each?

Response Time To

Site	A	B	C
1	10	6	8
2	6	7	10
3	8	8	8
4	15	15	7
5	4	5	6

11) The Xuma Corporation has five contracts to award for the coming fiscal year. Three companies have submitted bids on the various contracts and their bids are summarized in the table below in $1,000's.

CONTRACT

	1	2	3	4	5
Poppe, Inc.	5	3	X	8	9
Law Company	6	1	2	X	8
O'Donnel Bros.	8	6	6	10	X

An "X" means no bid was submitted on this contract from the corresponding contractor. It is Xuma's policy to award at least one contract to each bidder and not to award more than two contracts to any one bidder.

a) Formulate this problem as a linear program. What constraints are relaxed when using linear programming? Do you think this will affect the optimal solution?

b) Formulate as an assignment problem and solve. (Careful!)

W 12) Phil Smith, vice president of Quant Industries (QI) plans to make a three day trip to three cities and return to corporate headquarters. He is to spend one day in each city and return. Plane service to the cities does not always fit the executive's schedule to be in the city by 8:00 AM. Thus, in some cases he will have to rent a car to travel between the cities, which, considering his time, is more expensive.

Phil has given you the task of scheduling his trip. After taking into account plane schedules, fares, and rent-a-car prices, you have prepared the following matrix which gives the minimum city to city cost.

	Office	1	2	3
Office	–	60	120	75
1	60	–	155	85
2	120	100	–	95
3	75	125	105	–

What schedule do you recommend? What is the anticipated cost of this schedule?

SOLUTION:

STEP 1: The tour (óffice-1-2-3-office) costs 60 + 155 + 95 + 75 = 385. This is an upper bound for the problem.

STEP 2: Solve as an assignment problem with the cost of going from a city to itself = M.

MATRIX 1

	0	1	2	3
0	M	60	120	75
1	60	M	155	85
2	120	100	M	95
3	75	125	105	M

Subtract the minimum element in each row from all elements in that row to obtain:

MATRIX 2

	0	1	2	3
0	M	0	60	15
1	0	M	95	25
2	25	5	M	0
3	0	50	30	M

Subtract the minimum element in each column from all elements in that column to obtain:

MATRIX 3

	0	1	2	3
0	M	[0]	30	15
1	[0]	M	65	25
2	25	5	M	[0]
3	0	50	[0]	M

This gives an optimal assignment of value
60 + 60 + 95 + 105 = 320, but gives two subtours:

    SUBTOUR 1: 0-1-0
    SUBTOUR 2: 2-3-2

(Since this is not a tour go to STEP 4.)

STEP 4: Let us choose arbitrarily subtour 2 to branch on. Then the
branches are 2-3 unacceptable and 3-2 unacceptable. Thus the
branch and bound tree at this point is:

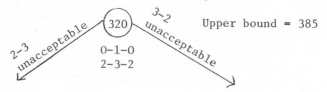

Upper bound = 385

Let us evaluate the 2-3 unacceptable branch and return to
STEP 2.

168

STEP 2:   Since 2-3 unacceptable this would give an M in the 2-3
          position in matrix 3. As this leaves no zeroes in the 2 row,
          subtract the minimum element in that row, 5, from all
          elements in that row. Similarly since there is no zero in
          column 3, subtract the minimum element, 15, from all elements
          in that column. This gives:

MATRIX 4

	0	1	2	3
0	M	0	30	[0]
1	[0]	M	65	10
2	25	[0]	M	M
3	0	50	[0]	M

The optimal assignment is the tour 0-3-2-1-0 whose value is
75 + 60 + 100 + 105 = 340. (Since this is a tour go to
STEP 3.)

STEP 3:   Change upper bound to 340 and now consider the 3-2 unaccept-
          able branch from 320. The branch and bound tree at this
          point is:

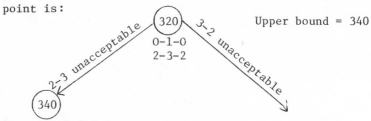

Upper bound = 340

320
0-1-0
2-3-2

340

2-3 unacceptable

3-2 unacceptable

Tour: 0-3-2-1-0

(GO TO STEP 2)

STEP 2:   Refer back to matrix 3 which generated the 320 node. Put M
          in the 3-2 position. This leaves no zeroes in column 2.
          Thus, subtract the minimum element in column 2, 30, from all
          elements in that column. This gives:

169

MATRIX 5

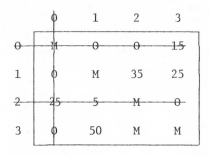

	0	1	2	3
0	M	0	0	15
1	0	M	35	25
2	25	5	M	0
3	0	50	M	M

Minimum unlined element = 25

MATRIX 6

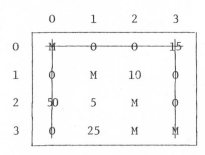

	0	1	2	3
0	M	0	0	15
1	0	M	10	0
2	50	5	M	0
3	0	25	M	M

Minimum unlined element = 5

MATRIX 7

	0	1	2	3
0	M	0	[0]	20
1	0	M	5	[0]
2	50	[0]	M	0
3	[0]	20	M	M

This gives a tour of 0-2-1-3-0 costing
120 + 100 + 85 + 75 = 380 (GO TO STEP 3).

STEP 3: This tour is higher than the upper bound. There are no more branches left. The final branch and bound tree is:

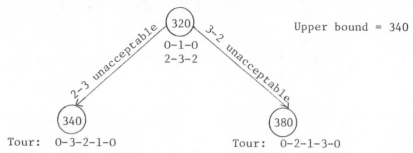

Upper bound = 340

Tour: 0-3-2-1-0   Tour: 0-2-1-3-0

Thus the optimal tour costs $340 and is from office-city 3-city 2-city 1-office.

O 13) A doctor must make rounds at three hospitals and return to his office each day. The distances are given in the following table.

TO

FROM	Office	St. Paul's	General	State
Office	-	10	12	14
St. Paul's	10	-	14	16
General	12	14	-	30
State	14	16	30	-

a) Solve as an assignment problem. Is this an optimal solution to the stated problem?

b) Suppose the distance from St. Paul's to General (and hence from General to St. Paul's) was 30 instead of 14. Solve again as an assignment problem. Show that this is not an optimal solution to the stated problem. What "relaxed" constraints are violated?

c) Solve for the optimal solution with the change in (b).

Outline of Solution:

a) Solve the problem as an assignment problem. Put M's for the distances for a city to itself. Note there are four optimal solutions but only two are tours (and one is the reverse of the other).

b) The only changes would be in the St. Paul's to General and General to St. Paul's position which would be increased by 16. This eliminates all but one of the "optimal" solutions to (a). Is it optimal?

c) Since O-SP-G-S-O is a tour = 72, this is an upper bound. The solution to (a) gives 56 which is a lower bound node from which we shall branch. Branch by letting route O-G be unacceptable and G-O be unacceptable.

(i) Branching on O-G unacceptable makes the entry an M in the final tableau. Since there are no zeroes for the G column, subtract the minimum entry in this column from all elements in the column, and solve as an assignment problem. This gives an optimal solution which is a tour of value 68. Reduce the upper bound to 68.

(ii) Now branch on G-O unacceptable making the entry an M in the G-O position in the final tableau (a) in part above. Since there are no zeroes in the G row, subtract the minimum entry in this row from all entries in the row. Solve as an assignment problem. This gives an optimal solution which is a tour (the reverse of the tour in (i)). This tour is optimal.

Answers:

a) Office-State-St. Paul's-General-Office = 56.

b) Optimal solution to assignment problem:
Office-General-Office;   St. Paul's-State-St. Paul's.
This is not a tour.   The relaxed constraint that was violated states that all locations be included on a tour.

c) Office-St. Paul's-State-General-Office = 68

14) Brent Willard is a distributor of plumbing supplies who must make deliveries to four retail outlets every week in Altland, Bringham, Colton, and Delphi and return to his dealership in Holtville. The table below gives the highway mileage distances between all cities. Brent had been making his deliveries to the cities in the above order.

	H	A	B	C	D
Holtville	–	50	65	85	100
Altland	50	–	25	40	60
Bringham	65	25	–	60	30
Colton	85	40	60	–	45
Delphi	100	60	30	45	–

a) What schedule would you recommend to Brent?

b) Suppose the route from Altland to Colton becomes closed in this direction only. What do you recommend?

c) Suppose the route from Altland to Colton becomes closed in both directions. What do you recommend?

* 15) Fielding Production has six different jobs that are to be sequenced for work in the production shop beginning with job #1. The time in hours for required changeovers from one job to the next is given in the following table. Note that because the sequence of jobs is not to be repeated, zeroes are placed in column 1 from all other jobs.

Jobs	1	2	3	4	5	6
1	–	5	8	13	11	1
2	0	–	8	6	9	1
3	0	12	–	7	9	2
4	0	10	8	–	2	3
5	0	8	6	4	–	2
6	0	2	2	3	1	–

Solve for the optimal sequencing of jobs.

16) A computerized drill press must be programmed to drill holes for part number 1037. The press drills six holes and returns to the position for drilling hole 1 for the next part. Given the following pattern for part 1037, in what sequence should the holes be drilled to minimize the total distance moved by the drill (and hence time). (Distances are in centimeters.)

FROM/TO	1	2	3	4	5	6
1	–	80	95	35	20	110
2	80	–	45	100	40	20
3	95	45	–	85	40	30
4	35	100	85	–	30	120
5	20	40	40	30	–	60
6	110	20	30	120	60	–

7 THE TRANSPORTATION PROBLEM

REVIEW

1. Formulation of the Transportation Problem

Given m origins with a supply of s_i goods at origin i, and n destinations with a demand d_j at destination j, the transportation problem is a problem which seeks to minimize the total shipping cost of items from the origins to the destinations in such a way that the supply and demand constraints are not violated. The key assumption of this model is that there is a unit cost, c_{ij}, of shipping items from origin i to destination j. Thus the total cost of shipping items from i to j is directly proportional to the amount of goods shipped between origin i and destination j. This model would be inappropriate when considering the shipping of individual boxes of cereal from Battle Creek, Michigan to Atlanta, Georgia by truck, as the cost of shipping two boxes of cereal is definitely not twice as much as the cost of shipping one box. However, in the same light, the cost of shipping two trucks full of cereal between the two cities is most likely approximately twice the cost of shipping one truck full of cereal.

In order to solve the transportation problem efficiently, the total supply at the origins must equal the total demand at the destinations. This can always be forced to occur by a convenient mathematical trick. If there is excess supply of k, a dummy destination is created. This destination has a demand of k and shipping costs from all origins of zero. Similarly if there is excess demand of k, a dummy origin is created with a supply of k and shipping costs to all destinations of zero. In a solution, a shipment from a dummy origin or to a dummy destination is simply a shipment that does not take place.

With total supply equal to total demand, the following is the mathematical model of the transportation problem. Letting x_{ij} equal the amount shipped from warehouse i to store j:

$$\text{MIN} \quad \sum_j \sum_i c_{ij} \, x_{ij}$$

$$\text{s.t.} \quad \sum_j x_{ij} = s_i \quad \text{for all } i$$

$$\sum_i x_{ij} = d_j \quad \text{for } j$$

$$x_{ij} \geq 0 \quad \text{for all } i \text{ and } j$$

Note that this is a linear program and can be solved by the simplex method. But due to the special structure of the problem, the form can be exploited so that the lengthy tableaus of the simplex method can be eliminated. The resulting algorithm is called the transportation algorithm.

2. Initialization: Starting Procedures for the Transportation Problem

The solution of a transportation problem is done in the format of a transportation tableau such as the one below with two origins and three destinations.

The transportation tableau has one row for each of the m origins and one column for each of the n destinations. This divides the tableau into m x n cells. In the upper right-hand corner of each cell is a box which gives the absolute cost of shipping one unit from the corresponding origin to the corresponding destination. In the rest of the cell will be placed one of two numbers: either a number representing the number shipped from the origin to the destination, or a circled number representing the <u>reduced</u> <u>cost</u> (or marginal cost) of altering the current shipping pattern by shipping one unit from that origin to that destination.

To get an initial assignment filling m + n - 1 cells (which correspond to the basic variables of the linear program) two methods are presented: (1) The Northwest Corner Method; (2) The Vogel Approximation Method.

The Northwest Corner Method is easier but neglects the effects of costs when selecting an initial solution.

Northwest Corner Starting Procedure

(1) Start with the upper left hand cell. Consider the supply at origin 1 and demand at destination 1, and assign the minimum of s_1 or d_1 to this cell.

(2) Reduce the supply and demand of this row and column by the amount allocated to this cell. Eliminate from further consideration that row or column reduced to zero. If all the supplies have been allocated, STOP.

(3) If a column has been eliminated, consider the cell immediately to the right of the last cell. If a row has been eliminated consider the cell immediately below the last cell considered. Allocate to this cell the minimum of the supply remaining in its row or the demand remaining in its column. GO TO STEP (2).

The Vogel Approximation Method (VAM) is more complex but takes into account the relative costs between the best and second best possible assignments in each row and column.

VAM Starting Procedure

(1) For each of the rows and columns not eliminated, calculate the difference between the best and second best costs in the row or column. This is the <u>penalty cost</u>.

(2) Select the row or column with the highest penalty cost (break ties arbitrarily) and allocate as many units as possible to the cell with the best cost in this row or column.

179

(3)   Reduce the row supply and column demand by this amount and eliminate the row or column whose supply or demand went to zero. Go to STEP (1).

3.   Solution Procedures

Once an initial shipping pattern has been obtained, the transportation algorithm moves toward optimality by a two-step procedure:

(1)   determine which unoccupied cell will most improve the value of the objective function per unit shipped over the corresponding route.

(2)   alter the current solution to ship as many as possible into that cell.

There are two methods for accomplishing STEP (1):   The Stepping Stone Method and the Modified Distribution (MODI) method presented below. In either method the goal is to place a circled number in each unoccupied cell denoting the <u>reduced</u> or marginal cost of altering the current shipping pattern by allocating one unit to this cell.

Stepping Stone Method for Obtaining Reduced Costs

(1)   For every unoccupied cell form a closed loop with this cell and occupied cells by drawing connected horizontal and vertical lines between them. (Note that lines may cross and may go through other occupied cells.)

(2)   Starting with the occupied cell, calculate the reduced cost, e_{ij}, by alternately adding and subtracting the numbers in the corners of the path. (Neglect crossovers. Note that for each calculation, for every row and column either: (i) there are no additions or subtractions in that row or column;   or, (ii) there is exactly one addition and one subtraction in that row or column.)

MODI Method for Obtaining Reduced Costs

(1)   Consider a number u_i associated with each row i and a number v_j associated with each column j. Let $u_1 = 0$. Then calculate the remaining u_i's and v_j's by using the relationship $u_i + v_j = c_{ij}$ for every occupied cell.

(2)   Compute the reduced costs, e_{ij}, for the unoccupied cells by:
$$e_{ij} = c_{ij} - u_i - v_j .$$

Regardless of which method is chosen for obtaining the reduced costs, the remaining steps of the transportation algorithm are the same:

Conclusion of Transporation Algorithm

(3) Select the most negative e_{ij}. If there are no negative e_{ij}, STOP; the current solution is optimal.

(4) Determine the stepping stone path for this cell (this is done by STEP (1) of stepping stone method). Consider each cell where a subtraction is to be made and select the one with the minimum allocation.

(5) For all cells that determine the stepping stone paths, subtract this number from the places where a subtraction was made and add it to places where additions were made. Go to STEP (1).

4. Special Cases

In a transportation problem with a maximization objective function, the procedure is the same except in STEP (3), the most positive e_{ij} is selected and the algorithm terminates when there are no positive e_{ij}.

Sometimes a transportation problem may have unacceptable routes, that is, places where shipments cannot be made in any real solution. Simply assign an extremely large cost, M, to this cell to force the algorithm not to ship any units to this cell.

Degeneracy occurs when there are less than $m + n - 1$ routes utilized in a solution. This can occur both in the starting procedure or in the course of the solution procedure. Degeneracy occurs in a starting procedure when both a supply and a demand determine the amount to be put into a cell. To resolve this, a zero allocation can be placed in any cell that does not form a closed loop with the other occupied cells.

Degeneracy occurs during the course of the solution procedure when two (or more) cells limit the number in STEP (4). In this case select any one of these cells to be unoccupied in the next tableau. The other cell(s) will be occupied with a zero.

During the course of the solution procedure, treat cells occupied with zeroes as you would any other occupied cell. Remember there are to be exactly $m + n - 1$ occupied cells at every iteration.

CELL – A section of a transportation tableau corresponding to a route between a specific origin and a specific destination.   (293)

DESTINATION – A demand location in a transportation problem.   (291)

DEGENERACY – Occurs when an allocation of zero must be assigned to obtain $M + n - 1$ occupied cells.   (314)

DUMMY ROWS OR COLUMNS – Rows or columns added with zero unit costs to force total supply to equal total demand.   (313)

MODI (Modified Distribution Method) – A solution procedure for solving transportation problems where the reduced costs are calculated by subtracting from the unit cost, c_{ij}. The row index u_i and the column index, v_j.   (309)

NORTHWEST CORNER METHOD – A starting procedure for determining an initial feasible solution in a transportation problem without any extra calculations.   (294)

OCCUPIED CELL – Cell indicating the current positive use of this shipping route (could be zero in the case of degeneracy).   (306)

ORIGIN – A supply location in a transportation problem.   (291)

REDUCED COST – The marginal cost of shipping any one unit into an unoccupied cell.   (305)

STEPPING STONE METHOD – A solution procedure for the transportation problem that calculates reduced costs by tracing a path between each unoccupied cell and a set of occupied cells.   (303)

VAM (Vogel's Approximation Method) – A starting procedure for determining an initial feasible solution htat takes into account relative costs.   (297)

Chapter 7 Check List

W 1) Building Brick Company (BBC) has orders for 80 tons of bricks at three suburban locations as follows: Northwood – 25 tons, Westwood – 45 tons; Eastwood – 10 tons. BBC has two plants which each produce 50 tons per week. How should end of week shipments be made to fill the above orders given the following delivery cost per ton data?

	Northwood	Westwood	Eastwood
Plant 1	24	30	40
Plant 2	30	40	42

SOLUTION:

Does supply = demand? No, add a dummy column with excess demand of 20, and shipping costs of zero.

Using NW corner starting procedure

Assign 25 tons from plant 1 – Northwood (reduce supply at plant 1 to 25).

Assign 25 tons from plant 1 – to Westwood (reduce demand at Westwood to 20).

Assign the remaining 50 tons at plant 2 so that Westwood receives 20, Eastwood 10, and Dummy 20.

	Northwood	Westwood	Eastwood	Dummy	Supply
Plant 1	25 [24]	25 [30]	[40]	[0]	50
Plant 2	[30]	20 [40]	10 [42]	20 [0]	50
Demand	25	45	10	20	

Using MODI Solution Procedure

$u_1 = 0$ Since x_{11}, x_{12} are occupied v_1 and v_2 are determined

$$v_1 = -u_1 + c_{11} = 24$$

$$v_2 = -u_1 + c_{12} = 30$$

184

Since x_{22} is occupied,

$$u_2 = -v_2 + c_{22} = -30 + 40 = 10$$

Since x_{23}, x_{24} are occupied,

$$v_3 = -u_2 + c_{23} = -10 + 42 = 32$$

$$v_4 = -u_2 + c_{24} = -10 + \ \ 0 = -10$$

Now $\quad e_{11} = c_{12} - u_1 - v_3 = 40 - \ \ 0 - \ \ \ 32 = 8$

$$e_{12} = c_{14} - u_1 - v_4 = \ \ 0 - \ \ 0 - (-10) = 10$$

$$e_{21} = c_{21} - u_2 - v_1 = 30 - 10 - \ \ \ 24 = -4$$

u_i \ v_j	24	30	32	-10
0	$-$ 25 $\boxed{24}$	$+$ 25 $\boxed{30}$	⑧ $\boxed{40}$	⑩ $\boxed{0}$
10	$+$ ④ $\boxed{30}$	$-$ 20 $\boxed{40}$	10 $\boxed{42}$	20 $\boxed{0}$

The closed loop with cell $(2, 1)$ is indicated above. 20 is the minimum assignment in an occupied subtracting cell. Modify the current assignment by 20 as indicated to get:

u_i \ v_j	24	30	36	-6
0	5 $\boxed{24}$	45 $\boxed{30}$	④ $\boxed{40}$	⑥ $\boxed{0}$
6	20 $\boxed{30}$	④ $\boxed{40}$	10 $\boxed{42}$	20 $\boxed{0}$

185

The u_i's and v_j's are obtained by:

$$u_1 = 0$$

$$v_1 = -u_1 + c_{11} = -0 + 24 = 24$$

$$v_2 = -u_1 + c_{12} = -0 + 30 = 30$$

$$u_2 = -v_1 + c_{21} = -24 + 30 = 6$$

$$v_3 = -u_2 + c_{23} = -6 + 42 = 36$$

$$v_4 = -u_2 + c_{24} = -6 + 10 = -6$$

The e_{ij}'s are obtained by:

$$e_{13} = c_{13} - u_1 - v_3 = 40 - 0 - 36 = 6$$

$$e_{14} = c_{14} = u_1 - v_4 = 0 - 0 - (-6) = 6$$

$$e_{22} = c_{22} = u_2 - v_2 = 40 - 6 - 30 = 4$$

Since all reduced costs are non-negative, this is the optimal shipment.

		Shipment	Cost
Optimal Solution:	Plant 1 – Northwood	5	$ 120
	Plant 2 – Westwood	45	1,350
	Plant 2 – Northwood	20	600
	Plant 2 – Eastwood	10	420
	Total		$2,490

W 2) Given the following minimum cost transportation problem

	D_1	D_2	D_3	D_4	Supply
O_1	5	5	9	12	40
O_2	11	8	13	13	30
O_3	15	18	16	20	30
Demand	5	15	35	45	

a) Use the Vogel Approximation Method to get an initial solution.

b) Use the Stepping Stone Method to determine the reduced costs for the unoccupied cells.

c) What is the value of the current solution?

d) By how much will the next transportation tableau improve on this solution?

e) Solve the problem.

SOLUTION:

a) Does supply = demand? Yes. The following is the VAM starting assignment. Explanation of row differences/column differences follows.

	D_1	D_2	D_3	D_4	Row Dif 1	Row Dif 2	Row Dif 3
O_1	5 · 5	5 · (−2)	9 · 5	− 12 · 30	0	4	3
O_2	11 · (+5)	− 8 · 15	13 · (+3)	+ 13 · 15	3	5	0
O_3	15 · (+3)	18 · (+4)	16 · 30	20 · (+1)	1	2	4
Col Dif 1	6	3	4	1			
Col Dif 2	−	−	4	1			

187

1) To get row and column differences subtract the smallest cost from the next to the smallest cost in each row and column of those remaining.

Row difference #1:   row 1:   5 -   5 = 0
                      row 2:   11 -   8 = 3
                      row 3:   16 - 15 = 1

Column difference #1:   column 1:   11 -   5 = 6
                        column 2:   8 -   5 = 3
                        column 3:   13 -   9 = 4
                        column 4:   13 - 12 = 1

6 is maximum difference (column 1). Thus assign the maximum possible to the smallest cost in column 1, i.e. assign 5 to cell (1, 1). This eliminates column 1's demand.

2) Get row difference #2 with column 1 eliminated:

Row difference #2:   row 1:   9 -   5 = 4
                      row 2:   13 -   8 = 5
                      row 3:   18 - 16 = 2

(Note that the column differences remain the same.)
Now the maximum row/column difference is 5 determined by row 2. Thus assign the maximum possible to the smallest remaining cost in row 2, i.e. assign 15 to cell (2, 2). This eliminates column 2's demand.

3) Get row difference #3 with columns 1 and 2 eliminated.

                      row 1:   12 -   9 = 3
                      row 2:   13 - 13 = 0
                      row 3:   20 - 16 = 4

Now the maximum row/column difference is 4 determined by both row 3 and column 3. Let us arbitrarily choose row 3. Thus assign the maximum possible to the smallest remaining cost in row 3, i.e., assign 30 to cell (3, 3). This eliminates row 3's supply.

4) Get column difference #2 for columns 3 and 4 with row 2 eliminated.

                      column 3:   13 -   9 = 4
                      column 4:   13 - 12 = 1

Now the maximum row/column difference is 4 determined by
column 3. Thus assign the maximum possible to the smallest
remaining cost in column 3, i.e., assign 5 to cell (1, 3).
This eliminates column 3's demand. Since column 4 is the only
column left, make the remaining assignment of 30 to cell (1, 4)
and 15 to cell (2, 3).

b) $e_{12} = c_{12} - c_{14} + c_{24} - c_{22} = 5 \quad 12 + 18 - 8 = -2$

$e_{21} = c_{21} - c_{11} + c_{14} - c_{24} = 11 - 5 + 12 - 13 = 5$

$e_{23} = c_{23} - c_{24} + c_{14} - c_{13} = 13 - 13 + 12 - 9 = 3$

$e_{31} = c_{31} - c_{33} + c_{13} - c_{11} = 15 - 16 + 9 - 5 = 3$

$e_{32} = c_{32} - c_{33} + c_{13} - c_{14} + c_{24} - c_{22} = 18 - 16 + 9 - 12 + 13 - 8$

$$= 4$$

$e_{34} = c_{34} - c_{14} + c_{13} - c_{33} = 20 - 12 + 9 - 16 = 1$

c) Value

$$5 \times 5 = 25$$

$$5 \times 9 = 45$$

$$30 \times 12 = 360$$

$$15 \times 8 = 120$$

$$15 \times 13 = 195$$

$$30 \times 16 = \underline{480}$$

$$\text{Total } 1225$$

d) The stepping stone path that gives the most negative e_{ij} shows that
15 can be reassigned around its loop. Since the reduced cost is
-2 per unit, a savings of 15 x 2 = 30 will be attained in the next
tableau.

e) Iteration 2

5 $\boxed{5}$	15 $\boxed{5}$	5 $\boxed{9}$	15 $\boxed{12}$
⊕5 $\boxed{11}$	⊕2 $\boxed{8}$	⊕3 $\boxed{13}$	30 $\boxed{13}$
⊕3 $\boxed{15}$	⊕6 $\boxed{18}$	30 $\boxed{16}$	⊕1 $\boxed{20}$

189

$$e_{21} = c_{21} - c_{11} + c_{14} - c_{24} = 11 - 5 + 12 - 13 = 5$$

$$e_{22} = c_{22} - c_{12} + c_{14} - c_{24} = 8 - 5 + 12 - 13 = 2$$

$$e_{23} = c_{23} - c_{13} + c_{14} - c_{24} = 13 - 9 + 12 - 13 = 3$$

$$e_{31} = c_{31} - c_{11} + c_{13} + c_{33} = 15 - 5 + 9 - 16 = 3$$

$$e_{32} = c_{32} - c_{12} + c_{13} + c_{33} = 18 - 5 + 9 - 16 = 6$$

$$e_{34} = c_{34} - c_{14} + c_{13} + c_{33} = 20 - 12 + 9 - 16 = 1$$

Thus the optimal solution is:

	Shipment	Cost
01 - D1	5	$ 25
01 - D2	15	75
01 - D3	5	45
01 - D4	15	180
02 - D4	30	390
03 - D3	30	480
	Total	$1,195

O 3) Given the following transportation problem:

	D1	D2	D3	D4	
01	20	30	15	16	33
02	14	18	12	18	16
03	19	16	14	14	21
	15	20	25	10	

a) Give the Northwest Corner starting solution. What is the advantage of this method?

b) Give the Vogel Approximation Method starting solution. What is the advantage of this method?

c) Use MODI solution procedure on (b) to show it gives the optimal solution.

d) Use MODI solution procedure on (a) to solve for the optimal solution.

Outline of Solution:

a) Does supply = demand? Yes.
Assign as much as possible to upper left hand cell (=15).
Assign as much as possible to new upper left hand cell (=18).
Assign as much as possible to new upper left hand cell (=2).
Assign as much as possible to new upper left hand cell (=14).
Assign remaining supply as required (11 and 10).

Advantage: Were any extra calculations required to make this assignment? No.

b) 1) Maximum row/column difference = 5, column 1, assignment = 15
2) Maximum row/column difference = 6, row 2, assignment = 1
3) Maximum row/column difference = 14, column 2, assignment = 20
4) Maximum row/column difference = 2, column 4, assignment = 1
5) Remaining assignments = 24, 9 in row 1

Advantage: Were costs considered in this assignment? Yes.

c) $u_1 = 0$, $u_2 = -3$, $u_3 = -2$, $v_1 = 17$, $v_2 = 18$, $v_3 = 15$, $v_4 = 16$ all

$e_{ij} \geq 0$.

d) <u>Iteration 1</u>

$u_1 = 0$, $u_2 = -12$, $u_3 = -10$, $v_1 = 20$, $v_2 = 30$, $v_3 = 24$, $v_4 = 24$.

Min $e_{ij} = e_{13} = -9$; Ship 14 around loop.

<u>Iteration 2</u>

$u_1 = 0$, $u_2 = -12$, $u_3 = -1$, $v_1 = 20$, $v_2 = 30$, $v_3 = 15$, $v_4 = 15$.

Min $e_{ij} = e_{32} = -13$; Ship 4 around loop.

<u>Iteration 3</u>

$u_1 = 0$, $u_2 = 1$, $u_3 = -1$, $v_1 = 20$, $v_2 = 17$, $v_3 = 15$, $v_4 = 15$.

Min $e_{ij} = u_{21} = -7$; Ship 7 around loop.

<u>Iteration 4</u>

$u_1 = 0$, $u_2 = -6$, $u_3 = -8$, $v_1 = 20$, $v_2 = 24$, $v_3 = 15$, $v_4 = 22$.

Min $e_{ij} = u_{14} = -6$; Ship 8 around loop.

<u>Iteration 5</u>

$u_1 = 0$, $u_2 = 0$, $u_3 = -2$, $v_1 = 14$, $v_2 = 18$, $v_3 = 15$, $v_4 = 16$.

Min $e_{ij} = u_{23} = -3$; Ship 1 around loop.

<u>Iteration 6</u>

See (c) above.

Answer: O1 – D3 = 24; O1 – D4 = 9; O2 – D1 = 15; O2 – D3 = 1;
         O3 – D2 = 20; O3 – D4 = 1; Total cost = $1,070.

4) Brewer's Department Store has orders from each of its four branches for 10 crates of the sale pillow cases. Brewer's two warehouses have 14 and 22 cases respectively. The following gives the distances in miles between the warehouses and stores.

	Store 1	Store 2	Store 3	Store 4
Warehouse 1	25	18	20	13
Warehouse 2	16	5	30	25

Shipping costs are figured at $2 per crate plus $.10 per mile per crate.

a) Set the problem up as a transportation problem with supply equal to demand.

b) Use the Northwest Corner Method to get an initial feasible solution.

c) Solve using the stepping stone method.

* 5) The Navy has 9,000 tons of materials in Albany, Georgia which it wishes to ship to three installations: San Diego, Norfolk, and Pensacola. They require 4,000, 2,500, and 2,500 tons respectively. The following gives a table of <u>hundred-ton</u> shipping costs for truck, train, and air in <u>hundreds</u> of dollars.

	San Diego	Norfolk	Pensacola
Truck	$12	$ 6	$ 5
Train	$20	$11	$ 9
Air	$30	$26	$28

Government regulations require equal distribution of the shipping among the three carriers.

a) Give the Vogel Approximation Method solution for this problem.

b) Solve use the MODI solution procedure.

6) There are four trucking companies which are bidding to haul Dangerly's Explosives from the manufacturing plant to the main warehouse. Dangerly makes three kinds of explosives: large blast stick explosives, low blast stick explosives, and, a highly volatile liquid explosive. Below are the shipping bids submitted by the four trucking firms per truckload as well as the weekly availability.

| Company | Explosives | | | Weekly |
	Large	Small	Liquid	Availability
Safety Haul	2,000	1,000	3,000	4
Federated Truckers	1,600	1,200	3,200	3
Intrastate Transport	1,400	1,400	2,800	2
Charles Kelley	1,800	1,600	3,600	3

Dangerly needs weekly hauls of three trucks for each of the stick explosives and five trucks for the liquid explosive.

a) Formulate as a transportation problem where supply = demand.

b) Give the VAM starting solution. Show by the MODI method that this gives an optimal solution.

c) Show there exists another optimal basic solution. Show how to construct a third optimal solution which uses seven combinations.

* 7) Consider the following cost-minimization transportation problem.

	D1	D2	D3	D4	Supply
01	6	4	3	7	12
02	6	8	5	8	14
03	2	3	3	2	24
Demand	5	10	15	20	

a) Give the Vogel Approximation Starting Solution.

b) Show by the stepping stone method that the solution in (a) is optimal.

c) Amending the tableau in (a), show that if an extra unit was found at origin #2, then the optimal solution does not change.

d) Show that if an extra unit was found at origin #1, the optimal solution does change, and give the new optimal solution.

e) By how much could the cost from 02 – D4 change and the current solution remain optimal?

f) By how much could the cost from 01 – D2 be increased and the current solution remain optimal?

W 8) Telly's Toy Company produces three kinds of dolls: the Bertha doll, the Holly dolly, and the Shari doll in quantities of 1,000, 2,000 and 2,000 per week respectively. These dolls are demanded at three large department stores: Shears, Nichols, and Words. Contracts requiring 1,500 total dolls per week are to be shipped to each store. However, Words does not want any Bertha dolls.

Because of past contract commitments and the size of other orders, profits vary from store to store on each kind of doll. A summary of the unit profit per doll is given below.

	Shears	Nichols	Words
Bertha	5	4	X
Holly	16	8	9
Shari	12	10	11

a) Set the problem up as a maximization transportation problem.

b) Give the Northwest Corner starting solution.

c) Use the MODI solution procedure to solve.

SOLUTION:

a) The origins are the dolls; the destinations are the stores. Since supply exceeds demand by 500, add a dummy store requiring 500 with all unit profits of zero. The profit of Bertha-Words is $-M$. (See first tableau below.)

b) The Northwest Corner starting solution in terms of hundreds of dolls: Bertha-Shears, 10; Holly-Shears, 5; Holly-Nichols, 15; (note degeneracy occurs here since a supply and demand are simultaneously satisfied); thus Holly-Words has a 0 basic allocation; Shari-Words, 15; Shari-Dummy, 5. (See first tableau below.)

197

c) Solving by MODI

Iteration 1

u_i \ v_j	S (5)	N (−3)	W (−2)	D (−13)
B (0)	− 10 [5]	(+7) [4]	(−M) [−M] +	(+13) [0]
H (11)	+ 5 [16]	15 [8]	− 0 [9]	(+2) [0]
S (13)	(−6) [12]	(0) [10]	+ 15 [11]	− 5 [0]

Since this is a profit maximization, most positive e_{ij} is taken.
Note the maximum shipment around the loop is zero, determined by cell (2, 3).

Iteration 2

u_i \ v_j	S (5)	N (−3)	W (11)	D (0)
B (0)	− 10 [5]	(+7) [4]	(−M) [−M]	+ 0 [0]
H (11)	+ 5 [16]	− 15 [8]	(−13) [9]	(−11) [0] −
S (0)	(+7) [12]	+ (+13) [10]	15 [11]	− 5 [0]

(Ship 5 around loop; note degeneracy disappears.)

Iteration 3

u_i \ v_j	S (5)	N (−3)	W (−2)	D (0)
B (0)	+ 5 [5]	− (+7) [4]	(−M) [−M]	5 [0]
H (11)	+ 10 [16]	− 10 [8]	(0) [9]	(−11) [0]
S (13)	(−6) [12]	5 [10]	15 [11]	(−13) [0]

(Ship 5 around loop.)

198

Iteration 4

	u_i / v_j	S 12	N 4	W 5	D 0
B	0	(-7) [5]	5 [4]	(-M) [-M]	5 [0]
H	4	15 [16]	5 [8]	(0) [9]	(-4) [0]
S	6	(-6) [12]	5 [10]	15 [11]	(-6) [0]

Optimal Solution

Doll	Store	Number	Profit
Bertha	Nichols	500	$ 2,000
Holly	Shears	1500	24,000
Holly	Nichols	500	4,000
Shari	Nichols	500	5,000
Shari	Words	1500	16,500
		Total	$51,500

* 9) Frederick's Tool Company has weekly orders for 2,400 cartons of tools from four wholesale outlets as follows: Dayton, 400 cartons; Jackson, 500 boxes; Omaha, 800 boxes; Phoenix, 700 boxes. Frederick's has three plants, each producing 800 items per week. The following shipping costs per box between the plants and cities are:

	Dayton	Jackson	Omaha	Phoenix
Plant 1	3	6	8	10
Plant 2	10	9	8	6
Plant 3	X	8	8	8

(Note Plant 3 has no easy mode of transportation to Dayton.)

a) Give the Northwest Corner starting solution.

b) Solve the problem using the Stepping Stone solution procedure.

10) Rocket Ice Cream Company has one plant in each of the three cities in the Tri-City area. Rocket receives orders daily from four major market chains: Beta Gamma Markets, Good Luck Markets, Zenith Markets, and Yankee Markets. Beta Gamma wants 2,000 half gallons daily, whereas Good Luck wants 3,000 daily, Zenith 1,500 daily, and Yankee 2,500 daily. Ice cream delivery trucks carry 250 half gallons and can make one delivery per day. Super market quality ice cream is produced at all three plants at the following daily rates: Lewiston Plant - 3,500 half gallons, Clarkson Plant - 3,000 half gallons, Expedition Plant - 2,500 half gallons.

The following is the truckload delivery cost between the plants and the supermarket distribution centers.

	Beta Gamma	Good Luck	Zenith	Yankee
Lewiston	100	80	70	40
Clarkson	90	75	80	55
Expedition	70	45	55	40

a) Set the problem up as a transportation problem giving the North-west Corner starting solution.

b) Solve using the Stepping Stone solution procedure.

c) What underlying assumptions would be violated if the trucks hold 300 half gallons of ice cream?

11) A plant has 14 machines which are to be allocated among three departments. The machines are of four types: there are 5 type A machines;
4 type B machines, 2 type C machines and 3 type D machines. The three
departments have 4, 8, and 2 machine operators respectively, each of
which can operate each kind of machine.

The following profit table is the accounting department's Thursday
prediction as to the profitability (in hundreds of dollars) of each
department-machine combination based on updated demands and needs of
current projects. These change daily.

	Machine A	Machine B	Machine C	Machine D
Dep't. 1	6	10	5	11
Dep't. 2	3	8	3	10
Dep't. 3	5	8	3	9

Give two optimal machine assignments for Thursday.

Suppose the city of Francene has 100 contracts up for bids equally divided between four different departments: sanitation, police services, parks department, and administration. Three different consulting firms are bidding on the contracts: Ace Consulting, Band Corporation, and QM Associates. Ace has personnel for 40 contracts, Band for 40, and QM for 30. Because contracts are similar within each department, each firm is able to bid on contracts based only on the department. The bid price (in hundreds of dollars per contract) is summarized below:

	Sanitation	Police	Parks	Administration
Ace	10	15	14	16
Band	15	18	8	10
QM	12	12	12	12

How should the contracts be awarded and how much will the city spend?

SOLUTION:

Although this problem has nothing to do with transportation, it can be thought of as a transportation problem with the supplies being the personnel at the various consulting firms and the demands the contracts.

Since supply = 110, demand = 100, a dummy destination with demand of 10 needs to be added. Using the Northwest Corner and the Stepping Stone method:

25 [10]	15 [15]	(+9) [14]	(+9) [16]	(+5) [0]	40
(+2) [15]	−10 [18]	25 [8] +	+ 5 [10]	(+2) [0]	40
(−3) [12]	+ (−8) [12]	(+2) [12] −	20 [12]	10 [0]	30
25	25	25	25	10	

25 ⌐10⌐ –	15 ⌐15⌐ (+1)	⌐14⌐ (+1)	⌐16⌐ (−3)	⌐0⌐
(+10) ⌐15⌐	(+8) ⌐18⌐	25 ⌐8⌐	15 ⌐10⌐	(+2) ⌐0⌐
(+5) ⌐12⌐ +	10 ⌐12⌐	(+2) ⌐12⌐	10 ⌐12⌐ –	10 ⌐0⌐

25 ⌐10⌐	5 ⌐15⌐ (+1)	⌐14⌐ (+1)	⌐16⌐ (+1)	10 ⌐0⌐
(+10) ⌐15⌐	(+8) ⌐18⌐	25 ⌐8⌐	15 ⌐10⌐	(+5) ⌐0⌐
(+5) ⌐12⌐	20 ⌐12⌐	(+2) ⌐12⌐	10 ⌐12⌐	(+3) ⌐0⌐

Optimal Solution

Ace Consulting	– 25 Sanitation contracts	=	$ 25,000
	– 5 Police contracts	=	7,500
Band Corporation	– 25 Parks contracts	=	20,000
	– 15 Administration contracts	=	15,000
QM Associates	– 20 Police contracts	=	24,000
	– 10 Administration contracts	=	12,000
	Total		$103,500

204

* 13) There are four marketing research firms (call them MR1, MR2, MR3, and MR4) that we have faith in to advertise our products. We have just come out with a new zizzle and wish to have 30 newspaper advertisements, 15 TV advertisements, and 25 radio advertisements prepared. Each of the firms has submitted bids for the ads. However, resources are limited and MR1 feels it can only produce 15 total ads, MR2 only 25, MR3 only 10, and MR4 only 20. The bids submitted in terms of <u>hundreds of dollars per ad</u> were:

FIRMS

		MR1	MR2	MR3	MR4
	Newspaper	16	10	12	12
MEDIA	TV	26	20	30	21
	Radio	22	15	23	14

a) Formulate this problem as a particular kind of mathematical model that we have studied and solve. Give an optimal solution of $106,500 using six media-firm combinations. Use Northwest Corner starting procedure.

b) Perhaps for consistency we want to use as few media-firm combinations as possible. Show that there exists another optimal solution of $106,500 using five media-firm combinations.

c) Perhaps for diversification we want to use as many combinations as possible. Give another optimal solution of $106,500 using seven media-firm combinations.

14) Consider the Brewer Department Store (see problem 4).

a) If every store is to get at least seven crates, write a linear program for this transportation problem.

b) Solve this problem as a transportation problem, in the following manner. For each store create two columns: (1) a column requiring seven units where shipping cost to the dummy store is M; and (2) a column requiring three units where the shipping cost to the dummy store is 0.

c) Show how the result could have been attained easily from the final tableau for problem #4 given below.

	S1	S2	S3	S4
W1	4.50 (+1.90)	3.80 (+2.30)	4.00 4	3.30 10
W2	3.60 10	2.50 10	5.00 2	4.50 (+1.20)
WD	0 (+1.40)	0 (+2.50)	0 4	0 (+.70)

206

15) Consider an ordinary assignment problem of 4 workers to 4 jobs. Show how this could be formulated and solved as a transportation problem. Explain why, in general, the transportation solution procedure is <u>not</u> an attractive way to solve this problem.

8

INTEGER
LINEAR
PROGRAMMING

KEY CONCEPTS

1. Structure of integer linear programs and the
    pitfalls of rounding off the optimal linear
    programming solution

2. Special applications that can be formulated
    as integer linear programs

3. The branch and bound solution procedure for
    solving integer linear programs

REVIEW

1. Structure of Integer Linear Programs

An integer linear program (ILP) has the same structure as a linear
program except that some or all of the variables are restricted to take on
integer values. That is, an ILP seeks to maximize or minimize a linear
objective function subject to linear inequalities or equalities, with some
or all of the variables designated to assume integer values. If all of
the variables are restricted to be integers the problem is called an
all integer linear program, while if some variables are still allowed to
take on non-integer values, the problem is called a mixed integer linear
program. An important class of ILP's are problems where the variables are
restricted to be 0 or 1. These problems are designated as binary or (0-1)
integer linear programs.

One incorrect approach for solving integer linear programs is to
relax the integer requirements for the variables, solve the resulting
linear program, and either round off or round down the resulting linear
programming optimal solution. Sometimes this will produce the optimal
integer solution but oftentimes this procedure will result in either a
suboptimal or even an infeasible solution for the ILP. However, because a
linear program is less constrained (it has no integer constraints), the
optimal solution to an LP maximization problem does provide an upper bound

for the optimal value of the objective function (a lower bound for a minimization problem) for the corresponding ILP.

Sensitivity analyses are often much more crucial in integer linear programming than in simple linear programming. This is because small changes in the coefficients may cause some variable(s) to deviate from an integer value, thereby forcing radical changes in the optimal solution for an ILP.

2. Special Formulations

Many problems automatically fit nicely into the framework of ILP's. These include problems in which variables represent numbers of people, vehicles or buildings. In these cases, non-integer values make no sense. However, some problems which violate the basic structure of linear programs can be modified to fit the structure of integer linear programs. For problems in which different projects, j, consume available resources only if the project is implemented, the problem can be formulated as an ILP as follows. Let x_j represent the number of projects, j, implemented and constrain $x_j \leq 1$, $x_j \geq 0$ and x_j to be integer. This forces x_j to take on the value 1 (implemented) or 0 (not implemented).

If at most K out of n projects are to be implemented, an additional constraint might be $\sum_{j=1}^{n} x_j \leq K$ with the constraint replaced by an equality if exactly K are to be implemented.

If two projects (i and j) are co-requisites (if one is implemented, the other must be) the constraint $x_i - x_j = 0$ would be added.

If implementation of project j is conditional upon implementation of project i (that is project j can only be done if project i is implemented) then the appropriate constraint would be $x_j - x_i \leq 0$.

If projects i and j are mutually exclusive (if one is implemented, the other must not be) then a constraint would be added of the form $x_i + x_j \leq 1$.

3. The Branch and Bound Algorithm

In Chapter 6 a branch and bound algorithm was introduced for solving the traveling salesman problem. This technique can also be applied to all integer and mixed integer linear programs. The algorithm first solves the problem with the integer constraints relaxed. If the solution happens to be an integer solution the ILP is solved. Otherwise additional constraints are added to the problem. Each constraint added is called a branch of the

"branch and bound tree." At the end of the branch a node is formed giving
the solution to the revised problem with the constraint added. Nodes
formed from branches are said to be descendant nodes from the node above.
The value of a node is the value of the objective function in the optimal
solution and provides an upper bound for all descendant nodes.

The algorithm for a maximization problem follows:

1.   Solve the problem as an LP. If the solution satisfies the
     integer constraints, STOP. Otherwise this provides an initial
     upper bound (UB) for the problem. Construct an initial node
     giving this solution.

2.   Find any feasible solution that satisfies the integer con-
     straints. This provides an initial lower bound (LB) for the
     problem.

3.   Consider the node with largest value in which a variable, x_j,
     that was restricted to be integer, assumed a value, $\overline{x}_j$, in
     the LP solution that was not integer. Form two branches: (1)
     one with the constraint $x_j \leq [\overline{x}_j]$ (where $[x_j]$ means the integer
     part of $\overline{x}_j$) added; and, (2) one with the constraint
     $x_j \geq [\overline{x}_j] + 1$ added.

4.   Form nodes at the ends of these branches by solving the new LP's.

5.   If a branch gives an infeasible solution to the LP, do not
     consider this branch further.

     If a branch gives a feasible solution to the ILP with objective
     function value z, form a node with this solution.
        i)   if z = UB, STOP. This solution is optimal.
       ii)   if z ≠ UB and z > LB, set LB = z. GO TO STEP 6.
      iii)   if z < LB, do not branch further from this node.
     If a branch gives a feasible solution to the LP that is not
     an integer solution, GO TO STEP 6.

6.   After both branches have been considered, set UB = max z value
     of all final descendant nodes considered thus far. If UB = LB,
     STOP. Otherwise GO TO STEP 3.

     The roles of upper and lower bounds are reversed for minimiza-
     tion problems.

ALL INTEGER LINEAR PROGRAM - A linear program in which all decision variables are restricted to be integers.   (334)

BRANCH AND BOUND - A method for solving integer linear programs which systematically adds relaxed constraints.   (347)

CO-REQUISITE PROJECTS - Projects i and j both of which must be completed or both not completed.   (343)

CONDITIONAL PROJECT - Project i is conditional on project j if project i can only be completed if project j is.   (343)

DESCENDANT NODE - Node generated by adding a constraint to the relaxed LP problem.   (349)

INTEGER LINEAR PROGRAM - A linear program where some or all of the variables must assume integer values.   (333)

LP RELAXATION - A method for making an initial attempt at solving an integer linear program with the integer constraints ignored.   (334)

MULTIPLE CHOICE CONSTRAINTS - A set of constraints at least one of which must be satisfied.   (341)

MUTUALLY EXCLUSIVE CONSTRAINTS - A set of constraints such that if one is satisfied the others must not be.   (342)

0 - 1 LINEAR PROGRAMMING - An integer linear program in which some or all of the variables must either be 0 or 1.   (334)

W 1) Solve the following problem by the graphical method of linear programming:

$$\text{MAX} \quad 3x_1 + 2x_2$$

$$\text{s.t.} \quad 3x_1 + x_2 \le 9$$

$$x_1 + 3x_2 \le 7$$

$$-x_1 + x_2 \le 1$$

$$x_1, x_2 \ge 0$$

Note that the optimal solution to this problem does not have integer values for x_1 and x_2. Now if these variables represented people, for example, fractional values would make no sense. There are two common practices which the novice may try in this case: (i) round-off; (ii) round-down.

a) By using the round-off rule that fractions greater than or equal to 1/2 will be rounded up and that those less than 1/2 will be rounded down, show that rounding off does not even give a feasible solution for this linear program.

b) Show that rounding down all fractions does not give the best integer solution in this case. Do this by listing all points in the feasible region of the linear program that have integer values for both x_1 and x_2. (HINT: There are eight of them.) Which point do you get by rounding down? Compute the objective function value for all eight points. Which one is optimal?

SOLUTION:

Solve the problem graphically.

a) Rounding off gives $x_1 = 3$, $x_2 = 2$ which is not in the feasible region.

b) Rounding down gives $x_1 = 2$, $x_2 = 1$ with $z = 8$.

However there are eight integer solutions to this problem.

x_1	x_2	z		
0	0	0		
1	0	3		
2	0	6		
3	0	9	←	optimal integer solution
0	1	2		
1	1	5		
2	1	8	←	rounding down solution
1	2	7		

Thus, neither rounding off nor rounding down gives the optimal integer solution to this problem.

0 2) Given the following problem

$$\text{MIN} \quad 2x_1 + x_2$$

$$\text{s.t.} \quad x_1 + 3x_2 \geq 5$$

$$8x_1 + 3x_2 \geq 17$$

$$x_1, \; x_2 \geq 0$$

a) Solve graphically for the optimal solution.

b) If x_2 were restricted to be an integer, what would be the optimal solution to the mixed integer program? Did rounding up x_2 or rounding off x_2 give this solution?

c) If x_1 and x_2 were both required to be integers, what would be the solution to the all integer linear program. Did rounding x_1 and x_2 give this solution?

Outline of Solution:

a) Graph the constraint region. Move the objective function parallel (towards origin) until it touches the last point of the feasible region.

b) Since x_2 must be an integer the feasible region is now the lines of integer x_2 values bounded by the feasible region. Determine the last of these points touched by moving the objective line toward the origin.

Round off and round up (since there are $\geq$ constraints) the value of x_2 of and in (a). Neither of these procedures will generate the above point.

c) Since x_1 and x_2 must both be integers the feasible region is all the integer points in the feasible region of (a). Consider moving our objective function line toward the origin again. Determine the last of these disjoint integer points to be touched.

Round off and round up both the values of x_1 and x_2 found in (a).

In this case rounding off provides the optimal integer solution.

Answers:

a) $x_1 = 12/7$, $x_2 = 23/21$, $z = 95/21$

b) $x_1 = 11/8$, $x_2 = 2$, $z = 19/4$

Rounding off gives $x_1 = 12/7$, $x_2 = 1$. Rounding up gives $x_1 = 12/7$, $x_2 = 2$. Neither is optimal.

c) $x_1 = 2$, $x_2 = 1$, $z = 5$.

Rounding off gives this solution (lucky). Rounding up gives $x_1 = 2$, $x_2 = 2$ which is not optimal.

* 3) Given the following all-integer linear program.

$$\text{MAX} \quad 15x_1 + 2x_2$$

$$\text{s.t.} \quad 7x_1 + x_2 \leq 23$$

$$3x_1 - x_2 \leq 5$$

$$x_1, x_2 \geq 0 \text{ and integer}$$

a) Solve for the optimal solution to the linear program ignoring the integer constraints.

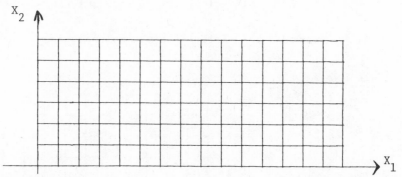

b) What solution do you get by rounding off? Is this the optimal integer solution? Explain.

c) What solution do you get by rounding down? Is this the optimal integer solution? Explain.

d) Show that the optimal solution to the all integer linear program gives a lower value of the objective function than the optimal solution to the linear program.

e) Explain why the optimal value of the objective function to the all integer program must always be less than or equal to the optimal value of the objective function of the corresponding linear program. When would they be equal? What could you say about the optimal value of the objective function of a mixed integer linear program?

4) Given the following problem.

$$\text{MAX} \quad 4x_1 + 7x_2$$

$$\text{s.t.} \quad 2x_1 + 7x_2 \leq 29$$

$$8x_1 + 3x_2 \leq 31$$

$$x_1, x_2 \geq 0$$

a) Solve for the optimal solution to the linear program.

b) What would be the optimal solution if x_1 and x_2 were restricted to be integers?

c) Suppose the objective function charged to MAX $3x_1 + 7x_2$

   (i) How would this affect the optimal solution to the linear program?

   (ii) How would this affect the optimal solution to the integer linear program?

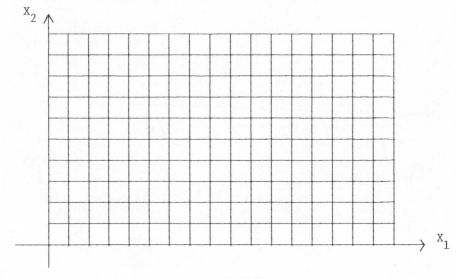

* 5) Given the following all-integer linear program.

$$\text{MAX} \quad 3x_1 + 10x_2$$

$$\text{s.t.} \quad 2x_1 + x_2 \le 5$$

$$x_1 + 6x_2 \le 9$$

$$x_1 - x_2 \ge 2$$

$$x_1, x_2 \ge 0, \text{ integer}$$

a) Solve the problem graphically as a linear program.

b) Show there is only one integer point and hence it must be the optimal solution.

c) Suppose the third constraint was changed to $x_1 - x_2 \ge 2.1$. What is the optimal solution to the linear program? What happens to the optimal solution of the integer linear program?

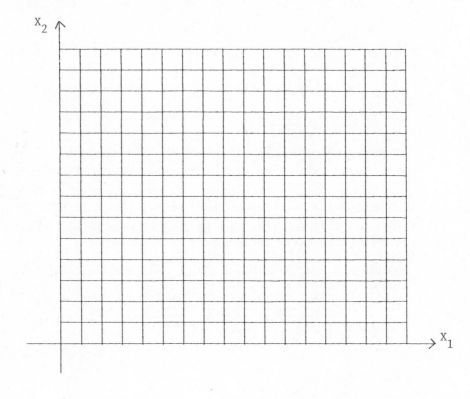

W 6) Consider TRI-CITY Trucking Company which serves four destinations. The destinations demand 100, 200, 300 and 400 items per week respectively. TRI-CITY has proposed four sites for distribution centers. Due to various restrictions the weekly output of these distribution centers would be 450, 500, 550, and 600 respectively. The unit shipping costs from the distribution centers to the destinations are summarized in the following table along with the expected weekly operating costs for each center. Management wants to meet the demands at the destinations while minimizing total operating and shipping costs. Formulate this as an integer program.

| | | Destination | | | | Weekly |
		D_1	D_2	D_3	D_4	Operating Costs
	C_1	10	12	14	15	$ 6,000
Distribution	C_2	12	13	18	17	$ 7,000
Center	C_3	20	16	13	15	$10,000
	C_4	18	18	18	18	$ 9,000

SOLUTION:

Let x_{ij} = the amount shipped from distribution center i to destination j.

Let y_i = the number of centers of type i built.

We want to restrict y_i to be 0 or 1. Thus we have $y_i \geq 0$, $y_i \leq 1$, and y_i integer. Also the supply that is available at center i is either the weekly output if this center is built or 0 if it is not. Therefore the supplies at each center must be multiplied by y_i. Additionally, the sum of all supplies must be greater than or equal to 1,000. Since we want to minimize total weekly costs we have:

MIN $10x_{11} + 12x_{12} + 14x_{13} + 15x_{14} + 12x_{21} + 13x_{22} + 18x_{23} + 17x_{24} +$

$20x_{31} + 16x_{32} + 13x_{33} + 15x_{34} + 18x_{41} + 18x_{42} + 18x_{43} + 18x_{44} +$

$6000y_1 + 7000y_2 + 10,000y_3 + 9000y_4$

s.t. $x_{11} + x_{12} + x_{13} + x_{14} - 450y_1 \leq 0$

$x_{21} + x_{22} + x_{23} + x_{24} - 500y_2 \leq 0$

$x_{31} + x_{32} + x_{33} + x_{34} - 550y_3 \leq 0$ } supply at distribution center, i, if built

$x_{41} + x_{42} + x_{43} + x_{44} - 600y_4 \leq 0$

$450y_1 + 500y_2 + 550y_3 + 600y_4 \geq 1000$ (Total Supply)

$x_{11} + x_{21} + x_{31} + x_{41} \qquad = 100$

$x_{12} + x_{22} + x_{32} + x_{42} \qquad = 200$

$x_{13} + x_{23} + x_{33} + x_{43} \qquad = 300$ } demand at destination j

$x_{14} + x_{24} + x_{34} + x_{44} \qquad = 400$

$y_1 \leq 1$

$y_2 \leq 1$

$y_3 \leq 1$

$y_4 \leq 1$

$x_{ij} \geq 0, \ y_i \geq 0 \quad i = 1,\ldots,4$

$\qquad\qquad\qquad\qquad j = 1,\ldots,4$

y_i integer

7) The Tower Engineering Corporation is considering undertaking several proposed projects for the next fiscal year. The projects, together with the number of engineers and number of support personnel required for each project and the expected project profit, are summarized in the table below.

	Project					
	1	2	3	4	5	6
Engineers Required	20	55	47	38	90	63
Support Personnel Required	15	45	50	40	70	70
Profit (Millions)	1	1.8	2.0	1.5	3.6	2.2

Formulate an integer linear program which maximize the company's profit subject to the following management constraints.

1) Use no more than 175 engineers.
2) Use no more than 150 support personnel.
3) If either project 6 or project 4 is done, both must be done.

4) Project 2 can only be done if project 1 is done.
5) If project 5 is done project 3 must not be done and vice versa.
6) No more than 3 projects are to be done.

W 8)   Solve problem 1) by the branch and bound method.

SOLUTION: The problem is:

$$MAX \quad 3x_1 + 2x_2$$

$$s.t. \quad 3x_1 + x_2 \leq 9$$

$$x_1 + 3x_2 \leq 7$$

$$- x_1 + x_2 \leq 1$$

$$x_1, x_2 \geq 0 \text{ and integer}$$

We redraw the graph so that the points may be easily identified.

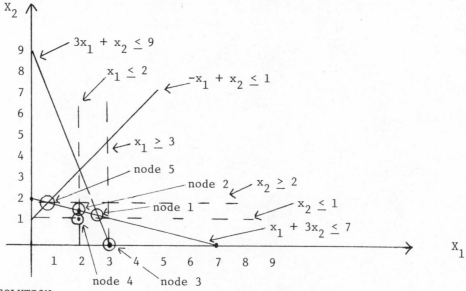

SOLUTION:

1.   Solve as L.P. This gives node 1: $x_1 = 2.5$, $x_2 = 1.5$, $z = 10.5$. This gives an UB.

2.   Note that rounding down gives $x_1 = 2$, $x_2 = 1$, $z = 8$ which is feasible. This gives a L.B. Thus the branch and bound tree at this point is

$$\begin{array}{l} 1 \\ \text{LP value} = 10.5 \\ \quad x_1 = 2.5 \\ \quad x_2 = 1.5 \end{array}$$

UB = 10.5
LB = 8

223

3. Consider branching on x_1. Thus the left branch is $x_1 \leq 2$ and the right branch is $x_1 \geq 3$.

4. The optimal solution when $x_1 \leq 2$ is added is $x_1 = 2$, $x_2 = 5/3$, $z = 9 \ 1/3$. (Node 2) The optimal solution when $x_1 \geq 3$ is added is $x_1 = 3$, $x_2 = 0$, $z = 9$. (Node 3)

5. Since the latter is an integer solution with $z > LB$, the LB is changed to 9.

6. Nodes 2 and 3 are the final descendant nodes so UB = max (node 2, node 3) = 9 1/3. The branch and bround tree is now:

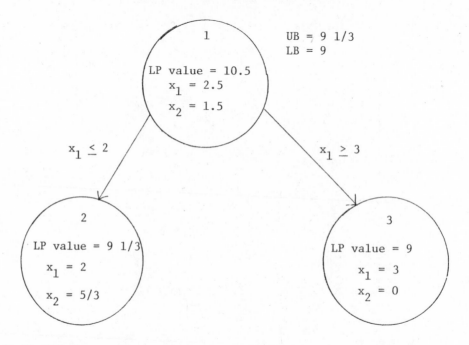

GO TO STEP 3.

3. Consider branching on x_2 from node 2. Thus the left branch is $x_2 \leq 1$ and the right branch is $x_2 \geq 2$.

4. Remember $x_1 \leq 2$ has already been added. Now also adding $x_2 \leq 1$ gives $x_1 = 2$, $x_2 = 1$, $z = 8$. When $x_2 \geq 2$ is added, this gives $x_1 = 1$, $x_2 = 2$, $z = 7$.

5. Since both are integer solutions they are to be compared with the current lower bound = 9. Since they are both smaller the LB remains unchanged.

6. Nodes 4, 5, and 3 are the final descendant nodes so UB = max (node 4, node 5, and node 3) = 9. Since UB = LB = 9, the problem is solved with node 3 giving the optimal integer solution of $x_1 = 3$, $x_2 = 0$, $z = 9$.

The final branch and bound tree would be:

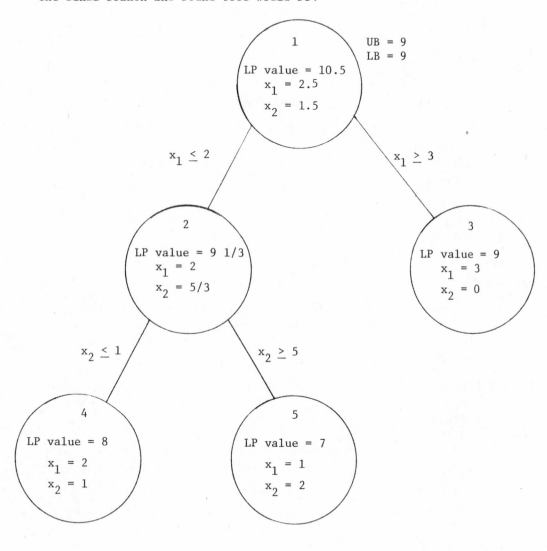

0 9)   Solve problem #2 by the branch and bound algorithm.

Outline of Solution:

The problem is

$$\text{MIN} \quad 2x_1 + x_2$$
$$x_1 + 3x_2 \geq 5$$
$$8x_1 + 3x_2 \geq 17$$
$$x_1, x_2 \geq 0$$

(i) Solving as a linear program gives:

$x_1 = 12/7$, $x_2 = 23/21$, $z = 95/21$.

(ii) Since only x_2 must be integer in this case round up $x_2 = 2$ so that $x_1 = 12/7$, $x_2 = 2$, $z = 38/7$. This gives an initial feasible solution. Thus LB = 95/21, UB = 38/7 (NOTE UB and LB calculations play reverse roles in a minimization problem). The solution to (a) gives node 1.

STEP 3:   Branch on $x_2 \leq 1$ (node 2) and $x_2 \geq 2$ (node 3).

STEP 4:   Node 2 gives $z = 5$, node 3 gives $z = 19/4$.

STEP 5:   Since both are feasible with x_2 an integer, recalculate UB = 19/4.

STEP 6:   LB = min z value of node 2 and node 3 = 19/4. Since LB = UB STOP.

(iii) Now both x_1 and x_2 must be integer. Node 2 gives an integer solution and hence gives an UB = 5 for the problem. The LB = 19/4 from node 3.

STEP 3:   Branch on $x_1 \leq 1$ and $x_1 \geq 2$ from node 3.

STEP 4:   For the $x_1 \leq 1$ branch, the problem is infeasible (node 4).
          For $x_1 \geq 2$ $z = 6$ (node 5).

STEP 5:   Although node 5 gives a feasible integer solution its value is greater than the upper bound.

STEP 6:   LB = min of z value of node 2 and node 5 = 5. Since UB = LB, STOP. Optimal solution at node 2.

226

* 10) Solve the following all integer linear program by the branch and bound algorithm.

$$\text{MAX} \quad 4x_1 + 3x_2$$

$$\text{s.t.} \quad 5x_1 + 6x_2 \leq 28$$

$$3x_1 + 2x_2 \leq 11$$

$$x_1, \, x_2 \geq 0 \text{ and integer}$$

11) Given the following problem

$$\text{MAX} \quad 5x_1 + 4x_2$$

$$\text{s.t.} \quad 4x_1 + x_2 \le 10$$

$$5x_1 + 3x_2 \le 15$$

$$x_1 + x_2 \le 4$$

$$x_1, x_2 \ge 0$$

a) Solve the linear program.

b) Use the branch and bound algorithm to solve the mixed integer linear program with x_2 required to be an integer.

c) Show that the branch and bound solution in (b) is also optimal for the all integer linear program.

d) Suppose the objective function changed to MAX $5x_1 + 3x_2$. Using the same branch and bound tree already calculated in (b) re-evaluate the optimal solution to both the mixed integer and all integer problems. Why can we use the same starting node?

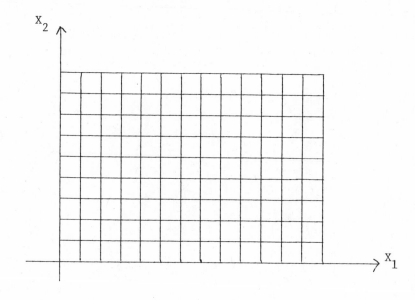

* 12) As a business manager for a grain distributor you are asked to decide
        how many containers of each of two grains to purchase to fill its
        1,600 pound warehouse. The table below summarizes the container size,
        availability, and expected profit per container upon distribution.

Grain	Container Size	Availability	Profit Per Container
A	500 Lbs.	3	$1,200
B	600 Lbs.	2	$1,500

a) What is the optimal decision if you are allowed to purchase
    fractional containers?

b) What is the optimal decision if fraction containers are not
    allowed?

13) Sloane Manufacturing has just obtained 30 additional tons each of the three metals needed to produce its basic and deluxe discombobulator machines. Given the following profit and resource table, what should be the mix of discombobulators produced? (Obviously a fraction of machine is useless.)

	Metal 1	Metal 2	Metal 3	Profit
Basic	4	6	7	$1,000
Deluxe	10	8	5	$1,500

* 14) Given the following linear program

$$\text{MAX} \quad 3x_1 + 2x_2 + 5x_3$$

$$\text{s.t.} \quad 2x_1 + x_2 + 2x_3 \le 9$$

$$3x_1 + x_2 + 5x_3 \le 26$$

$$x_1 + 2x_2 + 3x_3 \le 17$$

$$x_1, \ x_2, \ x_3 \ge 0$$

a) Solve by the simplex method.

b) Use the branch and bound algorithm to obtain the optimal solution to the all integer problem. (HINT: it is not necessary to solve the problem from scratch when a new constraint is added. Simply add the constraint and perform a row operation so that the result maintains tableau form. An artificial variable will have to be added to give this constraint a basic variable.)

9 NETWORK MODELS I: PERT/CPM

KEY CONCEPTS

1. Calculation of expected times and variances for each separate activity in a PERT network and for the entire project

2. Determination of a critical path, slack times, and earliest and latest start and finish times for all activities in a PERT network

3. Critical Path Method for determining the optimal allocation of additional resources for "crashing" activities to reduce project completion time

4. PERT/COST project managment technique for monitoring and controlling costs during the project

REVIEW

1. Activities in a PERT Network

When a project is being planned or analyzed, each individual activity must be identified and precedence relationships developed to show which activities must be completed before the given activity can commence. Estimates for the completion time of each activity must also be attained. PERT assumes the completion time for an activity follows a Beta distribution. This implies the mean or average completion time of an activity is $t = \frac{a + 4m + b}{6}$, and the variance of the completion time is

$\sigma^2 = \left(\frac{b - a}{6}\right)^2$ where a is the optimistic, m the most likely, and b the pessimistic estimate for completion times for the activity.

After the precedence relations and expected completion time for each activity have been determined, a PERT network or arrow diagram can be constructed. This network consists of nodes and directed arcs. The arcs represent the activities. It is labeled with a letter above the arc identifying the activity and a number below the arc denoting the activity's expected completion time. Each arc has an arrow indicating the beginning and end nodes (times) of the activity. Nodes represent points in time at which all immediate predecessor activities of a particular activity or set of activities have been completed. Nodes are numbered with integers beginning with 1, such that the arrows on the arcs point to higher numbered nodes from lower numbered nodes.

Occasionally an activity may have some but not all of its immediate predecessor activities in common with another activity. In these cases, dummy activities of time duration zero are drawn to construct nodes with the proper immediate predecessor relationship.

2. PERT Analyses

Given a PERT network the earliest start times (ES) and earliest finish time (EF) are determined by making a forward pass through the network. This consists of considering the nodes in ascending order (i.e. node 1, then node 2, etc.) as follows:

0. (Initialization) For all activities leaving node 1, ES = 0.

1. Consider all activities leaving the current node. For these activities EF = ES + t (where t is the expected completion time for the activity).

2. Consider the next highest node (if none, STOP). For all activities leaving this node ES = max (EF of activities entering this node). GO TO STEP 1.

To denote the ES and EF for each activity, [ES, EF] is placed next to the letter above the arc indicating the activity. The earliest project completion time, T, is the maximum of the EF's entering the last node.

The latest start time (LS) and latest finish time, (LF) are determined by making a backwards pass through network. This consists of considering the nodes in descending order as follows:

0. (Initialization) For all activities entering the final node, LF = T.

1. Consider all activities entering the current node. For these activities LS = LF - t.

2. Consider the next lower node (if none, STOP). For all activities entering this node, LF = min (LS of activities leaving this node). GO TO STEP 1.

To denote the LS and LF for each activity [LS, LF] is placed below.

Once the earliest and latest start and finish times have been calculated, the <u>slack time</u> for each activity can be calculated by subtracting its earliest start time from its latest start time (or subtracting its earliest finish time from its latest finish time). A sequence of consecutive activities with zero slack time form a <u>critical path</u>.

The expected completion time of the project, T, is the time corresponding to the highest numbered node. It equals the sum of the expected times along the critical path. The variance, σ^2, of the completion time of the entire project is the sum of the variances along the critical path. The completion time is assumed to have a normal distribution. Hence the probability that the project is completed by any particular time, s, is found by calculating the number of standard deviations that s is from T, $z = \dfrac{s - T}{\sigma}$, and using appendix A to determine the appropriate probability. Note that activities not on the critical path are assumed not to affect the overall completion time of the project; however, this assumption fails if, for example, there is a large delay on a non-critical activity.

3. <u>Critical Path Method</u>

If a manager needs additional resources to complete the project by a reduced expected time of s, he will want to know how to complete the project by time s at minimum additional cost. The <u>Critical Path Method</u> (CPM) accomplishes this by considering the expected times on a PERT network as fixed <u>normal times</u>, τ, which can be accomplished at normal cost C_n. CPM assumes: (1) if a maximum <u>crash cost</u>, C_c is spent, the activity can be reduced to a <u>crashed activity time</u> of τ'; (2) if some amount between C_n and C_c is spent on the activity, the time to do the activity will be reduced proportionally.

Let M be the maximum amount of time the activity can be reduced, i.e. $M = \tau - \tau'$. Also let K be the cost of reducing the activity by one unit, i.e. $K = \dfrac{C_c - C_n}{M}$. Thus, if we wish to crash (reduce) an activity's time by y units, the additonal cost would be Ky.

The following linear program, when solved, gives the minimum amount of additional resources that are needed to be spent to complete the project by time s.

Let x_i = time represented by node i

y_j = amount of crash time used on activity j

$$\text{MIN} \sum_j K_j y_j$$

s.t.

(1) The project must be completed by time s:

$x_N \leq s$ (where N is the highest numbered node)

(2) Each node represents the maximum of the earliest finish times of the activities with arrows into this node; thus for activity, j, between nodes k and i:

$x_i \geq x_k +$ (time to complete activity j), i.e.

$x_i \geq x_k + (\tau_j - y_j)$; (There is one constraint for each activity)

(3) For each activity, the amount of crash time cannot exceed the amount available; thus for each activity j:

$y_j \leq M_j$

(4) All variables are non-negative:

$x_i, y_j \geq 0$ for all i and j.

4. PERT/COST

PERT/COST is the name given to a technique for monitoring costs during the project. Work packages, which are groups of related activities (by one subcontractor for example), are used for planning and controlling project costs. Each work package has a budget or estimated cost and completion time.

Work packages can be treated like project activities in order to perform a PERT analysis giving earliest and latest start and finish times. Then by making the assumption that work package costs are distributed evenly throughout its duration, charts of projected costs can be developed based on earliest and latest start-times. These charts exhibit month by month (or week by week, etc.) projected distribution of funds. Thus at any point of the project, funds that have been already spent by month i should fall between the funds that should have been spent if all work packages had been started at their earliest times and at their latest times.

More specifically, for a given month, let V_i = the value of work for work package i, P_i = percent completion for work package i, B_i = budget for work package i, then

$$V_i = \left(\frac{P_i}{100}\right) B_i$$

Then if AC_i = the actual cost to date spent on work package i, the difference in the actual and budgeted values for work package i is:

$$D_i = AC_i - V_i$$

If D_i is positive, work package i is experiencing a <u>cost overrun</u>; if D_i is negative, work package i is experiencing a <u>cost underrun</u>. By summing the D_i's, the total cost overrun for the project may be found. If there is a substantial cost overrun, either the projected cost of the entire project should be revised or corrective action in uncompleted cost overrun activities should be taken.

ACTIVITIES - Specific jobs in a project represented by arcs in a PERT network. (365)

BACKWARDS PASS - A calculation procedure moving backwards through a PERT network to determine latest start and finish times for the activities. (377)

COST OVERRUN - Occurs when actual costs of performing a work package are greater than the budgeted cost.   (398)

COST UNDERRUN - Occurs when actual costs of performing a work package are less than the budgeted cost.   (398)

CRASH COST - The money spent to reduce the expected time of an activity. (385)

CRASH TIME - The time to complete an activity when extra money has been spent to complete this activity.   (385)

CRITICAL ACTIVITIES - Activities of a PERT project which cannot be delayed without delaying the entire project.   (375)

CRITICAL PATH - A sequence of consecutive critical activities from the beginning node to the ending node that determines the estimated completion time of the entire project.   (375)

CRITICAL PATH METHOD (CPM) - A network-based project management procedure which determines how to spend crash funds.   (384)

DUMMY ACTIVITY - A fictitious activity of time duration zero used to create a proper time sequence in a PERT network.   (368)

EARLIEST START (FINISH) TIME - The earliest time an activity may begin (be completed).   (375)

EVENTS - Points in time in a PERT network, represented by nodes, where certain activities must be completed before others are started. (367)

FORWARD PASS - A calculation procedure moving forward through a PERT network to determine the earliest start and finish times for the activities. (376)

IMMEDIATE PREDECESSOR - An activity which must be completed just before another activity is started. (366)

LATEST START (FINISH) TIME - The latest time an activity may be started (completed) without delaying the entire project.   (377)

NETWORK - A representation of a problem by a set of nodes and arcs. (367)

NORMAL COST - The money spent to complete an activity in its normal time. (386)

NORMAL TIME - The expected time to complete an activity without extra funds being allocated to this activity. (386)

PERT - Programmed Evaluation and Review Technique for project scheduling. (364)

PERT/COST - A technique designed to assist in the planning, scheduling, and controlling of project costs during completion of the project. (391)

SLACK TIME - The length of time an activity can be delayed without delaying the entire project. (377)

WORK PACKAGE - A grouping of interrelated project activities used in PERT/ COST systems for cost control. (392)

Chapter 9 Check List

W 1) Kraft's Kustom Kars is in the business of custom automobiles. In particular, Kraft operates a shop that builds and assembles the body and frame of the cars. The operations begin with the processing of the initial paperwork. This must be done before any other operations. Once the paperwork has been completed, the body and the frame can be built. After each piece is built, finishing work may begin on that piece. When both are built (although not necessarily finished) the final paperwork can be completed. When finishing work on both the body and the frame is completed, the body is mounted to the frame. In the frame building room certain chemicals are used which must be completely eliminated by a thorough washdown to prevent gaseous fumes from becoming a health hazard. The project is considered complete when the final paperwork has been completed, the body mounted to the frame, and the frame building room has been completely washed down. The table below gives the expected completion times in hours for each activity.

ACTIVITY	DESCRIPTION	COMPLETION TIME (HRS.)
A	Initial Paperwork	3
B	Build Body	3
C	Build Frame	2
D	Finish Body	3
E	Finish Frame	7
F	Final Paperwork	3
G	Mount Body to Frame	6
H	Frame Building Room Washdown	2

a) Draw the arrow diagram that gives the appropriate PERT network.

b) Find the earliest and latest start and finish times for the project.

c) How long should the project take?

d) Which activities cannot be delayed without delaying the entire project?

e) Suppose the body finish operation was delayed four hours. By how much would the entire project be delayed?

SOLUTION:

a) Before drawing the PERT network let us summarize the immediate predecessor in the following table.

ACTIVITY	IMMEDIATE PREDECESSOR	COMPLETION TIME (HRS.)
A	–	3
B	A	3
C	A	2
D	B	3
E	C	7
F	B,C	3
G	D,E	6
H	C	2

To draw a PERT network, there must be a node for the completion of each distinct entry in the immediate predecessor column as well as a beginning, and ending node. (There _may_ be others.) Recall, in numbering the nodes arrows must go from lower numbered nodes to higher numbered nodes.

Result:

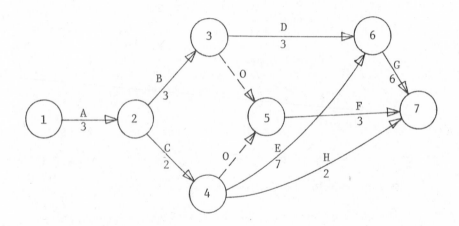

(NOTE: node 5 represents when both B and C are completed, node 3 represents B completed only, and node 4 represents C completed only. Thus dummy activities of time duration zero must connect nodes 3 and 5, and nodes 4 and 5 respectively.)

b) Remember earliest start times are the largest earliest finish times into the beginning node of an activity. The latest finish times are the minimum of the latest start times out of the ending node of an activity.

The forward pass

node 1: $ES_A = 0$. Then $EF_A = 0 + 3 = 3$.

node 2: ES_B and $ES_C = EF_A = 3$. Then $EF_B = 3 + 3 = 6$; $EF_C = 3 + 2 = 5$.

node 3: ES_D and $ES_O = EF_B = 6$. Then $EF_D = 6 + 3 = 9$; $EF_O = 6 + 0 = 6$.

node 4: ES_O and ES_E and $ES_H = EF_C = 5$. Then $EF_O = 5 + 0 = 5$;

$EF_E = 5 + 7 = 12$; $EF_H = 5 + 2 = 7$.

node 5: $ES_F = \max$ (EF into node 5) $= 6$. Then $EF_F = 6 + 3 = 9$.

node 6: $ES_G = \max$ (EF into node 6) $= 12$. Then $EF_G = 12 + 6 = 18$.

node 7: STOP, $T = \max$ (EF in to node 7) $= 18$.

The backwards pass

node 7: LF_H and LF_G and $LF_F = T = 18$. Then $LS_H = 18 - 2 = 16$;

$LS_G = 18 - 6 = 12$; $LS_F = 18 - 3 = 15$.

node 6: LF_D and $LF_E = LS_G = 12$. Then $LS_D = 12 - 3 = 9$; $LS_E = 12 - 7 = 5$.

node 5: $LF_{O(top)}$ and $LF_{O(bottom)} = LS_F = 15$. Then $LS_{O(top)} = 15 - 0 = 15$;

$LS_{O(bottom)} = 15 - 0 = 15$.

node 4: $LF_C = \min$ (LS out of 4) $= 5$. Then $LS_C = 5 - 2 = 3$.

node 3: $LF_B = \min$ (LS out of 3) $= 9$. Then $LS_B = 9 - 3 = 6$.

node 2: $LF_A = \min$ (LS out of 2) $= 3$. Then $LS_A = 3 - 3 = 0$.

node 1: STOP.

Thus the completed graph would be:

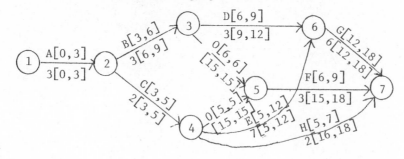

243

This leads to the following summary.

ACTIVITY	ES	EF	LS	LF	SLACK
A	0	3	0	3	0
B	3	6	6	9	3
C	3	5	3	5	0
D	6	9	9	12	3
E	5	12	5	12	0
F	6	9	15	18	9
G	12	18	12	18	0
H	5	7	16	18	11

Slack times are calculated by LF - EF or by LS - ES for each activity.

c) EF time at node 7 = 18 hours.

d) A, C, E, G have zero slack time - they form the critical path.

e) Body Finish is activity D. This has 3 hours of slack time.
Hence project would be delayed 4 - 3 = 1 hour.

W 2) The following project has been analyzed by your staff:

ACTIVITY	IMMEDIATE PREDECESSORS	OPTIMISTIC TIME (HRS.)	MOST LIKELY TIME (HRS.)	PESSIMISTIC TIME (HRS.)
A	–	4	6	8
B	–	1	4.5	5
C	A	3	3	3
D	A	4	5	6
E	A	.5	1	1.5
F	B,C	3	4	5
G	B,C	1	1.5	5
H	E,F	5	6	7
I	E,F	2	5	8
J	D,H	2.5	2.75	4.5
K	G,I	3	5	7

a) Construct the PERT network for this problem.

b) Solve for the expected earliest and latest start and completion times.

c) Identify the critical path and give the estimated project completion time.

d) What is the probability the project will be completed in one day (24 hours)?

SOLUTION:

a) We need nodes for beginning, the completion of A, B and C, E and F, D and H, G and I, and the end.

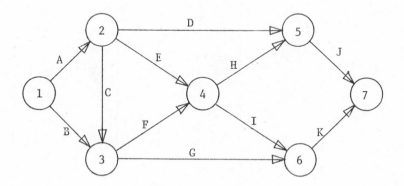

b) Calculate the expected time and variance for each activity, first

ACTIVITY	EXPECTED TIME	VARIANCE
A	6	4/9
B	4	4/9
C	3	0
D	5	1/9
E	1	1/36
F	4	1/9
*G	2	4/9
H	6	1/9
I	5	1
J	3	1/9
K	5	4/9

*Sample calculation for activity G,

$$t = \frac{a + 4m + b}{6} = \frac{1 + 4(1.5) + 5}{6} = \underline{\underline{2}}$$

$$\sigma^2 = (\frac{b - a}{6})^2 = (\frac{5 - 1}{6})^2 = (\frac{2}{3})^2 = 4/9$$

Thus we have,

ACTIVITY	ES	EF	LS	LF	SLACK
A	0	6	6	6	0
B	0	4	5	9	5
C	6	9	6	9	0
D	6	11	15	20	9
E	6	7	12	13	6
*F	9	13	9	13	0
G	9	11	16	18	7
H	13	19	14	20	1
I	13	18	13	18	0
J	19	22	20	23	1
K	18	23	18	23	0

Sample calculation for activity F,

$$ES = \max EF \text{ (activities into node 3)}$$

$$= \max (4, 9) = 9$$

$$EF = ES + 4 = 9 + 4 = 13$$

$$LF = \min LS \text{ (activities out of node 4)}$$

$$= \min (13, 14) = 13$$

$$LS = LF - 4 = 13 - 4 = 9$$

$$Slack = LS - ES = 9 - 9 = \underline{0}$$

c) Critical path (of zero slack) = A, C, F, I, K.

Estimated completion time = max EF (activities into node 7)

$$= \max (22, 23) = 23.$$

d) $z = \dfrac{s - T}{\sigma}$; $s = 24$, $T = 23$

$$\sigma^2 = \sigma_A^2 + \sigma_C^2 + \sigma_F^2 + \sigma_I^2 + \sigma_K^2$$

$$= 4/9 + 0 + 1/9 + 1 + 4/9 = \underline{\underline{2}}$$

$$= \sqrt{2} = 1.414$$

$$\therefore z = \frac{24 - 23}{1.414} = .71$$

From appendix B, Prob $(t \leq 24)$ = .5 + .2612 = $\underline{\underline{.7612}}$

0 3) Given the following PERT network showing the activities and expected completion times:

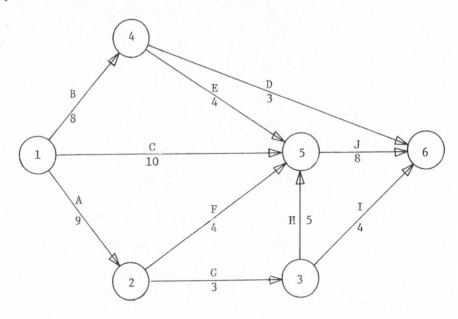

a) Construct a table giving the earliest and latest start and finish times for the project. Identify the slack times associated with each activity.

b) Give the estimated project completion time and identify the critical path.

c) Show that one man can do both E and H without delaying the entire project.

Outline of Solution:

a) For ES times, find max of EF times of all activities into the beginning node. Then EF = ES + (time to do activity).

Answer: ES for node 1 activities = 0
         ES for node 2 activities = 9
         ES for node 3 activities = 12
         ES for node 4 activities = 8
         ES for node 5 activities = 17

For LF times, find min of EF of all activities out of the ending node.

Answer: LF for activities ending at node 6 = 25
LF for activities ending at node 5 = 17
LF for activities ending at node 4 = 13
LF for activities ending at node 3 = 12
LF for activities ending at node 2 = 9

b) Critical path are activities with zero slack. Project completion time is max EF into node 6.

Answer: Critical Path = A, G, H, J; completion time = 25.

c) The same man can do both E and H if EF (activity E) $\leq$ LS (activity H).

Answer: EF (activity E) = 12, LS (activity H) = 12.

4) Given the following tabular description of a project, construct the PERT arrow diagram:

ACTIVITY	IMMEDIATE PREDECESSORS
A	–
B	A
C	–
D	B,C
E	B
F	D,E

* 5) Solve the following PERT scheduling problem for the earliest and latest start and finish times. Identify the critical path and give the estimated project completion time.

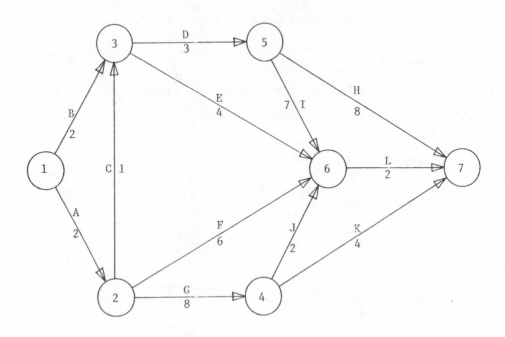

6) Consider the Kraft's Kustom Kar problem (see problem #1). The time estimates for the activities were derived from Beta distribution estimates for the mean. The following data was presented:

ACTIVITY	OPTIMISTIC TIME (HRS.)	MOST LIKELY TIME (HRS.)	PESSIMISTIC TIME (HRS.)
A	2	3	4
B	1	3	5
C	1.5	2	2.5
D	1.5	3	4.5
E	5	6	13
F	.5	3.25	4.5
G	5.5	5.75	7.5
H	1.75	2	2.25

a) Show that the expected times for the activities given in problem 1 are correct.

b) Calculate the variance for each activity.

c) What is the expected time and variance for the entire project? What distribution is assumed for the completion time of the entire project?

d) What is the probability that the project will be completed in 20 hours?

e) By what time will we be 50% sure of completing the project? 95%? 99%? 100%?

* 7)   A project consists of five activities:

ACTIVITY	OPTIMISTIC TIME (HRS.)	MOST LIKELY TIME (HRS.)	PESSIMISTIC TIME (HRS.)
Floor sanding	3	4	5
Floor buffing	1	2	3
Paint mixing	.5	1	1.5
Wall painting	1	2	9
Ceiling painting	1	5.5	7

Naturally the paint mixing preceeds the painting activities. Also, it is required that both ceiling painting and floor sanding be done before buffing is done.

a)   Construct and label the arrow diagram of the PERT network for this problem.

b)   What is the expected completion time of this project?

c)   What is the probability that the project will be finished in nine hours?

8)

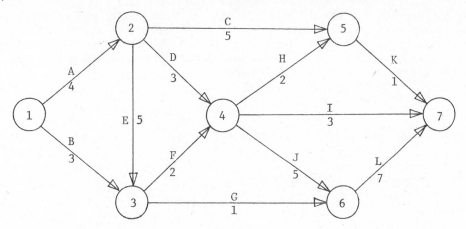

a) Given the above project starts at midnight (00:00 hours), construct
   a chart giving the earliest and latest start and finish times for
   each activity (times are in hours) and slack time.

ACTIVITY	ES	EF	LS	LF	SLACK
A					
B					
C					
D					
E					
F					
G					
H					
I					
J					
K					
L					

b) What is the critical path and expected project completion time?

c) If any man we hire can do all jobs and each man is willing to work
   24 hours straight, show that the entire project can be accomplished
   by two men. Give the two men's schedules so as not to violate (a)
   above. (HINT: One will do all jobs on the critical path.)

253

W 9) In the Kraft's Kustom Kar problem (see problems 1 and 6), suppose that
      the most optimistic times for activities A, B, C, and D can be attained
      for $3,000 each, and for activities E, F, G, and H for $2,000 each.
      Otherwise the normal times will be assumed to be the expected times.
      Write a linear program which when solved will give a minimum cost way
      of completing the project in 16 hours.

SOLUTION:

Summarizing, where $M = \tau - \tau'$ and $K = \dfrac{C_C - C_N}{M}$

ACTIVITY	τ	τ'	M	K
A	3	2	1	$\dfrac{3000}{1} = 3000$
B	3	1	2	$\dfrac{3000}{2} = 1500$
C	2	1.5	.5	$\dfrac{3000}{.5} = 6000$
D	3	1.5	1.5	$\dfrac{3000}{1.5} = 2000$
E	7	5	2	$\dfrac{2000}{2} = 1000$
F	3	.5	2.5	$\dfrac{2000}{2.5} = 800$
G	6	5.5	.5	$\dfrac{2000}{.5} = 4000$
H	2	1.75	.25	$\dfrac{2000}{.25} = 8000$

The problem is to:

Min: Total additional cost

s.t. (1) The project is completed in 16 hours.

      (2) No more crash time than is available is used on each activity.

      (3) Times at a node $\geq$ (time at preceding node) + (time to do
          activity including crash time).

Let x_i = time represented by node i;   i = 1,...,7

$\quad$ y_j = time activity j is reduced by crashing j = A,...,H

Then,

$$\text{Min } 3000y_A + 1500y_B + 6000y_C + 2000y_D + 1000y_E + 800y_F + 4000y_G$$
$$+ 8000y_W$$

s.t. $\quad$ $x_7 \leq 16$ $\qquad$ (1)

$$y_A \leq 1$$
$$y_B \leq 2$$
$$y_C \leq .5$$
$$y_D \leq 1.5 \left.\right\} \qquad (2)$$
$$y_E \leq 2$$
$$y_F \leq 2.5$$
$$y_G \leq .5$$
$$y_H \leq .25$$

$$x_7 \geq x_6 + (6 - y_G)$$
$$x_7 \geq x_5 + (3 - y_F)$$
$$x_7 \geq x_4 + (2 - y_H)$$
$$x_6 \geq x_4 + (7 - y_E)$$
$$x_6 \geq x_3 + (3 - y_D) \left.\right\} \qquad (3)$$
$$x_5 \geq x_4$$
$$x_5 \geq x_3$$
$$x_4 \geq x_2 + (2 - y_C)$$
$$x_3 \geq x_2 + (3 - y_B)$$
$$x_2 \geq x_1 + (3 - y_A)$$

$$x_i \geq 0 \quad i = 1,...,7$$
$$y_j \geq 0 \quad j = A,...,H$$

0 10) National Business Machines (NBM) has just developed a new minicomputer
that it plans to put into full scale production in a few months. The
table and arrow diagram below show the precedence relations and give
the normal and crash times (in hours) and costs for a daily operation
of the project. NBM plans three eight-hour shifts per day and desires
to know the minimum daily cost of producing the minicomputer. Set up
a linear program, which when solved would give the answer.

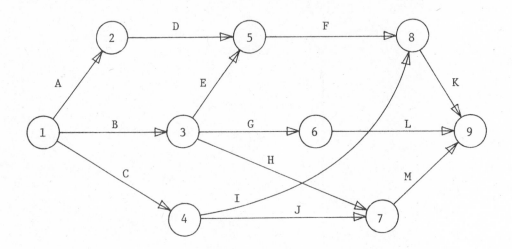

	NORMAL		CRASH	
ACTIVITY	TIME	COST	TIME	COST
A	2	$2,000	1.5	$3,000
B	4	3,000	3	3,500
C	1	1,500	1	1,500
D	4	5,300	2.5	8,000
E	6	5,400	5	7,000
F	10	6,000	8	9,000
G	8	4,800	5	9,900
H	2	2,800	1	2,900
I	5	4,500	4	5,000
J	12	6,000	6	9,600
K	7	7,000	4	9,700
L	11	8,800	9	9,200
M	4	1,000	1	7,000

Outline of Solution:

a) Solve the PERT problem using Normal Times.

   Answer: Critical Path Time = 27 hours. Thus crashing is required
   to complete the project in 24 hours.

256

b) Prepare a chart of the maximum time spent crashing activities and cost per unit of crash time for each activity.

c) Write an LP to minimize extra cost.

    s.t. (1) Project finished in 24 hours

        (2) No more crash time is used than is available for each activity.

        (3) Times at nodes $\geq$ (time at preceding node) + (time to do activity including crash time).

Answer:

Let x_i = time represented by node i

    y_j = amount of time activity j is crashed

$$\text{Min } 2000y_A + 500y_B + 0y_C + 1800y_D + 1600y_E + 1500y_F + 1700y_G$$
$$+ 100y_H + 500y_I + 600y_J + 900y_K + 200y_L + 2000y_M$$

s.t.
$$x_9 \leq 24 \qquad\qquad (1)$$

$$y_A \leq .5$$
$$y_B \leq 1$$
$$y_C \leq 0$$
$$y_D \leq 1.5$$
$$y_E \leq 1$$
$$y_F \leq 2$$
$$y_G \leq 3 \qquad\qquad (2)$$
$$y_H \leq 1$$
$$y_I \leq 1$$
$$y_J \leq 6$$
$$y_K \leq 3$$
$$y_L \leq 2$$
$$y_M \leq 3$$

257

$$x_9 \geq x_8 + (7 - y_K)$$

$$x_9 \geq x_7 + (4 - y_M)$$

$$x_9 \geq x_6 + (11 - y_L)$$

$$x_8 \geq x_5 + (10 - y_F)$$

$$x_8 \geq x_4 + (5 - y_I)$$

$$x_7 \geq x_4 + (12 - y_J)$$

$$x_7 \geq x_3 + (2 - y_H) \qquad\qquad (3)$$

$$x_6 \geq x_3 + (8 - y_G)$$

$$x_5 \geq x_3 + (6 - y_E)$$

$$x_5 \geq x_2 + (4 - y_D)$$

$$x_4 \geq x_1 + (1 - y_C)$$

$$x_3 \geq x_1 + (4 - y_B)$$

$$x_2 \geq x_1 + (2 - y_A)$$

$$x_i \geq 0 \quad i = 1,\dots,9$$

$$y_j \geq 0 \quad j = A,\dots,M$$

* 11) Joseph King has ambitions to be the mayor of Williston, North Dakota. Joe has determined the breakdown of the steps to the nomination and has estimated normal and crash costs and times for the campaign, as follows:

	ACTIVITY	NORMAL TIME (WEEKS)	COST	CRASH TIME (WEEKS)	COST	IMMED. PRED.
A.	Solicit Volunteers	6	$5,000	2	$10,000	-
B.	Initial "free" Exposure	3	4,000	3	4,000	-
C.	Raise Money	10	4,000	6	12,000	A
D.	Organize and Co-ordinate Schedule	4	1,000	2	2,000	A
E.	Hire Advertising Firm	2	1,500	1	2,000	B
F.	Arrange Major TV Interview	3	4,000	1	8,000	B
G.	Advertising Campaign	5	7,000	4	12,000	C,E
H.	Personal Campaigning	7	8,000	5	20,000	D,F

Joe King is not a wealthy man and would like to organize a four month (16 week) campaign at minimum cost. Write the linear program that would accomplish this task when solved.

12) Dan Wetzel is an independent who is also trying to make a bid to be
mayor of Williston (see problem 11). He has promised a clean campaign, one that he will initially finance on his own. He has $50,000
to invest in his campaign. Being a student of recent successful
political campaigns, he knows that his best chance to win is to be a
"fresh new face" at nomination time. Hence he wishes to keep the
entire campaign from beginning to end at a minimum. Write the linear
program that when solved will minimize the total time of the campaign
while keeping expenditures to a maximum of $50,000.

W 13) For the PERT network in problem 3, suppose the projected cost of each activity is $6,000. After the 11th week the following data concerning the progress of the project has been received at corporate head-quarters.

ACTIVITY	ACTUAL COST	PERCENT COMPLETION
A	$6,200	100%
B	5,700	100%
C	5,600	90%
D	0	0%
E	1,000	25%
F	5,000	75%
G	2,000	50%
H	0	0%
I	0	0%
J	0	0%

a) Prepare a graph of the maximum and minimum weekly expenditures.

b) Do the total expenditures by the end of week 11 represent an over-all cost overrun or cost underrun?

c) Is the project being completed on time by the end of week 11?

d) What corrective action, if any, do you recommend?

SOLUTION:

a) First prepare a chart of earliest finish costs, then one of latest finish costs. Spread activity cost evenly over duration of each activity. (See next page.)

EARLIEST FINISH

WEEK

ACTIVITY	1	2	3	4	5	6	7	8	9	10	11	12	13
A	666	667	667	666	667	667	666	667	667				
B	750	750	750	750	750	750	750	750					
C	600	600	600	600	600	600	600	600					
D									600	600			
E									2000	2000	2000		
F									1500	1500	1500	1500	
G										1500	1500	1500	1500
H										2000	2000	2000	
I													1200
J													1500
TOTAL	2016	4033	6050	8066	10083	12100	14116	16133	20900	28500	35500	40500	44700

EARLIEST FINISH (CONTINUED)

WEEK

ACTIVITY	14	15	16	17	18	19	20	21	22	23	24	25
A												
B												
C												
D												
E												
F												
G												
H	1200	1200	1200	1200								
I	1500	1500	1500									
J					750	750	750	750	750	750	750	750
TOTAL	47400	50100	52800	54000	54750	55500	56250	57000	57750	58500	59250	60000

LATEST FINISH

WEEK

ACTIVITY	1	2	3	4	5	6	7	8	9	10	11
A	666	667	667	666	667	667	666	667	667		
B						750	750	750	750	750	750
C								600	600	600	600
D											
E											
F											
G										2000	2000
H											
I											
J											
TOTAL	666	1333	2000	2666	3333	4750	6166	8183	10200	13550	16900

LATEST FINISH (CONTINUED)

WEEK

ACTIVITY	12	13	14	15	16	17	18	19	20	21	22	23	24	25
A														
B	750	750												
C	600	600	600	600	600	600								
D												2000	2000	2000
E			1500	1500	1500	1500								
F			1500	1500	1500	1500								
G	2000													
H		1200	1200	1200	1200	1200								
I							750	750	750	750	750	750	750	750
J											1500	1500	1500	1500
TOTAL	20250	22800	27600	32400	37200	42000	42750	43500	44250	45000	47250	51500	55750	60000

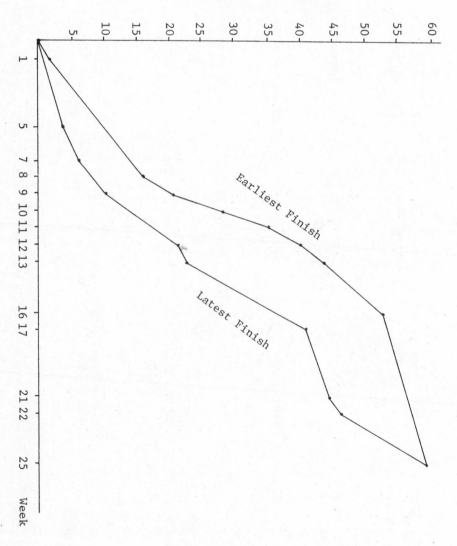

Expenditures in thousands

Earliest Finish

Latest Finish

Week

b)

ACTIVITY	A C	$V = \dfrac{P}{100}$ B	DIFFERENCE = D
A	$ 6,200	6,000	200
B	5,700	6,000	-300
C	5,600	5,400	200
D	0	0	0
E	1,000	1,500	-500
F	5,000	4,500	500
G	2,000	3,000	-1000
H	0	0	0
I	0	0	0
J	0	0	0
TOTALS	$25,500	26,400	-900

A $900 total cost <u>underrun</u>.

c) Consider each activity and its percent completion compared with its earliest and latest start and finish times. Note that G, a critical path job, should be 66 2/3% completed by the end of week 11 instead of just 50% completed. Hence the project will be delayed if G is not completed more rapidly.

d) Take some of cost underrun money and use it to take corrective action to speed up completion of activity G.

14) Consider the following PERT network:

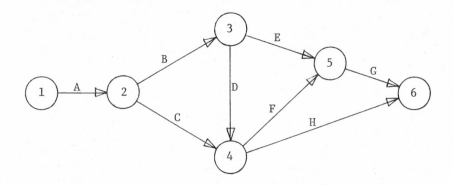

The estimated times and costs to do each activity are summarized below along with the actual status after 12 weeks.

ACTIVITY	TIME	EXPECTED COST	COST THROUGH 12 WEEKS	PERCENT COMPLETE IN 12 WEEKS
A	4	$200	$200	100%
B	3	600	525	100%
C	4	500	480	100%
D	2	500	515	100%
E	5	725	600	60%
F	2	250	130	50%
G	5	800	0	0%
H	6	780	400	50%

a) Is the project going to be completed in the minimum expected time given the current status of the project?

b) Is the project currently in a cost overrun or cost underrun posture?

c) What corrective action do you recommend if any? Should the manager report to management that an overall cost overrun is inevitable?

* 15) Dennis Stollard is also entering the race for mayor of Williston, North Dakota (see problem 11). Dennis has decided to run his campaign at minimum cost regardless of the completion time. Thus he will not crash any activities. Dennis has demanded of his staff a graph depicting the range of expenditures he can expect over the course of the campaign. Suppose that after 10 weeks the following status report was submitted to campaign headquarters.

ACTIVITY	ACTUAL COST	% COMPLETION
A	$5,400	100%
B	3,900	100%
C	2,000	40%
D	1,000	75%
E	400	50%
F	400	10%

a) Give the graph of the range of expenditures of the campaign.

b) After 10 weeks, is the overall project experiencing cost overruns or underruns? Do you recommend any corrective action?

16) The following is a project for developing and testing a new product by introducing it in a small geographical area.

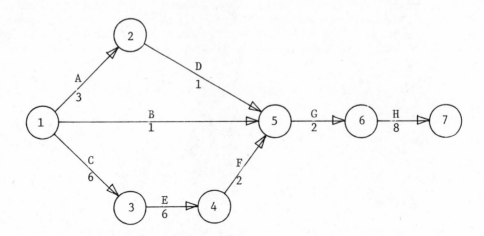

The times given on the arcs are the estimated time to do each activity in weeks. The <u>standard deviation</u> of each activity is 1/4 of the estimated completion time. It is important for the product to be on the market (which means the above project must be completed) in 1/2 year (= 26 weeks). If not, a "competition cost" of $10,000 will be incurred. For $1,000 an experienced marketing research team can be hired reducing the market test time (activity H) from an estimated eight weeks to an estimated six weeks. Should this experienced team be employed?

* 17) Consider the following PERT network. Times are estimated times in
       weeks. The variance on each activity is .8.

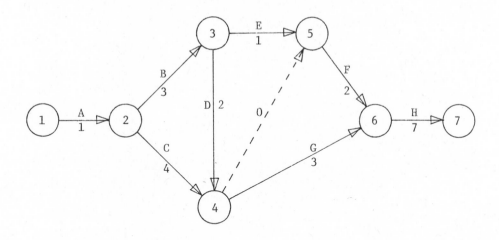

a) Give the expected project completion time.

b) What is the critical path?

c) If the project begins on May 1, by what date are we 99% sure the
    project will be completed.

d) The project has a target completion date of August 28 (17 weeks).
    If the project is completed by August 28, the profit on the
    project will be $10,000. There is a clause in the contract that
    if work is not completed by August 28, a $5,000 penalty will be
    incurred by the manufacturer, decreasing his profit to $5,000.
    If for $2,000 a more experienced firm can reduce the estimated
    time on activity H from seven to five weeks, should the manu-
    facturer accept this offer?

18) Given the following PERT network:

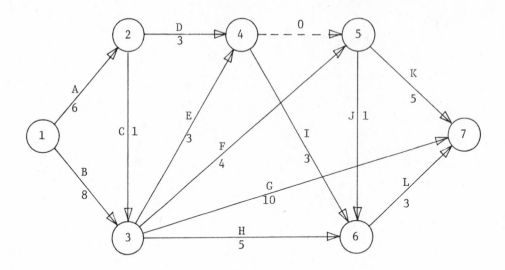

a) Prepare a chart showing the earliest and latest start and finish times and slack time for each activity.

b) What is the critical path and the expected completion time?

c) Suppose Reliable Plumbers, the subcontractor doing activity J, is going to be delayed five weeks. If the project is delayed, it costs us $2,000 per week of delay. As the prime contractor, you can:

   i) Keep Reliable Plumbers.

   ii) Cancel the contract with Reliable Plumbers and hire Local Plumbers, Inc. However, Local Plumbers will take two weeks instead of one and will charge us $3,500 per week to do the job. Reliable was charging only $3,000 per week.

   iii) You can train the people doing activity E to do the work. This involves a two week training period beginning as soon as E is done, and then three weeks for them to do activity J. The cost of training is $800 per week. The cost of them doing activity J is $1,000 per week.

Which alternative would you select? Justify.

10 NETWORK MODELS II: OTHER TOPICS

REVIEW

1. Shortest Route Problem

There are many different problems in management science which can be modeled by a network. A network is a representation of a problem by a set of nodes which are connected by a set of arcs. The numerical values of the arcs in the network can represent physical distance, time, cost, capacity, etc.

The shortest route problem is concerned with finding the shortest path in a network from one node (or set of nodes) to another node (or set of nodes). If all arcs in the network have nonnegative values then a labeling algorithm can be used to find the shortest paths from a particular node (designated as node 1) to all other nodes in the network.

The labeling algorithm gives each node a label consisting of two parts. The first part of the label indicates the distance from node 1. The second part of the label indicates the preceeding node which is on that route from node 1 to that particular node.

Because in most network problems there are a number of different alternative routes possible between node 1 and other nodes, the labeling algorithm uses both tentative labels and permanent labels. Initially the label assigned to each node (other than node 1) is tentative. The label becomes permanent when the distance given in the first part of the label equals the shortest route distance between node 1 and the particular node (the algorithm will automatically determine this). Once a label becomes permanent, it remains permanent for the remainder of the algorithm.

Shortest Path Algorithm

Step 1: Assign node 1 a permanent label of $[0, S]$. If a particular node, j, is connected to node 1 by just <u>one</u> arc, assign that node a temporary label of $[d_{ij},\ 1]$ (where d_{ij} is the arc length between node i and node j). If a particular node, k, is not connected to node 1 by just one arc then give that node a tentative label of $[M, -]$ (where M represents a large number).

Step 2: Determine the tentatively labeled node with the smallest distance value (the first part of the label). Declare this node permanently labeled. If all nodes are permanently labeled go to step 4.

Step 3: Consider the new permanently labeled node found in step 2. For each node which has a tentative label <u>and</u> is connected to the permanently labeled node by just <u>one</u> arc, compute the sum of that arc length and the distance value of the permanently labeled node. If this sum is less than the current distance value of the tentatively labeled node then (1) make this sum the new distance value of the tentatively labeled node and (2) make the permanently labeled node found in step 2 the predecessor (second part of the label) of the tentatively labeled node. Go to step 2.

Step 4: The permanent labels identify the shortest distance from node 1 as well as the preceding node for each node. The shortest route to a given node can be found by starting at the given node and moving to its preceding node and then continuing this backward movement through the network to node 1.

To find the shortest path between every pair of nodes in a network with N nodes apply the algorithm (N - 1) times, each time designating a different node as node 1.

2. Maximal Flow Problem

The <u>maximal flow</u> problem is concerned with determining the maximal volume of flow in a network from one node, designated as the <u>source</u>, to another node, designated as the <u>sink</u> through arcs in the network. Each arc has a maximum <u>arc flow capacity</u> which limits the total flow through the arcs. It is possible that an arc (i, j), may have a different capacity from i to j than from j back to i. The following algorithm can be used to find the maximal flow through a network.

Maximal Flow Algorithm

Step 1:   Find any path from the source node to the sink node that has
positive flow capacities (in the direction of the flow) for <u>all</u>
arcs on the path. If no path is available then the optimal
solution has been reached.

Step 2:   Find the smallest arc capacity, P_f, on the path selected in step 1.
Increase the flow through the network by sending an amount P_f over
this path.

Step 3:   For the path selected in step 1 reduce all arc flow capacities in
the direction of the flow by P_f and increase all arc flow capacities in the opposite direction of the flow by P_f. Go to step 1.

One way to find a path in step 1 of the algorithm is to give each
directed arc with a positive flow capacity a distance of 1 and each directed
arc with zero flow capacity a distance of M (some very large number). Use
the shortest path algorithm on this new network to find the shortest path
from the source to the sink. If the distance is greater than or equal to
M then there is no path with a positive flow capacity. Otherwise, use this
shortest path as the path for step 1.

3. Minimal Spanning Tree Problem

A tree is a set of connected arcs that does not form a cycle. The
word "spanning" indicates that all nodes are connected. Thus, the <u>minimal</u>
<u>spanning tree</u> problem seeks to determine the minimum sum of arc lengths
necessary to connect all nodes in a network.

The following algorithm can be used to find the minimal spanning tree
in a network.

Minimal Spanning Tree Algorithm

Step 1:   Prepare a table of direct distances. This is a table with a row
and a column for each node. The entry in the row i and column j
will be 0 if i = j; $d_{i,j}$ if node i is connected to node j by an
arc; or M if node i is not connected to node j. Add a column to
the left-hand side of the table and label this column with the
word "connected."

Step 2:   Select any arbitrary node and consider it connected. Place a "√"
in the left-hand column beside the node number and cross out the
column corresponding to this connected node.

Step 3:   For all rows corresponding to the connected nodes (that is, the √
rows), find the smallest value and circle it. The column con-
taining the circled element is the new connected node.

Step 4: Place a √ in the left-hand column beside the new connected node number and cross out the column corresponding to this connected node. Return to step 3 until all nodes are connected.

Step 5: The minimal spanning tree solution is given by the connections identified by the circled elements; the total length of the connection is given by the sum of the circled elements.

GLOSSARY

ARC FLOW CAPACITY - The maximum flow for an arc of the network. It is possible that the arc capacity in one direction may not equal the capacity in the reverse direction.   (427)

MAXIMAL FLOW - The maximum amount of flow possible from a source to a sink in a network.   (427)

MINIMAL SPANNING TREE - The spanning tree with the minimum length.   (433)

SHORTEST ROUTE - Shortest path between two nodes in a network.   (416)

SINK - A destination node (that is, no following nodes exist).   (427)

SOURCE - An origin node (that is, no prior nodes exist).   (427)

SPANNING TREE - A set of arcs that connect every node in the network with all other nodes.   (433)

Chapter 10 Check List

W 1) Find the shortest path from node (1) to all other nodes.

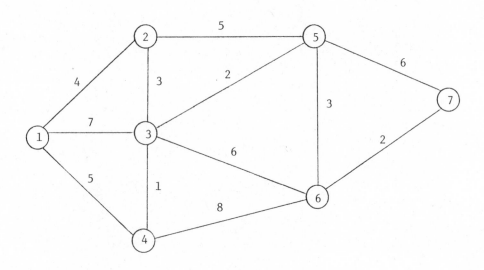

SOLUTION:

NOTE: The notation [ ] will denote a permanent label and ( ) will
denote a temporary label.

Iteration 1

Step 1: a) Assign node 1 the permanent label [0, S].

b) Since nodes 2, 3, and 4 are connected to node 1 by only one
arc assign the temporary label of (4, 1) to node 2, (7, 1) to
node 3, and (5, 1) to node 4. The first part of this
temporary label indicates the distance between node 1 and the
node in question while the second part indicates that the
preceeding node was node 1.

c) Assign all other nodes the temporary label of (M,-)

The network should now appear as follows.

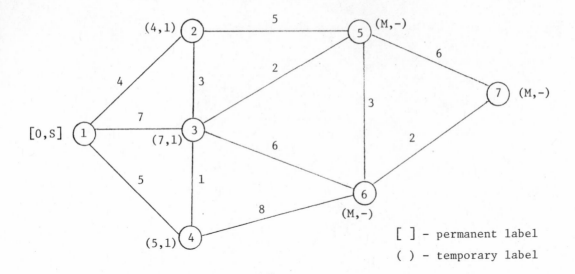

[ ] - permanent label
( ) - temporary label

Step 2: Because node 2 is the temporary labeled node with the smallest distance value (4) it becomes permanently labeled.

Step 3: For each node with a temporary label which is connected to node 2 by just one arc, compute the sum of that arc length plus the distance value of node 2. Hence for node 3 this is 3 + 4 = 7 and for node 5 this is 5 + 4 = 9. Because 7 is the same as the current distance value for node 3 do not change the label for node 3.

For node 5, however, the value of 9 is less than the current distance label of M. Hence the temporary label for node 5 is changed to (9, 2). Here the 2 indicates that node 2 preceeds node 5 on the route between 1 and 5 which has a distance of 9.

The network now appears as follows.

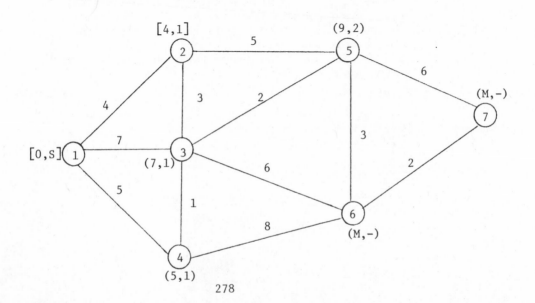

Iteration 2

Step 2: Because node 4 is the temporary labeled node with the smallest distance value (5) it becomes permanently labeled.

Step 3: For each node with a temporary label which is connected to node 4 by one arc, compute the sum of that arc length plus the distance value of node 4. Hence for node 3 this is 1 + 5 = 6 and for node 6 this is 8 + 5 = 13. Because 6 is less than 7, (the current distance value for node 3) the new node 3 label becomes (6, 4). Similarly, the new node 6 label becomes (13, 4).

The network now appears as follows.

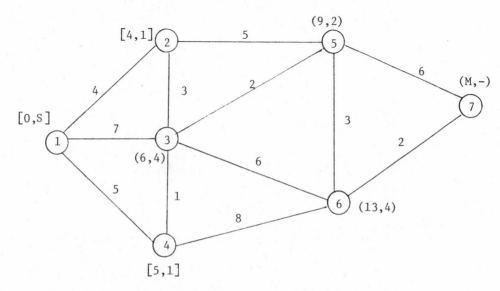

Iteration 3

Step 2: Because node 3 is now the temporary labeled node with the smallest distance value (6) it becomes permanently labeled.

Step 3: For each node with a temporary label which is connected to node 3 by one arc, compute the sum of that arc length plus the distance value for node 3. Hence for node 5 this is 2 + 6 = 8 and for node 6 this is 6 + 6 = 12. Because 8 is less than 9 (the current distance value for node 5) the new label for node 5 becomes (8, 3). Similarly because 12 is less than 13, the new label for node 6 becomes (12, 3).

The network now appears as follows.

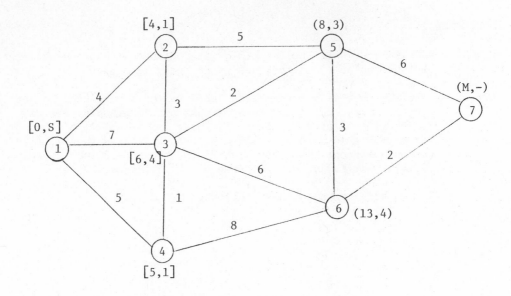

Iteration 4

Step 2: Node 5 receives a permanent label.

Step 3: The label for node 6 becomes (11, 5) since 3 + 8 = 11 is less than the current distance value of node 6 (13). Similarly, the label of node 7 becomes (14, 5).

The network now appears as follows.

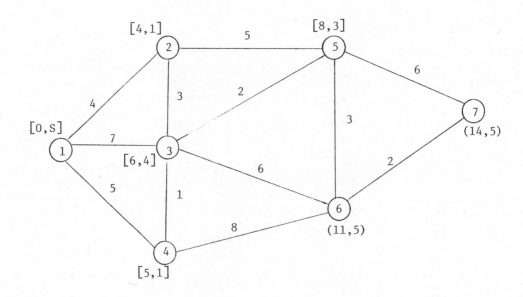

Iteration 5

Step 2: Node 6 receives a permanent label.

Step 3: The label for node 7 becomes (13, 6) since 2 + 11 = 13 is less than the current distance value of node 7 (14).

The network now appears as follows.

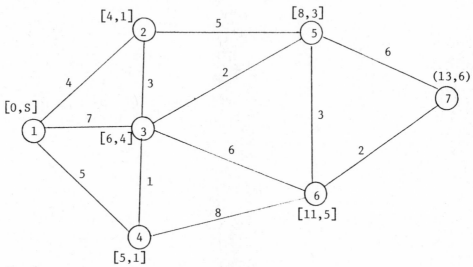

Iteration 6

Step 2: Node 7 receives a permanent label. Because all nodes now have a permanent label go to step 4 of the algorithm.

Step 4: For each node we have the following.

Node	Minimum Distance	Shortest Route
2	4	1-2
3	6	1-4-3
4	5	1-4
5	8	1-4-3-5
6	11	1-4-3-5-6
7	13	1-4-3-5-6-7

For example, to find the minimum distance and shortest route to node 6 we observe from the network that the label for node 6 is [11, 5]. This indicates that the minimum distance path to node 6 is of distance 11. The 5 in the label indicates that node 5 preceeds node 6 on the shortest path. Looking then at the label for node 5, [8, 3], we see node 3 preceeds node 5 on the shortest path. The label for node 3, [6, 4], indicates that node 4 preceeds node 3 on the shortest path. Finally the label for node 4, [5, 1] indicates that node 1 preceeds node 4 on the shortest path.

0 2) Susan Winslow has an important business meeting in Paducah this evening. She has a number of alternate routes by which she can travel from company headquarters in Lewisburg, city 1, to Paducah, city 6. The network below summarizes the various routes.

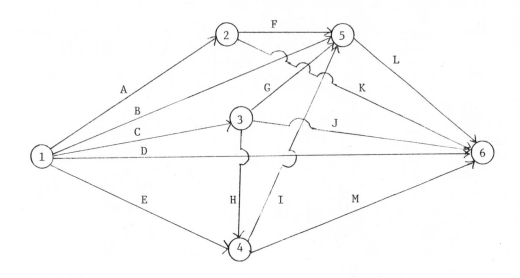

The following table gives the method of travel, travel time, and cost of going on each of the different branches of the network.

Route	Method	Time (in hours)	Cost
A	Train	4	$ 20.
B	Plane	1	$115.
C	Bus	2	$ 10.
D	Taxi	6	$ 90.
E	Train	3 1/3	$ 30.
F	Bus	3	$ 15.
G	Bus	4 2/3	$ 20.
H	Taxi	1	$ 15.
I	Train	2 1/3	$ 15.
J	Bus	6 1/3	$ 25.
K	Taxi	3 1/3	$ 50.
L	Train	1 1/3	$ 10.
M	Bus	4 2/3	$ 20.

If Susan earns a salary of $15 per hour. What route should she take to minimize her total travel costs?

(i)   Determine the cost of traveling on each branch of the network.
       COST = (TRAVEL TIME) x ($15) + TRAVEL COST

(ii)   Permanently label node 0 and give each other node a temporary label.

(iii) Choose the node with the smallest temporary label to make permanently
       labeled (Node 3). Recalculate all other temporary labels.

(iv)   Continue choosing the next smallest temporary label to make permanent
       and recomputing the values of all other temporary labels.

(v)   The completed network will be as follows.

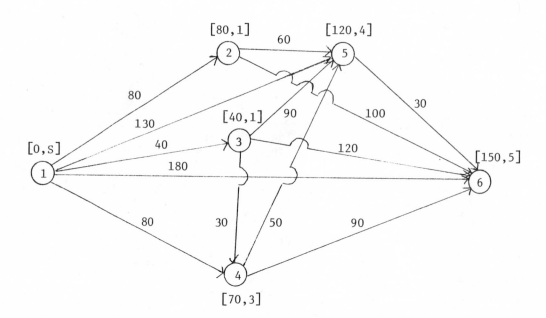

Answer:

The minimum cost route Ms. Winslow should travel is C-H-I-L (or from node
1 to 3 to 4 to 5 to 6) at a total cost of $150.

3) Suppose in problem 2) Susan Winslow earned only $6 per hour. Which path should she take to travel from Lewisburg to Paducah? What would be the answer if she earned $60 per hour?

4) Ted Kraft must drive from his home office in Tustin, city 1, to visit a customer in Alta Loma, city 8. The following network is a model of the roads connecting these cities, together with the estimated travel times. Which route should Ted travel to minimize his total travel time?

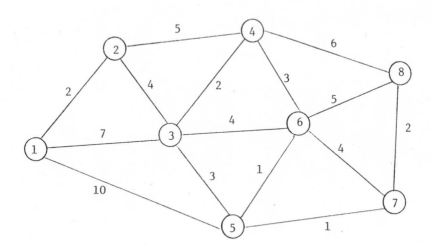

* 5) C and P Railroad serves the mid-Atlantic states with terminals in 8
      cities. The following network is a representation of the various
      C and P routes together with distances between terminals (as expressed
      in hundreds of kilometers). The company is considering building a new
      headquarters building adjacent to an existing terminal. The site
      selection committee has narrowed the choices down to either city 3, 4,
      or 6. Management's objective in locating its headquarters is to
      minimize the necessary travel distance between headquarters and the
      farthest terminal from headquarters. In which of the three cities
      should the headquarters be located?

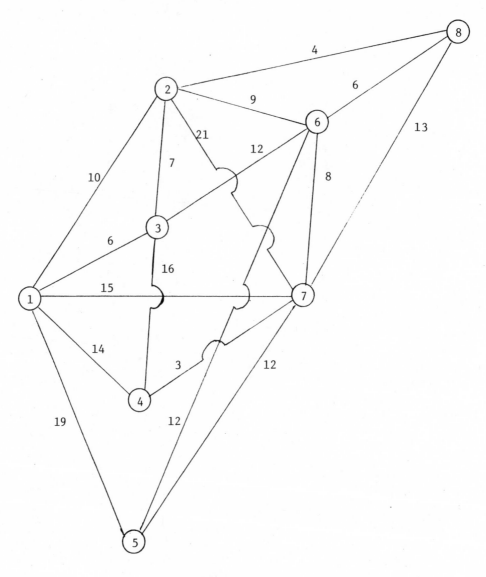

6) Bidwell Valve has just received an order for 10 gross of its model 1073 lawn sprinkler. Essentially the sprinklers must go through four processes before they are considered a complete product: manufacturing, finishing, assembly, and packaging.

While all three of the plant's shifts are capable of performing the four processing operations the costs vary according to the table below.

Shift	Manufacturing	Finishing	Assembly	Packaging
Day	$500	$320	$420	$130
Evening	$450	$280	$450	$200
Night	$405	$330	$500	$ 80

Current management policy at Bidwell dictates that the preferred policy is to have the same shift work on consecutive jobs. Hence there is a $20 penalty imposed by delaying consecutive operations by one shift (day to evening, evening to night, night to day) and a $50 penalty for delaying consecutive operations by two shifts (day to night, evening to day, night to evening). For example, if manufacturing is assigned to evening, finishing to day, assembly to day, and packaging to evening, then the total cost would be
($450) + ($320 + $50) + ($420) + ($200 + $20) = $1,460. Which production schedule will minimize the total cost of producing the lawn sprinklers?

(HINT: Set up as a shortest path problem with a node corresponding to each shift for each phase of processing.)

* 7) Union Dye and Detergent, UNIDYDE, is in the business of manufacturing specialized bleaching polymers for the textile industry. One of UNIDYDE'S major sources of revenues is a product called Lustretex. The manufacture of Lustretex involves five sequential chemical processes: blending, reduction, purification, fabrication, and distillation. Because of the relatively short shelf life of Lustretex, UNIDYDE maintains a small inventory of the product and encourages customers to place backorders. The time required and cost per gallon for each chemical process is as follows.

Process		Time	.	Cost Per Gallon
Blending	(B)	3 days		$.10
Reduction	(R)	2 days		$.20
Purification	(P)	1 day		$.15
Fabrication	(F)	4 days		$.35
Distillation	(D)	2 days		$.25

The raw material costs of Lustretex is $.85 per gallon; administrative sales, packaging, and other expenses amount to $.30 per gallon; and each gallon sells for $2.80 per gallon

UNIDYDE has just received a rush order for 10,000 gallons of Lustretex from one of their large customers. The order must be produced in 9 days to meet the customer's deadline and the customer will pay a 20¢ per gallon premium if the order can be produced in 7 days.

Because the normal time required to produce Lustretex is 12 days, if UNIDYDE wishes to fill the order it must somehow institute some alternative actions in the production schedule. Company management has determined any of the 5 following possible actions can be undertaken.

(1) Purchase the raw materials required for Lustretex after they have gone through the first 3 stages of processing and are ready for fabrication. The cost of the raw materials would increase to $1.01 per gallon and delivery time is 2 days.

(2) Add special reagents to decrease blending time to 1 day at an additional cost of $.09 per gallon.

(3) Using additional energy, decrease the reduction time to 1 day at an additional cost of $.05 per gallon.

(4) Increase the purification time to 2 days. This will eliminate the need for distillation thus saving 2 days (and $.25 per gallon). The cost of this action is, however. $.40 per gallon.

288

(5) Adding special polymers can reduce the fabrication time to 1 day. The cost is $.18 per gallon.

These options can be summarized in the following network chart. The letter on each arc indicates the processing operation and the number on each arc indicates the option undertaken (0 for normal operation).

For example, the top path on the chart, (B-1), (F-5), (D-0) indicates that option 1 was taken for blending (raw materials purchased after having gone through the first 3 stages of processing), option 5 was taken for fabrication (special polymers added to reduce time), and distillation followed as normal (requiring 2 days). The total processing time is 5 days.

Using the shortest path algorithm, determine what course of action UNIDYDE management should follow to maximize profit on this order. What will be the profit on this order?

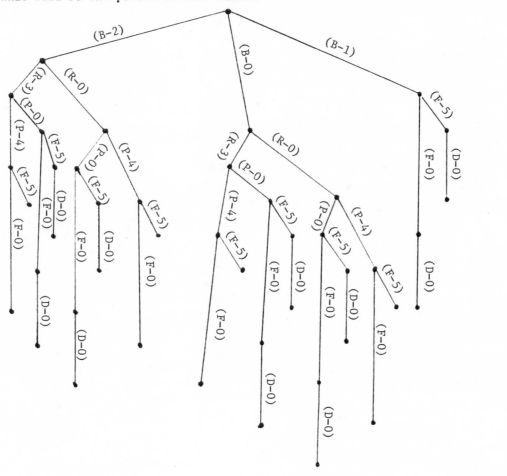

8) Suppose in problem 7) that because of a shortage of special polymers option 5) was no longer available. Instead fabrication time could be reduced 2 days at a cost of $.15 per gallon. What would be UNIDYDE's optimal policy and the resulting profit on the order?

W 9) Find the maximal flow from node 1 to node 7 in the following network.

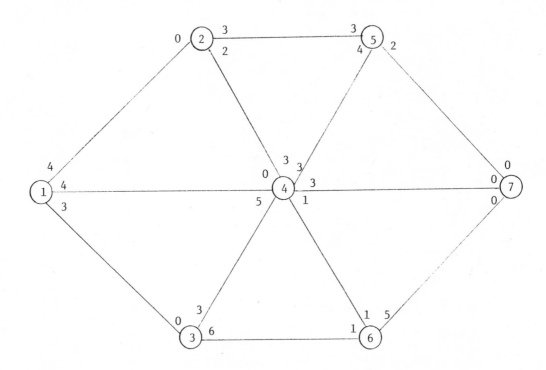

SOLUTION:

Iteration 1

Step 1: Find a path from the source node, 1, to the sink node, 7, that
         has flow capacities greater than zero on all arcs of the path.
         One such path is 1-2-5-7.

Step 2: The smallest arc flow capacity on 1-2-5-7 is the minimum of
         {4, 3, or 2} = 2.

Step 3: Reduce all arc flow capacities in the direction of flow by 2
         and increase all arc flow capacities in the reverse direction
         by 2. The new network is as follows.

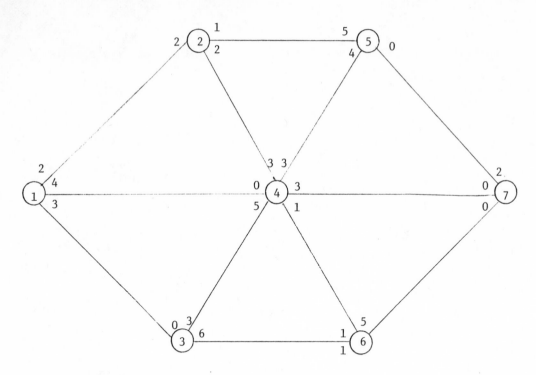

Iteration 2

Step 1: Path 1-4-7 has flow capacity greater than zero on all arcs.

Step 2: The minimum arc flow capacity on 1-4-7 is 3.

Step 3: Reducing all arc flow capacities in the direction of flow by 3 and increasing these capacities in the reverse direction of flow by 3 gives the following network.

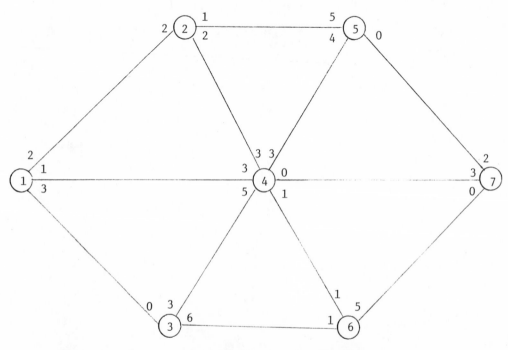

Iteration 3

Step 1: Path 1-3-6-7 has flow capacity greater than zero on all arcs.

Step 2: The minimum arc flow capacity on 1-3-6-7 is 3.

Step 3: Reducing all arc flow capacities in the direction of flow by
         3 and increasing these capacities in the reverse direction
         of flow by 3 gives the following network.

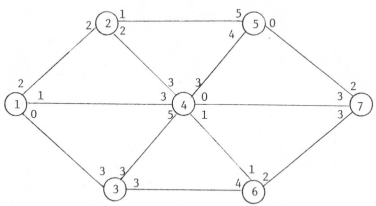

Iteration 4

Step 1: In order to find another path which has positive flow capacity
         on all arcs use inspection or construct a new, but related,
         network. This network will have directed arcs of length 1 for
         each arc with positive flow capacity. Hence, the new network
         will be as follows.

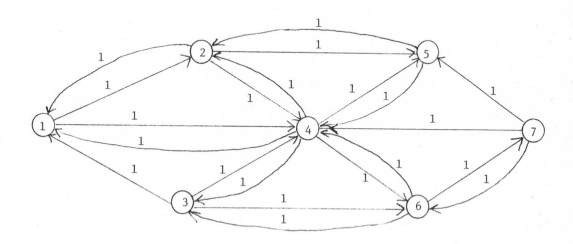

Using the shortest path algorithm on this network gives 1-4-6-7 as the shortest path between 1 and 7.

Step 2: The minimum arc flow capacity (of the original network) is equal to the minimum of {1, 1, 2} or 1.

Step 3: Reducing all arc flow capacities in the direction of flow by 1 and increasing these capacities in the reverse direction of flow by 1 gives the following network.

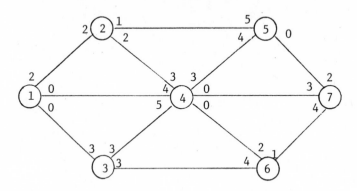

Iteration 5

Step 1: Again construct a related network with directed arcs of length 1 corresponding to all arcs which have positive flow capacity. This gives the following network.

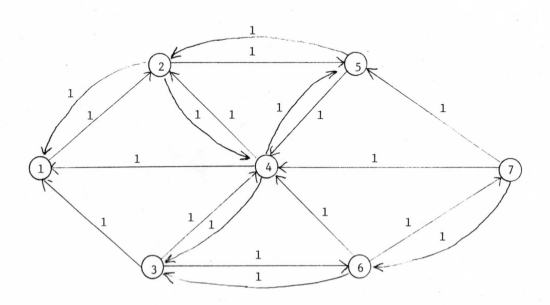

Using the shortest path algorithm the shortest path
from node 1 to 7 is 1-2-4-3-6-7.

Step 2: The smallest arc flow capacity on 1-2-4-3-6-7 is the minimum
of {2, 2, 5, 3, 1} = 1.

Step 3: Reducing all arc flow capacities in the direction of flow by
1 and increasing these capacities in the reverse direction of
flow by 1 gives the following network.

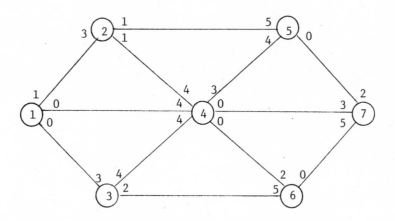

Iteration 6

Step 1: Again construct a related network with directed arcs of length
1 corresponding to all arcs which have positive flow capacity.
This gives the following network.

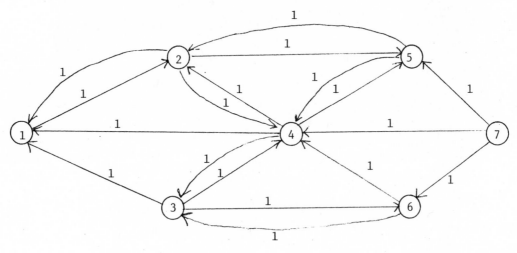

295

Applying the shortest path algorithm to this network indicates
that there is no path from node 1 to node 7. Hence the
optimal solution to the problem has been found. The maximal
possible flow between nodes 1 and 7 is the sum of the reduc-
tions found in step 2 of each iteration, that is
2 + 3 + 3 + 1 + 1 = 10.

O 10)   IMC, Independent Microwave Corporation, operates a private line
        telephone communications system for large businesses. IMC serves
        New York, Boston, Philadelphia, Washington, and Chicago. The number
        of telephone circuits currently available on each route of their
        network is as follows.

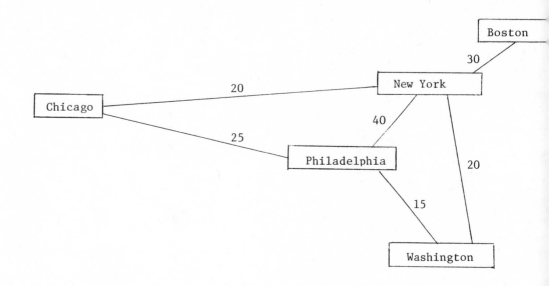

Additionally, IMC can lease 30 satellite telephone circuits between
Washington and Chicago, 20 satellite telephone circuits between
Boston and Chicago and 10 satellite telephone circuits between New
York and Chicago.

Major Electric is interested in renting 110 telephone circuits from
IMC to handle communications between its company headquarters in New
York and its manufacturing facility in Chicago. How many telephone
circuits can IMC rent to Major Electric?

Outline of Solution:

    (i)   Construct a network to represent the total capacity of IMC.

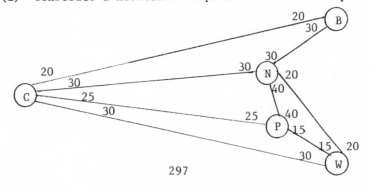

297

(ii) Assign a flow between New York and Chicago.

(iii) Assign a flow from New York to Boston to Chicago.

(iv) Assign a flow from New York to Philadelphia to Chicago.

(v) Assign a flow from New York to Washington to Chicago.

(vi) Assign a flow from New York to Philadelphia to Washington to Chicago.

(vii) Since there are no other paths between New York and Chicago with positive flow capacity the algorithm is finished. The network should look as follows.

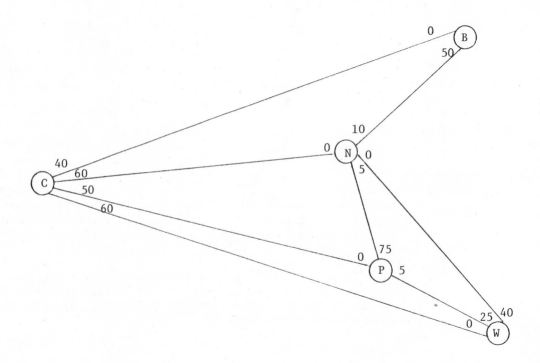

Answer: 30 + 20 + 25 + 20 + 10 = 105 circuits

* 11) Find the maximal flow from node A to node B.

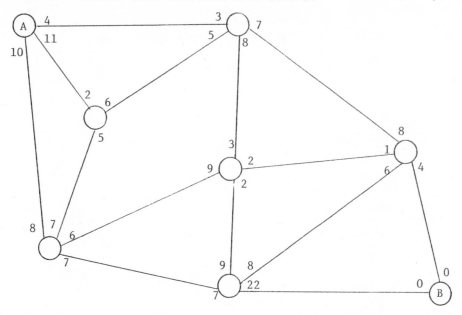

12) Navesink Brewing Company has decided to introduce a new light beer to be called Navesink Natural. The secret to Navesink's remarkable flavor is in the sparkling clear water of the Navesink River.

Management has decided to manufacture the new beer on production line 8. The network below gives the current spare capacity on each of the water lines in the brewery in gallons per hour. What is the maximum amount of water (as measured in gallons per hour) that can be obtained for production line 8?

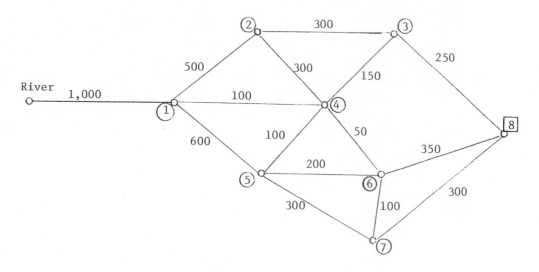

299

13) Trans Oceanic Shipping Company has 5 cargo ships which sail between New York and Tel Aviv. Trans Oceanic has been offered a contract to ship up to 120,000 pounds of Jaffa oranges from Tel Aviv to New York in April. After a careful analysis management has determined the following relevant ship capacities in 1,000's of pounds during April.

		TO					
		Tel Aviv	Athens	Rome	Paris	London	N. Y.
	Tel Aviv	–	60	20	40	–	–
	Athens	–	–	15	40	–	20
FROM	Rome	–	10	–	20	40	–
	Paris	–	40	30	–	30	40
	London	–	–	10	25	–	60
	N. Y.	–	–	–	–	–	–

How many pounds of oranges can Trans Oceanic ship?

* 14)   The Iris-Rose Cup Company manufactures paper cups for use in vending
        machines. Cup manufacturing consists of five separate operations;
        printing the paper, cutting the paper, forming the cup, waxing the
        cup, and packaging the cup. The cup factory is arranged with one
        printing area, two cutting areas, six cup forming machines, three cup
        waxing machines, and one packaging area. After the cups are formed,
        pneumatic tubes move the cups throughout the factory.

        An analysis done on the Iris-Rose Cup factory has indicated that the
        cup production process can be represented as a network with the
        following flow capacities (as represented in hundreds of cups per
        minute). What is the maximum number of cups which can be produced
        per hour?

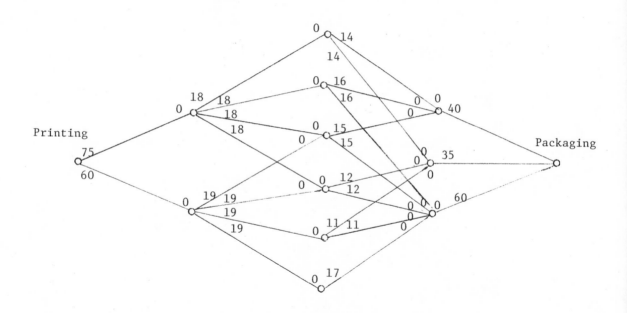

W 15) Find the minimal spanning tree in the following network.

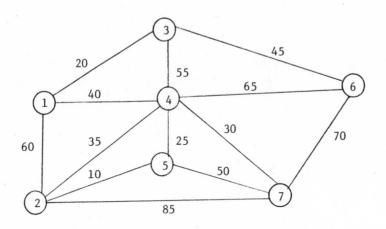

SOLUTION:

(i) Step 1. Prepare a table of direct distances between nodes as given below. (If there is no direct branch let the distance = M)

TO NODE

Connected	1	2	3	4	5	6	7
1	0	60	20	40	M	M	M
2	60	0	M	35	10	M	85
3	20	M	0	55	M	45	M
4	40	35	55	0	25	65	30
5	M	10	M	25	0	M	50
6	M	M	45	65	M	0	70
7	M	85	M	30	50	70	0

FROM NODE

302

ii) <u>Iteration 1</u>

Step 2. Select node 1 as the arbitrary node to call connected.
Placing a √ next to node 1 and crossing out column 1 gives the
following.

TO NODE

Connected	1	2	3	4	5	6	7
√ 1	0	60	20	40	M	M	M
2	60	0	M	35	10	M	85
FROM 3	20	M	0	55	M	45	M
NODE 4	40	35	55	0	25	65	30
5	M	10	M	25	0	M	50
6	M	M	45	65	M	0	70
7	M	85	M	30	50	70	0

Steps 3 & 4. The smallest unlined element in the checked row is
20 under column 3. Circle 20, check row 3, and cross out column
3. This gives the following.

TO NODE

Connected	1	2	3	4	5	6	7
√ 1	0	60	(20)	40	M	M	M
2	60	0	M	35	10	M	85
FROM √ 3	20	M	0	55	M	45	M
NODE 4	40	35	55	0	25	65	30
5	M	10	M	25	0	M	50
6	M	M	45	65	M	0	70
7	M	85	M	30	50	70	0

iii) Iteration 2

Steps 3 & 4. The smallest unlined element in the checked rows is 40 in row 1, column 4. Circle 40, check row 4 and cross out column 4. This gives the following.

TO NODE

Connected		1	2	3	4	5	6	7
	✓ 1	0	60	20	40	M	M	M
	2	60	0	M	35	10	M	85
FROM	✓ 3	20	M	0	55	M	45	M
NODE	✓ 4	40	35	55	0	25	65	30
	5	M	10	M	25	0	M	50
	6	M	M	45	65	M	0	70
	7	M	85	M	30	50	70	0

iv) Iteration 3

Steps 3 & 4. The smallest unlined element in the checked rows is 25 in row 4, column 5. Circle 25, check row 5 and cross out column 5.

v) Iteration 4

Steps 3 & 4. The smallest unlined element in the checked rows is 10 in row 5, column 2. Circle 10, check row 2, and cross out column 2. The table now will appear as follows.

TO NODE

Connected		1	2	3	4	5	6	7
	✓ 1	0	60	20	40	M	M	M
	✓ 2	60	0	M	35	10	M	85
FROM	✓ 3	20	M	0	55	M	45	M
NODE	✓ 4	40	35	55	0	25	65	30
	✓ 5	M	10	M	25	0	M	50
	6	M	M	45	65	M	0	70
	7	M	85	M	30	50	70	0

304

vi) <u>Iteration 5</u>

Steps 3 & 4. The smallest unlined element in the checked rows is 30 in row 4, column 7. Circle 30, check row 7, and cross out column 7.

vii) <u>Iteration 6</u>

Steps 3 & 4. The smallest unlined element in the checked rows is 45 in row 3, column 6. Circle 45, check row 6, and cross out column 6.

The final table is as follows.

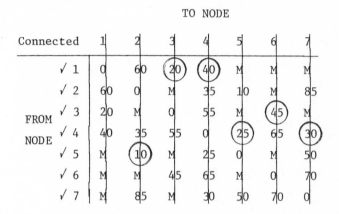

TO NODE

Connected		1	2	3	4	5	6	7
	✓ 1	0	60	(20)	(40)	M	M	M
	✓ 2	60	0	M	35	10	M	85
FROM	✓ 3	20	M	0	55	M	(45)	M
NODE	✓ 4	40	35	55	0	(25)	65	(30)
	✓ 5	M	(10)	M	25	0	M	50
	✓ 6	M	M	45	65	M	0	70
	✓ 7	M	85	M	30	50	70	0

The minimal spanning tree for this network can be found by connecting node i with node j if element (i, j) of the table is circled. For this problem it is as follows.

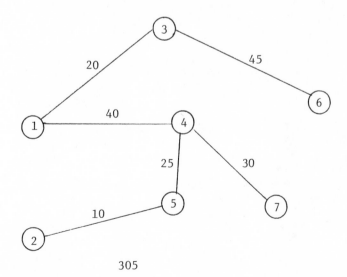

O 16) Griffith's Cherry Preserve is a combination wild animal habitat and amusement park. Besides their phenomenally successful wild animal safari tour there are eight different theme areas in the amusement park.

One problem encountered by management is to develop a method by which people can efficiently travel between each area of the park. Management has learned that a people mover can be constructed at a cost of $50 per foot. If the following network represents the distances between each area of the park for which a people mover is possible, determine the minimum cost for such a system.

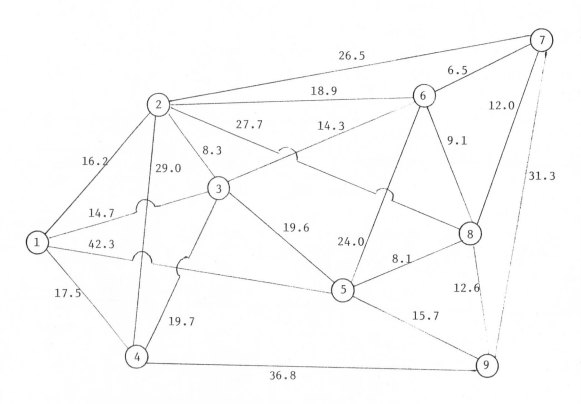

DISTANCES GIVEN IN 100's OF FEET

(i) Construct a table of direct distances corresponding to the network.

Connected	1	2	3	4	5	6	7	8	9
1	0	16.2	14.7	17.5	42.3	M	M	M	M
2	16.2	0	8.3	29.0	M	18.9	26.5	27.7	M
3	14.7	8.3	0	19.7	19.6	14.3	M	M	M
4	17.5	29.0	19.7	0	M	M	M	M	36.8
5	42.3	M	19.6	M	0	24.0	M	8.1	15.7
6	M	18.9	14.3	M	24.0	0	6.5	9.1	M
7	M	26.5	M	M	M	6.5	0	12.0	31.3
8	M	27.7	M	M	8.1	9.1	12.0	0	12.6
9	M	M	M	36.8	15.7	M	31.3	12.6	0

(ii) Choose node 1 to be connected. Check node 1 and cross out column 1.

(iii) Find the minimum uncovered element in the checked row(s). Circle this element, cross out that column, and check the row corresponding to that column.

(iv) Continue step (iii) until all columns are crossed out. The final table will look as follows.

Connected	1	2	3	4	5	6	7	8	9
✓ 1	0	16.2	(14.7)	(17.5)	42.3	M	M	M	M
✓ 2	16.2	0	8.3	29.0	M	18.9	26.5	27.7	M
✓ 3	14.7	(8.3)	0	19.7	19.6	(14.3)	M	M	M
✓ 4	17.5	29.0	19.7	0	M	M	M	M	36.8
✓ 5	42.3	M	19.6	M	0	24.0	M	8.1	15.7
✓ 6	M	18.9	14.3	M	24.0	0	(6.5)	(9.1)	M
✓ 7	M	26.5	M	M	M	6.5	0	12.0	31.3
✓ 8	M	27.7	M	M	(8.1)	9.1	12.0	0	(12.6)
✓ 9	M	M	M	36.8	15.7	M	31.3	12.6	0

(v) From this table the following minimal spanning tree can be identified.

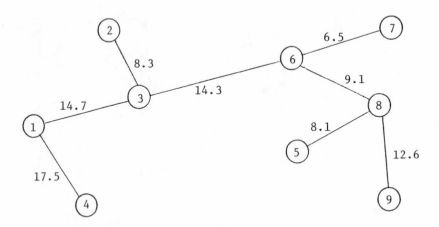

Answer:

The total cost of installing a people mover will be

$(14.7 + 17.5 + 8.3 + 14.3 + 6.5 + 9.1 + 8.1 + 12.6)$ x 100 x $50 = $4,551.

Distance of people mover in feet

* 17) Find the minimal spanning tree of this network.

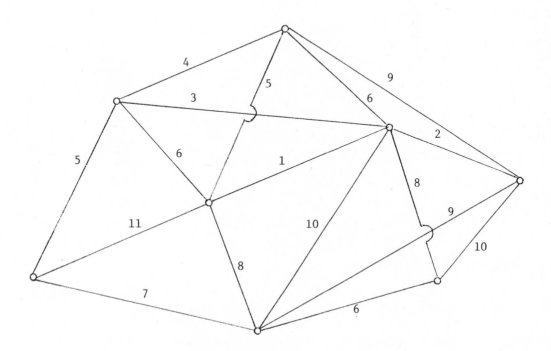

18) Metropolitan Cable TV has recently been awarded the cable TV franchise for Tangerine County. After a careful economic analysis Metropolitan has decided to offer its service to 8 towns in the county. Metropolitan plans to construct an antenna in Oldport (city 1) and use existing telephone routes to transmit the cable TV signal. The following network represents the possible routes between the towns and their corresponding distances in miles.

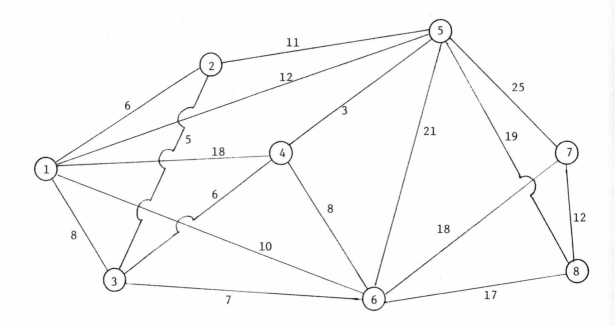

Metropolitan must pay the telephone company $500 per mile for use of the telephone company's poles. How should Metropolitan construct its route to minimize this cost?

* 19) Alaska Gas Transmission Company is planning to construct a pipeline
to supply gas from Alaska's north slope to eight United States gas
companies. The following table gives the right of way distances
between each pair of gas companies and between the gas companies and
the north slope drilling site.

	North Slope	Company							
		A	B	C	D	E	F	G	H
North Slope	0	32	43	41	44	45	53	56	61
Company A	32	0	12	15	16	17	31	25	32
Company B	43	12	0	18	12	11	32	26	28
Company C	41	15	18	0	10	14	23	15	18
Company D	44	16	12	10	0	5	22	13	16
Company E	45	17	11	14	5	0	23	15	12
Company F	53	31	32	23	22	23	0	7	14
Company G	56	25	26	15	13	15	7	0	8
Company H	61	32	28	18	16	12	14	8	0

Distance in 100's of miles

Each mile of right of way purchased for the pipeline costs an average
of $100. Use the minimal spanning tree algorithm to determine how
Alaska Gas Transmission should construct its pipeline to minimize its
total right of way costs.

11 DECISION THEORY

REVIEW

1. Payoff Tables and Decision Trees

A problem in decision theory is characterized by <u>decision alternatives</u>, <u>states of nature</u>, and <u>resulting payoffs</u>. The decision alternatives refer to the feasible actions which may be considered by the decision maker. The states of nature refer to future events, not under the control of the decision maker, which may occur. The states of nature are defined so that one and only one state of nature will occur. Given the decision maker has chosen a specific decision alternative, corresponding to each state of nature there is a resulting payoff or profit for the decision maker. These are often shown in a matrix called a <u>payoff table</u>.

When the decision maker knows which state of nature will occur this is called making <u>decisions under certainty</u>. More commonly, the state of nature which will occur is not known and therefore the decision maker is making <u>decisions under uncertainty</u>.

Decision problems involving a modest number of decision alternatives and states of nature can be analyzed using a graphical representation of the decision making process called a <u>decision tree</u>. Starting from the root of the tree, designated by a square node, a branch is drawn for each decision alternative (decision branches). At the end of each decision branch a round node is drawn. Connected to each round node are additional branches for each feasible state of nature. At the end of these branches the payoffs corresponding to the particular decision alternative and state of nature are shown. Working backwards along the tree, from the payoffs back to the root node, it is possible to determine the best decision alternative.

2. Decision Criteria Not Using Probability

There are three commonly used criteria for decision making which do not rely on a knowledge of the probabilities of the states of nature.

The maximin decision criterion is a pessimistic or conservative approach to arriving at a decision. In this approach the decision maker attempts to maximize the minimum possible profit. That is, this policy gives the best lower bound on profit. Thus, the decision is made by listing the minimum payoff for each decision alternative, and choosing the best (maximum) of these.

Alternatively, the maximax decision criterion is an optimistic approach. For this criterion the decision maker selects the decision which maximizes the maximum payoff. That is, this policy gives the best upper bound on profit. Hence, to obtain the maximax decision, list the maximum payoff for each decision alternative and choose the best (maximum).

Corresponding to each state of nature there is a best decision alternative, that which gives the maximum payoff. The difference between the payoff for this best decision alternative and the payoff for each of the other decision alternatives is called the regret or opportunity loss. Under the minimax regret criterion the decision maker chooses the decision alternative corresponding to the minimum of the maximum regret values. Thus the minimax regret decision is gotten by: (1) preparing a regret table by subtracting each entry in a column from the maximum in the column; (2) listing the maximum regret for each alternative; (3) choosing the best (minimum) of the values found in step (2).

3. Decision Criteria Using Probabilities

In many situations probability estimates can be developed for the states of nature. In using the expected monetary value (EMV) criterion the analyst (1) computes the expected value for each decision and then, (2) selects the alternative yielding the best expected value. In using the expected opportunity loss criterion the decision maker computes the expected regret or opportunity loss for each decision and chooses the decision with the minimum expected opportunity loss. The decision alternative chosen under the expected opportunity loss criterion will always be the same as the decision alternative chosen using the expected monetary value criterion. The expected value of perfect information (EVPI) is the expected improvement in profit if the decision maker knows the true state of nature with certainty. It can be shown that the expected value of perfect information is equivalent to the expected opportunity loss for the optimal decision. Hence, EVPI is obtained by 1) finding the optimal decision under the expected opportunity loss criterion or the expected monetary value criterion and 2) computing the expected opportunity loss for this decision. Alternatively, EVPI can be derived by (1) determining the optimal return corresponding to each state of nature, (2) computing the expected value of these optimal returns, and (3) subtracting the EMV of the optimal decision from the amount determined in step (2).

4. Decision Making With Experimentation

In some decision making problems it is possible to gain additional information regarding the probabilities of the states of nature through experimentation. Prior to the experiment the probabilities are known as prior probabilities. Conditional probabilities for the outcomes of the experiment, given each particular state of nature, are assumed to be known. These conditional probabilities, together with the prior probabilities are combined using Bayes' Theorem to obtain posterior probabilities , probabilities for the states of nature conditioned upon the outcome of the experiment. In this way the sample information gained through the experiment affects the probabilities for the states of nature and thereby the optimal decision under the expected monetary value criterion.

The decision making process using experimentation can be represented by a tree diagram. The root of the tree (designated by a circle) is called the indicator node. From this node emanate arcs known as indicator branches. Each branch corresponds to a specific result of the experiment. At the other end of each indicator branch is a square shaped node representing a decision is to be made based on the indicated information. From this node there is an arc (branch) corresponding to each possible decision. At the end of each decision branch there is another circular node denoting that if the corresponding decision has been made, a state of nature will occur and a payoff will be obtained. Hence, from each of these nodes there is an arc (branch) for each state of nature, and finally, at the end of each state of nature branch there is the payoff associated with that particular decision and state of nature. Using the posterior probabilities for the states of nature (e.g. conditioned upon the specific experimental outcome), the decision maker can work backwards from the payoffs to the root of tree and determine the optimal decision corresponding to each experimental result (indicator branch).

The expected value of sample information (EVSI) is calculated by subtracting the expected monetary value of the optimal decision policy before experimentation from that value after experimentation. The efficiency of sample information is computed by taking the ratio of the EVSI to the EVPI. Since it is clear that sample information can never be better than perfect information, the efficiency will always be a number between 0 and 1.

BAYESIAN REVISION - The process of adjusting the prior probabilities to create the posterior probabilities based upon information obtained by experimentation.   (462)

BRANCHES - Lines or arcs connecting nodes of the decision tree.   (456)

DECISION MAKING UNDER CERTAINTY - The process of choosing a decision alternative when the state of nature is known.   (449)

DECISION MAKING UNDER UNCERTAINTY - The process of choosing a decision alternative when the state of nature is not known.   (449)

DECISION TREE - A graphical representation of the decision making situation from decision to state of nature to payoff.   (456)

EFFICIENCY - The ratio of EVSI to EVPI; perfect information is 100% efficient.   (475)

EXPECTED MONETARY VALUE - A decision criterion for decisions under uncertainty. Under this criterion the payoff for each decision is weighted by the probability of occurrence of the states of nature. (453)

EXPECTED VALUE OF SAMPLE INFORMATION (EVSI) - The difference between the expected monetary value of an optimal strategy utilizing experimental information and the "best" expected value without any experimental information. It is a measure of the economic value of experimental information.   (474)

EXPECTED OPPORTUNITY LOSS - A criterion for decision making under uncertainty. Under this criterion the regret for each decision is weighted by the probability of occurrence of the states of nature.(455)

EXPECTED VALUE OF PERFECT INFORMATION (EVPI) - The expected value of the information of exactly which state of nature is going to occur (that is, perfect information). EVPI is equal to the expected opportunity loss of the best decision alternative when no additional information is available.   (460)

INDICATOR - Information about the states of nature obtained by experimentation.   (462)

MAXIMAX - A maximization decision criterion for decisions under uncertainty that seeks to maximize the maximum payoff.   (450)

MAXIMIN - A maximization decision criterion for decisions under uncertainty that seeks to maximize the minimum payoff.   (450)

MINIMAX – A minimization decision criterion for decisions under uncertainty that seeks to minimize the maximum cost.   (450)

MINIMAX REGRET – A maximization or minimization decision criterion for decisions under uncertainty that seeks to minimize the maximum regret.   (451)

MINIMIN – A minimization decision criterion for decisions under uncertainty that seeks to minimize the minimum cost.   (451)

NODES – The intersection or junction points of the decision tree.   (456)

OPPORTUNITY LOSS OR REGRET – The amount of loss (either the lower profit or higher cost) due to not making the best decision for each state of nature.   (451)

PAYOFF – The outcome measure such as profit, cost, etc.   Each combination of a decision alternative and a state of nature has a specific payoff.   (448)

PAYOFF TABLE – A tabular representation of the payoffs for a decision problem.   (448)

POSTERIOR (REVISED) PROBABILITIES – The conditional probabilities of the states of nature after adjusting the prior probabilities based upon given indicator information.   (462)

PRIOR PROBABILITIES – The probabilities of the states of nature prior to obtaining experimental information. (461)

SAMPLE INFORMATION – An indicator, usually the result of taking a statistical sample.   (462)

STATES OF NATURE – The uncontrollable future events that can affect the outcome of a decision.   (447)

Chapter 11 Check List

W 1) Consider the following problem with three decision alternatives, three states of nature and the following payoff table.

States of Nature

		s_1	s_2	s_3
	d_1	4	4	-2
Decisions	d_2	0	3	-1
	d_3	1	5	-3

What is the optimal decision under

a) the maximin criterion?

b) the maximax criterion?

c) the minimax regret criterion?

Suppose that the probabilities for the states of nature were as follows: $P(s_1) = .20$, $P(s_2) = .50$, $P(s_3) = .30$.

d) Using a decision tree diagram find the optimal decision under the expected monetary value criteria.

e) Find the optimal decision using the expected opportunity loss criterion.

f) What is the expected value of perfect information?

SOLUTION:

a) To find the maximin criterion decision we must first find the minimum payoff for each decision. For d_1 this is -2, for d_2 this is -1, and for d_3 this is -3. Since the maximum of these three values is -1, $\underline{d_2}$ is the optimal decision.

b) To find the maximax criterion decision all we need really do is look for the largest value of the payoff table and the resulting decision is the optimal one. For this example the largest value of the payoff table is 5 and the optimal decision is $\underline{d_3}$.

c) To find the decision using the minimax regret criterion we first must compute the regret table. To do this,

319

1) for each state of nature identify the maximum payoff.

2) compute the difference between this payoff and the other payoffs.

In this example, for s_1 the maximum payoff is 4 (decision d_1), for s_2 the maximum payoff is 5 (d_3), and for s_3 the maximum payoff is -1 (d_2). We therefore compute the regret table by subtracting each payoff in the s_1 column from 4, each payoff in the s_2 column from 5, and each payoff in the s_3 column from -1. This gives the following regret table:

	s_1	s_2	s_3
d_1	0	1	1
d_2	4	2	0
d_3	3	0	2

We next compute the maximum regret for each decision. For d_1 this is 1, for d_2 it is 4, and for d_1 it is 3. Choosing the decision with the minimum maximum regret gives d_1.

Note that for this example each decision criterion gives a different optimal decision.

d) The tree diagram will look as follows:

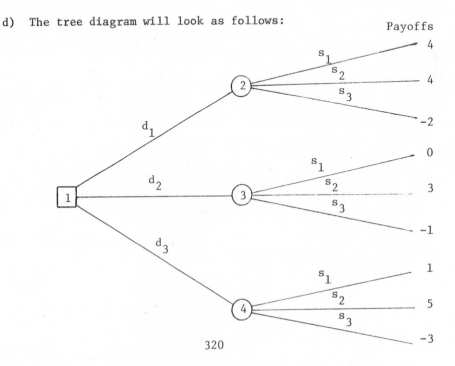

Using the fact that $P(s_1) = .20$, $P(s_2) = .50$ and $P(s_3) = .30$ we can compute the expected value associated with nodes 2, 3, and 4

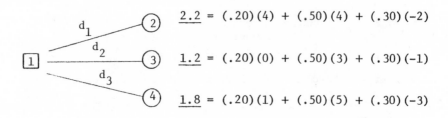

$$2.2 = (.20)(4) + (.50)(4) + (.30)(-2)$$

$$1.2 = (.20)(0) + (.50)(3) + (.30)(-1)$$

$$1.8 = (.20)(1) + (.50)(5) + (.30)(-3)$$

Choosing the decision with the maximum node value gives the solution d_1 with an expected value of 2.2

e) We note the optimal decision criteria must also be d_1 using the expected loss criteria. To show this compute the expected regret for each decision using the above state of nature probabilities.

Expected Regret $(d_1) = (.20)(0) + (.50)(1) + (.30)(1) = .8$

Expected Regret $(d_2) = (.20)(4) + (.50)(2) + (.30)(0) = 1.8$

Expected Regret $(d_3) = (.20)(3) + (.50)(0) + (.30)(2) = 1.2$

Choose the decision with the minimum expected regret, d_1.

f) The expected value of perfect information is the expected opportunity loss under the optimal decision, d_1. Thus EVPI $= .8$.

0 2) Jim has been employed at Gold Key Realty at a salary of $1,200 per
       month for the past year. Because Jim is considered a top salesman, the
       manager of Gold Key is offering him one of three salary plans for the
       next year.

       Plan I - $1,500 per month
       Plan II - $1,000 per month and $200 per house sold
       Plan III - $100 per month and $450 per house sold

       Over the past year Jim has sold up to six homes per month.

       a) Compute the monthly salary payoff table for this problem.

       b) For this payoff table find the optimal decision under the follow-
           ing criterion.

           1) Minimax regret

           2) Maximin

       c) Suppose during the past year in 1 month Jim sold no homes, in 2
           months he sold 1 home, in 1 month he sold 2 homes, in 2 months he
           sold 3 homes, in 1 month he sold 4 homes, in 3 months he sold 5
           homes, and in 2 months he sold 6 homes. Under the expected mone-
           tary value criterion which is the best salary plan for Jim?

Outline of Solution:

       a)   i) Determine the different decisions that Jim can make and the
                 resulting states of nature.
            ii) Evaluate Jim's salary under each decision and state of nature.

    b-1)   i) Calculate the regret table.
          ii) Determine the maximum regret for each decision.
         iii) Choose the decision with the minimum value found in step ii).

    b-2)   i) Determine the minimum payoff for each decision.
          ii) Choose the decision with the maximum value found in step i).

       c)   i) Determine the probability distribution for the states of
                 nature.
            ii) Using these probabilities compute the expected monetary
                 values of the three plans.
           iii) Select the plan with the largest expected monetary value.

322

Answers:

a)

Payoff Table

Number of Houses Sold

	0	1	2	3	4	5	6
Plan I	1500	1500	1500	1500	1500	1500	1500
II	1000	1200	1400	1600	1800	2000	2200
III	100	550	1000	1450	1900	2350	2800

b)

Regret Table

Number of Houses Sold

	0	1	2	3	4	5	6
Plan I	0	0	0	100	400	850	1300
II	500	300	100	0	100	350	600
III	1400	950	500	150	0	0	0

1 - Plan II - 600
2 - Plan I - 1500

c) Plan III - EMV = $1,758.33

3) Consider the following problem with three decision alternatives, four states of nature and the following payoff table.

	s_1	s_2	s_3	s_4
d_1	200	600	-600	200
d_2	0	200	-200	200
d_3	-200	-400	0	200

What is the optimal decision under

a) the maximin criterion?

b) the maximax criterion?

c) the minimax regret criterion?

If the probabilities for the states of nature are as follows:
$P(s_1) = .10$, $P(s_2) = .40$, $P(s_3) = .30$ and $P(s_4) = .20$ find

d) the optimal decision under the expected monetary value criterion. What is this value?

e) the expected value of perfect information.

* 4) Mark Investment Advisors has just completed an analysis on the returns of five utility stocks for the next year. Mark hypothesizes that next year the economy will either be in a depression (s_1), recession (s_2), upward cycle (s_3), or a major expansionary period (s_4). The per dollar growth for the five stocks corresponding to each state of the economy are as follows:

	s_1	s_2	s_3	s_4
Stock A	-.40	-.20	+.10	+.60
Stock B	-.30	-.10	0	+.30
Stock C	-.10	0	+.05	+.30
Stock D	0	+.05	+.10	+.15
Stock E	.05	+.15	-.10	-.20

a) If you had a chance to purchase shares of Stock B or Stock C which would you purchase? Why?

b) Find the best stock to purchase under the

1) maximax criterion.

2) the minimax regret criterion.

3) the maximin criterion.

c) Suppose the probabilities of the various future states of the economy are as follows:

$P(s_1) = .20$

$P(s_2) = .40$

$P(s_3) = .20$

$P(s_4) = .20$

Using the expected monetary value criterion which stock would you select for purchase?

325

* 5) The Super Cola Company must decide whether or not to introduce a new diet soft drink. Management feels that the diet soda will either have sales of 100 million bottles, 50 million bottles or 1 million bottles. If the company does introduce the diet soda sales of 100 million bottles will result in a profit of $1 million, sales of 50 million bottles will mean a profit of $200 thousand, and sales of 1 million will mean a loss of $2 million. If the company does not market the soda it will have a loss of $400 thousand.

a) Construct the payoff table for this problem.

b) Construct the regret table for this problem.

c) What is the company's optimal decision if the company

   1) is extremely pessimistic?

   2) is extremely optimistic?

   3) wanted to minimize its maximum disappointment?

Stanton Marketing has been hired by Super Cola to do a marketing study. They estimate the probability of sales of the new diet soda to be as follows:

   P(100 million bottles in sales) = 1/3
   P(50 million bottles in sales) = 1/2
   P(1 million bottles in sales)   = 1/6

d) Using the expected monetary value criterion, should Super Cola introduce the diet soda?

e) Stanton informs Super Cola management that it can do a more thorough market study which will tell with certainty which of the three sales projections is correct. The cost of the study will be $275,000. Should management have the study performed?

6) The manager of the research division of Super Cola must decide whether or not to continue work on a new sugar-free sweetener. He estimates that if the project proves successful this will be worth $2.5 million to the company, but if it proves unsuccessful it will entail a loss of $1.8 million. If the project is discontinued when the sweetener could have been developed successfully the company will entail a loss of $1.2 million, while if the project is discontinued but would have failed there is a gain of $0.1 million. The research manager estimates the probability of the sweetener being a success is .35.

a) Construct the payoff table for this problem.

b) Construct the regret table for this problem.

c) What is the research manager's optimal action according to the

    1) maximin criterion?

    2) maximax criterion?

    3) minimax regret criterion?

d) If you were the research manager, what decision would you make? Why?

W 7) Dollar Department Stores is planning a two day sale on the new <u>Home</u> <u>Kitchen Center</u> appliance. The cost of advertising for the sale is $950. Dollar expects to sell either 60, 80, 100 or 120 units. The units cost Dollar $300 per dozen and Dollar sells them at $36 each. Any units remaining after the sale will be returned to the factory for a full refund less a postage cost of $2 per unit. The sales manager wants to either order 6, 8, 10 or 12 dozen units.

a) Construct the payoff table for this problem

b) What is the optimal decision under the following criterion

   1) maximin?

   2) maximax?

   3) minimax regret?

c) Should the sales manager ever order 12 dozen units? Why?

SOLUTION:

a) There are 4 decisions, order 6, 8, 10 or 12 dozen, and 4 states of nature, sell 60, 80, 100 or 120 units.

Payoff = (profit on item sold) - (cost of returns) - (advertising expense)

(Profit on goods sold is sales revenue less cost.)

For example, if the company orders 8 dozen and the demand is for 60 units the profit is $60(11) - (36)(2) - 950 = -362$. Or if the company orders 6 dozen and the demand is for 100 units the profit is $(72)(11) - (36)(0) - 950 = -158$. In a similar manner we can calculate the payoff table as follows:

		Sales			
		60	80	100	120
Order	6 doz.	−314	−158	−158	−158
	8 doz.	−362	−102	106	106
	10 doz.	−410	−150	110	370
	12 doz.	−458	−198	62	322

b) Maximin – order 6 dozen
    Maximax – order 10 dozen
    Minimax Regret:

Regret Table

Sales

	60	80	100	120
Order 6 doz.	0	56	268	528
8 doz.	48	0	4	264
10 doz.	96	48	0	0
12 doz.	144	96	48	48

Compute the maximum regret for each decision.

    6 doz. – 528
    8 doz. – 264
    10 doz. – 84
    12 doz. – 144

The minimum is 84 – therefore order 10 dozen.

c) The sales manager should not order 12 dozen because he would always be better off ordering 10 dozen.

8) For the Dollar Department Store (problem 7), the sales manager estimates there is an equal likelihood of selling either 60, 80, 100 or 120 units (i.e. probability = .25 for each case).

a) What is the optimal ordering decision under the expected monetary value criterion?

b) How much is it worth to Dollar to know the exact sales (i.e. the expected value of perfect information)?

c) If you were the sales manager, would you run the sale? Why?

* 9) Metropolitan Cable Vision is investigating the installation of a cable TV system in town. The engineering department estimates the cost of the system (in present worth dollars) to be $700,000. The sales department has investigated four pricing plans. For each pricing plan the marketing division estimates the profit (in present worth dollars) per household to be as follows:

Plan	Profit Per Household
I	$15
II	$18
III	$20
IV	$24

The sales department estimates that the number of subscriber households will be either 10,000, 20,000, 30,000, 40,000, 50,000, or 60,000.

a) Construct the payoff table for the problem.

b) What is the company's optimal decision under

   1) the maximax criterion?

   2) the maximin criterion?

   3) the minimax regret criterion?

c) Suppose the sales department has determined that the number of subscribers to the sytem will be a function of the pricing plan. The probability distribution for the pricing plans are as follows:

Number of Subscribers	Probability Under Pricing Plan			
	I	II	III	IV
10,000	0	.05	.10	.20
20,000	.05	.10	.20	.25
30,000	.05	.20	.20	.25
40,000	.40	.30	.20	.15
50,000	.30	.20	.20	.10
60,000	.20	.15	.10	.05

Using a decision tree analysis, determine which pricing plan is optimal under the expected monetary value criterion.

10) The firm of Cashman Engineering Associates is considering ordering a new office copier. The company is investigating four leasing plans. These are as follows:

Plan I   - $100 per month plus 2¢ per copy for the first 10,000 copies and 1.6¢ per copy for each copy over 10,000.

Plan II - $200 per month plus 1.2¢ per copy.

Plan III - $150 per month with the first 5,000 copies free and 2.2¢ per copy for each copy greater than 5,000.

Plan IV - $300 per month plus .5¢ per copy.

The company has determined it will either make 12,600;   14,400; 16,200;   18,000;   19,800;   or 21,600 copies per month.

a) Construct the monthly payoff table for this problem in terms of costs.

b) What is the optimal cost leasing plan using the

   1) minimin cost criterion?

   2) minimax cost criterion?

c) The company estimates that the probability of making x copies per month, $P(x)$, is as follows:

   $P(12,600) = .05$
   $P(14,400) = .10$
   $P(16,200) = .15$
   $P(18,000) = .25$
   $P(19,800) = .25$
   $P(21,600) = .20$

What is the optimal leasing plan using the expected monetary value criterion to determine the least cost alternative?

W 11) Consider the following three state, four action decision problem with the following payoff table.

	s_1	s_2	s_3
d_1	1	3	-4
d_2	-2	4	1
d_3	3	2	2
d_4	3	1	3

The prior probabilities for the states are $P(s_1) = .2$ and $P(s_2) = .5$.

a) Find the optimal decision using the expected monetary value criterion.

An experiment having two outcomes, I_1 and I_2, is run. The following probabilities are known for the experiment.

$P(I_1|s_1) = .2$

$P(I_1|s_2) = .4$

$P(I_1|s_3) = .7$

b) Find the posterior probabilities for s_1, s_2 and s_3.

c) Using a tree diagram determine the optimal decision policy.

d) What is the expected value of sample information?

SOLUTION:

a) Since $P(s_1) = .2$, $P(s_2) = .5$ we know that $P(s_3) = 1 - .2 - .5 = .3$. We can therefore compute the expected monetary value of each decision:

$EMV(d_1) = (.2)(1) + (.5)(3) + (.3)(-4) = .5$

$EMV(d_2) = (.2)(-2) + (.5)(4) + (.3)(1) = 1.9$

$EMV(d_3) = (.2)(3) + (.5)(2) + (.3)(2) = 2.2$

$EMV(d_4) = (.2)(3) + (.5)(1) + (.3)(3) = 2.0$

Thus, decision d_3 is optimal.

b)

State	Prior Prob.	Conditional Prob. $P(I_1|s_j)$	Joint Prob.	Posterior Prob. $P(s_j|I_1)$
s_1	.2	.2	.04	.089
s_2	.5	.4	.20	.444
s_3	.3	.7	.21	.467
			$P(I_1) = .45$	

State	Prior Prob.	$P(I_2|s_j)$	Joint Prob.	$P(s_j|I_2)$
s_1	.2	.8	.16	.291
s_2	.5	.6	.30	.545
s_3	.3	.3	.09	.164
			$P(I_2) = .55$	

Note that $P(I_2|s_j) = 1 - P(I_1|s_j)$ for all s_j.

334

c)

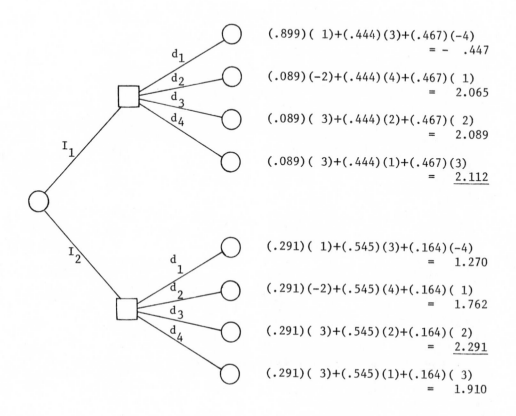

$(.899)(\ 1)+(.444)(3)+(.467)(-4)$
$$= -\ \ .447$$

$(.089)(-2)+(.444)(4)+(.467)(\ 1)$
$$=\ \ 2.065$$

$(.089)(\ 3)+(.444)(2)+(.467)(\ 2)$
$$=\ \ 2.089$$

$(.089)(\ 3)+(.444)(1)+(.467)(3)$
$$=\ \ \underline{2.112}$$

$(.291)(\ 1)+(.545)(3)+(.164)(-4)$
$$=\ \ 1.270$$

$(.291)(-2)+(.545)(4)+(.164)(\ 1)$
$$=\ \ 1.762$$

$(.291)(\ 3)+(.545)(2)+(.164)(\ 2)$
$$=\ \ \underline{2.291}$$

$(.291)(\ 3)+(.545)(1)+(.164)(\ 3)$
$$=\ \ 1.910$$

If the experiment outcome is I_1 the optimal decision is d_4 and if the experiment outcome is I_2 the optimal decision is d_3.

d) We see from the probability table that $P(I_1) = .45$ and $P(I_2) = .55$. Therefore the expected return from this decision policy is $(.45)(2.112) + (.55)(2.291) = 2.21$ as compared to the expected return for the decision without using the indicator information being 2.20. Therefore the EVSI = 2.21 − 2.20 = .01.

335

O 12) The payoff table for a decision problem involving three actions and four states is as follows:

	s_1	s_2	s_3	s_4
d_1	10	5	15	-10
d_2	12	4	12	2
d_3	8	8	8	8

The prior probabilities are

$P(s_1) = .4$

$P(s_2) = .3$

$P(s_3) = .2$

$P(s_4) = .1$

a) Find the optimal decision using the expected monetary value criterion.

b) Find the EVPI.

Suppose some indicator information, I, is obtained with $P(I_1|s_1)$ = .6, $P(I_1|s_2) = .3$, $P(I_1|s_3) = .2$, and $P(I_1|s_4) = .9$.

c) Find the posterior probabilities $P(s_1|I_1)$, $P(s_2|I_1)$, $P(s_3|I_1)$, $P(s_4|I_1)$.

d) Recommend a decision alternative based on these probabilities.

e) Find the EVSI.

Outline of Solution:

a) Use the probability distribution to calculate EMV for each decision alternative. Choose the decision alternative with the largest EMV.

b) Determine the expected regret of the decision found in part a).

c) i) Determine $P(I_2|s_i)$ for all i by noting that $P(I_2|s_i) =$

1 - $P(I_1|s_i)$.

ii) Calculate the posterior probabilities using the tabular
approach.

d) For each indicator, calculate the EMV using the posterior probabilities found in part c). Choose the decision alternative which
gives the largest EMV for that indicator.

e) i) Determine the expected value of the optimal solution by
weighting the answers in part d) by $P(I_1)$ and $P(I_2)$.

ii) Subtract the EMV for the optimal decision found in part a)
from the expected value of the optimal solution found above.

Answers:

a) d_2, EMV = 8.6

b) $ER(d_2) = (.4)(0) + (.3)(4) + (.2)(3) + (.1)(6) = 2.4$

c)

State	Prior Prob. $P(s_j)$	Conditional Prob. $P(I_1\|s_j)$	Joint Prob. $P(I_1 \cap s_j)$	Posterior Prob. $P(s_j\|I_1)$
s_1	.4	.6	.24	.52
s_2	.3	.3	.09	.20
s_3	.2	.2	.04	.09
s_4	.1	.9	.09	.20
			$P(I_1) = .46$	

State	Prior Prob. $P(s_j)$	$P(I_2\|s_j)$	$P(I_2 \cap s_j)$	$P(s_j\|I_2)$
s_1	.4	.4	.16	.30
s_2	.3	.7	.21	.39
s_3	.2	.8	.16	.30
s_4	.1	.1	.01	.02
			$P(I_2) = .54$	

d)

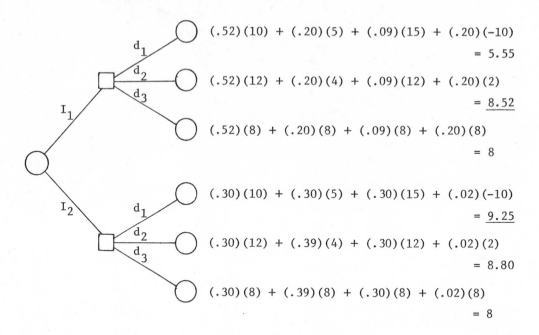

(.52)(10) + (.20)(5) + (.09)(15) + (.20)(−10)

= 5.55

(.52)(12) + (.20)(4) + (.09)(12) + (.20)(2)

= 8.52

(.52)(8) + (.20)(8) + (.09)(8) + (.20)(8)

= 8

(.30)(10) + (.30)(5) + (.30)(15) + (.02)(−10)

= 9.25

(.30)(12) + (.39)(4) + (.30)(12) + (.02)(2)

= 8.80

(.30)(8) + (.39)(8) + (.30)(8) + (.02)(8)

= 8

If the indicator is I_1 choose d_2 and if the indicator is I_2 choose d_1.

e)   EVSI = (.46)(8.52) + (.54)(9.25) − 8.6 = .3142

338

* 13) For the payoff data in problem 11) suppose we have a different indicator J such that.

$P(J_1|s_1) = .1$ $P(J_2|s_1) = .9$

$P(J_1|s_2) = .8$ $P(J_2|s_2) = .2$

$P(J_1|s_3) = .2$ $P(J_2|s_3) = .8$

a) What is the new optimal policy?

b) What is the EVSI?

c) Compare the efficiency of the J indicator to that of the I indicator in problem 11).

14) For the payoff table in problem 12) suppose we have a different indicator function J, for which we know

$$P(J_1|s_1) = .8 \quad , \quad P(J_1|s_2) = .1$$

$$P(J_1|s_3) = .5 \text{ and } P(J_1|s_4) = .2$$

a) What is the new optimal policy?

b) What is the EVSI?

c) Compare the efficiency of the J indicators to that of the I indicators in problem 12).

*15) Consider the following decision tree representation of a decision problem with three indicators, two decision alternatives and two states of nature.

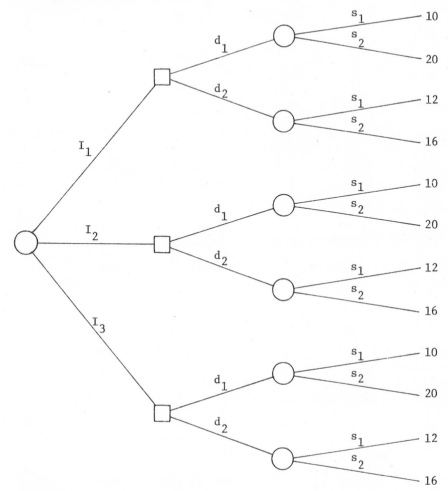

Assume the following probability information is given:

$P(s_1) = .6$ $P(I_1|s_1) = .5$ $P(I_2|s_1) = .3$

$P(s_2) = .4$ $P(I_1|s_2) = .3$ $P(I_2|s_2) = .4$

a) Find the values for $P(I_1)$, $P(I_2)$ and $P(I_3)$.

b) Find the posterior probabilities.

c) Using the decision tree approach, determine the optimal decision strategy. What is the expected value of the solution?

341

16) In problem 15) the payoff table is as follows:

	s_1	s_2
d_1	10	20
d_2	12	16

Using the data in problem 15)

a) Find the optimal decision using the expected monetary value criterion without the indicator information.

b) Find the expected value of perfect information.

c) Find the expected value of sample information.

d) What is the efficiency of the indicator information?

W 17) Burger Prince Restaurant is contemplating opening a new restaurant on Main Street. It has three different models, each with a different seating capacity. Burger Prince estimates that the average number of customers per hour will be 80, 100, or 120. The payoff table for the three models is as follows:

Average # of Customers Per Hour

	80	100	120
Model A	$10,000	$15,000	$14,000
Model B	$ 8,000	$18,000	$12,000
Model C	$ 6,000	$16,000	$21,000

Burger Prince estimates the probability of 80 customers per hour is the same as the probability of 120 customers per hour and twice as much as the probability of 100 customers per hour.

a) Using the expected monetary value criterion what is the optimal decision?

b) What is the expected value of perfect information?

c) Burger Prince must decide whether or not to purchase a marketing survey from Stanton Marketing for $1,000. The results of the survey are "favorable" or "unfavorable". The conditional probabilities are:

P(favorable/80 customers per hour) = .2
P(favorable/100 customers per hour) = .5
P(favorable/120 customers per hour) = .9

Should Burger Prince buy the survey?

SOLUTION:

a)   i)   Determine the probabilities for 80, 100, and 120 customers.

$$P(80) + P(100) + P(120) = 1$$
$$P(80) = P(120)$$
$$P(80) = 2P(100)$$

implies $P(80) = .4$, $P(100) = .2$, $P(120) = .4$

   ii)   Calculate the EMV for each model.

EMV(Model A) = \$12,600
EMV(Model B) = \$11,600
EMV(Model C) = \$14,000

   iii)   Choose the model with the largest EMV, Model C.

b)   i)   Find the regret of the Model C decision.

	80	100	120
Model C	\$4,000	\$2,000	0

EVPI = $(.4)(\$4,000) + (.2)(\$2,000) = \$1,800$

c)   i)   Find the posterior probabilities

State	Prior	Conditional	Favorable Joint	Posterior
80	.4	.2	.08	.15
100	.2	.5	.10	.19
120	.4	.9	.36	.67
			.54	

State	Prior	Conditional	Unfavorable Joint	Posterior
80	.4	.8	.32	.70
100	.2	.5	.10	.22
120	.4	.1	.04	.09
			.46	

344

ii) Evaluate the EVSI

If outcome "favorable"

$EMV(d_1) = \$13,730$

$EMV(d_2) = \$12,660$

$EMV(d_3) = \underline{\$18,010}$ - choose d_3

If outcome "unfavorable"

$EMV(d_1) = \underline{\$11,560}$ - choose d_1

$EMV(d_2) = \$10,640$

$EMV(d_3) = \$\ 9,610$

$EVSI = (.54)(\$18,010) + (.46)(\$11,560) - \$14,000 = \$927.40$

iii) Compare EVSI with the cost of the survey.

Since the survey will cost more than the EVSI it should not be purchased.

18) An appliance dealer must decide how many (if any) new microwave ovens to order for next month. The ovens cost $220 and sell for $300. Because the oven company is coming out with a new product line in two months, any ovens not sold next month will have to be sold at the half price clearance sale. Additionally, the dealer feels that he suffers a loss of $25 for every oven demanded when he is out of stock. On the basis of past month's sales data the dealer estimates the probabilities of demand for 0, 1, 2 or 3 ovens to be .3, .4, .2 and .1.

The dealer is considering conducting a telephone survey on customers attitudes towards microwave ovens. The results of the survey will be either "favorable", "unfavorable" or "no opinion". The dealer estimates the following conditional probabilities for the survey results.

P(favorable/demand = 0 ovens)   = .1
P(favorable/demand = 1 oven)   = .2
P(favorable/demand = 2 ovens)   = .3
P(favorable/demand = 3 ovens)   = .9
P(unfavorable/demand = 0 ovens) = .8
P(unfavorable/demand = 1 oven) = .3
P(unfavorable/demand = 2 ovens) = .1
P(unfavorable/demand = 3 ovens) = .1

a) Compute the payoff matrix for this problem.

b) What is the appliance dealer's optimal decision without conducting the telephone survey using the EMV criterion?

c) What is the EVPI?

d) What is the optimal decision strategy for the dealer if he conducts the telephone survey?

e) What is the maximum amount he should pay for the telephone survey?

* 19) Super Cola is considering the introduction of a root beer soft drink. The company feels that the probability the product will be a success is .6. The payoff table for the decision analysis is as follows:

	s_1 Success	s_2 Failure
Produce	$250,000	-$300,000
Do Not Produce	-$ 50,000	-$ 20,000

The company has a choice of hiring two market research firms to obtain additional information. Stanton Marketing claims it has developed market indicators, I_1 and I_2, for which $P(I_1|s_1) = .7$ and $P(I_1|s_2) = .4$. New World Marketing claims it has developed market indicators J_1 and J_2, for which $P(J_1|s_1) = .6$ and $P(J_1|s_2) = .3$.

a) Using the expected monetary value criterion, without hiring a market research firm what is the optimal decision for Super Cola?

b) What is the EVPI?

c) Find the EVSI for Stanton.

d) Find the EVSI for New World.

e) If both firms charge $5,000, which should Super Cola hire?

f) If Stanton charges $10,000 while New World charges $4,000, which firm should Super Cola hire? Why?

* 20) For the Mark Investment Advisors problem, problem 4, the payoff
table for the five stocks was as follows:

	s_1	s_2	s_3	s_4
d_1 - Stock A	-.40	-.20	+.10	+.60
d_2 - Stock B	-.30	-.10	0	+.30
d_3 - Stock C	-.10	0	+.05	+.30
d_4 - Stock D	0	+.05	+.10	+.15
d_5 - Stock E	.05	+.15	-.10	-.20

and $P(s_1) = .20$, $P(s_2) = .40$ and $P(s_3) = .20$. Mark is considering
developing an econometric model for the economy which will have one
of three outcomes I_1 - good; I_2 - average; or I_3 - poor. Mark
estimates the following conditional probabilities.

$$P(I_j|s_k)$$

	s_1	s_2	s_3	s_4
I_1	.1	.3	.5	.4
I_2	.1	.4	.4	.6
I_3	.8	.3	.1	.0

What is the optimal decision policy associated with this econometric
model?

21) Dollar Department Stores has just acquired the chain of Wenthrope and Sons Custom Jewelers. Dollar has received an offer from Harris Diamonds to purchase the Wenthrope store on Grove Street for $120,000. Dollar has determined that the profit potential for this store will depend on the economy. Estimates of the stores future profitability are either $80,000, $100,000, $120,000 or $140,000 with the following probabilities.

$P(\$80,000) = .2$
$P(\$100,000) = .3$
$P(\$120,000) = .1$
$P(\$140,000) = .4$

a) On the basis of this information should Dollar sell the store?

b) What is the EVPI?

c) Dollar can have an economic forecast performed at a cost of $10,000. The economic forecast produces indicators I_1 and I_2, for which

$P(I_1|80,000) = .1$, $P(I_1|100,000) = .2$
$P(I_1|120,000) = .6$, $P(I_1|140,000) = .3$

Should the company have the forecast performed?

* 22) A part of Dollar Department Stores' recent acquisition (problem 21) was a five acre parcel of land on Cedar Street. Dollar can either sell the land, build a shopping center, or build an apartment complex. The profitability of each venture is closely tied to the population growth rate in town. Dollar has determined the following payoff table.

Population Growth Rate

	$s_1 = 5\%$	$s_2 = 10\%$	$s_3 = 15\%$
Sell Land	$150,000	$150,000	$150,000
Build Shopping Center	$100,000	$160,000	$200,000
Build Apartment	$120,000	$160,000	$180,000

A preliminary estimate by Dollar is that

P(5% growth rate) = .2
P(10% growth rate) = .5
P(15% growth rate) = .3

Dollar is contemplating purchasing an econometric study of the region for $3,000. The results of the study will be classified as either I_1 - excellent, I_2 - fair, I_3 - below average, or I_4 - poor. The conditional probabilities for the study are as follows:

$$P(I_j | s_k)$$

	s_1	s_2	s_3
I_1	.1	.2	.7
I_2	.2	.3	.1
I_3	.2	.4	.1
I_4	.5	.1	.1

a) Without purchasing the econometric study, what should the decision be under the expected monetary value criterion?

b) What is the EVPI?

c) Find the optimal decision policy using the econometric study.

d) Should the company purchase the econometric study?

* 23)   Dicom Corp. has developed a new high speed computer which it intends
to sell at $150,000. The company's salesmen have lined up demon-
strations with four clients for next month and they estimate that the
probability of each client purchasing a computer is .4. Because the
company cannot completely shut down its assembly line it plans to
make at least one computer for next month. The cost of producing
computers next month is as follows:

1 computer $100,000
2 computers $190,000
3 computers $260,000
4 computers $310,000

Any unsold computers must be sold at $60,000. Additionally, if a
client wants to purchase a computer, but all available computers have
been sold, the company estimates it loses $20,000.

a)   Determine the payoff table for this problem.

b)   What is the optimal strategy using the expected monetary value
criterion?

c)   Dicom can have a survey performed as to the general market impres-
sion of this new computer, favorable or not. If the reaction is
favorable the following probabilities are believed to hold.

P(favorable/0 computers sold) = .1
P(favorable/1 computer sold) = .2
P(favorable/2 computers sold) = .6
P(favorable/3 computers sold) = .9
P(favorable/4 computers sold) = 1.0

How much should Dicom pay for this survey?

24) The payoff for the Dollar Department Store, <u>Home Kitchen Center</u> <u>Appliance</u> sale, problem 7, is as follows:

	$s_1 = 60$	$s_2 = 80$	$s_3 = 100$	$s_4 = 120$
6 doz.	−314	−158	−158	−158
8 doz.	−362	−102	106	106
10 doz.	−410	−150	110	370
12 doz.	−458	−198	62	322
Probability	.25	.25	.25	.25

Order Size

The manager selects two persons at random to question whether or not they like the Home Kitchen Center Appliance. He believes that the following probabilities are true.

P(0 people like the appliance/60 units in sales)   = .40
P(1 person likes the appliance/60 units in sales) = .40
P(0 people like the appliance/80 units in sales)   = .30
P(1 person likes the appliance/80 units in sales) = .40
P(0 people like the appliance/100 units in sales) = .20
P(1 person likes the appliance/100 units in sales) = .50
P(0 people like the appliance/120 units in sales) = .10
P(1 person likes the appliance/120 units in sales) = .30

Find the optimal decision for the sales manager based on the results of his questioning.

12 INVENTORY MODELS WITH DETERMINISTIC DEMAND

REVIEW

1. Inventory Models

The study of inventory models is concerned with two basic questions:
(1) how much should be ordered each time, and (2) when should reordering
take place. The objective is to minimize total costs over a specified
period of time (such as a year). Total costs include: (1) <u>reordering
costs</u>, including salaries and expenses of processing an order; (2) <u>hold-
ing costs</u>, usually a percentage of the value of the item, assessed for
keeping an item in inventory (including finance costs, insurance, security
costs, taxes, warehouse overhead, etc.); (3) <u>backorder costs</u> or goodwill
associated with being out of stock when an item is demanded; (4) purchase
costs--the actual price of the items; (5) negative costs, such as
<u>quantity discounts</u>; (6) other costs such as seasonal costs.

The simplest inventory models are assumed to be deterministic and
linear; that is, demand is known to be fixed at D items per year and
is constant throughout the year. The decision maker must determine if
these assumptions are appropriate for his particular problem. Another
simplifying assumption is that delivery is instantaneous or that there is a

fixed lead time for delivery. If these assumptions are approximately correct, employing them will greatly simplify the model and facilitate the solution procedure.

2. Deterministic Inventory Models

(i) EOQ Model

Assumptions:

(1) Demand is constant throughout the year at D items per year;
(2) Delivery time is instantaneous;
(3) Reorder cost: $\$C_o$ per order;

(4) Holding cost: $\$C_h$ per item per year in inventory.

Results:

(1) Optimal Order Quantity: $Q^* = \sqrt{\dfrac{2DC_o}{C_h}}$

(2) Number of Reorder Times Per Year $= \dfrac{D}{Q^*}$

(3) Time Between Orders $= \dfrac{Q^*}{D}$ years

(4) Total Annual Variable Cost: $TC = (1/2)Q^*C_h + \dfrac{DC_o}{Q^*}$

(ii) Economic Production Lot-Size Model

Assumptions:

(1) Demand constant throughout the year at D items per year;
(2) Production rate is P items per year (and P > D);
(3) Instantaneous set up time;
(4) Set up cost: $\$C_o$ per run;

(5) Holding cost: $\$C_h$ per item per year in inventory.

Results:

(1) Optimal Production Lot-Size: $Q^* = \sqrt{\dfrac{2DC_o}{(1 - D/P)C_h}}$

(2) Number of Production Runs Per Year $= \dfrac{D}{Q^*}$

(3) Time Between Set-Ups: $\frac{Q^*}{D}$ years

(4) Total Annual Variable Cost: $TC = (\frac{1}{2})(1 - D/P)Q^*C_h + \frac{DC_o}{Q^*}$

(iii) **Planned Shortage Model**

Assumptions:

(1) Demand is constant throughout the year at D items per year;
(2) Delivery time is instantaneous;
(3) Reorder cost: $\$C_o$ per order;
(4) Holding cost: $\$C_h$ per item per year in inventory;
(5) Backorder costs: $\$C_b$ per item backordered per year;
(6) Customers do not withdraw an order when supplier is out of stock; the order is filled upon delivery of next shipment.

Results:

(1) Optimal Order Quantity: $Q^* = \sqrt{\dfrac{2DC_o}{C_h}\left(\dfrac{C_h + C_b}{C_b}\right)}$

(2) Maximum Number of Backorders: $S^* = Q^*\left(\dfrac{C_h}{C_h + C_b}\right)$

(3) Number Orders Per Year: $\dfrac{D}{Q^*}$

(4) Time Between Orders: $\dfrac{Q^*}{D}$ years

(5) Total Annual Variable Cost:

$$TC = \frac{(Q^* - S^*)^2}{2Q^*}\,C_h + \frac{D}{Q^*}\,C_o + \frac{S^{*2}}{2Q^*}\,C_b \; .$$

(iv) **Quantity Discount Model**

Assumptions:

(1) Demand is constant throughout the year at D items per year;
(2) Delivery time is instantaneous;
(3) Reorder cost: $\$C_o$ per order;

(4) Purchase cost: $\$C_1$ per item if the quantity ordered is between 0 and X_1 (price level 1), $\$C_2$ per item if the quantity ordered is between $(X_1 + 1)$ and X_2 (price level 2), etc.

(5) Holding costs: $\$C_h$ per item per year in inventory, where $C_h = IC_i$ for appropriate price level i (I is the annual inventory carrying charge).

Results:

The optimal order quantity and total annual cost are determined in the following manner.

(1) For each price level, i, compute Q_i^* using the EOQ formula $\left(Q_i^* = \sqrt{\dfrac{2DC_o}{C_h}} \right)$ (note that C_h may change for each price level).

(2) For those Q^* which are too small to qualify for the discounted price, adjust the order quantity upward, to the nearest order quantity which will allow the product to be purchased at the discounted price.

(3) For each of the order quantities resulting from steps 1 and 2, compute the total annual cost using the unit price from the appropriate price category. Total cost for price level i =

$$TC_i = \frac{Q_i^*}{2} C_h + \frac{D}{Q_i^*} C_o + DC_i$$

$$\left(\text{Total Cost} \right) = \begin{pmatrix} \text{Annual} \\ \text{Inventory} \\ \text{Holding} \\ \text{Cost} \end{pmatrix} + \begin{pmatrix} \text{Annual} \\ \text{Inventory} \\ \text{Order} \\ \text{Cost} \end{pmatrix} + \begin{pmatrix} \text{Annual} \\ \text{Inventory} \\ \text{Purchase} \\ \text{Cost} \end{pmatrix}$$

(4) Choose Q_i^* which gives the minimum total cost found in step 3.

These models have built-in restrictive assumptions concerning instantaneous delivery and fixed demand. Hence the results from these models should only be used as guidelines. However, if lead time can be assumed to be fixed at m years, then reordering should begin when Dm items remain in inventory. Also, if the decision maker desires to have a

356

safety stock of y items to make up for any unforeseen delays or higher than expected demands, the order should be placed an additional y/D years in advance. It should be emphasized again that these models only serve as guidelines for the decision maker. There could be secondary reasons, not built in to the model, for modifying the decision generated. If, for example, the model gave an optimal time between orders of 12.8 days, there would probably be good reason to place orders every 14 days (2 weeks). This would make bookkeeping and control easier. Small changes in the model will have a small effect on the overall total costs.

3. Material Requirements Planning

The Material Requirements Planning Method (MRP) is used to control a manufacturing inventory system. The major function of an MRP system is to translate the demand for finished goods into detailed inventory requirements for all components.

Among the inputs to an MRP system are the master production schedule and the bill of materials. The master production schedule summarizes requirements and deadlines for finished goods. The bill of materials is a structured parts list detailing the sequencing of the assembly of the product.

In manufacturing there is often a dependent demand between different components. Because of this dependence, the net inventory requirements for the different components are determined using the following formula.

$$\begin{pmatrix} \text{Net Component} \\ \text{Requirements} \end{pmatrix} = \begin{pmatrix} \text{Gross Component} \\ \text{Requirements} \end{pmatrix} - \begin{pmatrix} \text{Number of} \\ \text{Components} \\ \text{in Inventory} \end{pmatrix}$$

Here the gross component requirement is the quantity of the component necessary to support production at the next higher level of assembly.

In addition to determining demand requirements for components, an MRP system also calculates the date that net requirements are needed. This is done using a procedure referred to as time phasing. In time phasing, a production plan for components is developed by working backwards from the desired completion date of the finished product through the various manufacturing stages.

Because of the large amount of data which must be recorded and maintained, large scale computers are used to implement MRP systems. Many computer manufacturers offer programs which will perform such calculations. Hence, MRP serves as part of a data processing and management information system whose function is to monitor and control the status of production and inventory.

357

BACKORDER - The receipt of an order for a product when there are no units on hand; these are accumulated and satisfied upon arrival of the next shipment.   (513)

BILL OF MATERIALS - A structured parts list that shows the manner in which the product is actually put together.   (522)

COST OF CAPITAL - The cost a firm incurs, usually interest payments on borrowed funds or dividend payments on stocks, in order to obtain capital for investment. The cost of capital, which may be stated as an annual percentage rate, is part of the holding cost associated with maintaining inventory levels.   (496)

CYCLE TIME - Length of time between two consecutive orders.   (505)

DEPENDENT DEMAND - The demand for one component depends upon the demand for another component.   (523)

ECONOMIC ORDER QUANTITY (EOQ) - The order quantity which minimizes the total annual costs in a problem with only reordering and holding costs.   (497)

GOODWILL COST - Cost associated with a backorder, or stockout.   (514)

HOLDING COST - All costs associated with maintaining an inventory investment including cost of capital, inventory, insurance, security, taxes, etc.; this is usually figured as a percentage of purchase cost.   (496)

LEAD TIME - Time between placing an order and the receipt of that order.   (504)

MASTER PRODUCTION SCHEDULE - A statement of how many finished items are to be produced and when.   (522)

MATERIAL REQUIREMENTS PLANNING (MRP) - A computerized data processing system whose function is to schedule production and control the level of inventory.   (521)

ORDERING COST - The fixed cost of placing an order including staff salaries, paper, transportation, etc.   (499)

PLANNED SHORTAGE MODEL - Inventory model where ordering is done when there is a fixed number of backorders.   (512)

PRODUCTION LOT-SIZE PROBLEM - Problem concerning the number of items to produce during a production run and the length of time between production runs.   (508)

QUANTITY DISCOUNTS - Discounts on purchase price of items offered for larger order quantities.   (518)

SAFETY STOCK - Additional inventory maintained to reduce the number of stockouts during the lead time.   (507)

TIME PHASING - Determining when components must be ordered for production.   (525

Chapter 12 Check List

W 1) Barry's Barometer Business (BBB) is a retail outlet which deals exclusively with weather equipment. Currently BBB is trying to decide on an inventory and reorder policy for super deluxe home barometers. These cost BBB $50 each and demand is about 500 per year distributed fairly evenly throughout the year. Reordering costs are $80 per order and holding costs are figured at 20% of the cost of the item.

a) Build a total cost mathematical model for this system.

b) What is the optimal reorder quantity according to the model?

c) How many times per year would BBB reorder?

d) What total cost does the model give?

e) Given the answer in parts (b), and (c), choose a more convenient order quantity. What is the total cost of this decision? Compare this with (c) and comment.

SOLUTION:

a) Total Cost = (Holding Costs) + (Reorder Costs) + (Purchase Costs)

$$TC = C_h \left(\frac{Q}{2}\right) + C_o \left(\frac{D}{Q}\right) + \$50D$$

$C_h = .2(50) = 10; \quad C_o = 80, \quad D = 500$

Thus, $\quad TC = 5Q + \dfrac{40,000}{Q} + 25,000$

b) $\quad Q* = \sqrt{\dfrac{2DC_o}{C_h}} = \sqrt{\dfrac{2(500)(80)}{10}} = 89.44 = \underline{\underline{90}}$

c) Number of reorder times per year $= \dfrac{500}{90} = 5.56$

d) $\quad TC = 5(90) + \dfrac{40,000}{90} + 25,000 =$

$$450 + 444 + 25,000 = 25,894$$

e) It is probably more convenient to order 100 at a time and order 5 times per year.

$$TC = 5(100) + \dfrac{40,000}{100} + 25,000 = 25,900$$

This $6 difference represents only a .6% change in variable costs and a .02% change in total costs.

O 2) BBB also sells standard outside thermometers which it purchases from a different company for $10. Demand for these thermometers is 2,000 per year (=300 selling days). Consider reorder costs of $40 per order and holding costs based on 20% of the purchase costs.

a) What is the optimal order quantity?

b) What is the total annual variable cost?

c) If the lead time for delivery is two weeks (=12 days) at what inventory level should an order be placed?

Outline of Solution:

This is a simple EOQ model.

a) $Q* = \sqrt{\dfrac{2DC_o}{C_h}}$

Answer: 283 (rounded off)

b) $TC = \dfrac{Q* \, C_h}{2} + \dfrac{DC_o}{Q*}$

Answer: $563 (rounded off)

c) Demand per day = ?

Inventory level = (Demand per day) x (12 days)

Answer: 80

362

* 3) A small clinic must keep on hand supplies of a heroin treatment drug, which itself is a drug. Because of the sensitivity of the program, extra precautions are taken to keep the drug in inventory. However these precautions incur additional expense. The drug comes in 100 unit containers and inventory costs are estimated at $2 per container per day (=$730 per year). Transportation costs are also high--$130 per order. Paperwork to process an order is $20 per order. If demand is relatively constant at 100,000 units (=1,000 containers) per year, develop a reorder policy for the clinic. If lead time is one day, at what inventory level should an order be placed?

4) Terri's Tie Shop (TTS) is the exclusive retail outlet for Trophy Ties. Although demand is slightly higher in December (Christmas) and June (Father's Day), it is relatively constant throughout the year as last year's sales figures show:

MONTH	DEMAND	MONTH	DEMAND
JAN	75	JUL	68
FEB	70	AUG	75
MAR	72	SEP	74
APR	76	OCT	70
MAY	69	NOV	76
JUN	85	DEC	90

The average cost of a Trophy Tie is $4 to TTS. TTS figures inventory costs at 15% yearly and reorder costs are $25 per order. There is no reason to assume demand will change this year.

a) What is the average demand per month?

b) Assume demand is constant throughout the year and determine an optimal inventory policy for the model.

c) What is the total annual variable costs of the model?

d) Make some suggestions to modify the inventory policy of the model to fit the "real" problem. Comment.

* 5) Hammering Hank's Hardware needs to develop an inventory policy for stocking Better Made Tools. Demand is for 10,000 items per year. Presently Hank does his own bookkeeping and ordering. He figures his reorder costs at $2 per order not including the cost of his time. However Hank is considering hiring a full time bookkeeper and this will raise the per order cost to $18 per order. If holding costs are $1/item per year of storage, what value should Hank put on his book-keeping time (per year) to justify adding the bookkeeper.

W 6) Non-Slip Tile Company (NST) has been using production runs of 100,000 tiles, 10 times per year to meet the demand of 1,000,000 tiles annually. The set-up cost is $5,000 per run and holding costs are estimated at 10% of the manufacturing cost of $1 per tile. The production capacity of the machine is 500,000 tiles per month (=6,000,000) per year.

a) Develop a mathematical model for the total annual cost for this problem.

b) What production schedule do you recommend?

c) How much is NST losing annually by using their present production schedule?

d) How long is the machine idle between runs?

SOLUTION:

This is an economic production lot size problem with $D = 1,000,000$, $P = 6,000,000$ $C_h = .10$, $C_o = 5,000$.

a) TC = (Holding Costs) + (Set-Up Costs) + (Manufacturing Costs)

$$= (C_h)\left(\frac{Q}{2}\right)\left(1 - \frac{D}{P}\right) + \frac{DC_o}{Q} + (1,000,000)(1)$$

$$= .04167Q + \frac{5,000,000,000}{Q} + 1,000,000$$

b) $$Q^* = \sqrt{\frac{2DC_o}{C_h\left(1 - \frac{D}{P}\right)}} = \sqrt{\frac{2(1,000,000)(5,000)}{(.0833)}} = 346,479 \text{ per run}$$

runs per year $= \frac{D}{Q^*} = 2.89$ times per year

c) TC of optimal policy $= .04167(346,479) + \frac{5,000,000,000}{346,479} + 1,000,000$

$$= \$1,028,868$$

TC of current policy $= .04167(100,000) + \frac{5,000,000,000}{100,000}$

$$+ 1,000,000 = \$1,054,167$$

difference $= \$25,299$

d) There are 2.89 cycles per year. Thus each cycle lasts $\frac{365}{2.89}$ = 126.3 days.

Time to produce 346,479 per run is $\frac{346,479 \text{ (tiles/run)}}{6,000,000 \text{ (tiles/year)}} \times 365$ (days/year) = 21.1 days. Thus, the machine is idle for 126.3 - 21.1 = 105.2 days between runs.

7) Rancher Jim's Luncheon Meat Company produces fresh luncheon meats. Demand is for 300,000 pounds of meat per year. Rancher Jim has his choice of two machines to process the meats. The annual lease costs and annual processing capacities are given below.

	ANNUAL LEASE COST	ANNUAL PROCESSING CAPACITY
Machine I	$10,000	250,000 lbs.
Machine II	$12,000	1,000,000 lbs.

Set-up costs are $1,000 per run and holding costs are $.10 per lb. per year. Rancher Jim's profit is .20 per pound.

a) Show that Machine II gives the maximum profit for processing.

b) Consider the time between cycles. Why would you most likely recommend Machine I for Rancher Jim?

* 8) National Business Machines (NBM) is trying to develop the effective
      use of one of its production lines which produces transistors for
      circuits of computers. In general, allowing for defectives, NBM needs
      1,000,000 transistors per year for their NBM 470 series. A production
      rate of 3,000,000 per year is possible if the production line were in
      continuous operation 24 hours a day, 365 days per year. The cost of
      storing a transistor is $1 per year. Production start-up costs $4,000
      and takes two weeks.

   a) What is the optimal number of transistors NBM should make per
       production run?

   b) What will be the number of production runs per year?

   c) What is the duration of a production run?

   d) If workers have (and must take) vacation between the end of one
       production run and the start-up of another, how much vacation time
       do they get per year?

9) Zak's Zippers is contemplating manufacturing their own zippers rather than distributing the zippers it receives from ZZZ Distributors. Zak's figures it must sell the zipper at the same price or else the yearly demand of 4,000 dozen zippers will be greatly affected. Presently the purchase cost per dozen zippers is $10, whereas the proposed manufacturing cost for labor and raw materials is estimated at $8 per dozen. In any event, the holding costs are estimated at 20% of the purchase cost or manufacturing cost of the item. Reorder costs are currently $40 per order. However, start-up costs for each production cycle are estimated at $400. If Zak's can lease a machine with a production capacity of 8,000 dozen zippers per year at an annual cost of $5,000, should Zak's convert to manufacturing their own zippers?

W 10) Barry's Barometer Business (see problem 1) has been so successful selling super deluxe barometers that BBB has no fear of losing much business if he runs short. BBB figures the backorder cost is $4. (All other relevant data is the same as problem 1.)

Identify the following:

a) Minimum cost order quantity
b) Maximum number of backorders
c) Maximum inventory level
d) Time between orders
e) Total annual costs (including purchase costs)
f) What percentage of variable costs is saved by allowing shortages?

SOLUTION:

This is an EOQ problem with planned shortages with $D = 500$, $C_h = \$10$, $C_o = \$80$, $C_b = \$4$.

a) $Q^* = \sqrt{\dfrac{2DC_o}{C_h}\dfrac{\left(C_h + C_b\right)}{C_b}} = \sqrt{\dfrac{2(500)(80)}{10}}\left(\dfrac{14}{4}\right) = 167$ (rounded)

b) $S^* = Q^* \dfrac{C_h}{C_h + C_b} = 167\left(\dfrac{10}{14}\right) = 119$ (rounded)

c) $Q^* - S^* = 48$

d) Time between orders $= \dfrac{Q^*}{D} = \dfrac{167}{500} = 1/3$ year (every 4 months)

e) $TC = \dfrac{(Q^* - S^*)^2}{2Q^*} C_h + \dfrac{DC_o}{Q^*} + \dfrac{S^*}{2Q^*} C_b + \$25,000$

$= \dfrac{(48)^2}{2(167)} (\$10) + \dfrac{(500)(80)}{167} + \dfrac{(119)^2}{2(167)} (4) + \$25,000$

$= \$25,478$

f) Variable cost (no shortage) $= 894$ (problem #1)

Variable cost (with shortage) $= 478$

difference $= 416$

% difference $= \dfrac{416}{894}$ x 100% = 46.5%.

11) Raspby Records, the only record store in a small midwest town is trying to determine an optimal order quantity of Stevie Wonder albums. Assume demand is constant at 2,000 per year. Holding costs are approximately 10% of the list price of $8 per album. If order costs are $10 per order, and Raspby figures a $1 stockout cost, what should be Raspby's ordering policy of Stevie Wonder records? Assume back-orders will be filled when a new shipment is received at Raspby's and that lead time is one week. Why is the model not a particularly good one for popular music?

* 12) Andy's Auto Parts has been stocking an unusually fine grade of racing oil on which it makes a 10¢ per quart profit. Demand has been 2,000 quarts per week. Storage costs are 1¢ per quart per week. Andy wants to develop an inventory policy. Reordering costs are $10 per order. If Andy allows backorders, he figures demand will drop to 1,900 quarts per week. Andy gives a 3¢ per week discount per can backordered. Derive an optimal inventory policy for Andy.

W 13) Barry's Barometer Business (problem 1) has been offered a 10%
       purchase discount from the manufacturer on orders of 100 or more.
       What should BBB's purchase decision be under those circumstances?

SOLUTION:

From problem 1, the optimal order quantity without the discount is
90, for a total annual cost of $25,894.

If 10% discount is given then D = 500, C_o = 80, C_h = .2(45) = 9

$$Q^* = \sqrt{\frac{2DC_o}{C_h}} = \sqrt{\frac{2(500)(80)}{9}} = 94.3$$

This is less than the quantity discount order point, thus BBB must
consider the total cost right at Q^* = 100.

$$\text{Total Cost} = \begin{pmatrix} \text{Annual} \\ \text{Inventory} \\ \text{Costs} \end{pmatrix} + \begin{pmatrix} \text{Annual} \\ \text{Inventory} \\ \text{Order} \\ \text{Costs} \end{pmatrix} + \begin{pmatrix} \text{Annual} \\ \text{Inventory} \\ \text{Purchase} \\ \text{Cost} \end{pmatrix}$$

Total Cost = $4.5Q^* + \frac{40,000}{Q^*} + 22,500 = \$23,350.$

Since this is a lower total cost than the optimal figure without the
discount, 100 is the optimal order quantity and orders should be
placed five times per year (every 2.4 months).

14) A small 24 hour grocery store is trying to decide on an order policy for Super Cola. Demand seems to be constant at 48 cases per week. Inventory holding costs are $1 per case per week and reordering costs are $10 per order.

a) What is the optimal order quantity?

b) The cost of soda is $4 per case, but there is a 10% discount for orders of 40 or more cases and a 20% discount on orders of 80 or more cases. In view of these discounts, what should be the order quantity?

* 15) A company has the following choices for purchasing a product for which demand is 100 per week.

OPTION	PURCHASE COST/ITEM	QUANTITY
I	$10.00	0 - 599
II	$ 9.80	600 or more
III	$ 9.90	exactly 100

Under option III, the ordering company will have no paperwork as the 100 items will be delivered every week automatically. Thus under option III the only work associated with an order is in filing an invoice which is assumed to have zero cost. Otherwise reorder costs are $75 per order. If holding costs are figured at 1/2 of 1% per week, what is the optimal order quantity?

W 16) Columbia Mopeds has just received an order for 10,000 mopeds from Shears Department Stores. To meet the contract requirements the mopeds must be completed in 10 weeks. The following is a bill of materials chart for the Columbia moped.

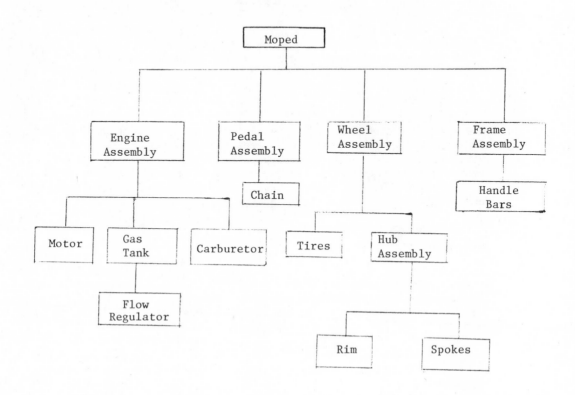

The following table gives the current inventory and lead time necessary for each component in the manufacturing process.

Component	Units in Inventory (per moped)	Lead Time in Weeks
Moped	2,200	1
Engine Assembly	1,500	2
Motor	900	5
Gas Tank	2,000	1
Carburetor	800	4
Flow Regulator	1,600	3
Pedal Assembly	600	6
Chain	900	3
Wheel Assembly	1,700	4
Tires	1,000	4
Hub Assembly	2,000	1
Rim	6,000	3
Spokes	3,200	2
Frame Assembly	8,000	4
Handle Bars	600	7

On the basis of this information, use MRP to determine the net requirements and order times for each component.

SOLUTION:

The contract calls for 10,000 mopeds, but the company only has 2,200 in stock. Therefore, it needs to manufacture 7,800 mopeds. Using the formula

$$\begin{pmatrix} \text{Net Component} \\ \text{Requirements} \end{pmatrix} = \begin{pmatrix} \text{Gross} \\ \text{Components} \\ \text{Requirements} \end{pmatrix} - \begin{pmatrix} \text{Number of} \\ \text{Components} \\ \text{in Inventory} \end{pmatrix}$$

we have the following net component requirements:

```
Engine Assemblies    7,800 - 1,500 = 6,300
Motor                6,300 -   900 = 5,400
Gas Tank             6,300 - 2,000 = 4,300
Carburetor           6,300 -   800 = 5,500
Flow Regulator       4,300 - 1,600 = 2,700
Pedal Assembly       7,800 -   600 = 7,200
Chain                7,200 -   900 = 6,300
Wheel Assembly       7,800 - 1,700 = 6,100
Tires                6,100 - 1,000 = 5,100
Hub Assembly         6,100 - 2,000 = 4,100
Rim                  4,100 - 6,000 =   0*
Spokes               4,100 - 3,200 =   900
Frame Assembly       6,300 - 8,000 =   0*
Handle Bars            0* -   600 =   0 *
```

*Current inventory exceeds demand requirements.

For example, in order to deliver the 10,000 mopeds it will be
necessary to produce 6,300 chains which will bring the total number
of chains available to 7,200. These 7,200 chains will be used to
manufacture 7,200 pedal assemblies. This will bring the total
number of pedal assemblies available to 7,800 which will allow
7,800 mopeds to be built.

To determine the order times we work backwards. Since the order
must be completed in 10 weeks the moped assembly must begin by week
9 (10 - 1). Continuing in this fashion we have

	Week
Complete time for engine assembly	9
- Lead time for engine assembly	2
Place order for engines	7
Complete time for motors	7
- Lead time for motors	5
Place order for motors	2
Complete time for gas tank	7
- Lead time for gas tank	1
Place order for gas tank	6
Complete time for flow regulator	6
- Lead time for flow regulator	3
Place order for flow regulator	3
Complete time for carburetor	7
- Lead time for carburetor	4
Place order for carburetor	3

	Week
Complete time for pedal assembly	9
− Lead time for pedal assembly	6
Place order for pedal assembly	3
Complete time for chain	3
− Lead time for chain	3
Place order for chain	0 (immediately)
Complete time for wheel assembly	9
− Lead time for wheel assembly	4
Place order for wheel assembly	5
Complete time for tires	5
− Lead time for tires	4
Place order for tires	1
Complete time for hub assembly	5
− Lead time for hub assembly	1
Place order for hub assembly	4
Complete time for spokes	4
− Lead time for spokes	2
Place order for spokes	2

Note that it is unnecessary to calculate the order placement date for rims, frames, or handles since current inventory exceeds the demand requirements.

Summarizing our results gives the following table:

Component	Net Requirements	Lead Time (in Weeks)	Order Date (in Weeks)
Moped	7,800	1	9
Engine Assembly	6,300	2	7
Motor	5,400	5	2
Gas Tank	4,300	1	6
Carburetor	5,500	4	3
Flow Regulator	2,700	3	3
Pedal Assembly	7,200	6	3
Chain	6,300	3	0
Wheel Assembly	6,100	4	5
Tires	5,100	4	1
Hub Assembly	4,100	1	4
Rim	0	3	
Spokes	900	2	2
Frame Assembly	0	4	
Handle Bars	0	7	

0 17) Thorton Industries Corporation is planning to begin distributing its
new model 712 microwave oven in 12 weeks. At the National Appliance
Dealer's Show the oven was such a success that Thorton has contracted
to deliver an initial 26,000 units. The following is the bill of
materials chart for the model 712.

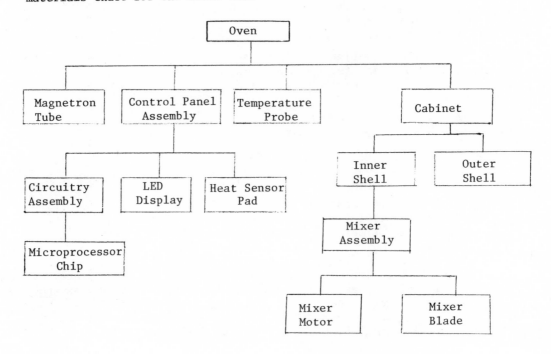

Because the company manufactures all of its components, lead times
will be a function of the quantity of the orders.

The following is a list of the current inventory and lead time for each component in the model 712.

Component	Units in Inventory	Lead Time (in weeks) per 10,000 Units
Oven	1,000	1
Magnetron Tube	10,000	4
Control Panel Assembly	2,000	2
Circuitry Assembly	4,000	1
Microprocessor Chip	9,000	3
LED Display	6,000	2
Heat Sensor Pad	3,000	2
Temperature Probe	20,000	6
Cabinet	5,000	1
Inner Shell	3,000	2
Mixer Assembly	8,000	3
Mixer Motor	3,000	1
Mixer Blade	2,000	2
Outer Shell	7,000	4

On the basis of this information use MRP to determine the net requirements and order times for each component.

Outline of Solution:

i) Determine the net component requirements using the formula

$$\begin{pmatrix} \text{Net Component} \\ \text{Requirements} \end{pmatrix} = \begin{pmatrix} \text{Gross Component} \\ \text{Requirements} \end{pmatrix} - \begin{pmatrix} \text{Number of} \\ \text{Components} \\ \text{in Inventory} \end{pmatrix}$$

ii) For each component which has a positive net components requirement determine the lead time. This can be calculated by multiplying the lead time given in the table times the answer determined in part i) and dividing by 10,000.

iii) Working backwards, using time phasing and the lead times determined in step ii), determine the order dates for each component.

Answer:

Components	Net Requirements	Lead Time (in weeks)	Order Date (in weeks)
Oven	25,000	2.5	9.5
Magnetron Tube	15,000	6.0	3.5
Control Panel Assembly	23,000	4.6	4.9
Circuitry Assembly	19,000	1.9	3.0
Microprocessor Chip	10,000	3.0	0
LED Display	17,000	3.4	1.5
Heat Sensor Pad	20,000	4.0	.9
Temperature Probe	5,000	3.0	6.5
Cabinet	20,000	2.0	7.5
Inner Shell	17,000	3.4	4.1
Mixer Assembly	9,000	2.7	1.4
Mixer Motor	6,000	.6	.8
Mixer Blade	7,000	1.4	0
Outer Shell	13,000	5.2	2.3

18) Weber Appliance Company is gearing up for Christmas production of its La Guillotine food processor. The following is a bill of material chart for the food processor.

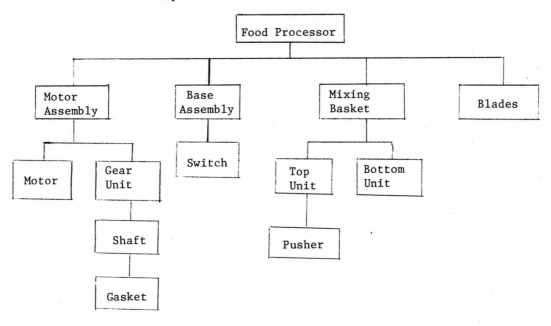

The company wishes to manufacture 15,000 additional units within the next 13 weeks. The following table gives the current inventory and lead time for each component in the food processor.

Component	Current Inventory	Lead Time (in weeks)
Food Processor	0	1
Motor Assembly	5,000	2
Motor	2,000	5
Gear Unit	6,000	3
Shaft	1,000	4
Gasket	4,000	5
Base Assembly	3,000	4
Switch	3,000	3
Mixing Basket	5,000	1
Top Unit	2,000	9
Pusher	1,000	2
Bottom Unit	4,000	8
Blades	7,000	10

Use MRP to determine the net requirements and order times for each component.

* 19) Dicom Corporation is planning to manufacture a personal micro computer for home and office use. Dicom has obtained a contract from Radio Hut to deliver 3,000 units. The following is the bill of material chart for the personal micro computer.

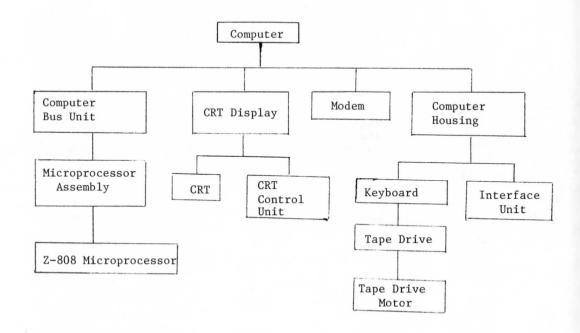

Dicom's objective is to manufacture the 3,000 computers as quickly as possible. The following table gives the current inventory and lead time for each component going into the computer.

Component	Units in Inventory	Lead Time per 1,000 Units (in weeks)
Computer	0	2
Computer Bus Unit	500	3
Microprocessor Assembly	200	1
Z-808 Mircoprocessor	1,000	4
CRT Display	300	2
CRT	200	5
CRT Control Unit	400	2
Modem	1,600	1
Computer Housing	0	3
Keyboard	2,100	2
Tape Drive	700	4
Tape Drive Motor	800	5
Interface Unit	500	4

On the basis of this information, how quickly can Dicom manufacture the 3,000 computers?

13 INVENTORY MODELS WITH PROBABILISTIC DEMAND

KEY CONCEPTS

1. Order quantity--reorder point models

2. Single period inventory models with a small
    number of possible demand values

3. Single period inventory models with a large
    number of possible demand values

REVIEW

1. Order Quantity--Reorder Point Models

In most cases demand in an inventory problem is not known in advance. For these situations a probabilistic demand inventory model should be used. Because of the mathematical complexity of such models approximation techniques are often employed. One method of obtaining a good approximation for the solution is to solve the problem assuming that the demand is known and equal to the expected or average demand. For example, in the EOQ model one would use the expected demand as the value for D to calculate Q*. Because Q* does not vary significantly with moderate changes in D in the EOQ model, this solution will be very close to optimal.

To decide when to reorder, a service level giving the proportion of time a stockout will be tolerated must be specified and an estimated lead time must be given. If the lead time demand distribution is assumed to be a normal distribution, with μ = the average demand during the lead time, and σ = the standard deviation of demand during lead time then the reorder point, r, is:

$$r = \mu + z\sigma .$$

Here z is the number of standard deviations necessary to achieve the acceptable stockout probability. The quantity $z\sigma$ is called the <u>safety stock</u>.

2. Single Period Inventory Model With a Small Number of Demands

The <u>single period inventory model</u>, sometimes referred to as the <u>newsboy problem</u>, deals with a situation in which demand is probabilistic. Additonally, only one order is placed for the item and any unsold items at the end of the period are sold for salvage value (which could be 0 or even a negative amount). Hence, for this model there are no inventory holding costs.

When there are a small number of possible demand values for this model then it is practical to develop a payoff table. The payoffs will depend both upon the action taken (the quantity ordered) and the state of nature (the actual demand). These payoffs are therefore referred to as <u>conditional payoffs</u> or profits. Then, given the probabilistic distribution for demand, the expected monetary value criterion can be used to determine the optimal order quantity.

3. Single Period Inventory Model With a Large Number of Demands

In many single period inventory problems there are a large number of different values that the demand and order quantity can take on. In these cases it is best to approximate the demand by a continuous probability distribution. The technique used to obtain the optimal decision alternative in such cases is called <u>incremental analysis</u>. In incremental analysis the opportunity loss incurred in not increasing the decision alternative by one unit is divided by the sum of this opportunity loss and the opportunity loss incurred by increasing the decision alternative by one unit. The optimal decision, Q^*, is the smallest value such that the probability of the state of nature being less than or equal to Q^* is greater than or equal to this opportunity loss ratio. For example, if we are trying to determine the optimal order quantity, Q^*, we must first determine L_S, the loss of stocking one unit and finding it would not be sold, and L_{NS}, the loss of not stocking one unit and finding it could have been sold. If the demand is known to be D then Q^* is the smallest value such that $P(D \leq Q^*) \geq \dfrac{L_{NS}}{L_S + L_{NS}}$.

GLOSSARY

INCREMENTAL OR MARGINAL ANALYSIS - The solution technique whereby the
analyst considers the marginal profit or cost associated with
incrementing the order quantity by 1 unit.   (547)

LEAD TIME DEMAND DISTRIBUTION - Probability distribution of demand during
lead time.   (540)

PROBABILISTIC DEMAND - Situations in which demand for an item is given
by a probability distribution rather than a fixed number.   (538)

SINGLE-PERIOD INVENTORY MODELS - Inventory models in which it is assumed
that only one order is placed for the product, and at the end of
the period the item has either sold out or there is a surplus of
unsold items which will be sold for a salvage value.   (542)

SERVICE LEVEL - The percentage of stockouts that are allowed per year.   (541)

Chapter 13 Check List

W 1) Roberts Drugs is a drug wholesaler supplying 55 independent drug
stores. Roberts wishes to determine an optimal inventory policy for
COMFORT brand headache remedy. Sales of COMFORT are relatively
constant as the past 10 weeks of data indicate.

Week	Sales	Week	Sales
1	110 cases	6	120 cases
2	115 "	7	130 "
3	125 "	8	115 "
4	120 "	9	110 "
5	125 "	10	130 "

a) Each case of COMFORT costs Roberts $10.00 and Roberts uses a 14%
annual holding cost rate for its inventory. If the cost to
prepare a purchase order for COMFORT is $12.00 determine the
optimal inventory order quantity for COMFORT.

b) The lead time for a delivery of COMFORT has averaged four working
days. Lead time demand has therefore been estimated to have a
normal distribution with a mean of 80 cases and a standard
deviation of 10 cases. Roberts wants at most a 2% probability of
selling out of COMFORT. What should the reorder point be?

c) On the basis of parts a) and b) determine the total annual
inventory cost for COMFORT.

SOLUTION:

a) The average sales over the 10 week period is (110 + 115 + 125 +
120 + 125 + 120 + 130 + 115 + 110 + 130)/10 = 120 cases. Hence,
D = 120 x 52 = 6,240 cases per year
C_h = IC = .14(10.) = $1.40 per item per year in inventory
C_o = $12.00 per order

and $Q* = \sqrt{\dfrac{2DC_o}{C_h}} = \sqrt{\dfrac{2(6240)(12)}{1.40}} \approx 327$.

b) Lead time demand is normally distributed with μ = 80, σ = 10.
Since Roberts wants at most a 2% probability of selling out of
COMFORT the corresponding z value (see Appendix A) is 2.06. That
is, $P(z > 2.06)$ = .0197. Hence, Roberts should reorder COMFORT
when its supply reaches $\mu + z\sigma$ = 80 + 2.06(10) = 101 cases.
Safety stock is 21 cases.

391

c) The total annual costs of this solution are

ORDERING COST: $\quad (\frac{D}{Q})\ C_o = (\frac{6240}{327})12 \qquad\qquad = \$229.$

HOLDING COST—NORMAL INVENTORY: $\quad (\frac{Q}{2})\ C_o = (\frac{327}{2})1.40 = \$229.$

HOLDING COST—SAFETY STOCK: $\quad 21C_h = 21(1.40) \qquad = \$\ 29.$

$$\text{TOTAL} \qquad \$487.$$

O 2) Allied Sound is the distributor for Welsh cassette recording tape in Tangerine County. Demand for cassettes has been averaging 50 gross per week and the company purchases the recording tape from Welsh at $100 per gross. Allied uses a 19% annual holding cost rate for inventory and the order cost is $20 per order. Delivery time for an order of Welsh cassette tape is approximately 3 days during which time sales are normally distributed with a mean of 30 gross and standard deviation of 16 gross. If Allied wishes to experience an average of only two stockouts per year, determine an optimal inventory policy for Allied and the cost of such a policy.

Outline of Solution:

    i)   Solve for Q* using the EOQ formula.

    ii) Determine the number of orders per year (= D/Q*).

    iii) Determine the probability of a stockout (= 2/(number of orders per year)).

    iv) Find the z value which gives this probability in the upper tail area.

    v)   Calculate $r = \mu + z\sigma$.

    vi) Calculate the total cost = ordering cost + holding cost of normal inventory + holding cost of safety stock.

Answers:

    Q* = 74 gross

    r = 55 gross

    TC = $1,881.

3) Tennis Man's World has noted that its sales of tennis balls in Southern California is relatively constant at about 104,000 per year. The balls cost Tennis Man's World .75 each. Holding costs are figured at 10% per year and reorder costs amount to $35 per order with a lead time of two weeks. Although in two weeks the average amount ordered is (104,000/52 x 2) = 4,000 the distribution of demand is approximately normally distributed with a standard deviation of 1,400 balls. Develop an inventory policy for Tennis Man's World that will allow stockouts on only 2% of the orders. Why would this not be a good model if Tennis Man's World were in North Dakota?

* 4) Kelley's Service Station does a large business in tune-ups. Demand has been averaging 210 spark plugs per week. Holding costs are $.01 per plug per week and reorder costs are estimated at $10 per order. Kelley does not want to be out of stock on any more than 1% of his orders. There is one day delivery time. The standard deviation is five plugs per day. Assume a normal distribution of demand during lead time.

a) What inventory policy do you suggest for Kelley's Service Station?

b) What is the average amount of safety stock for the reorder point in (a)?

c) What are the total weekly costs including safety stock costs?

5) Barry's Barometer Business (problem 1 of Chapter 12) has experienced more fluctuation in the demand than at first predicted. Although demand still averages about 500 super deluxe barometers per year, the assumed constant demand during the lead time has been approximately normally distributed with a mean of 30 and a standard deviation of 8.

a) What is the reorder point if BBB will tolerate no more than an average of one stockout per year?

b) What is the safety stock level and the annual safety stock costs for the reorder point in (a)?

W 6) AML Vending has just received a contract from the city to install a vending machine for bus route maps at the corner of Main and Vine Streets. The vending machine can hold 200 maps and sales per day are normally distributed with a mean of 10 maps and a standard deviation of 2 maps. (Note that this implies that over a K day period sales will be normally distributed with a mean of 10K maps and a standard deviation of $2\sqrt{K}$ maps.)

AML's contract with the city specifies that the vending machines must be filled at regular intervals. Also they must be filled frequently enough so that on average at most twice per year the company will be filling an empty machine. How frequently should AML fill the vending machine?

SOLUTION:

Suppose AML fills the machine every 20 days. Sales during these 20 days will be normally distributed with $\mu = 200$, $\sigma = 8.9$. Hence, on the average half the time the company would fill an empty machine.

If AML fills the machine every 19 days sales during the 19 days will be $N(\mu = 190, \sigma = 8.72)$. Hence the probability of selling 200 or more maps is $P(z \geq \frac{200 - 190}{8.72}) = P(z \geq 1.15) = .1251$. Therefore there is a 12.1% chance of the machine running out of maps in 19 days. If the company fills the machine every 19 days then they are filling the machine an average of 19.2 times per year. Hence the average number of times a year the machine will be empty is 2.4 (= .125 x 19.2).

If AML fills the machine every 18 days sales during this period will be $N(\mu = 180, \sigma = 8.49)$. Hence the probability of selling 200 or more routes is $P(z \geq \frac{200 - 180}{8.49})$. $= P(z \geq 2.36) = .0091$. If the company fills the machine every 18 days, it will be filling the machine 20.28 times per year and will therefore fill an empty machine on the average of .18 times per year. Since .18 is less than 2, the company should fill the machine every 18 days.

7) Suppose in problem 6) that the sales per day of bus route maps is normally distributed with a mean of 15 maps and a standard deviation of 5 maps. This implies that over a K day period sales will be normally distributed with a mean of 15K maps and a standard deviation of $5\sqrt{K}$ maps. If all other data is the same as in problem 6) determine how frequently AML must fill the vending machines.

W 8) A newstand must order the same number of newspapers each day. On a good newsday it figures it can sell 500 papers, on an average newsday 300 papers, and on a slow newsday 200 papers. The papers come in batches of 50 and the distributor will not split the batches. The papers cost 5¢ each and sell for 15¢. If demand is greater than supply the newstand figures a goodwill cost of 3¢ per paper it is short. If supply is greater than demand, the papers can be sold for recycling at a rate of 2¢ each. If the probabilities for a good, average, or slow newsday are .3, .5 and .2 respectively, what order quantity should be used?

SOLUTION:

There are three possible demands for paper

$$P(200 \text{ demanded}) = .3$$
$$P(300 \text{ demanded}) = .5$$
$$P(500 \text{ demanded}) = .2$$

The newstand can order in quantities of 50 papers. Since demand will never be less than 200 nor greater than 500 it only makes sense to order a quantity between 200 and 500. If the newstand orders an amount of papers d_i and the amount of papers demanded are s_j then the profit equals the revenue on the papers sold ($.15s_j$) minus the cost of the papers ($.05d_i$) plus salvage value (0 if $d_i \le s_j$ and $.02(d_i - s_j)$ otherwise) minus the goodwill cost (0 if $d_i \ge s_j$ and $.03(s_j - d_i)$ otherwise). Hence

$$\text{Profit } (d_i, s_j) = .15s_j - .05d_i + \max[0, .02(d_i - s_j)]$$
$$- \max[0, .03(s_j - d_i)]$$

For example, if the newstand orders 400 papers and sells 300 its profit equals $.15(300) - .05(400) + .02(100) - 0 = \$27$. Using this profit formula we get the following payoff table.

States of Nature

Decisions	s_1 200 sold	s_2 300 sold	s_3 500 sold
d_1 = orders 200	20	17	11
d_2 = " 250	18.50	23.50	17.50
d_3 = " 300	17	30	24
d_4 = " 350	15.50	28.50	30.50
d_5 = " 400	14	27	37
d_6 = " 450	12.50	25.50	43.50
d_7 = " 500	11	24	50

Using the probability distribution for demand we have

$$EV(d_1) = .3(20) \quad + .5(17) \quad + .2(11) \quad = \$16.70$$

$$EV(d_2) = .3(18.50) + .5(23.50) + .2(17.50) = \$20.80$$

$$EV(d_3) = .3(17) \quad + .5(30) \quad + .2(24) \quad = \$24.90$$

$$EV(d_4) = .3(15.50) + .5(28.50) + .2(30.50) = \$25.00$$

$$EV(d_5) = .3(14) \quad + .5(27) \quad + .2(37) \quad = \$25.10$$

$$EV(d_6) = .3(12.50) + .5(25.50) + .2(43.50) = \$25.20$$

$$EV(d_7) = .3(11) \quad + .5(24) \quad + .2(50) \quad = \$25.30$$

Therefore the optimal decision for the newstand is to order 500 papers.

0 9) Williams Supply Company is the authorized retail dealer for Husky Tractors. Williams must place its order for tractors four months prior to delivery and is unable to obtain additional tractors during the principal sales season. Williams estimates that its demand for the Husky model 2413 tractor will be between 0 and 4 tractors for the season. The tractors cost Williams $12,000 each plus a delivery charge of $3,000 which is independent of the quantity ordered. After subtracting overhead and related expenses Williams nets $14,200 on each tractor sold. Tractors unsold by the end of the season are marked down in price so that Williams nets $11,500 each. For each customer Williams loses because of a shortage of tractors the company estimates it incurs a goodwill cost of $350.

Williams' management believes that they are as likely to encounter a demand for 0 tractors as they are for 4 tractors. They believe that the demand for 2 tractors will be equal to the demand for 3 tractors and will be twice as great as the demand for 1 tractor. The demand for 1 tractor will be three times as great as the demand for 0 tractors. Determine an optimal inventory policy for Williams Supply Company.

Outline of Solution:

   i)   Solve for the state of nature probabilities by noting the relative likelihoods of demand and that the probabilities must sum to 1.

   ii) Determine the payoff table. Note that the cost of buying x tractors = $3,000 + $12,000 x if x > 0 and $0 if x = 0 and PROFIT = SALES REVENUE − COST OF GOODS − GOODWILL COST.

   iii) Calculate the expected profit for each order quantity by multiplying for each decision the probabilities found in i) by the payoffs found in ii) and summing.

   iv) Choose the decision with the largest payoff found in (iii).

Answer: Order 3 tractors, expect profit = $1,197.

10) Bill Gale operates a small contracting firm specializing in single family dwellings. Bill has learned through a friend that one of his competitors is leaving the business and has 20 new kitchen stoves to sell. The stoves normally cost Bill $375 each, but the competitor is willing to sell them for $340 each. Bill estimates that any stoves purchased from the competitor which are unused by the end of the year will have to be sold at a discounted price of $300. Bill expects to build between 6 and 9 homes this year with the following probability estimates:

$$P(6 \text{ built}) = .20$$
$$P(7 \text{ built}) = .30$$
$$P(8 \text{ built}) = .40$$
$$P(9 \text{ built}) = .10 \ .$$

How many stoves should Bill purchase from his competitor?

* 11) The Chez Paul Restaurant is an exclusive French restaurant which serves only 10 couples for dinner. Paul is famous for his "truffle salad for two" which must be prepared one day in advance. It costs Paul $7 to prepare each salad and its menu price is $20. Unsold salads are thrown away in the garbage. Paul believes that if a couple orders the salad and he is sold out he suffers a goodwill cost of $15. Demand for the salads has the following distribution.

$$P(1 \text{ salad ordered}) = .05$$
$$P(2 \text{ salads ordered}) = .15$$
$$P(3 \quad " \quad " \quad) = .20$$
$$P(4 \quad " \quad " \quad) = .30$$
$$P(5 \quad " \quad " \quad) = .20$$
$$P(6 \quad " \quad " \quad) = .10$$

Based on this information, how many "truffle salads for two" should Paul prepare?

W 12)   The publishers of the <u>Fast Food Restaurant Menu Book</u> wish to determine how many copies to print. It costs \$5,000 to produce the book
and the profit per book is \$.45. Sales for this edition are
estimated to be normally distributed. The most likely sales volume
is 12,000 copies and they believe there is a 5% chance that sales
will exceed 20,000.

   a)   If any unsold copies of the book can be sold at salvage at a
        \$.55 loss, how many copies should be printed?

   b)   If any unsold copies of the book can be sold at a \$.65 loss,
        how many copies should be printed?

SOLUTION:

   a) μ = 12,000.   To find σ note that z = 1.65 corresponds to a 5%
        probability.   Therefore (20,000 – 12,000) = 1.65σ or σ = 4848.
        Using incremental analysis

$$L_S = .55$$

$$L_{NS} = .45$$

$$\frac{L_{NS}}{L_{NS} + L_S} = .45$$

Find Q* such that $P(D \leq Q^*)$ = .45

Z = –.12

Q* = 12,000 – .12(4848) = 11,418 books.

   b)   Using incremental analysis

$$L_S = .65$$

$$L_{NS} = .45$$

$$\frac{L_{NS}}{L_S + L_{NS}} = \frac{.45}{1.1} = .4091$$

Therefore we wish to find Q* such that

$P(D \leq Q^*)$ = .4091

Z = –.23

Q* = 12,000 – (.23)(4848) = 10,885

However, since this is less than the breakeven volumne
($\frac{5,000}{.45}$ = 11,111) no copies should be printed.   That is,
if the company only prints 10,885 copies it will not recoup
the \$5,000 fixed cost of producing the book.

O 13) In order to obtain a sales contract for a nuclear generator Eastern
Electric has agreed to supply uranium to the utility for one year.
Eastern estimates that the demand of the utility for uranium will be
uniformly distributed between 1 and 4 tons. Eastern currently has
the option of purchasing uranium in bulk at $60 per pound. Uranium
bought after this time will cost $70 per pound. At the end of the
year Eastern plans to sell all remaining uranium at $55 per pound.
If Eastern charges the utility $62 per pound for uranium use incre-
mental analysis to determine the amount of uranium Eastern should
purchase in bulk.

Outline of Solution:

  i) L_S = (cost of uranium − salvage value)

      L_{NS} = (selling price − cost of uranium) + goodwill cost

  ii) Determine $P(D < Q^*) = \dfrac{L_{NS}}{L_S + L_{NS}}$

  iii) Since demand is uniform between 1 and 4 tons,
        $Q^* = 1 + P(D < Q^*)(4-1)$.

  Answer: $Q^* = 3$ tons.

14) Dollar Department Stores is contemplating ordering a quantity of designer's original scarves for the fall fashion season. The scarves will sell for $3.00 each. Dollar can purchase the scarves at $1.75 each and dispose of any unsold scarves at its one-half price clearance sale. Dollar estimates the demand for scarves to be normally distributed.

a) If μ = 500 and σ = 100, how many scarves should Dollar purchase?

b) If μ = 500 and σ = 50, how many scarves should Dollar purchase?

c) If μ = 500, σ = 50 and there is an opportunity cost of $.30 for every customer who desires a scarf when Dollar has sold out, then how many scarves should Dollar order?

15) Amazing Bakers sells bread to 40 supermarkets. It costs Amazing $1,250 per day to operate its plant. The profit per loaf of bread sold in the supermarket is $.025. Any unsold bread is returned to be sold at the Amazing Thrift Store at a loss of $.015.

a) If sales follow a normal distribution with μ = 70,000 and σ = 5,000. How many loaves should Amazing bake?

b) Amazing is considering a different sales plan for which the profit per loaf of bread sold in the supermarket is $.030 and the loss per loaf of bread returned equals $.018. If μ = 60,000 and σ = 4,000 how many loaves should Amazing now bake?

* 16) Winkies Donuts is a small chain of donut shops in Lemon County.
Winkies' success is built largely around its jelly donut. Recently,
Winkies management has received a number of complaints concerning
store #17 running out of jelly donuts in the late afternoon.
Consequently, Winkies has undertaken a study of the store's opera-
tions.

The study has indicated the following:

(1) Demand for jelly donuts each afternoon is approximately
normally distributed with a mean of 150 donuts and a standard
deviation of 30 donuts.

(2) The cost to manufacture a jelly donut is 9¢.

(3) The selling price is 20¢.

(4) Donuts unsold at the end of the day are donated to a local
charity which gives Winkies a tax savings of 3¢ per donut.

Additionally, Winkies management feels that there is a goodwill loss
of 75¢ for each customer who comes into the shop wanting a jelly
donut, but cannot buy one because the store is sold out. Based on
this information, how many jelly donuts should the baker prepare for
the afternoon selling period?

14

COMPUTER SIMULATION

REVIEW

1. Setting Up the Computer Model

Computer simulation is a procedure that attempts to recreate a
problem situation under study by developing a computer model of the process.
Typically it is used to model random processes that are too complex to be
solved by analytic techniques. The advantage of using the computer is that
many different policies and scenarios can be compared in a relatively short
amount of time.

The first step in a computer simulation is to develop a mathematical statement of the problem. This model should be as realistic as
possible with the only limitations imposed by the time and storage requirements of the resulting program. Following the construction of the mathematical model, values for each of the variables must be determined. In
cases where one or more of the problem inputs are random variables, it is
necessary to obtain estimates for the probability distributions of these
variables.

2. Monte Carlo Simulation

Inputs of the random variables for the computer simulation are determined to correspond to their estimated probability distributions. Random numbers are generated by the computer program, with each number being matched to a specific random variable value. The matching is done in such a way that the resulting random variables follow the estimated probability distributions. This procedure is called Monte Carlo simulation. To incorporate Monte Carlo simulation into a computer program it is necessary to generate the random numbers by using mathematical formulae. Because the "random numbers" used in a computer simulation are not truly random, they are called pseudo-random numbers.

3. Use of The Computer

For each policy under consideration by the decision maker, the computer program evaluates that policy by considering many different sequences of input data. Each sequence is determined by the random variable values obtained through the pseudo-random number generation. The number of different sequences of input data which should be considered for each policy should be determined so that the results are meaningful. The primary consideration in this regard is the amount of time required by the computer program to perform the calculations. For each policy the same set of pseudo-random numbers should be used so that comparisons between policies do not differ due to different sample distributions for the random variables.

It is common terminology to refer to the computer program that performs the simulation as the simulator. Special programming languages have been developed to enable analysts to more easily input simulation models into a computer. Two of the more common languages in use today are GPSS (General Purpose Simulation System) and SIMSCRIPT.

4. Advantages and Disadvantages of Computer Simulation

The biggest advantage of computer simulation is that is is a useful solution procedure for problems that are too complex to be solved by other management science techniques. Another advantage is that the simulation provides a convenient experimental laboratory. Once the computer program has been developed it is usually relatively easy to experiment with the model. Sensitivity analysis on the parameters and random variables can be conveniently performed.

There are two major disadvantages to computer simulation: (1) a large amount of time may be required to develop the program; and, (2) there is no guarantee that the solution obtained by the simulation will actually be optimal. Typically however, the solution will be either optimal or near optimal.

GPSS AND SIMSCRIPT - Two commonly used computer programming languages used for simulation studies. (578)

MONTE CARLO SIMULATION - Simulations that use a random number procedure to create values for the probabilistic components of a simulation model. (576)

PSEUDO-RANDOM NUMBERS - Computer-generated numbers developed from mathematical formulae which have the properties of random numbers. (576)

SIMULATION - A procedure that involves developing a model to recreate the process or system under study. Most often this technique employs a computer model (computer program) to recreate the process and then, by trial-and-error experiments, identifies near-optimal solutions. (561)

SIMULATOR - The computer program written to perform the simulation calculations. (578)

Chapter 14 Check List

W 1) The price change of shares of Probaballistics, Inc. has been observed over the past 50 trades. The frequency distribution is as follows:

PRICE CHANGE	FREQUENCY (Number of Trades)
-3/8	4
-1/4	2
-1/8	8
0	20
1/8	10
1/4	3
3/8	2
1/2	1
	50

a) Develop a relatively frequency distribution for this data.

b) If the current price per share of Probaballistics, Inc. is 23, use random numbers to simulate the price per share over the next 20 trades.

c) Compare this price with the expected price one would obtain based on the probability distribution.

SOLUTION:

a) To develop a relative frequency distribution for this data we divide the frequency of each price change by the total number of trades.

Answer:

PRICE CHANGE	RELATIVE FREQUENCY
-3/8	.08
-1/4	.04
-1/8	.16
0	.40
1/8	.20
1/4	.06
3/8	.04
1/2	.02
	1.00

b) To develop a simulation for the future price we must assign a random number to each price change so that the probability of seeing a certain price change corresponds to its probability. One such assignment for numbers between 00 and 99 is as follows:

PRICE CHANGE	RANGE OF NUMBERS
-3/8	00-07
-1/4	08-11
-1/8	12-27
0	28-67
1/8	68-87
1/4	88-93
3/8	94-97
1/2	98-99

Let us choose our pseudo-random numbers from column one beginning at the bottom and moving up. Thus, the first random number chosen is 21 (bottom left hand corner of Appendix B), and the price of the stock will decrease from 23 to 22 7/8. Continuing moving up the left hand column of Appendix B we have the following results:

TRADE #	RANDOM NUMBER	PRICE CHANGE	STOCK PRICE
1	21	-1/8	22 7/8
2	84	1/8	23
3	07	-3/8	22 5/8
4	30	0	22 5/8
5	94	3/8	23
6	57	0	23
7	57	0	23
8	19	-1/8	22 7/8
9	84	1/8	23
10	84	1/8	23 1/8
11	62	0	23 1/8
12	32	0	23 1/8
13	71	1/8	23 1/4
14	94	3/8	23 5/8
15	04	-3/8	23 1/4
16	97	3/8	23 5/8
17	58	0	23 5/8
18	67	0	23 5/8
19	78	1/8	23 3/4
20	14	-1/8	23 5/8

c) Based on the probability distribution, the expected price change per
    trade = (.08)(-3/8) + (.04)(-1/4) + (.16)(-1/8) + (.40)(0)
          + (.20)(1/8) + (.06)(1/4) + (.04)(3/8) + (.02)(1/2) = .005.

    Hence, after 20 trades we would expect a price of 23 + 20(.005)
    = 23.10.

0 2) Shelly's Supermarket has just installed a postage stamp vending machine.
      Based on a month of operation, Shelly's estimates the number of postage
      stamps sold per day can be approximated by the following distribution.

NUMBER SOLD PER DAY	PROBABILITY
20	.10
30	.15
40	.20
50	.25
60	.20
70	.10

Shelly's makes a profit of 2¢ per postage stamp. The vending machine
holds 230 stamps and it costs Shelly's $2.00 in labor to fill the
machine.

a) Determine the mean number of stamps sold per day.

b) Determine the mean time until the machine empties.

c) Assume Shelly's adopts the policy of filling the machine at the
    beginning of every nth day, where n is the answer in part b).
    Conduct a 20 day simulation and determine the expected profit per
    day. Assume the machine is filled on the first day.

Outline of Solution:

a) Mean number of stamps sold per day = (.10)(20) + (.15)(30)
                                       + (.20)(40) + (.25)(50)
                                       + (.20)(60) + (.10)(70) = 46.

b) Mean time until the machine empties equals

    $$\frac{\text{Machine capacity}}{\text{Mean number of stamps sold per day}} = \frac{230}{46} = 5 \text{ days}.$$

c) Assume Shelly's fills the machine every 5th day.

    i) Determine a set of random numbers corresponding to each sales
        level.

NUMBER SOLD PER DAY	RANGE OF NUMBERS
20	00-09
30	10-24
40	25-44
50	45-69
60	70-89
70	90-99

ii) Starting with, for example, the first two numbers of column 3 in Appendix B and working down the column we have the following simulation:

DAY	NUMBER	DEMAND	NUMBER OF STAMPS LEFT IN MACHINE	PROFIT ON SALE OF STAMPS	COST OF REFILLING MACHINE	DAILY PROFIT
1	71	60	170	1.20	2.00	-.80
2	95	70	100	1.40	0	1.40
3	83	60	40	1.20	0	1.20
4	44	40	0	.80	0	.80
5	34	40	0*	0	0	0
6	49	50	180	1.00	2.00	-1.00
7	88	60	120	1.20	0	1.20
8	56	50	70	1.00	0	1.00
9	05	20	50	.40	0	.40
10	39	40	10	.80	0	.80
11	75	60	170	1.20	2.00	-.80
12	12	30	140	.60	0	.60
13	03	20	120	.40	0	.40
14	59	50	70	1.00	0	1.00
15	29	40	30	.80	0	.80
16	77	60	170	1.20	2.00	-.80
17	76	60	110	1.20	0	1.20
18	57	50	60	1.00	0	1.00
19	15	30	30	.60	0	.60
20	53	50	0	.60**	0	.60

TOTAL PROFIT $9.60

EXPECTED PROFIT PER DAY $\frac{\$9.60}{20} = \$ .48$

*Since machine is empty
**Since machine only has 30 stamps left

416

3) Suppose in problem 2) Shelly's Supermarket decides to fill the postage machine every 4th day. Conduct a 20 day simulation and determine the expected profit per day for this policy. Compare this answer to that in problem 2). Which policy would you recommend?

4) Global Airlines is trying to determine how often to perform routine maintenance on its jet engines. After any maintenance is performed the number of days until failure is a random variable with the following distribution.

NUMBER OF DAYS AFTER MAINTENANCE THAT FAILURE WILL OCCUR	PROBABILITY
1	.10
2	.20
3	.30
4	.40

If a jet engine fails before its next routine maintenance, it costs Global $10,000 for a major overhaul maintenance job. Routine maintenance however only costs $1,000. On the basis of this information simulate the maintenance cost of a jet over a 20 day period where routine maintenance is performed

a) Two days after the last maintenance
b) Three days after the last maintenance
c) Four days after the last maintenance

* 5) Consider the following PERT problem.

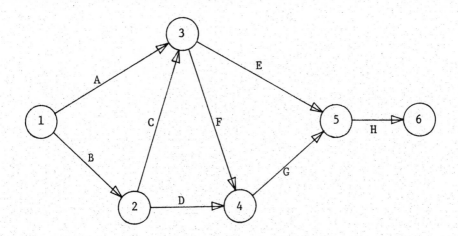

The expected completion line of each job is given as follows:

JOB	EXPECTED COMPLETION TIME IN WEEKS
A	7
B	4
C	3
D	6
E	5
F	3
G	3
H	4

a) Determine the critical path(s) and expected completion time of this
project.

b) Suppose that each job has a 25% chance of being completed in a week
less than its expected completion time and a 25% chance of being
completed in a week more than its expected completion time. Do a
5 trial simulation to determine the average completion time of this
project. Compare this answer to the answer in part a).

W 6) Wilson Motors currently has 10 Mini Cars in stock. Five gold, 3 silver, and 2 blue. Each day there will be between 0 and 3 car purchases with the following probabilities.

$$P(0 \text{ customers}) = .1$$
$$P(1 \text{ customer}) = .4$$
$$P(2 \text{ customers}) = .3$$
$$P(3 \text{ customers}) = .2$$

The probability of a customer wanting a particular colored car is as follows:

$$P(\text{gold}) = .4$$
$$P(\text{silver}) = .3$$
$$P(\text{blue}) = .3$$

If Wilson is out of a particular colored car, the customer leaves without purchasing a car.

a) Simulate Wilson's car sales over a 5-day interval (choose random numbers from columns 1 and 2).

b) If Wilson earns $200 on each car sold and suffers a goodwill loss of $50 for each customer who leaves without purchasing a car, how much do they earn on Mini Cars during these 5 days?

c) Repeat this simulation choosing the random numbers from columns 3 and 4. Compare with your answer to (b). Comment.

SOLUTION:

Develop random number mappings for both the number of customers arriving per day and the choice of colors.

# of Customers	Random #
0	0
1	1,2,3,4
2	5,6,7
3	8,9

Color	Random #
Gold	0,1,2,3,
Silver	4,5,6
Blue	7,8,9

Each day a random number must be selected to determine the number of customers and <u>for each</u> customer a random number must be selected to determine the color choice.

a) Choosing the random numbers from columns 1 and 2 gives the following simulation.

Day	Random #*	Customer	Random #**	Color Desired	Gold	Silver	Blue	Profit
1	6	1	5	silver	5	2	2	$200
		2	0	gold	4	2	2	$200
2	8	3	5	silver	4	1	2	$200
		4	8	blue	4	1	1	$200
		5	0	gold	3	1	1	$200
3	5	6	9	blue	3	1	0	$200
		7	2	gold	2	1	0	$200
4	4	8	2	gold	1	1	0	$200
5	5	9	6	silver	1	0	0	$200
		10	3	gold	0	0	0	$200

*First digit of column 1, Appendix B
**First digit of column 2, Appendix B

b) The profit from this simulation is $2,000.

c) Choosing the random numbers from columns 3 and 4 gives the following simulation.

Day	Random #*	Customer	Random #**	Color Demanded	Remaining Inventory Gold	Silver	Blue	Profit
1	7	1	5	silver	5	2	2	$200
		2	7	blue	5	2	1	$200
2	9	3	0	gold	4	2	1	$200
		4	6	silver	4	1	1	$200
		5	1	gold	3	1	1	$200
3	8	6	5	silver	3	0	1	$200
		7	0	gold	2	0	1	$200
		8	7	blue	2	0	0	$200
4	4	9	3	gold	1	0	0	$200
5	3	10	5	silver	1	0	0	$-50

*First digit of column 3, Appendix B
**First digit of column 4, Appendix B

c) For this simulation the profit is $1,750.

422

7) The soda vending machine at Shelly's Supermarket stocks 3 flavors of soda: Cola, Root Beer, and Lemon-Lime. The probability of a customer selecting one of the three flavors is as follows:

$$P(Cola) = .5$$
$$P(Root\ Beer) = .2$$
$$P(Lemon-Lime) = .3$$

The following is the probability distribution of the number of customers in a <u>five minute</u> interval.

$$P(0\ customers) = .3$$
$$P(1\ customer) = .4$$
$$P(2\ customers) = .3$$

Assume initially the vending machine has 3 bottles of Cola, 2 bottles of Root Beer and 4 bottles of Lemon Lime. A customer desiring a flavor which is sold out will leave without making a purchase. Conduct a 40 minute simulation of the soda vending machine. How much of each of the 3 types of soda will be left at the end of the 40 minutes?

W 8) Global Airlines must decide how many reservations to accept on its
evening transatlantic flight. Global earns a profit of $20 per
passenger, however there is only a 90% probability of a person holding
a reservation actually showing up for the flight. Because of government regulations any passenger holding a reservation who is bumped from
a flight because of overbooking will cause a loss to Global of $450.
Assume the plane can carry 200 passengers. Also assume that if Global
accepts reservations for n seats, the number of passengers who actually
fly will be normally distributed with mean equal to .9n and variance
equal to .09n. Using simulation determine the average profit per
flight over 15 trips if the company accepts n = 220 reservations.

SOLUTION:

Since n = 220 the number of passengers who actually fly is normally

distributed with mean μ = .9(220) = 198, and σ^2 = .09(220) = 19.8
(σ = 4.45).
To conduct a simulation of the normal distribution we must

  1) Choose a random value, y, between 0 and 1.

  2) Determine, using Appendix A, the largest value of z such that
      $P(Z \leq z) \leq y$.

  3) Convert this value of z into the actual X value using the
      formula $X = \mu + z\sigma$.

  4) Once we have the value for X we evaluate the resulting profit
      per flight using the formula: PROFIT = (PROFIT PER PASSENGER) x
      (NUMBER PASSENGERS FLYING) - (LOSS PER PASSENGER DUE TO
      OVERBOOKING) x (NUMBER PASSENGERS OVERBOOKED)
      = (20)(min[X, 200]) - (450)(max[0, X - 200])

For example, let us use for our simulation the left hand column of
Appendix B. Then our first random number is y = .6327. Using Appendix
A we see that this value corresponds to z = .34; e.g. P(z $\leq$ .34) = .5
+ .1293 = .6293 < .6327. Our first simulation trial value for X is therefore 198 + (.34)$\overline{(4.45)}$ = (199.5). The expected profit of this flight
is therefore (199.5)($20) = $3,990. Continuing down the column we have
the following simulation.

TRIP	(APPENDIX B) RANDOM #	(APPENDIX A) Z	X	PROFIT
1	.6327	.34	199.5	3,990
2	.8854	1.21	203.4	2,470
3	.5595	.15	198.7	3,974
4	.4627	-.09	197.6	3,952
5	.5536	.14	198.6	3,972
6	.6939	.51	200.3	3,865
7	.1318	-1.11	193.1	3,862
8	.1772	-.92	193.9	3,878
9	.3652	-.34	196.5	3,930
10	.8162	.91	202.0	3,100
11	.8464	1.03	202.6	2,830
12	.6329	.34	199.5	3,990
13	.7050	.54	200.4	3,820
14	.0642	-1.52	191.2	3,824
15	.2071	-.81	194.4	3,888

$$\text{AVERAGE DAILY PROFIT} = \frac{55,345}{15} = \$3,689.67$$

9) For Global Airlines (problem 8), suppose the company wishes to accept X = 222 reservations. Use simulation to compute the average profit per flight over 15 trips for this decision. Compare the answer to problem 8). Which of the two reservations policies would you recommend that the company adopt?

* 10) Susan Winslow has two alternative routes to travel from her home in Oldport to her office in Lewisburg. She can travel on the 5 freeway to the 57 freeway or on the 55 freeway to the 91 freeway. The time distributions are as follows:

Freeway 5		Freeway 57		Freeway 55		Freeway 91	
Time	Relative Frequency	Time	Relative Frequency	Time	Relative Frequency	Time	Relative Frequency
5	.30	4	.10	6	.20	3	.30
6	.20	5	.20	7	.20	4	.35
7	.40	6	.35	8	.40	5	.20
8	.10	7	.20	9	.20	6	.15
		8	.15				

Do a five day simulation of each of the two routes. On the basis of this simulation, which route should Susan take if her objective is to minimize travel time?

O 11) The Rumson Post Office serves a small rural town. In any one minute interval during a Saturday morning either 0, 1, 2 or 3 customers arrive with the following probabilities.

$$P(0) = .40$$
$$P(1) = .30$$
$$P(2) = .20$$
$$P(3) = .10$$

The only clerk working on Saturday at the post office is Mrs. Smith. Her service time per customer is also a random variable with the following distribution.

$$P(\text{service} = 1 \text{ minute}) = .80$$
$$P(\text{service} = 2 \text{ minutes}) = .15$$
$$P(\text{service} = 3 \text{ minutes}) = .05$$

If the system starts empty, simulate the waiting line over a 10 minute interval. What is the average number of customers in the waiting line per minute?

Outline of Solution:

  i) Determine a random number mapping for both the number of arrivals per minute and the service time.

  ii) Develop a simulation keeping track of the number of customers arriving in each minute, the number of customers in the waiting line in each minute, the service time of each customer, and the time when the customer currently being served leaves the post office. (Use random numbers from column 1 of Appendix B to generate the number of arrivals, and from column 2 to generate service times).

Answer: Average number of people in waiting line is 1.

427

12) As the owner of a rent-a-car agency you have determined the following statistics.

NUMBER OF CARS RENTED DAILY	PROBABILITY	LENGTH OF CAR RENTAL PER RENT	PROBABILITY
0	.10	1 day	.50
1	.15	2 days	.30
2	.20	3 days	.15
3	.30	4 days	.05
4	.25		

The net profit is $40 per car per day rented. When there is demand for a car and none is available there is a shortage cost (good-will loss) of $80 and the rental is lost. Each day a car is unused costs $5 per car. Your firm has four cars initially.

a) Conduct a 10 day simulation of this business.

b) If your firm can obtain another car for $200 per 10 days, should you take the extra car?

.

* 13) Suppose you run a store that carries an inventory of a certain item.
Over the weeks you have collected the following data concerning
demand:

WEEKLY DEMAND	PROBABILITY
0	.10
1	.20
2	.20
3	.20
4	.20
5	.10

Now, your policy has been to reorder 8 units whenever your inventory
reached 4 items or less at the end of a week. Current inventory is 5
items. The cost of reordering is $40 and holding costs are $2 per
item per week. Lead time for an order has been observed to be:

WEEKS	PROBABILITY
1	.40
2	.50
3	.10

Stockout costs are $10 per occurrence. (These sales are lost.)

Conduct an 8 week simulation of this situation and determine the total
cost for this period.

14) Consider the store inventory situation (problem 13). The company you order items from has just offered you a new policy. They will automatically deliver 3 items per week for a weekly charge of $12. This policy will therefore eliminate reorder costs and lead times. Assuming the same data as in problem 13) conduct an 8 week simulation of this policy. Comparing the cost of this policy to the answer in problem 13, would you adopt the new policy?

* 15) You are considering an inventory system for your office machine business. You have ascertained the following costs:

> Holding Costs: $2/machine/week
> Reorder Costs: $160/order
> Building Rental Costs: $1/week/machine

Building costs are based on the size of the building rented and if you figure the maximum number will be in inventory, then the size of the building will be one more than this number. You have found the following distribution for weekly demand:

19	30%
20	50%
21	10%
22	10%

a) Since demand is relatively constant (what is average weekly demand?), formulate an inventory policy which will minimize total weekly cost of your model? (HINT: Compare the factor multiplying Q in the total cost equation for this model to the EOQ model, or use calculus).

b) Now consider the implementation of the policy determined in part a) for 10 weeks. If there is a stockout cost of $5 per item, and a surcharge of $10 per item that arrives at the warehouse when there is no space for it, calculate the average weekly cost. Comment.

15 WAITING LINE MODELS

REVIEW

1. Description of Queuing Process

Queuing theory is the study of waiting lines. For a given waiting line process we may be interested in a number of characteristics in order to develop an economically attractive system. These may include the percent of time the service facility is idle, the probability of a specific number of units in the system, the average number of units in the system, etc. Some typical situations where queuing analysis is employed are determining the number of tellers at a bank, the number of toll booths on a highway, and the type of waiting line at a post office.

The queuing process operates as follows. Customers, or units, enter the system and are either served immediately or find the server(s) busy and join the queue (waiting line). When a customer completes service he leaves the system and, depending on the priority rule in effect, another customer from the queue begins being serviced. Four characteristics of a queuing model are: (1) the manner in which customers arrive; (2) the time required for service; (3) the priority determining the order of service; and, (4) the number and configuration of servers in the system.

2. General Assumption for Arrivals and Service Times

In general, the arrival of customers into the system is a random event. Typically the arrival distribution is characterized as a Poisson process. The Poisson distribution is defined as the probability of x arrivals during a specific time, P(x), and equals $\frac{\lambda^x e^{-\lambda}}{x!}$. Here λ equals the expected number of arrivals for the specific period of time and e equals 2.71828... Values of $e^{-\lambda}$ are provided in Appendix C. Sample data should be used to determine the appropriateness of the Poisson distribution as well as the value for λ.

Most often, the service time is also a random variable. The distribution most commonly used to describe the service time is the exponential distribution with a probability density function $f(t) = \mu e^{-\mu t}$. Here t is the service time and μ is the average (mean) number of customers that can be served by the facility in a specific period of time. For the exponential distribution, the probability that a customer completes service before some time T, $P(t \leq T)$, equals $1 - e^{-\mu T}$. The most common queue discipline is first come, first served (FIFO). However in many cases other disciplines more appropriately describe the service system.

3. Analysis of Queuing Systems

i) Single Server Queues

Consider the waiting line model characterized as follows:

    Arrival process: Poisson with mean arrival rate λ
    Service process: Exponential with service rate μ
    Queue discipline: FIFO
    Maximum queue length: infinite
    Number of servers: 1

The following results have been obtained for this model.

(1) The probability that the service facility is idle:
$P_o = 1 - \frac{\lambda}{\mu}$.

(2) The probability of n units in the system: $P_n = (\frac{\lambda}{\mu})^n (1 - \frac{\lambda}{\mu})$.

(3) The average number of units in the system: $L = \frac{\lambda}{\mu - \lambda}$.

(4) The average time a unit spends in the system (waiting time + service time): $W = \frac{1}{\mu - \lambda} = L/\lambda$.

(5) The average number of units in the queue waiting for service: $L_q = \lambda^2 / \mu(\mu - \lambda)$.

(6) The average time a unit spends in the queue waiting for service: $W_q = \dfrac{\lambda}{\mu(\mu - \lambda)} = L_q / \lambda$.

(7) The probability that an arriving unit must wait for service: $P_w = 1 - P_o = \lambda / \mu$.

The ratio of the mean arrival rate to the mean service rate, λ / μ, is called the <u>utilization factor</u> for the queue. From above, we see that the utilization factor is equal to the probability that an arrival must wait for service, i.e. the probability the server is busy (in use). In order for the queue not to grow infinitely large in size we must have the service rate, μ, be greater than the arrival rate, λ. Hence, the utilization factor must be less than 1. Using the above formulae, together with cost estimates it is possible to determine the most economical single server waiting line system.

ii) <u>Multiple Server Queues</u>

If in the above waiting line process we had k servers (each with a mean potential service rate of μ), one line (a waiting customer is served by the first available server), and $k\mu$ is greater than λ, then the following results can be shown:

(1) The probability that all k service channels are idle:

$$P_o = \cfrac{1}{\left[\displaystyle\sum_{n=o}^{k-1} \frac{1}{n!} \left(\frac{\lambda}{\mu}\right)^n\right] + \frac{1}{k!} \left(\frac{\lambda}{\mu}\right)^k \frac{k\mu}{k\mu - \lambda}}$$

(2) The probability of n units in the system:

$$P_n = \frac{1}{k! \, k^{n-k}} \left(\frac{\lambda}{\mu}\right)^n P_o \text{ for } n > k$$

$$P_n = \frac{1}{n!} \left(\frac{\lambda}{\mu}\right)^n P_o \text{ for } n \leq k$$

(3) The average number of units in the system:

$$L = \frac{\lambda\mu(\lambda/\mu)^k}{(k - 1)!(k\mu - \lambda)^2} P_o + \frac{\lambda}{\mu}$$

(4) The average time a unit spends in the system (waiting time + service time): $W = L/\lambda$.

(5) The average number of units in the queue waiting for service:
$$L_q = L - \frac{\lambda}{\mu} \ .$$

(6) The average time a unit spends in the queue waiting for service: $W_q = L_q/\lambda$.

(7) The probability that an arriving unit must wait for service:
$$P_w = \frac{1}{k!} \ (\frac{\lambda}{\mu})^k \ \frac{k\mu}{k\mu - \lambda} \ P_o \ .$$

It is interesting to note that it is more efficient to have one server with a mean service rate of $k\mu$ rather than k servers, each with a mean service rate of μ.

4. Extensions

A three part code has been developed to represent certain aspects of the particular queuing model under study. The first part of the code identifies the arrival distribution, the second part identifies the service distribution, while the third part indicates the number of servers in the system. Because both the Poisson and the exponential distribution give rise to a Markov process the letter M is used to represent both of these distributions. Hence, a single server queue with a Poisson arrival process and exponential service time distribution would be represented as M/M/1. If there were K servers in this system the representation would be M/M/K.

Queuing models have been developed to handle assumptions other than the Poisson arrival distribution, exponential service distribution, infinite queue lengths, and the FIFO queue discipline. In cases where analytical methods have failed to yield results, insight has been gained through simulation.

EXPONENTIAL DISTRIBUTION - A probability distribution used to describe the pattern or service time for some waiting lines. For this distribution the probability density function, $f(x) = \mu e^{-\mu t}$ where μ is the expected number of units the service facility can handle in a specific period of time. (602)

FIFO - A queue discipline for which units are served on a first come first served basis. (604)

MEAN ARRIVAL RATE - The expected number of customers or units arriving or entering the system in a given period of time. (601)

MEAN SERVICE RATE - The expected number of customers or units that can be serviced by one server in a given period of time. (603)

MULTIPLE-CHANNEL - A waiting line with two or more parallel identical servers. (610)

OPERATING CHARACTERISTICS - The performance characteristics of a waiting line such as average number of customers in the system, average queue size, average waiting time, and so on. (598)

POISSON DISTRIBUTION - A probability distribution, used to describe the random arrival pattern for some waiting lines, characterized by $P(x) = \dfrac{\lambda^x e^{-\lambda}}{x!}$, where x = the number of arrivals in a specific period of time and λ = the average or expected number of arrivals for the specific period of time. (601)

QUEUE - A waiting line. (598)

QUEUE DISCIPLINE - The way in which customers in the waiting line are ordered for service. (604)

QUEUING THEORY - The operations research term for the study of waiting lines. (598)

SINGLE-CHANNEL - A waiting line with only one server. (600)

STEADY STATE - The normal operation of the waiting line after an initial transient or startup period of time. (605)

UTILIZATION FACTOR - The ratio of the mean arrival rate to the mean service rate, λ/μ. It indicates the proportion of the time the service facilities are in use. (606)

Chapter 15 Check List

NOTE: The following waiting line problems are all based upon the assumptions of Poisson arrivals and exponential service times and an unlimited queue length.

W 1) Joe Ferris is a stock trader on the floor of the New York Stock Exchange for the firm of Smith, Jones, Johnson, and Thomas, Inc. Assuming stock transaction orders arrive at a mean rate of 20 per hour find the following:

a) No orders are received within a 15 minute period.

b) Exactly 3 orders arrive in a 15 minute period.

c) More than 6 orders arrive in a 15 minute period.

SOLUTION:

Orders arrive at a mean rate of 20 per hour or one order per 3 minutes. Therefore, in a 15 minute interval the average number of orders arriving will be $\lambda = 15/3 = 5$. Using Appendix C to determine $e^{-5} = .007$,

a) $P(x = 0) = \dfrac{5^0 e^{-5}}{0!} = e^{-5} = .007$

b) $P(x = 3) = \dfrac{5^3 e^{-5}}{3!} = \dfrac{125(.007)}{6} = .140$

c) $P(x > 6) = 1 - P(x = 0) - P(x = 1) - P(x = 2) - P(x = 3) - P(x = 4)$

$- P(x = 5) - P(x = 6) = 1 - .762 = .238$

O 2) Each order received by Joe Ferris (see problem 1) requires an average of 2 minutes to process.

a) What is the mean service rate per hour?

b) What percentage of the orders will take less than 1 minute to process?

c) What percentage of the orders will be completed in exactly 2 minutes?

d) What percentage of the orders will require more than 3 minutes for processing?

439

3) Assuming Joe Ferris receives stock transaction orders at the mean rate of 20 per hour and his average service time per order is 2 minutes find the following:

a) The probability Joe is idle.

b) The average number of orders waiting to be filled.

c) The average turnaround time per order (waiting time plus service time).

d) The utilization rate for this system.

* 4) Customers arrive at the Roney Tax Preparation office on the average of once per hour. The average time it takes Ms. Roney to prepare a customer's income tax form is 45 minutes.

a) What is the probability of no customers arriving in 2 hours?

b) What is the probability that an income tax form is finished within 45 minutes from the time it is started?

c) What is the average time a customer spends waiting to see Ms. Roney?

d) What is the probability that Ms. Roney has 3 people in her office (2 waiting and 1 being served)?

5) Cars travel down Main Street at the rate of 20,000 per hour. The probability of a car pulling into the drive-in window at the Burger Prince Restaurant is .002. Cars are serviced at the mean rate of 60 per hour.

a) What is the arrival rate of cars at the drive-in window?

b) What is the average number of cars waiting to be served?

c) What is the average number of cars both in the queue and being served?

d) What is the probability that an arriving car must wait for service?

W 6)   Smith, Jones, Johnson, and Thomas, Inc. (see problem 1) has begun a
major advertising campaign which it believes will increase its business
by 50%.

   a)   If orders do increase by 50%, what will the new arrival rate of
   stock orders be for Joe Ferris?

   b)   Assume Joe Ferris continues to process orders in an average time
   of 2 minutes. Will he be able to handle the increase in orders?
   Why or why not?

   The company has hired an additonal floor trader who works at the
   same speed as Joe Ferris.

   c)   What is the probability that neither person will be working on an
   order?

   d)   What is the average turnaround time for an order?

   e)   What is the average number of orders waiting to be filled?

SOLUTION:

   a)   Since previously λ = 20 per hour, the new λ = 20(1.50) = 30 per
   hour.

   b)   Since Joe Ferris processes orders at a mean rate of μ = 30 we have
   $\mu = \lambda$ = 30 and a utilization factor of 1. This implies the queue
   will become infinitely large and hence he cannot handle this
   increase in demand.

   c)   We now have a k = 2 person queue with $\lambda = \mu$ = 30.

$$P_o = \frac{1}{\left[\sum_{n=0}^{1} \frac{1}{n!} (1)^n\right] + \frac{1}{2!} (1)^2 \left(\frac{2}{2-1}\right)}$$

$$= \frac{1}{\left[2 + \frac{1}{2} (2)\right]} = \frac{1}{3}$$

   d) $W = \dfrac{30(1)^2}{(60-30)^2} \cdot \left(\dfrac{1}{3}\right) + \dfrac{1}{30} = \dfrac{2}{45}$ hour = 2.67 minutes

   e) $L_q = L - \dfrac{\lambda}{\mu} = \lambda W - \dfrac{\lambda}{\mu} = 30\left(\dfrac{2}{45}\right) - 1 = \dfrac{1}{3}$

* 7)   Due to the recent increase in business at the Frederick's Auto Co.,
       the office typist is now receiving an average of 22 letters per day
       to type. On average, it takes 20 minutes to type each letter and the
       typist works 8 hours a day.

   a)   What is the typist's utilization rate?

   b)   What is the average time required to have a letter typed (waiting
        time plus typing time)?

   c)   What is the probability that the typist will have at least 3
        letters to type?

   d)   What is the average number of letters waiting to be typed?

* 8) The management at the Burger Prince Restaurant feels that the waiting line at the drive-in window is too long, causing a loss of potential customers. Management believes that if the average number of cars in the queue waiting to be served was less than 1, the probability of cars stopping at the restaurant would increase to .003. Burger Prince is therefore developing procedural changes for its staff in order to speed up service. How fast must the service rate be increased to in order to achieve the objective of having the average number of waiting cars be less than or equal to 1? Assume 20,000 cars per hour drive down Main Street and the probability of a car stopping at the Burger Prince drive-in window is .003.

9) The grocery department at Dollar Department Store currently has 5 check out positions. On average one customer per minute enters the store and spends an average of 55 minutes choosing his items. Each checker can check out a customer in an average time of 4 minutes.

a) What is the average time a customer will spend in the grocery department?

b) Management is considering reducing the number of check out positions to 3 and hiring baggers. This will reduce the average time required to check out a customer to 2.5 minutes. Would this reduce the average waiting time?

W 10) The advertising campaign of Smith, Jones, Johnson, and Thomas, Inc. (see problems 1 and 6) was so successful that business actually doubled. The mean rate of stock orders arriving at the exchange is now 40 per hour and the company must decide how many floor traders to employ. Each floor trader hired can process an order in an average time of 2 minutes.

Based on a number of factors the brokerage firm has determined the average waiting cost per minute for an order as $.50. Floor traders hired will earn $20 per hour in wages and benefits. Using this information determine the total hourly cost of hiring.

a) 2 traders.

b) 3 traders.

SOLUTION:

For each value of k we must determine the average number of units in the system, L.

$$\lambda = 40 \atop \mu = 30 \;,\; \frac{\lambda}{\mu} = \frac{4}{3}$$

a) $k = 2$

$$P_o = \cfrac{1}{\left[\displaystyle\sum_{n=0}^{1} \frac{1}{n!}\left(\frac{4}{3}\right)^n\right] + \frac{1}{2}\left(\frac{4}{3}\right)^2 \left(\frac{60}{20}\right)}$$

$$= \cfrac{1}{\left[1 + \frac{4}{3} + \frac{8}{3}\right]} = \frac{1}{5}$$

$$L = \cfrac{(30)(40)\left(\frac{40}{30}\right)\left(\frac{40}{30}\right)}{(20)(20)} \; \frac{1}{5} + \frac{4}{3} = \frac{12}{5}$$

$$\text{Hourly cost} = \left(\frac{12}{5}\right)(60)(.50) + (2)(20) = \$112$$

447

b) $k = 3$

$$P_o = \frac{1}{\left[\sum_{n=0}^{2} \frac{1}{n!} \left(\frac{4}{3}\right)^n\right] + \frac{1}{6}\left(\frac{4}{3}\right)^3 \left(\frac{90}{50}\right)} = \frac{1}{1 + \frac{4}{3} + \frac{8}{9} + \frac{32}{45}}$$

$$= \frac{45}{45 + 60 + 40 + 32} = \frac{45}{177} = \frac{15}{59}$$

$$L = \frac{(30)(40)\left(\frac{4}{3}\right)^3}{(2)(50)(50)} \cdot \left(\frac{15}{59}\right) + \frac{4}{3}$$

$$= \frac{128}{885} + \frac{4}{3} = \frac{1308}{885}$$

$$\text{Total cost} = \left(\frac{1308}{885}\right)(60)(.50) + (3)'(20) = 104.34$$

11) The Chez Paul Restaurant is contemplating the purchase of microwave ovens. It is considering two different models. Model I costs $400 and Model II costs $600. The average cooking time for an item in Model I is 6 minutes and in Model II is 4 minutes. Paul estimates he will want to cook 20 items per hour. If he is willing to spend $1,200 on ovens should he purchase 3 Model I ovens or 2 Model II ovens? Why?

* 12) Shear's Department Store has 2 catalog order desks, one at each entrance to the store. On average a customer arrives at each order desk once every 12 minutes. The service rate of each order desk is on average 8 customers per hour.

   a) What is the average number of customers waiting to be served at each order desk?

   b) What is the probability that both order clerks will not have any customers?

   c) What is the average time a customer spends at an order desk (waiting plus service time)?

   d) What is the probability that both order clerks are busy?

13) Shear's Department Store is considering consolidating its 2 catalog order desks (see problem 12) into one location staffed by the two clerks. The clerks will continue to work individually, at the same speed of 8 customers per hour. Customers will now arrive at the mean rate of once every 6 minutes. Under this plan find the following:

a) What is the average number of customers waiting to be served?

b) What is the probability of no customers being present at the order desk?

c) What is the average time a customer spends at the order desk (waiting time plus service time)?

d) What is the probability that both order clerks are busy?

e) Comparing the answers to problems 12 and 13 do you think the company should consolidate its catalog order desks? Explain.

W 14) Frederick's Auto Company is considering relief action for its typist (see problem 7). It can either hire an additional typist (who also works at the average rate of one letter per 20 minutes) at a cost of $40 per day or it can lease an automated typewriter. There are three models of the typewriter, each with a different daily cost and resulting increase in the typist's efficiency. This information is summarized in the following table.

Model	Cost Per Day	Increase in Typist's Efficiency
I	$37	50%
II	$39	75%
III	$43	150%

The company has determined that the cost of a letter waiting to be mailed out is $.80 per hour. If letters continue to arrive at the typist at a rate of 22 per day, what action should the company take to minimize total costs.

SOLUTION:

For each of the 4 alternatives determine the average number of units in the system and the total cost.

Alternative a) Hire another typist. This is a 2 person queue with $\lambda = 22$ and $\mu = 24$.

Compute $P_o = \dfrac{39}{80}$

Compute $L = 1.24$

Total cost = Wages + $\begin{pmatrix}\text{Cost per letter} \\ \text{per hour}\end{pmatrix}\begin{pmatrix}\text{Number of hours} \\ \text{in a day}\end{pmatrix}\begin{pmatrix}\text{Average number} \\ \text{of letters}\end{pmatrix}$

= 40 + (.80)(8)(1.24) = $\underline{\$47.94}$

ALTERNATIVE b) Lease Model I. This is a single server queue with $\mu = (1.5)(24) = 36$ and $\lambda = 22$.

Compute $L = \dfrac{22}{14} = 1.57$

Total cost = 37 + (.80)(8)(1.57) = $\underline{\$47.05}$

451

ALTERNATIVE c) Lease Machine II. This is a single server queue with
μ = (1.75)(24) = 42 and λ = 22.

Compute L = $\frac{22}{20}$ + 1.1

Total cost = 39 + (.80)(8)(1.1) = $\underline{\$46.04}$

ALTERNATIVE d) Lease Machine III. This is a single server queue with
μ = (2.5)(24) = 60 and λ = 22.

Compute L = $\frac{22}{38}$ = .58

Total cost = 43 + (.80)(8)(.58) = $\underline{\$46.70}$

Choose the minimum total cost system – <u>Lease Machine II</u>.

* 15) Shear's Department Store has completed the catalog order desk consoli-
dation plan (see problem 13) and now has 2 order clerks, each working
at a mean speed of 8 customers per hour. Customers arrive at the
order desk at the mean rate of once every 6 minutes. Management
believes that some customers are going to find the wait at the order
desk too long and take their business to Word's, Shear's competition.
In order to reduce the time required by an order clerk to serve a
customer, Shear's is contemplating installing one of two new minicomputer systems. System A leases for \$18 per day and will increase
the clerks' efficiency by 25%. System B leases for \$23 per day and
will increase the clerks' efficiency by 50%. Assume the clerks work
8 hours. Shear's estimates its cost of having a customer in the system
at \$3 per hour. Determine if Shear's should install a minicomputer
system and if so, which type.

16) Assume Frederick's Auto Company is considering a fifth alternative
for the typist relief action (see problem 14). The company is contemplating hiring a student typist who can type a letter in an average
time of 30 minutes. The student typist will work for $30 per day.
Discuss, in a step by step fashion, the procedure you would use to
develop a simulation model to determine the economic benefit of such
a decision.

W 17)   Jerry's Jewelry Store is seeking a salesman for its evening shift.
Three applicants with former experience have applied for the position,
each demanding different salaries. You have contacted the former
supervisor of each who has supplied you with information on the
average service times for each applicant. The applicants' demands
and service times are as follows:

Applicant	Hourly Wage Demanded	Average Service Time
Martha Miller	$ 6	6 min.
Kenneth Weeks	$10	5 min.
Edith Schneider	$14	4 min.

Customers arrive at the store at an average rate of 8 per hour and
you have estimated that the cost of having a person in the system
(for security, customer relations, etc.) is $4/hour/customer. Which
applicant should you hire?

SOLUTION:

Total hourly cost = Hourly wage + $4 (average number of customers
                    in system)

= Wages + 4L

In each case $L = \dfrac{\lambda}{\mu - \lambda}$

Martha Miller

$\lambda = 8$, $\mu = 10$

Then,

$$L = \frac{8}{10 - 8} = 4$$

Thus, Total Hourly Cost = 6 + 4(4) = $22

<u>Kenneth Weeks</u>

$\lambda = 8$, $\mu = 12$

Then,

$$L = \frac{8}{12 - 8} = 2$$

Thus, Total Hourly Cost = $10 + 4(2) = \$18$

<u>Edith Schneider</u>

$\lambda = 8$, $\mu = 15$

Then,

$$L = \frac{8}{15 - 8} = 1.14$$

Thus, Total Hourly Cost = $14 + 4(1.14) = \$18.56$

Hire Kenneth Weeks.

18) A company has tool cribs where workmen must draw parts. Two men have applied for the position of distributing parts to the workmen. Man A is fresh out of trade school and wants $6 per hour. His average service time is 4 minutes. A veteran (Man B) wants $12 per hour and has an average service time of 2 minutes. A workman's time is figured at $10 per hour and they arrive to draw parts at a rate of 12 per hour.

a) What would be the average waiting time a workman would spend in the system under each applicant?

b) Since workmen arrive at a rate of 12 per hour, what is the waiting cost per hour under each applicant (not including distributor's cost)?

c) Which applicant would you hire?

16 DYNAMIC PROGRAMMING

KEY CONCEPTS

1. General formulation and structure of dynamic
    programming problems

2. Principal of optimality and recurrence rela-
    tions

3. The solution of shortest route, knapsack, and
    production and inventory control problems by
    dynamic programming

REVIEW

1. General Formulation

Dynamic programming is an approach to problem solving which
permits decomposing the original problem into a series of several smaller
subproblems. By sequentially solving these subproblems it is possible to
obtain the solution to the original problem.

To successfully apply dynamic programming the original problem
must be viewed as a multistage decision problem. This stage decomposi-
tion may be obvious in some instances (e.g. for time dependent problems
the stages can be thought of as different time periods). However, in
other instances the best way to define the stages must be determined
through subtle reasoning. A dynamic programming problem can be solved
by starting at the final stage and working backwards through the problem
to the initial stage. This is called backwards recursion.

Perhaps the hardest aspect of learning dynamic programming is in
understanding the notation. At each stage, n, of the process there is a
known input, x_n (called the state variable of the process at stage n),
and an optimal decision variable, d_n, which takes on a value according to
some decision criteria. The input and decision results in an output,

x_{n-1} (the state at the previous stage) and a particular <u>return function</u>, $r_n(x_n, d_n)$. The output is determined by a <u>stage transformation function</u>. $x_{n-1} = t_n(x_n, d_n)$, which is dependent upon the actual problem.

The <u>optimal value function</u>, $f_n(x_n)$ is the cumulative return starting at stage n with state x_n and proceeding to stage 1, under an optimal policy (strategy).

If the problem consists of N stages with initial state x_N then the solution will be $f_N(x_N)$. One way of determining the information included in the state variable is to imagine being a consultant called in to help solve the problem at a particular stage. The information one would have to know to finish solving the problem is the state information.

2. Principle of Optimality and Recurrence Relation

One reason dynamic programming is such a powerful procedure is that it is possible to solve the original problem without having to solve every possible subproblem. This follows from an insightful observation known as Bellman's "<u>principle of optimality</u>". This principle states that regardless of what decisions were made at previous stages, if the decision made at stage n is to be part of an overall optimal solution, then the decision made at stage n must be optimal for all remaining stages. Hence, at stage n, given state x_n, we wish to choose the decision, d_n, so as to maximize the sum of the current return $r_n(x_n, d_n)$ plus the best return from all subsequent stages, $f_{n-1}(x_{n-1})$. (Here x_{n-1} is determined by $x_{n-1} = t_n(x_n, d_n)$). This result is called the <u>recurrence relation</u>.

$$f_n(x_n) = \max_{d_n} \left\{ r_n(x_n, d_n) + f_{n-1}(t_n(x_n, d_n)) \right\}$$

The solution procedure begins by starting at stage 0 with the <u>boundary condition</u> $f_0(x_0) = 0$ for all feasible values of x_0. At each stage, n, $f_n(x_n)$ is computed for all feasible values of x_n. The solution is found by working towards stage N.

3. Shortest Route, Knapsack, and Production and Inventory Control Problems

Three classes of problems which conveniently lend themselves to a dynamic programming solution are shortest route problems, <u>knapsack</u> or <u>cargo loading</u> problems, and production and inventory control problems.

To solve a shortest route problem using dynamic programming it is necessary to be able to consider the network as a series of stages. At each stage there are a number of different nodes in the network. Each arc in the network connects a node of one stage, n, with a node of the next stage, n + 1. The states correspond to the different nodes in the stage. The distances of each arc can be thought of as negative returns (as the objective is to minimize the distance through the network). At each stage the decision is to choose the best arc for the path.

The knapsack problem seeks to determine the optimal number of each of N items (which must not be fractional) to maximize profit subject to an overall capacity constraint. That is, each type of item has a value and a measurement (e.g., weight, volume, etc.). The objective is to select items which maximize the total value subject to a total allowable measurement. There are a number of different approaches which can be used in solving this problem via dynamic programming. One way is to let the stages be defined to correspond to the different types of items. Thus, the subproblem at stage n is to determine the optimal allocation of item types 1, 2, 3,...,n given a total capacity constraint of x_n. At each stage n, this problem is solved for all feasible values of x_n. The optimal solution is found by solving the problem at stage N for x_N equal to the total allowable measurement.

In production and inventory control problems the stages correspond to time periods. A production decision must be made for each stage subject to constraints on the production and storage capacity of that period. The objective is to satisfy the demand during each time period, subject to the constraints of the problem, at the minimum cost. The state at each stage will be the amount of inventory on hand at the beginning of the period.

GLOSSARY

BACKWARDS RECURSION - The process of solving a dynamic programming problem by starting at the final stage and working backwards towards the initial stage.   (625)

BOUNDARY CONDITION - A set value of the optimal value function for the initial stage under consideration.

DECISION VARIABLE, d_n - A variable representing the possible decisions that can be made at stage n.   (631)

DYNAMIC PROGRAMMING - An approach to problem solving that permits decomposing one large mathematical model which may be very difficult to solve into a number of smaller subproblems which are easier to solve.   (624)

KNAPSACK OR CARGO LOADING PROBLEM - A problem in which N types of items, each with a particular value and measurement, are to be chosen to maximize total value subject to a total measurement constraint.   (634)

OPTIMAL VALUE FUNCTION, $f_n(x_n)$ - The sum of the return functions starting at stage n with state x_n and going to stage 1 using the optimal decision policy at each stage.   (633)

PRINCIPLE OF OPTIMALITY - Regardless of the decisions that have been made at the previous stages, if the decision made at stage n is to be part of an overall optimal solution, the decision made at stage n must be optimal for all remaining stages.   (625)

RECURRENCE RELATION - The relationship which defines the optimal value function at stage n in terms of the return function at stage n plus the optimal value function at stage n - 1.   (637)

RETURN FUNCTION, $r_n(x_n, d_n)$ - A value (such as a profit or loss) associated with making decision d_n at stage n given state variable x_n.   (633)

STAGE - When a large problem is decomposed into smaller subproblems each subproblem corresponds to a stage.   (624)

STAGE TRANSFORMATION FUNCTION, $t_n(x_n, d_n)$ - The rule or equation that relates the output state variable x_{n-1} for stage n to the input state variable x_n and decision variable d_n.   (632)

STATE VARIABLES, x_n and x_{n-1} - An input state variable x_n and an output state variable x_{n-1} together define the condition of the process at the beginning and end of stage n.   (632)

460

Chapter 16 Check List

W 1) Consider the following network.

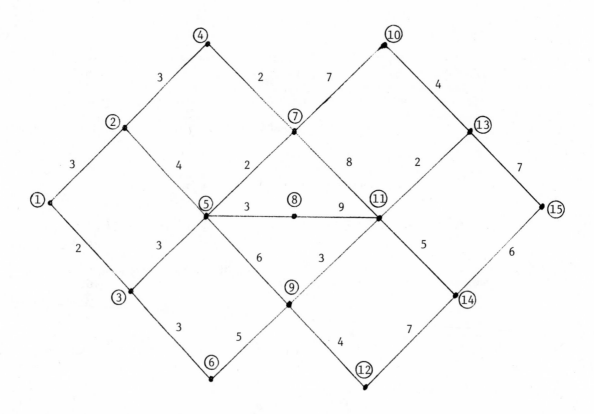

Find the shortest path(s) from node 1 to node 15 assuming that you can only travel from left to right.

<u>SOLUTION</u>:

This problem can be viewed as a six stage decision problem. Working backwards through the network, let stage 1 correspond to nodes 13 and 14; stage 2 correspond to nodes 10, 11, and 12; stage 3 correspond to nodes 7, 8, and 9; stage 4 correspond to nodes 4, 5, and 6; stage 5 correspond to nodes 2 and 3; and stage 6 correspond to node 1.

At each stage a decision will be made as to how to move from the particular state to the final state (node 15) in the shortest possible distance. For example, at stage 1 there are 2 states: node 13 and node 14. Because there is no choice of how to reach node 15 from either node 13 or 14 the decision is automatic. This can be summarized in the following table.

Input Nodes	ARC Decision	Shortest Distance to Node 15
13	13-15	7
14	14-15	6

In the table, column one gives the particular states of this stage, column 2 gives the optimal arc decision, and column 3 gives the shortest distance to reach the final node. The information in the third column is used at the next stage and the information in the second column is used to determine the optimal strategy.

At stage 2 there are three states, nodes 10, 11, and 12. From nodes 10 and 12 there is no decision required to determine the shortest path, however a decision must be made at node 11. From node 11 there are two possibilities: travel on arc 11-13 to Node 13 or travel on arc 11-14 to node 14. The distance of arc 11-13 is 2 and from the table in stage 1 we see that the distance from 13 to 15 (column 3) is 7 for a total of 9. Similarly the distance of arc 11-14 is 5 and the distance from 14 to 15 is 6 for a total of 11. Since 9 is less than 11 the optimal decision if one were at node 11 is to travel on arc 11-13 to reach node 13. This can be represented in the following table.

Stage 2

Input Nodes	Arc Decision	Output Nodes	Shortest Distance to Node 15
10	10-13	13	11
11	11-13	13	9
12	12-14	14	13

Note that a new column has been added to the table to list the output
node. For this problem this information is redundant since it can be
determined by the arc decision. In many problems, however, the output
node can not be determined from the arc decision easily and should therefore be listed.

At stage 3 a decision must be made at nodes 7 and 9 regarding the best
route. From 7 one could either move to node 10 or node 11. The distance
from node 7 to 10 is 7 and from the table for stage 2 we see the distance
from node 10 to node 15 (column 4) is 11 for a total of 18. Similarly
the total distance from node 7 taking path 7-11 can be determined to be 17.
Hence the best decision from node 7 is to go to node 11. The complete
results for stage 3 can be summarized by the following table.

Stage 3

Input Nodes	Arc Decision	Output Nodes	Shortest Distance to Node 15
7	7-11	11	17
8	8-11	11	18
9	9-11	11	12

Writing the shortest distances to node 15 next to each node gives the
following network.

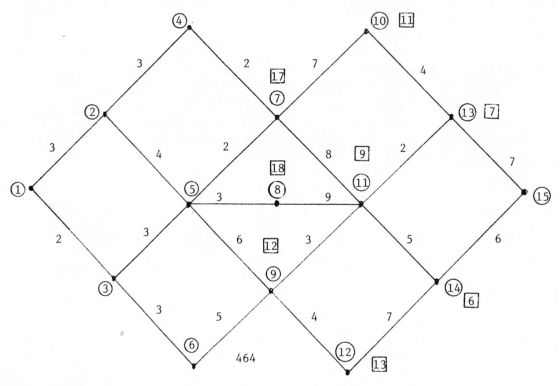

At stage 4 there are three possible arcs to travel on from node 5. The best decision is found by calculating the minimum of $\{(2 + 17), (3 + 18), (6 + 12)\} = 18$. Hence, the table at stage 4 is as follows.

Stage 4

Input Nodes	Arc Decision	Output Nodes	Shortest Distance to Node 15
4	4-7	7	19
5	5-9	9	18
6	6-9	9	17

At stage 5 decisions must be made for both nodes 2 and 3. From node 2 moving to node 4 requires a distance of 3 and from the table at stage 4 we see the minimum distance from 4 to 15 is 19 for a total of 22. Similarly going from node 2 to node 5 gives a total distance of 22. Completing the calculations for node 3 gives the following table at stage 5.

Stage 5

Input Nodes	Arc Decision	Output Nodes	Shortest Distance to Node 15
2	2-4 or 2-5	4 or 5	22
3	3-6	6	20

At stage 6 one must choose to either travel from node 1 to 2 or from node 1 to 3. The shortest distance is the minimum of $\{(3 + 22), (2 + 20)\} = 22$. Hence the best decision is to travel from 1 to 3. Working forwards through the network (backwards through the stages) we see the best route is 1-3-6-9-11-13-15 with a total distance of 22. The final network, including the shortest distance value to node 15 at each node will look as follows.

See next page.

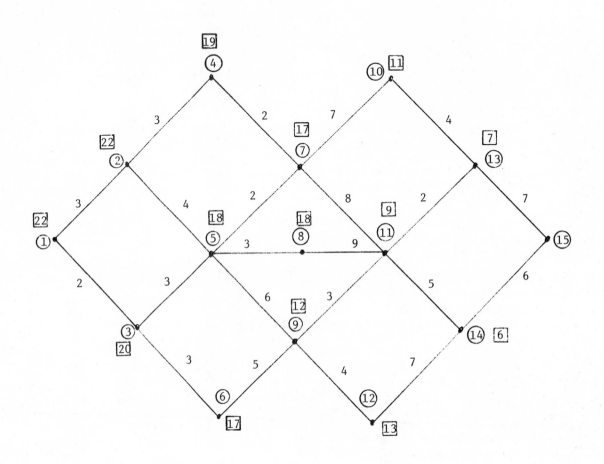

0 2) Consider the following network.

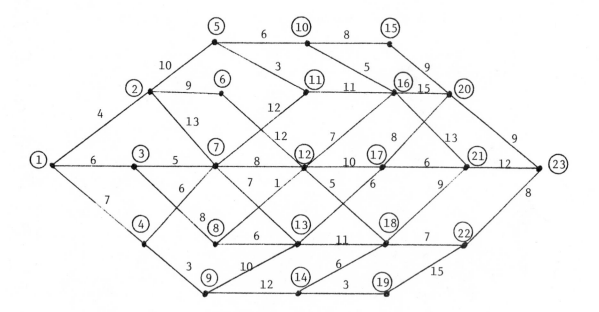

Find the longest path(s) from node 1 to node 23 assuming that you
can only travel from left to right.

<u>Outline of Solution:</u>

   i)   Identify the number of stages in the problem and the states (nodes) corresponding to each stage.

  ii)   Begin at the right of the graph working backwards towards the left of the graph. At each node determine the longest distance possible to travel from that node to the end node, 23, using the recurrence relation (previous stage values plus arc lengths). Also determine the optimal arc decision for each node.

 iii)   Stop when you reach node 1.

Answer: The final network should look as follows:

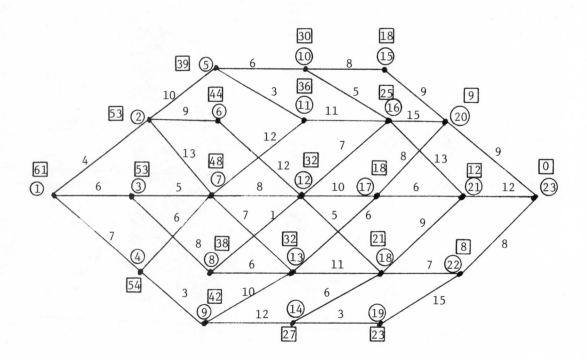

The longest path is 1-4-7-11-16-21-23 with a distance of 61.

3) Universal Telephone and Television has 6 million dollars earmarked for investment among 3 divisions which are having earnings difficulties. The 3 divisions are Bolivia Telephone Company, Camden Insurance Corporation, and Host Baking Company. The company is considering either giving Bolivia Telephone 0, 2, 4, or 6 million dollars or selling the company for 2 million dollars. It is considering giving Camden Insurance either 0, 2, 4, or 6 million dollars. Finally, it is considering either giving Host Bakery 0, 4 or 6 million dollars or selling the company for 4 million dollars. The following tables give estimates of the long term present value return of each action.

Bolivia Telephone		Camden Insurance		Host Baking	
Action (millions)	Long Term Return (millions)	Action (millions)	Long Term Return (millions)	Action (millions)	Long Term Return (millions)
sell	$ 2			sell	$4
give $0	$-1	give $0	$ 1	give $0	$3
give $2	$ 4	give $2	$ 5	give $4	$5
give $4	$ 7	give $4	$ 8	give $6	$8
give $6	$10	give $6	$12		

The following network representation corresponds to this investment problem. The arc distances are the long term returns associated with each investment alternative. Using dynamic programming, find the longest path(s) through this network and determine how Universal Telephone and Telegraph should disperse the $6 million.

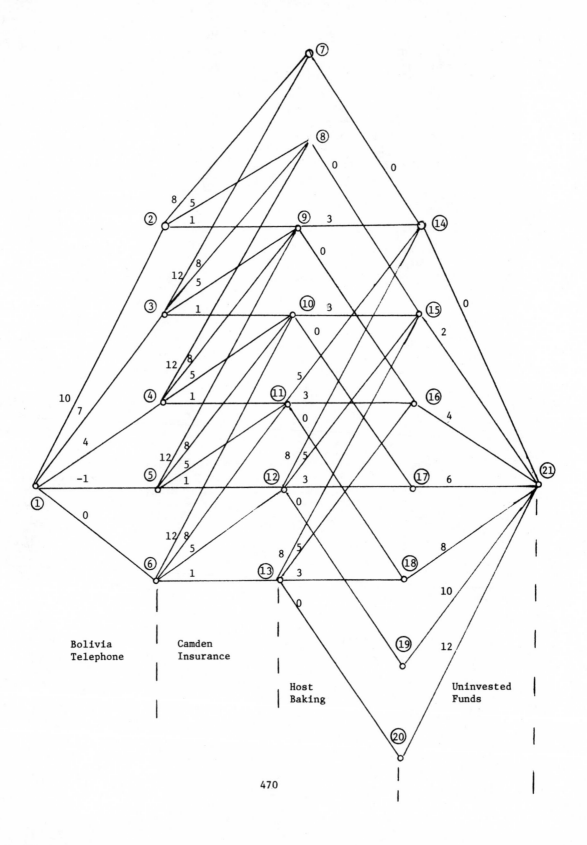

470

* 4) UNIDYDE'S Wainright Arms Division has just obtained a 7 year contract
from the Army to manufacture bullets for the M-21 training rifle.
Wainright has just purchased a cartridge stamping machine for $2
million which will be used in making the bullets. Because cartridge
stamping machines tend to wear with age, as the machine becomes older
the percentage of defective cartridges increases. The following
table gives the cost to Wainright of operating a machine of various
ages.

Age of Machine at Beginning of Year	Operating Cost per Year
New	$ 200,000
1 year	$ 300,000
2 years	$ 600,000
3 years	$ 700,000
4 years	$ 800,000
5 years	$1,100,000
6 years	$2,000,000

Each year Wainright has a choice of doing a major overhaul on the
machine or trading in the machine for a new model. If Wainright has
a major overhaul performed this is equivalent to the machine not
aging during the past year.

Also, at the end of the seven years Wainright plans to sell the
machine for its salvage value. The following table summarizes these
values as a function of the machines age.

Age at end of year	Major Overhaul Cost	Trade In Cost	Salvage Value
1 year	$300,000	$ 300,000	$1,500,000
2 years	$300,000	$ 400,000	$1,200,000
3 years	$300,000	$ 600,000	$1,100,000
4 years	$300,000	$ 800,000	$1,000,000
5 years	$400,000	$1,000,000	$ 900,000
6 years	$500,000	$1,300,000	$ 800,000
7 years			$ 300,000

The following network represents the costs (in $100,000) incurred
by Wainright over the 7 year period for the different policy options.
Using dynamic programming, find the minimum cost path(s) to go from
node 1 to node 29.

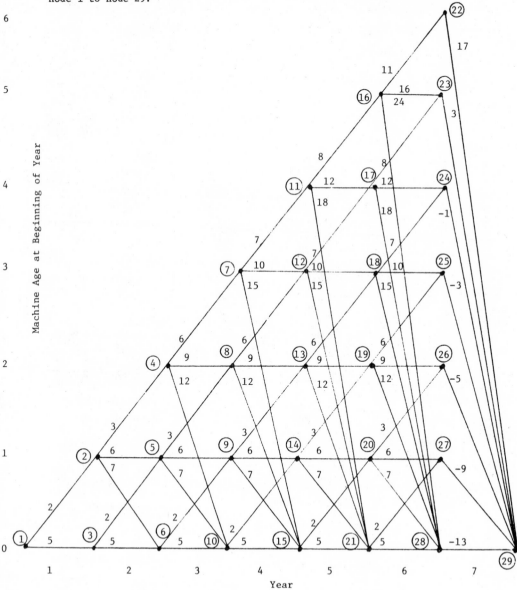

5) In problem 4) if the operating cost for a new and a one year old
   machine both increase to $600,000 per year then the following net-
   work would represent the problem faced by Wainright Arms. Find the
   minimum cost path(s) in this network.

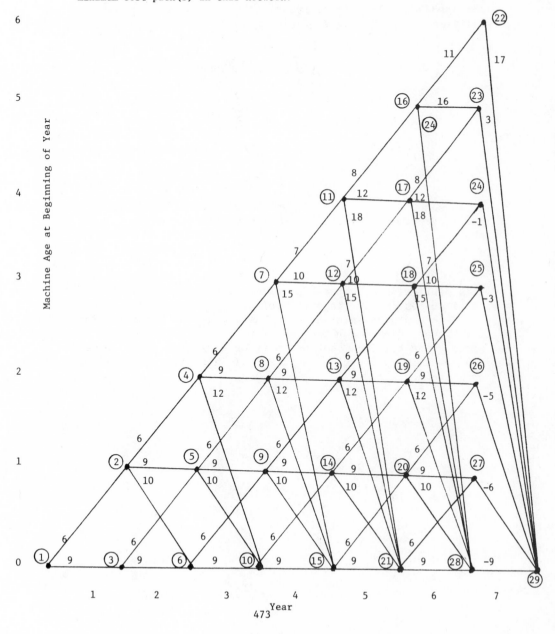

W 6) Ajax Sound is in the business of fabricating phonograph connection
wire. They purchase 30 foot spools of wire from National Electric
at $3.00 per spool and cut the wire into various lengths. Each
length of wire is fitted with phono connector jacks at both ends and
then packaged. The phono connectors cost $.40 per pair (one pair is
used in each package of wire) and packaging and labor together cost
$.20 per package.

Because of Ajax's superior marketing skills they are in the enviable
position of being able to sell all the phonograph connection wire
they produce. They are currently contemplating offering four
different sized packages of wire. These are as follows.

Size	Wholesale Package Price
5'	$1.30
8'	$1.80
12'	$2.50
16'	$3.30

If unused wire from a spool can be sold for scrap at $.03 per foot,
how many packages of each size wire should Ajax make from a 30 foot
spool?

SOLUTION:

This problem is a knapsack problem. The different sized packages of
wire will correspond to the items going into the knapsack. The first
step in determining a solution is to determine the value to Ajax of each
sized package. Since each package of wire will have the same packaging
and phono connector jack cost we subtract this cost ($.60) from the
wholesale selling price of each package. This gives the following values
for each package.

Size	Value
5'	$ .70
8'	$1.20
12'	$1.90
16'	$2.70

Note, that it is unnecessary to subtract out the cost of the wire since once the wire has been purchased this is a "sunk" cost independent of how it is cut up.

Since there are four different sized packages this will be a four stage dynamic programming problem. At stage 1 we must decide how many of the 5' size packages to make, at stage 2 how many of the 8' size packages to make, etc. In dynamic programming notation we will let d_n be the number of packages of size n to produce. The state, x_n will be the number of spare feet on the spool remaining when we reach stage n. The stage transformations are defined as follows.

$$\text{Stage 4} \quad x_3 = t_4(x_4, d_4) = x_4 - 16d_4$$

$$\text{Stage 3} \quad x_2 = t_3(x_3, d_3) = x_3 - 12d_3$$

$$\text{Stage 2} \quad x_1 = t_2(x_2, d_2) = x_2 - 8d_2$$

$$\text{Stage 1} \quad x_0 = t_1(x_1, d_1) = x_1 - 5d_1$$

The return at each stage is as follows.

$$\text{Stage 4} \quad r_4(x_4, d_4) = \$2.70d_4$$

$$\text{Stage 3} \quad r_3(x_3, d_3) = \$1.90d_3$$

$$\text{Stage 2} \quad r_2(x_2, d_2) = \$1.20d_2$$

$$\text{Stage 1} \quad r_1(x_1, d_1) = \$ .70d_3$$

At stage 1 we compute the value associated with producing different amounts of the 5' size packages of wire. The inputs, x_1, at stage 1 are the different amounts of wire still available on the spool to make 5' sized wire. These can range from 0' to 30'. For each value of x_1 we wish to compute how many packages of 5' wire can be made, d_1^*, and the resulting return from this action, $f_1(x_1)$. These values are given in the following table.

x_1	d_1^*	$f_1(x_1)$
0	0	0
1	0	0
2	0	0
3	0	0
4	0	0
5	1	.70
6	1	.70
7	1	.70
8	1	.70
9	1	.70
10	2	1.40
11	2	1.40
12	2	1.40
13	2	1.40
14	2	1.40
15	3	2.10
16	3	2.10
17	3	2.10
18	3	2.10
19	3	2.10
20	4	2.80
21	4	2.80
22	4	2.80
23	4	2.80
24	4	2.80
25	5	3.50
26	5	3.50
27	5	3.50
28	5	3.50
29	5	3.50
30	6	4.20

At stage 2 we must determine how many 8' size packages to produce. The input, x_2, at stage 2 will be the number of feet of wire available for making both 8' and 5' sized packages of wire. Again this amount can range from 0 to 30'. The decision, d_2^*, will be the optimal number of 8' sized packages to produce. Since there are at most 30' available d_2 can have a value of either 0, 1, 2, or 3.

For each value of x_2 we compute the return for each possible value of d_2. For example if $x_2 = 17$ we can produce 0, 1 or 2 packages of 8' wire. If we produce 0 packages this leaves 17' available for 5' wire.

From the stage 1 table we see that the value of this is 2.10. If we produce 1 package of 8' wire we will have 9' left over for 5' size wire. The total value of this solution is 1.20 (the value of one 8' package) + .70 (the value of having 9' available for 5' wire) = 1.90. Finally if we produce 2 packages of 8' wire the value is 2.40 and we have 1' left over to make 5' sized wire. Since we cannot therefore make any 5' sized wire the value of this solution is 2.40.

For each value of x_2 we choose the decision d_2 which gives the largest total value. This decision is designated as d_2^* and the largest value is designated as $f_2(x_2)$. Since the stage transformation at stage 2 is $x_1 = x_2 - 8d_2$, we can calculate the value of x_1 for each value of x_2. This will be helpful in tracing back a solution. The table at stage 2 will therefore look as follows.

x_2	d_2: $r_2(x_2, d_2) + f_1(x_1)$				d_2^*	$f_2(x_2)$	$x_1 = t_2(x_2, d_2^*) = x_2 - 8d_2^*$
	0	1	2	3			
0	0				0	0	0
1	0				0	0	1
2	0				0	0	2
3	0				0	0	3
4	0				0	0	4
5	.70				0	.70	5
6	.70				0	.70	6
7	.70				0	.70	7
8	.70	1.20			1	1.20	0
9	.70	1.20			1	1.20	1
10	1.40	1.20			0	1.40	10
11	1.40	1.20			0	1.40	11
12	1.40	1.20			0	1.40	12
13	1.40	1.90			1	1.90	5
14	1.40	1.90			1	1.90	6
15	2.10	1.90			0	2.10	15
16	2.10	1.90	2.40		2	2.40	0
17	2.10	1.90	2.40		2	2.40	1
18	2.10	2.60	2.40		1	2.60	10
19	2.10	2.60	2.40		1	2.60	11
20	2.80	2.60	2.40		0	2.80	20
21	2.80	2.60	3.10		2	3.10	5
22	2.80	2.60	3.10		2	3.10	6
23	2.80	3.30	3.10		1	3.30	15
24	2.80	3.30	3.10	3.60	3	3.60	0
25	3.50	3.30	3.10	3.60	3	3.60	1
26	3.50	3.30	3.80	3.60	2	3.80	10
27	3.50	3.30	3.80	3.60	2	3.80	11
28	3.50	4.00	3.80	3.60	1	4.00	20
29	3.50	4.00	3.80	4.30	3	4.30	5
30	4.20	4.00	3.80	4.30	3	4.30	6

478

At stage 3 we must determine how many 12' size packages to produce. The input at stage 3 will be the number of feet of wire remaining on a spool to be used for 5', 8' and 12' sized packages. The decision, d_3, will be the number of 12' sized packages to produce. $f_3(x_3)$ will be the optimal value from producing 5', 8', and 12' sized packages having x_3 feet of wire available..

d_3	$r_3(x_3,\ d_3) + f_2(x_2)$					
x_3	0	1	2	d_3^*	$f_3(x_3)$	$x_2 = t_3(x_3,\ d_3^*) = x_3 - 12d_3^*$
0	0			0	0	0
1	0			0	0	1
2	0			0	0	2
3	0			0	0	3
4	0			0	0	4
5	.70			0	.70	5
6	.70			0	.70	6
7	.70			0	.70	7
8	1.20			0	1.20	8
9	1.20			0	1.20	9
10	1.40			0	1.40	10
11	1.40			0	1.40	11
12	1.40	1.90		1	1.90	0
13	1.90	1.90		0 or 1	1.90	1 or 13
14	1.90	1.90		0 or 1	1.90	2 or 14
15	2.10	1.90		0	2.10	15
16	2.40	1.90		0	2.40	16
17	2.40	2.60		1	2.60	5
18	2.60	2.60		0 or 1	2.60	6 or 18
19	2.60	2.60		0 or 1	2.60	7 or 19
20	2.80	3.10		1	3.10	8
21	3.10	3.10		0 or 1	3.10	9 or 21
22	3.10	3.30		1	3.30	10
23	3.30	3.30		0 or 1	3.30	11 or 23
24	3.60	3.30	3.80	2	3.80	0
25	3.60	3.80	3.80	1 or 2	3.80	1 or 13
26	3.80	3.80	3.80	0, 1 or 2	3.80	2 or 14 or 26
27	3.80	4.00	3.80	1	4.00	15
28	4.00	4.30	3.80	1	4.30	16
29	4.30	4.30	4.50	2	4.50	5
30	4.30	4.50	4.50	1 or 2	4.50	6 or 18

The calculations at stage 4 are as follows.

x_4 \ d_4	$r_4(x_4, d_4) + f_3(x_3)$ 0	1	d_4^*	$f_4(x_4)$	$x_3 = t_4(x_4, d_4^*) = x_4 - 16d_4^*$
0	0		0	0	0
1	0		0	0	1
2	0		0	0	2
3	0		0	0	3
4	0		0	0	4
5	.70		0	.70	5
6	.70		0	.70	6
7	.70		0	.70	7
8	1.20		0	1.20	8
9	1.20		0	1.20	9
10	1.40		0	1.40	10
11	1.40		0	1.40	11
12	1.90		0	1.90	12
13	1.90		0	1.90	13
14	1.90		0	1.90	14
15	2.10		0	2.10	15
16	2.40	2.70	1	2.70	0
17	2.60	2.70	1	2.70	1
18	2.60	2.70	1	2.70	2
19	2.60	2.70	1	2.70	3
20	3.10	2.70	0	3.10	20
21	3.10	3.40	1	3.40	5
22	3.30	3.40	1	3.40	6
23	3.30	3.40	1	3.90	7
24	3.80	3.90	1	3.90	8
25	3.80	3.90	1	3.90	9
26	3.80	4.10	1	4.10	10
27	4.00	4.10	1	4.10	11
28	4.30	4.60	1	4.60	12
29	4.50	4.60	1	4.60	13
30	4.50	4.60	1	4.60	14

Here we see that the company will earn the same value (4.60) if it uses 28, 29 or 30 feet of the wire. Since unused wire can be sold for scrap the company should therefore use only 28 feet of wire and sell the remaining 2 feet for scrap.

We can use the various tables to work backwards and obtain the optimal solutions. From the stage 4 table we see that the value of d_4^* for $x_4 = 28$ is 1. Hence the company should produce one package of 16 wire.

The value of x_3 corresponding to $x_4 = 28$ is 12. Looking at the stage 3 table for $x_3 = 12$ we see that $d_3^* = 1$ and $x_2 = 0$. Hence the company should also make 1 size 12' package. Since $x_2 = 0$ the company should not make any sized 5' or 8' packages.

The total net profit of this solution is ($1.90) + ($2.70) + ($.06) − ($3.00) = $1.66 [(value of 12' package) + (value of 16' package) + (value of scrap wire) − (cost of wire spool)] per 30' spool of wire.

0 7)   The Dreyfus Advertising Agency is currently handling the Super-Cola
account. Super-Cola has earmarked $15,000 for next month's adver-
tising of Burple powdered soft drink. Dreyfus has determined a value,
in terms of long term profitability, for each form of advertising.
Also, Super-Cola management has placed restrictions on the maximum
number of times a particular advertising medium can be used. This is
summarized in the following table.

Medium	Cost Per Use	Value Per Use	Maximum # of Uses
TV	$ 7,000	11	2
Radio	$ 2,000	5	3
Newspaper	$ 1,000	2	6
Burple Challenge	$ 12,000	18	1
Magazine	$ 4,000	9	2

How should Dreyfus spend the $15,000 to maximize the total value
rating?

Outline of Solution:

i)   Begin by considering giving each possible dollar amount from
$0 to $15,000 (in units of $1,000) to TV advertising. Calcu-
late the return of each of these assignments. This is $f_1(x_1)$

ii) Next consider each possible dollar amount going to both TV and
radio advertising. The recurrence relation is
$$f_2(x_2) = \max_{d_2 \leq 3} \{5d_2 + f_1(x_2 - 2d_2)\}$$

iii) Calculate the stage 3 (newspapers) optimal value function
$$f_3(x_3) = \max_{d_3 \leq 6} \{2d_3 + f_2(x_3 - d_3)\}$$

iv) Calculate the stage 4 (Burple Challenge) optimal value function
$$f_4(x_4) = \max_{d_4 \leq 1} \{18d_4 + f_3(x_4 - 12d_4)\}$$

v)   Calculate the stage 5 (magazine) optimal value function for $x_5 = 15$
$$f_5(x_5) = \max_{d_5 \leq 2} \{9d_5 + f_4(x_5 - 4d_5)\}$$

Answer: Purchase 3 radio commercials, 1 newspaper advertisement, and
2 magazine advertisements. Total value = 35.

8) Suppose in problem 7) that the Super-Cola company had $20,000 to spend on advertising. How should this be spent to maximize the total value rating?

* 9) Suppose in problem 6) Ajax Sound also offered two additional sized packages of wire: a 6' size with a wholesale package price of $1.50 and an 11' size with a wholesale package price of $2.40. Assume all other data is the same as given in problem 6). How many packages of each size should Ajax now produce from a 30 foot spool of wire?

W 10) Dollar Department Stores has four operating divisions; Dollar Stores, Wenthrope Jewelry, Fidelity Insurance, and the newly acquired chain of Burger Prince Restaurants. Dollar management is currently planning its yearly budget and has decided to allocate $20,000,000 to the four divisions. The four division vice presidents have prepared various requests for funds together with the estimated future discounted after tax profitability to Dollar. These amounts (in millions of dollars) are as follows:

Dollar Stores		Wenthrope Jewelry		Fidelity Insurance		Burger Prince Restaurants	
Request	Profit	Request	Profit	Request	Profit	Request	Profit
3	5	3	7	3	2	3	7
4	7	4	10	4	5	4	10
5	8	5	13	5	10	5	15
6	11	6	15	6	14	6	19
7	13	7	18	7	17	7	23
8	14	8	22	8	20	8	25
9	16			9	23	9	29
10	18			10	26		
				11	28		

If each division must receive at least $3 million in funds, how should the money be allocated to each division so as to maximize Dollar's total future discounted after tax profitability?

i) At stage 1 we consider the allocation to Dollar Stores only. This gives the following table.

x_1	$f_1(x_1)$
0	$-\infty$
1	$-\infty$
2	$-\infty$
3	5
4	7
5	8
6	11
7	13
8	14
9	16
10	18
11	18
12	18
13	18
14	18
15	18
16	18
17	18
18	18
19	18
20	18

ii) At stage 2 we consider an allocation of funds to both Wenthrope
     Jewelry and Dollar Stores.

x_2	\$ to Wenthrope Jewelry						d_2^*	$f_2(x_2)$	$x_1 = x_2 - d_2^*$
	3	4	5	6	7	8			
0								$-\infty$	
1								$-\infty$	
2								$-\infty$	
3	$-\infty$							$-\infty$	
4	$-\infty$	$-\infty$						$-\infty$	
5	$-\infty$	$-\infty$	$-\infty$					$-\infty$	
6	(12)	$-\infty$	$-\infty$	$-\infty$			3	12	3
7	14	(15)	$-\infty$	$-\infty$	$-\infty$		4	15	3
8	15	17	(18)	$-\infty$	$-\infty$	$-\infty$	5	18	3
9	18	18	(20)	(20)	$-\infty$	$-\infty$	5,6	20	4,3
10	20	21	21	22	(23)	$-\infty$	6	23	3
11	21	23	24	23	25	(27)	8	27	3
12	23	24	26	26	26	(29)	8	29	4
13	25	26	27	28	29	(30)	8	30	5
14	25	28	29	29	31	(33)	8	33	6
15	25	28	31	31	32	(35)	8	35	7
16	25	28	31	33	34	(36)	8	36	8
17	25	28	31	33	36	(38)	8	38	9
18	25	28	31	33	36	(40)	8	40	10
19	25	28	31	33	36	(40)	8	40	11
20	25	28	31	33	36	(40)	8	40	12

iii) At stage 3 we consider an allocation of funds to Fidelity
Insurance, Wenthrope Jewelry, and Dollar Stores.

x_3 \ d_3	3	4	5	6	7	8	9	10	11	d_3^*	$f_3(x_3)$	$x_2 = x_3 - d_3^*$
	\$ to Fidelity Insurance											
0												
1												
2												
3	$-\infty$											
4	$-\infty$	$-\infty$										
5	$-\infty$	$-\infty$	$-\infty$									
6	$-\infty$	$-\infty$	$-\infty$	$-\infty$								
7	$-\infty$	$-\infty$	$-\infty$	$-\infty$	$-\infty$							
8	$-\infty$	$-\infty$	$-\infty$	$-\infty$	$-\infty$	$-\infty$						
9	⑭	$-\infty$	$-\infty$	$-\infty$	$-\infty$	$-\infty$	$-\infty$			3	14	6
10	⑰	⑰	$-\infty$	$-\infty$	$-\infty$	$-\infty$	$-\infty$	$-\infty$		3,4	17	7,6
11	20	20	㉒	$-\infty$	$-\infty$	$-\infty$	$-\infty$	$-\infty$	$-\infty$	5	22	6
12	22	23	25	㉖	$-\infty$	$-\infty$	$-\infty$	$-\infty$	$-\infty$	6	26	6
13	25	25	28	㉙	㉙	$-\infty$	$-\infty$	$-\infty$	$-\infty$	6,7	29	7,6
14	29	28	30	㉜	㉜	㉜	$-\infty$	$-\infty$	$-\infty$	6,7,8	32	8,7,6
15	31	32	33	34	㉟	㉟	㉟	$-\infty$	$-\infty$	7,8,9	35	8,7,6
16	32	34	37	37	37	㊳	㊳	㊳	$-\infty$	8,9,10	38	8,7,6
17	35	35	39	㊶	40	40	㊶	㊶	40	6,9,10	41	11,8,7
18	37	38	40	43	㊹	43	43	㊹	43	7,10	44	11,8
19	38	40	43	44	46	㊼	46	46	46	8	47	11
20	40	41	45	47	47	49	㊿	49	48	9	50	11

iv) At stage 4 we consider the allocation of funds to all divisions.

$ to Burger Prince Restaurant

x_4 \ d_4	3	4	5	6	7	8	9	d_4^*	$f_4(x_4)$	$x_3 = x_4 - d_4^*$
20	48	48	50	51	(52)	51	51	7	52	13

Answer: Give Burger Prince $7 million
           Fidelity Insurance $6 million
           Wenthrope Jewelry $4 million
           Dollar Stores $3 million

     or Burger Prince $7 million
           Fidelity Insurance $7 million
           Wenthrope Jewelry $3 million
           Dollar Stores $3 million

Discounted Future After Tax Profitability = $52 million

11) Mission Bay Development Corporation is engaged in developing an exclusive 25 acre parcel of property. They have received bids from 5 builders to purchase construction lots. Because of the different nature of the builders, they desire different sized lots. The data is as follows.

Builder	Lot Size Requested	Offered Price Per Lot	Maximum Number of Lots Desired
1	3 acre	50,000	6
2	1 acre	15,000	5
3	6 acre	105,000	8
4	20 acre	350,000	1
5	5 acre	91,000	2

How should Mission Bay sell their land to maximize total sales revenue?

W 12) Dicom Corporation wishes to determine a production schedule for its new Model 44/12 virtual memory computer. Because of differences in parts availability and spare production capacity the cost of producing the machines will vary from month to month. The following table gives these costs together with the sales demand over the next 5 months and the maximum possible production level per month.

Month	Cost of Production Per Machine (in $100,000)	Maximum Production Level for Month	Sales Demand (in units)
July	42	5	3
August	32	4	2
September	18	3	1
October	26	4	5
November	45	5	3

The holding cost for each unsold machine still in inventory at the end of a month is $500,000. Corporate policy dictates that the maximum number of machines allowed in inventory at the end of any month is 8. Determine an optimal 5 month production schedule for the Dicom Model 44/12.

SOLUTION:

This is an $N = 5$ period dynamic programming problem with each period corresponding to one month. Working backwards let stage 1 correspond to November, stage 2 to October, etc. The following data is given.

Month	Demands	Production Capacity	Storage Capacity	Production Cost Per Unit*	Holding Cost Per Unit*
November	$D_1 = 3$	$P_1 = 5$	$W_1 = 8$	$C_1 = 45$	$H_1 = 5$
October	$D_2 = 5$	$P_2 = 4$	$W_2 = 8$	$C_2 = 26$	$H_2 = 5$
September	$D_3 = 1$	$P_3 = 3$	$W_3 = 8$	$C_3 = 18$	$H_3 = 5$
August	$D_4 = 2$	$P_4 = 4$	$W_4 = 8$	$C_4 = 32$	$H_4 = 5$
July	$D_5 = 3$	$P_5 = 5$	$W_5 = 8$	$C_5 = 42$	$H_5 = 5$

*in $100,000

491

If, at some month between July and November, you were called in as a consultant to solve this problem you would have to know (besides the above data) how many machines were currently in inventory. This will be the state variable. Hence x_1 = inventory at the beginning of November, x_2 = inventory at the beginning of October, etc. Since the computer is new, there is no inventory at the beginning of July and $x_5 = 0$. The state transformations are determined by the relationship: beginning inventory at one month = beginning inventory of the preceeding month + production – demand. Since we have numbered the months in reverse, we have the following stage transformations.

$$x_5 = 0$$

$$x_4 = x_5 + d_5 - D_5 = x_5 + d_5 - 3$$

$$x_3 = x_4 + d_4 - D_4 = x_4 + d_4 - 2$$

$$x_2 = x_3 + d_3 - D_3 = x_3 + d_3 - 1$$

$$x_1 = x_2 + d_2 - D_2 = x_2 + d_2 - 5$$

$$x_0 = x_1 + d_1 - D_1 = x_1 + d_1 - 3$$

Here the d_i represent the amount of production decision for each month. For example, the equation $x_3 = x_4 + d_4 - D_4$ states that the beginning inventory in September (x_3) equals the beginning inventory in August (x_4) plus the amount produced in August (d_4) minus the amount demanded in August (D_4).

The return at each stage will represent the sum of the production and holding costs for the month and will therefore be a function of the inventory at the beginning of the month and the amount produced during the month. For example if we begin in November with x_1 computers in inventory and produce d_1 computers the cost will be $45d_1$ to build the d_1 computers plus a holding cost of $5(x_1 + d_1 - D_1)$ since there will be $x_1 + d_1 - D_1$ computers remaining at the end of the month. This can be expressed as

$$r_1(x_1, d_1) = 45d_1 + 5(x_1 + d_1 - D_1)$$

or $\qquad r_1(x_1, d_1) = 50d_1 + 5x_1 - 15$

since $\qquad\qquad D_1 = 3$

Similarly,

$$r_2(x_2, d_2) = 26d_2 + 5(x_2 + d_2 - D_2) = 31d_2 + 5x_2 - 25$$

$$r_3(x_3, d_3) = 18d_3 + 5(x_3 + d_3 - D_3) = 23d_3 + 5x_3 - 5$$

$$r_4(x_4, d_4) = 32d_4 + 5(x_4 + d_4 - D_4) = 37d_4 + 5x_4 - 10$$

$$r_5(x_5, d_5) = 42d_5 + 5(x_5 + d_5 - D_5) = 47d_5 + 5x_5 - 15$$

There are, however, certain restrictions on the values that the x and d variables can assume.

1) Since backordering is not allowed we must be able to meet the sales demand. That is, for period n, it must be true that $x_n + d_n \geq D_n$

2) Because there is a maximum storage capacity of W_n at each stage n, the total inventory at the end of any month can't exceed W_n. Hence for each stage n it must be true that $x_n + d_n - D_n \leq W_n$ or $x_n + d_n \leq W_n + D_n$.

3) The amount produced at each stage cannot exceed the production capacity. This can be expressed as $d_n \leq P_n$.

Let the optimal value function $f_n(x_n)$ represent the optimal return for stages 1 through n given that one starts stage n with an inventory x_n. The recurrence relation is therefore

$$f_n(x_n) = \min_{d_n}\{r_n(x_n, d_n) + f_{n-1}(x_{n-1})\}$$

What this relationship states is that the return from stages 1 through n given state x_n can be determined as follows. Choose the production quantity at stage n which minimizes the return at stage n plus the returns for stages 1 through n given state x_{n-1}. The constraints

1) $x_n + d_n \geq D_n$

2) $x_n + d_n \leq W_n + D_n$

and   3) $d_n \leq P_n$

place certain restrictions on the values d_n can assume.

Starting at stage 1 (November) we have

$$f_1(x_1) = \min_{d_1} r_1(x_1, d_1)$$

(since $f_0(x_0) = 0$ is the boundary condition.)

Using our expression for $r_1(x_1, d_1)$ together with restrictions 1) 2) and 3) we have

$$f_1(x_1) = \min 50d_1 + 5x_1 - 15$$

$$\text{s.t.} \qquad x_1 + d_1 \geq 3$$

$$x_1 + d_1 \leq 11$$

$$d_1 \leq 5$$

Note that $d_1 \geq 0$ (we can't have negative production), $d_1 \leq 5$, and we have from $x_1 + d_1 \leq 11$ that $x_1 \leq 11$. Using the tabular approach gives the following

$$50d_1 + 5x_1 - 15$$

$x_1 \backslash d_1$	0	1	2	3	4	5	d_1^*	$f_1(x_1)$
0				(135)	185	235	3	135
1			(90)	140	190	240	2	90
2		(45)	95	145	195	245	1	45
3	(0)	50	100	150	200	250	0	0
4	5	55	105	155	205	255		

We note that although one might want to consider all possible values of x_1 up to 11 this is unnecessary. Having x_1 any larger than 3 would result in DICOM having computers in inventory at the end of November. This is not desired in this problem and will actually cause an increase in costs (as indicated in the calculation for $x_1 = 4$).

At stage 2 of the problem we have the recurrence relation

$$f_2(x_2) = \min 31d_2 + 5x_2 - 25 + f_1(x_1)$$

or

$$f_2(x_2) = \min\ 31d_2 + 5x_2 - 25 + f_1(x_2 + d_2 - 5)$$

$$\text{s.t.}\qquad x_2 + d_2 \geq 5$$

$$x_2 + d_2 \leq 13$$

$$d_2 \leq 4$$

The table will look as follows

d_2 x_2	$31d_2 + 5x_2 - 25 + f_1(x_1)$					d_2^*	$f_2(x_2)$	$x_1 = x_2 + d_2^* - 5$
	0	1	2	3	4			
1					239	4	239	0
2				213	199	4	199	1
3			187	173	159	4	159	2
4		161	147	133	119	4	119	3
5	135	121	107	93		3	93	3
6	95	81	67			2	67	3
7	55	41				1	41	3
8	15					0	15	3

Note that $x_2 = 0$ is infeasible and therefore there is no row corresponding to $x_2 = 0$

At stage 3 of the problem we have the following recurrence relation and table.

$$f_3(x_3) = \min\ 23d_3 + 5x_3 - 5 + f_2(x_3 + d_3 - 1)$$

$$\text{s.t.}\qquad x_3 + d_3 \geq 1$$

$$x_3 + d_3 \leq 9$$

$$d_3 \leq 3$$

| | $25d_3 + 5x_3 - 5 + f_2(x_3 + d_3 - 1)$ | | | | | | |
x_3 \ d_3	0	1	2	3	d_3^*	$f_3(x_3)$	$x_2 = x_3 + d_3^* - 1$
0			280	(263)	3	263	2
1		257	245	(228)	3	228	3
2	243	222	210	(193)	3	193	4
3	209	187	175	(172)	3	172	5
4	174	152	154	(151)	3	151	6
5	139	131	133	(130)	3	130	7
6	118	110	112	(109)	3	109	8
7	97	(89)	91		1	89	7
8	76	(68)			1	68	8
9	(55)				0	55	8

At stage 4 of the problem we have the following recurrence relation and table

$$f_4(x_4) = \min \quad 37d_4 + 5x_4 - 10 + f_3(x_4 + d_4 - 2)$$

$$\text{s.t.} \quad x_4 + d_4 \geq 2$$

$$x_4 + d_4 \leq 10$$

$$d_4 \leq 4$$

x_4 \ d_4			$37d_4 + 5x_5 - 10 + f_3(x_4 + d_4 - 2)$			d_4^*	$f_4(x_4)$	$x_3 = x_4 + d_4^* - 2$
	1	2	3	4	5			
0			(327)	329	336	2	327	0
1		(295)	297	299	320	1	295	0
2	(263)	265	267	283	304	0	263	0
3	(233)	235	251	267	288	0	233	1
4	(203)	219	235	251	272	0	203	2
5	(187)	203	219	235	257	0	187	3
6	(171)	187	203	220	241	0	171	4
7	(155)	171	188	204	233	0	155	5
8	(139)	156	172	196		0	139	6
9	(124)	141	164			0	124	7
10	(108)	132				0	108	8

Finally, at stage 5 of the problem we have the recurrence relation

$$f_5(x_5) = \min\ 47d_5 + 5x_5 - 15 + f_4(x_5 + d_5 - 3)$$

$$\text{s.t.} \qquad x_5 + d_5 \leq 3$$

$$x_5 + d_5 \geq 11$$

$$d_5 \leq 5$$

Since we wish to start out in July with $x_5 = 0$ inventory on hand we need only compute this one row in the table.

x_5 \ d_5			$47d_5 + 5x_5 - 15 + f_4(x_5 + d_5 - 3)$				d_3^*	$f_x(x_5)$	$x_4 = x_5 + d_5 - 3$
	0	1	2	3	4	5			
0				(453)	468	483	3	453	0

Working backwards through the tables we see that $f_5(x_5 = 0) = 453$

497

$$d_5^* = 3$$

$$d_4^* = 2$$

$$d_3^* = 3$$

$$d_2^* = 4$$

$$d_1^* = 2$$

Hence the company should build 3 computers in July, 2 in August, 3 in September, 4 in October and 2 in November for a total cost of $45.3 million.

0 13) UNIDYDE Corporation is currently planning the production of red dye
number 56 for the next 4 months. Because of the volatile nature of
the dye, special production and handling procedures must be followed.
This causes the production and handling costs, as well as production
and storage capacity, to vary from month to month. This data is
given in the following table.

Month	Production Cost Per Batch*	Maximum Production Level (in Batches)	Holding Cost Per Batch in Inventory at End of Month*	Maximum Storage Capacity (in Batches)
February	11	3	3	4
March	15	4	2	3
April	16	3	2	5
May	9	2	1	2

*in thousands of dollars

The sales department has received the following orders. February - 2
batches, March - 4 batches, April - 2 batches, May - 3 batches. At the
end of May the FDA has ruled that red dye #56 can no longer be produced
because it may cause cancer. Hence the company does not wish any red dye
#56 in inventory at the end of May. Current inventory is 2 batches.
Determine a production schedule for the next 4 months.

Outline of Solution:

   i)   Determine the parameter values for each stage, letting stage 1
correspond to May, stage 2 correspond to April, etc.

   ii) Calculate the return and stage transformation function for each
stage.

   iii) Begin at stage 1 and determine $f_1(x_1)$ for all feasible values
of x_1.

$$f_1(x_1) = \min \; r_1(x_1, d_1)$$

$$\text{s.t.} \quad x_1 + d_1 \geq D_1$$

$$x_1 + d_1 \leq P_1 + W_1$$

$$d_1 \leq P_1$$

iv) Work backwards to stage 4 by using the recurrence relation at each stage n.

$$f_n(x_n) = \min \quad r_n(x_n, d_n) + f_{n-1}(x_{n-1})$$

$$\text{s.t.} \quad x_n + d_n \geq D_n$$

$$x_n + d_n \leq P_n + D_n$$

$$d_n \leq P_n$$

v) The value of the optimal solution is $f_4(2)$ since the current inventory is 2 batches. Work backwards through the tables to determine the optimal solution.

Answer: Produce 3 batches in February, 1 batch in March, 3 batches in April, and 2 batches in May for a total cost of $125,000.

500

14) Walt's Custom Boats manufactures luxury yachts. Walt is phasing
out production of his 42' Sportfisher which he plans to replace
with a 44' Sportfisher. Walt currently has orders for the next 4
months for the 42' model after which he will cease production. The
following data is given for the next 4 months.

Month	Production Cost Per Boat*	Maximum Production Level	Holding Cost Per Boat in Inventory at End of Month*	Maximum Storage Capacity	# of Boats to be Delivered in Month
May	25	4	1	6	1
June	27	3	1	5	3
July	30	2	2	3	3
August	29	3	1	4	4

*In thousands of dollars

If Walt's current inventory of 42' Sportfishers is 1 boat, how should
Walt manufacture the 42' Sportfisher over the next four months to
minimize total production and inventory holding costs?

* 15) Suppose in problem 13) the production cost for UNIDYDE to manufacture red dye #56 did not vary from month to month. Instead, the
production cost in each month was 8 + 3x thousand dollars, where x
was the number of batches produced. That is, if the company makes
0 batches the cost is $0, 1 batch costs $11,000, 2 batches cost
$14,000, etc. If all other data is the same as in problem 13),
determine UNIDYDE's production schedule for the next 4 months.

* 16) IMC, has estimates that there will be substantial growth on its telecommunications route between New York and Philadelphia. The estimated growth in circuits over the next ten years is as follows.

Year	Growth in Circuits	Year	Growth in Circuits
1	200	6	800
2	400	7	1,000
3	600	8	1,200
4	800	9	1,400
5	1,000	10	1,600

The telecommunications route currently has no spare capacity. IMC has a number of different systems available to satisfy the demand growth, however some systems will not be available until a number of years in the future. The systems data is as follows.

System	Year of Availability	Circuit Capacity	System Cost in $100,000
T46	3	1,200	22
S1240	1	1,000	25
SS13	7	2,000	25
VF78	5	1,000	18

Because of budget constraints, management has determined that the maximum number of spare capacity circuits allowed on the route at any time is 800. Management has also determined that any spare circuits installed on the route at the end of year 10 will be valued at $500 each.

Determine a 10 year growth plan for the New York–Philadelphia route.

17) The AML Vending Machine Company has just signed a 6 year nonrenew-
able lease to install a coffee vending machine in a Dollar Department Store's tire center.

AML estimates that the yearly net profit will be a function of the
age of the machine. AML currently has a choice of several different
aged machines to purchase, each with a different cost. In any year
AML can also trade in its machine for a new model. Also, because
of the nature of the lease, AML plans to sell the machine at the end
of the 6 years for its salvage value (this is also a function of the
machine's age). The following pertinent data is known by AML.

Machine Age	Purchase Cost	Yearly Net Profit	Trade In Cost for New Machine	Salvage Value
New	$400	$200	–	$360
1	$290	$170	$140	$270
2	$260	$150	$170	$230
3	$215	$120	$200	$190
4	$180	$110	$225	$170
5	$150	$105	$260	$140
6+	$130	$100	$300	$120

Determine an equipment purchase plan for AML over the 6 year
period which will minimize its total costs.

18)   Use dynamic programming to solve problem 6) of Chapter 10.

19)   Use dynamic programming to solve problem 12) of Chapter 8.

17 MARKOV PROCESSES

REVIEW

1. Definition of Markov Chains

Markov process models are useful in studying the evolution of systems over repeated trials or sequential time periods. In such a process, a set of transition probabilities govern the manner in which the state of the system changes from one period or stage to the next. A system is said to have a finite Markov chain with stationary transition probabilities if the system possesses the following properties:

1) There are a finite number of states;
2) The transition probabilities remain constant for each stage;
3) The probability of the process being in a particular state at
   stage n + 1 is completely determined by the state of the
   process during stage n.

2. Transition and State Probabilities

The transition probability of going from state i at one period to state j at the next period is denoted by p_{ij}. Usually such probabilities are represented in matrix form, called a <u>transition matrix</u>, denoted P. They are generally obtained using the relative frequency method. The <u>state probability</u>, denoted by $\Pi_i(n)$, is the probability of the process being in state i at stage n. The state probabilities for any period are determined by a matrix multiplication of the previous period's state probabilities times the transition probabilities. Using vector notation we have $\Pi(n + 1)$, the vector of state probabilities at stage n + 1, equals $\Pi(n) \times P$. Using recursive logic, it is clear that the state probabilities at any stage will be a function of the initial state probabilities, denoted $\Pi(o)$. In certain cases, as the number of stages (n) becomes large the state probabilities approach limiting values, independent of the initial state probabilities. These limiting probabilities, denoted Π_i, are called <u>steady-state proba-bilities</u>. They can be obtained by solving the series of equations, $\Pi = \Pi P$ and $\Sigma \Pi_i = 1$. By determining the steady-state probabilities an economic analysis of the long range behavior of the system is possible.

3. <u>Fundamental Matrix</u>

If the probability of the process remaining in a particular state at each transition equals 1 the state is called an <u>absorbing state</u>. For a Markov process which has some absorbing and some nonabsorbing states the transition matrix can be thought of being comprised of four submatrices $\begin{bmatrix} I & 0 \\ R & Q \end{bmatrix}$. The upper left hand square submatrix, I, corresponding to the absorbing states, is an identity matrix. The upper right hand submatrix, 0, is a zero matrix. The lower left hand submatrix, R, contains the transition probabilities between the nonabsorbing and absorbing states. The lower right hand square submatrix, Q, represents the transition proba-bilities between the nonabsorbing states. The inverse matrix of the dif-ference between the identity matrix and the lower right hand submatrix, $N = (I - Q)^{-1}$, is called the <u>fundamental matrix</u>. The product of the fundamental matrix and the lower left hand submatrix, NR, gives the proba-bility of eventually moving from a nonabsorbing state into each absorbing state. Multiplying a vector of initial nonabsorbing state probabilities by this matrix gives the probabilities of eventually being in the absorb-ing states. Such computations enable economic analyses of systems and policies.

506

ABSORBING STATE - A state is said to be absorbing if the probability of
making a transition out of that state is zero. Thus once the system has made a transition into an absorbing state, it will remain
there forever. (669)

FUNDAMENTAL MATRIX - A matrix necessary for the computation of probabilities associated with absorbing states of a Markov process. (669)

MARKOV PROCESS (MARKOV CHAIN) - A probability model of a system in which
the state of the system at one trial determines the probabilities
for the system being in particular states at the next trial. (656)

STATE OF THE SYSTEM - The condition of the system at any particular trial
or time period. (657)

STATE PROBABILITY - The probability the system will be in any particular
state. ($\pi_i(n)$ is the probability that the system will be in state
i during period n.) (659)

STEADY-STATE PROBABILITY - The probability that the system will be in any
particular state after a large number of transitions. Once steady
state has been reached, the state probabilities do not change from
period to period. (π_i is the steady state probability of the system being in state i.) (664)

TRANSITION MATRIX - A matrix consisting of the transition probabilities for
the Markov chain. (658)

TRANSITION PROBABILITY - Given the system is in state i during one period,
the transition probability p_{ij} is the probability that the system
will be in state j during the next period. (658)

TRIALS OF THE PROCESS - The events that trigger transitions of the system
from one state to another. In many applications successive time
periods represent the trials of the process. (657)

Chapter 17 Check List

W 1) The weather conditions in the resort town of Ocho Rios are dependent upon the previous day's weather. Conditions are classified as either sunny or cloudy by the tourist board. If the weather is sunny on one day the probability it will be sunny on the next day is .9. If it is cloudy on one day, the probability it will be cloudy on the next day is .2.

a) Construct the transition matrix for this problem.

b) What is the expected number of sunny days per year?

c) What is the probability of it being cloudy for the next two days if today is cloudy?

d) What is the probability of it being cloudy for exactly one of the next two days if today is cloudy?

SOLUTION:

a) Transition matrix

<table>
<tr><td></td><td></td><td colspan="2">Weather Tomorrow</td></tr>
<tr><td></td><td></td><td>Sunny</td><td>Cloudy</td></tr>
<tr><td rowspan="2">Weather Today</td><td>Sunny</td><td>.9</td><td>.1</td></tr>
<tr><td>Cloudy</td><td>.8</td><td>.2</td></tr>
</table>

b) To find the expected number of sunny days per year we must first find the long-run proportion (probability) of sunny days.

Let Π_1 = long-run proportion of sunny days

Π_2 = long-run proportion of cloudy days

We have

$$[\Pi_1 \ \Pi_2] \begin{bmatrix} .9 & .1 \\ .8 & .2 \end{bmatrix} = [\Pi_1 \ \Pi_2]$$

509

or in equation form,

1) $.9\Pi_1 + .8\Pi_2 = \Pi_1$

2) $.1\Pi_1 + .2\Pi_2 = \Pi_2$

3) $\Pi_1 + \Pi_2 = 1$

Solving for equations (2) and (3) we have

$$.1\Pi_1 = .8\Pi_2$$

or $\quad\quad \Pi_1 = 8\Pi_2$

and since $\quad \Pi_1 + \Pi_2 = 1$

$$8\Pi_2 + \Pi_2 = 1$$

Thus, $\quad\quad \Pi_2 = 1/9$

and $\quad\quad \Pi_1 = 8/9$

Therefore the expected number of sunny days per year equals $(365)(8/9) = 324$ days.

c) Let us construct a tree diagram

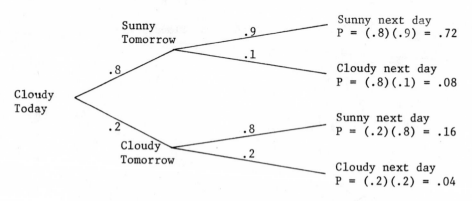

510

Hence, the probability of the next two days being cloudy = .04.

d) The probability of exactly one cloudy day can also be found from the tree diagram. It equals .08 + .16 = .24.

0 2) Joe Ferris, a stock trader at the brokerage firm of Smith, Jones, Johnson, and Thomas, Inc. has noticed that the price changes in the shares of Dollar Department Stores at each trade are dependent upon the previous trade's price change. His observations can be summarized by the following transition matrix.

Next Price Change

		+ 1/8	0	− 1/8
	+ 1/8	.70	.20	.10
Current Price Change	0	.30	.40	.30
	− 1/8	.20	.10	.70

a) What is the long-run average change in the value of a share of Dollar Department Stores' stock per trade?

b) If the shares of Dollar Department Stores are currently traded at $18 and the last trade was at 17 7/8 what is the probability the shares will sell at 18 in two trades?

Outline of Solution:

a) Let Π_1 = long-run probability stock price change = + 1/8

Π_2 = long-run probability stock price change = 0

Π_3 = long-run probability stock price change = − 1/8

Solve

$$[\Pi_1 \; \Pi_2 \; \Pi_3] \begin{bmatrix} .70 & .20 & .10 \\ .30 & .40 & .30 \\ .20 & .10 & .70 \end{bmatrix} = [\Pi_1 \; \Pi_2 \; \Pi_3]$$

or

(1) $\quad .7\Pi_1 + .3\Pi_2 + .2\Pi_3 = \Pi_1$

(2) $\quad .2\Pi_1 + .4\Pi_2 + .1\Pi_3 = \Pi_2$

(3) $\quad .1\Pi_1 + .3\Pi_2 + .7\Pi_3 = \Pi_3$

(4) $\quad \Pi_1 + \Pi_2 + \Pi_3 = 1$

This is done by solving equation (4) together with any 2 of the first 3 equations.

For example, using equations (2), (3) and (4) gives

$$2\Pi_1 + 6\Pi_2 + \Pi_3 = 0$$

$$\Pi_1 + 3\Pi_2 - 3\Pi_3 = 0$$

$$\Pi_1 + \Pi_2 + \Pi_3 = 1$$

Answer: $\quad \Pi_1 = \dfrac{15}{34} \qquad \Pi_2 = \dfrac{7}{34} \qquad \Pi_3 = \dfrac{12}{34}$

The long-run average change in the value of a share of Dollar Department Stores' stock per trade equals:

$$(\frac{15}{34})(\frac{1}{8}) + \frac{7}{34}(0) + \frac{12}{34}(-1/8) = \frac{2}{272} = \$.011$$

b) Note that the price of the last trade is irrelevant - a fundamental property of Markov chains. Construct a tree diagram.

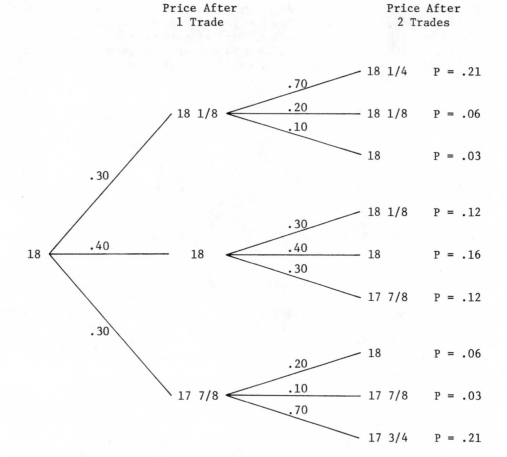

Price After 1 Trade   Price After 2 Trades

The probability that the stock will sell at 18 after 2 trades
equals .03 + .16 + .06 = .25

3) Leisure World Travel Agency never has more than two people waiting to be served (customers finding two people already waiting go down the street to Leisure's competitor, Worldwide Travel). The number of people waiting to be served is a Markov process which can be summarized by the following transition probability table.

Number of People Waiting
15 Minutes Later

		0	1	2
Number of	0	.70	.20	.10
People Currently	1	.30	.50	.20
Waiting	2	.30	.10	.60

a) What is the long-run expected number of people waiting for service?

b) Suppose there is currently no one waiting for service. Determine the probability of having 0, 1, and 2 people waiting for service for each interval over the next hour and a half.

* 4) There are currently only two fast food restaurants in the Main Street area, Burger Prince and Feisty Fowl. The probability of a customer eating at one restaurant is dependent upon which restaurant he ate at previously. The probabilities can be summarized by the following matrix.

Next Restaurant

		Burger Prince	Feisty Fowl
Last Restaurant Eaten At	Burger Prince	.7	.3
	Feisty Fowl	.4	.6

Colonel Mustard's Hot Dogs is planning to open a new restaurant next to Burger Prince. Burger Prince management estimates the new restaurant will result in the following transition probabilities.

Next Restaurant

		Burger Prince	Feisty Fowl	Col. Mustard's
	Burger Prince	.5	.3	.2
Last Restaurant Eaten At	Feisty Fowl	.3	.5	.2
	Col. Mustard's	.3	.3	.4

By how much will the long-run market share of Burger Prince and Feisty Fowl change with the opening of Col. Mustard's?

5) In order to retain its market share after the opening of Colonel
   Mustard's Restaurant (see problem 4), Burger Prince is planning to
   offer 2 new entrees - Roast Beef and Fish Filet. Management believes
   this will increase the probability of a customer eating at Burger
   Prince. In particular they believe the new transition probabilities
   will be as follows:

Next Restaurant

		Burger Prince	Feisty Fowl	Col. Mustard's
	Burger Prince	.60	.25	.15
Last Restaurant Eaten At	Feisty Fowl	.35	.45	.20
	Col. Mustard's	.30	.30	.40

What will Burger Prince's long-run market share be if management does
introduce the 2 new entrees?

W 6) The vice president of personnel at Jetair Aerospace has noticed that yearly shifts in personnel can be modeled by a Markov process. The transition probabilities are as follows:

Next Year

		Remain in same position	Promotion	Retire	Quit	Fired
	Remain in same position	.55	.1	.05	.2	.1
Current Year	Promotion	.7	.2	.0	.1	.0
	Retire	0	0	1	0	0
	Quit	0	0	0	1	0
	Fired	0	0	0	0	1

a) Determine the transition probability matrix for this problem in the form $\begin{bmatrix} I & | & 0 \\ - & + & - \\ R & | & Q \end{bmatrix}$.

b) Compute the fundamental matrix for this problem.

What is the probability of an employee just promoted eventually

c) retiring?

d) quitting?

e) being fired?

SOLUTION:

a) Since we must have the identity matrix in the upper left hand corner, our transition matrix will be as follows:

$$\begin{array}{c} \\ \\ \text{Current} \\ \text{State} \\ \\ \end{array} \begin{array}{c} 1 \\ 2 \\ 3 \\ 4 \\ 5 \end{array} \begin{array}{ccccc} 1 & 2 & 3 & 4 & 5 \\ \left[\begin{array}{ccccc} 1 & 0 & 0 & 0 & 0 \\ 0 & 1 & 0 & 0 & 0 \\ 0 & 0 & 1 & 0 & 0 \\ .05 & .2 & .1 & .55 & .1 \\ 0 & .1 & 0 & .7 & .2 \end{array}\right] \end{array}$$

State 1–Retire

State 2–Quit

State 3–Fired

State 4–Remain in same position

State 5–Promotion

$$Q = \begin{bmatrix} .55 & .1 \\ .7 & .2 \end{bmatrix}$$

$$R = \begin{bmatrix} .05 & .2 & .1 \\ 0 & .1 & 0 \end{bmatrix}$$

b) $N = (I - Q)^{-1} = \left(\begin{bmatrix} 1 & 0 \\ 0 & 1 \end{bmatrix} - \begin{bmatrix} .55 & .1 \\ .7 & .2 \end{bmatrix} \right)^{-1}$

$$= \begin{bmatrix} .45 & -.1 \\ -.7 & .8 \end{bmatrix}^{-1}$$

The determinant, $d = a_{11} a_{22} - a_{21} a_{12} = (.45)(.8) - (-.7)(-.1)$

$$= .29$$

Hence,

$$N = \begin{bmatrix} .8/.29 & .1/.29 \\ .7/.29 & .45/.29 \end{bmatrix} = \begin{bmatrix} 2.76 & .34 \\ 2.41 & 1.55 \end{bmatrix}$$

518

c) through e)

$$NR = \begin{bmatrix} 2.76 & .34 \\ 2.41 & 1.55 \end{bmatrix} \begin{bmatrix} .05 & .2 & .1 \\ 0 & .1 & 0 \end{bmatrix}$$

		Retire	Quit	Fire
=	Same	.14	.58	.28
	Promote	.12	.64	.24

The probability of someone just being promoted eventually being in one of the absorbing states is given by the bottom row of this probability matrix. The answers are therefore

c) Eventually retiring   = .12

d) Eventually quitting   = .64

e) Eventually being fired = .24

7) Suppose Jetair Aerospace (problem 6) reduces the probability of a worker being fired down to .05. The new transition probability matrix will be as follows:

Next Year

		Remain in same Position	Promotion	Retire	Quit	Fired
Current Year	Remain in same position	.6	.1	.05	.2	.05
	Promotion	.7	.2	0	.1	0
	Retire	0	0	1	0	0
	Quit	0	0	0	1	0
	Fired	0	0	0	0	1

Determine the probability of an employee just promoted eventually

a) retiring?

b) quitting?

c) being fired?

Compare with the answers in problem 6).

* 8) Fidelity Insurance has modeled its life insurance business as a Markov process. Each year a customer either pays his premium, borrows against his policy to pay the premium, cashes in his policy, or dies. The transition probability table is as follows:

Next Year

		Pays Premium	Borrows on Policy	Cashes Policy In	Dies
	Pays Premium	.65	.23	.10	.02
Current Year	Borrows on Policy	.42	.34	.21	.03
	Cashes Policy In	0	0	1	0
	Dies	0	0	0	1

What is the probability of an insured eventually cashing in his policy if

a) he pays premium in current year?

b) he borrows against the policy to pay the premium in the current year?

c) Suppose this year 60% of Fidelity's customers who paid their premium borrowed against their policy. What percentage of the customers will eventually cash in their policy?

9) As owner of the LASF Truck Rental Agency, you rent trucks which operate exclusively in two cities: LA and SF. The following table gives the probabilities of transitions in a given week:

	TO LA	TO SF	Wrecked	Stolen
From LA	.5	.2	.2	.1
From SF	.6	.2	.2	0

a) Set the problem up as a Markov Chain in the form

$$\begin{bmatrix} I & | & 0 \\ - & + & - \\ R & | & Q \end{bmatrix}$$

b) What is the probability that a truck from SF is eventually wrecked?

c) Suppose we buy 200 trucks and put half of them in SF and half in LA. What is the expected distribution of the trucks after two weeks?

0 10) The evening television news broadcast that individuals view on one
evening is influenced by which broadcast they viewed previously. An
executive at the C network has determined the following transition
probability table describes this phenomenon.

News Program Watched Next

	Network	A	C	N
Current News Program Watched	A	.80	.12	.08
	C	.08	.85	.07
	N	.08	.09	.83

a) Which network has the most loyal viewers?

b) What are the long-run market shares of the three networks?

c) Suppose each network earns \$1,250 in daily profit from advertising
revenue for each million viewers it has. If on average 40 million
people watch the evening television news, compute the average
daily profit for each network.

Outline of Solution:

a) Determine which network has the viewers with the highest probability of watching it again.

Answer: Network C.

b) Let Π_1 = long-run market share of Network A

Π_2 = long-run market share of Network C

Π_3 = long-run market share of Network N

Solve for

$$[\Pi_1\ \Pi_2\ \Pi_3] \begin{bmatrix} .80 & .12 & .08 \\ .08 & .85 & .07 \\ .08 & .09 & .83 \end{bmatrix} = [\Pi_1\ \Pi_2\ \Pi_3]$$

Answer: Π_1 = .286

$\quad\quad\quad\quad$ Π_2 = .381

$\quad\quad\quad\quad$ Π_3 = .333

c)   i)   Compute the average daily number of viewers for Networks A, C and N.

$\quad\quad$ Answer: A - 11.44 million
$\quad\quad\quad\quad\quad\quad$ C - 15.24 $\quad$ "
$\quad\quad\quad\quad\quad\quad$ N - 13.32 $\quad$ "

$\quad$ ii)   Multiply these values by \$1,250 to obtain daily profit.

$\quad\quad$ Answer: A - \$14,300
$\quad\quad\quad\quad\quad\quad$ C - \$19,050
$\quad\quad\quad\quad\quad\quad$ N - \$16,650

11) Consider the evening news broadcast market problem (problem 10).
Network A believes that by hiring a new woman anchorperson it will
increase its market share. It feels that by taking this action the
transition probabilities will be as follows:

		News Program Watched Next		
Network		A	C	N
Current News Program Watched	A	.82	.09	.09
	C	.10	.84	.06
	N	.08	.10	.82

The network must pay the new anchorperson $2,750 per day.

The network earns $1,250 in daily profit from advertising revenues
for each million viewers and an average of 40 million people watch
the news. What will the new average daily profit for Network A be?
Comparing this answer to that of problem 10), part c, should the
network hire the anchorperson?

* 12) Three airlines compete on the route between New York and Los Angeles. Stanton Marketing has performed an analysis of first class business travelers to determine their airline choice. Stanton has modeled this choice as a Markov process and has determined the following transition probabilities:

Next Flight

Airline	A	B	C
A	.50	.30	.20
B	.30	.45	.25
C	.10	.35	.55

Last Flight

a) Determine the long-run share for each of the three airlines.

Determine the probability of a passenger flying on three different airlines on his next three consecutive flights if

b) his next flight is on Airline A,

c) his next flight is on Airline B,

d) his next flight is on Airline C.

e) The weekly profit of each airline is estimated to be (y − .28) times $1,000,000, where y is the airlines' market share. The management of Airline A is contemplating an advertising campaign which it believes will result in new business. Stanton Marketing has projected that such an advertising campaign will result in the following transition probability matrix.

Next Flight

Airline	A	B	C
A	.50	.25	.25
B	.35	.45	.20
C	.15	.30	.55

Last Flight

What is the maximum amount that management could spend per week on this advertising plan?

W 13) On any particular day an individual can take one of two routes to work. Route A has a 25% chance of being congested whereas route B has a 40% chance of being congested. The probability of the individual taking a particular route one day depends on his previous day's experience. If he takes route A and it is not congested he is likely to take route A again with probability .8. If A is congested he will take route B the next day with probability .7. Similarly if he takes route B and it is not congested he will take route B again with probability .9 whereas if route B is congested he will take route A with probability .6.

a) Construct the transition matrix for this problem. (HINT: There are 4 states.)

b) Determine the long-run percent of time route A is taken.

SOLUTION:

a) Let state 1 = route A not congested
state 2 = route A congested
state 3 = route B not congested
state 4 = route B congested

The transition matrix is

$$
\begin{array}{c c c c c}
 & 1 & 2 & 3 & 4 \\
1 & \left[(.75)(.8)\right. & (.25)(.8) & (.6)(.2) & (.4)(.2) \\
2 & (.75)(.3) & (.25)(.3) & (.6)(.7) & (.4)(.7) \\
3 & (.75)(.1) & (.25)(.1) & (.6)(.9) & (.4)(.9) \\
4 & (.75)(.6) & (.25)(.6) & (.6)(.4) & \left.(.4)(.4)\right]
\end{array}
$$

(The first term of each product is the probability of the route being congested or not, and the second term represents the transition probabilities between routes.)

Multiplying through we get the following:

527

$$
\begin{array}{c c c c c}
 & 1 & 2 & 3 & 4 \\
1 & \begin{bmatrix} .6 & .2 & .12 & .08 \\ .225 & .075 & .42 & .28 \\ .075 & .025 & .54 & .36 \\ .45 & .15 & .24 & .16 \end{bmatrix}
\end{array}
$$

b) We must solve the following set of equations to determine the steady state probabilities.

$$.6\pi_1 + .225\pi_2 + .075\pi_3 + .45\pi_4 = \pi_1$$

$$.2\pi_1 + .075\pi_2 + .025\pi_3 + .15\pi_4 = \pi_2$$

$$.12\pi_1 + .42\pi_2 + .54\pi_3 + .24\pi_4 = \pi_3$$

$$.08\pi_1 + .28\pi_2 + .36\pi_3 + .16\pi_4 = \pi_4$$

$$\pi_1 + \pi_2 + \pi_3 + \pi_4 = 1$$

Answer: $\pi_1 = .36$

$\pi_2 = .12$

$\pi_3 = .312$

$\pi_4 = .208$

Hence the long run percent of time route A is taken = .36 + .12 = .48.

* 14) If the Dow Jones Industrial Average increases one day, the probability it will increase, remain the same, or decrease the next day is .3, .4, and .3 respectively, <u>except</u> if it has increased two days in a row. In this case the respective probabilities are .4, .3, and .3.

If it remains unchanged one day, the probabilities it will increase, remain the same, or decrease the next day are .2, .4, .4 respectively.

If it decreases one day the probabilities it will increase, remain the same, or decrease the next day are .2, .5, and .3 respectively, <u>except</u> if it has decreased two days in a row. In this case the respective probabilities are .1, .2, and .7.

a) Explain why the states - increase, remain the same, and decrease, do not form the states of a Markov chain.

b) Define appropriate states and construct the transition matrix, P.

18 CALCULUS-BASED SOLUTION PROCEDURES

REVIEW

1. Unconstrained Optimization in One Decision Variable

Sometimes it is possible to formulate problems which require only one decision variable in the objective function and are otherwise unconstrained. Other problems which at first are formulated in more than one decision variable may, with appropriate substitutions, be reduced to one variable problems. Calculus based solution procedures employing derivatives (see Appendix D) are used to solve problems with one or more variables in which the objective function is nonlinear.

For functions in one variable, either the function has no finite maximum or a local maximum is optimal. A local maximum occurs at a value x* of the variable such that any very small change in the value of x either positively or negatively will result in a lower value of the objective function. A necessary condition for a function f(x) to obtain a local maximum at x* is that $\frac{df(x^*)}{dx} = 0$. Sufficient conditions for x* to be a local maximum are (1) $\frac{df(x^*)}{dx} = 0$, and (2) $\frac{d^2f(x^*)}{dx^2} < 0$. A point is called a global maximum if it yields the highest value of f(x) for all values of x. Local and global minima are defined analogously; the only difference is that sufficient condition (2) is $\frac{d^2f(x^*)}{dx^2} > 0$.

531

The global maximum of a continuous function over an interval for x, $a \leq x \leq b$, occurs either at (1) an end point a or b; or (2) a local maximum. Hence the procedure to find the global maximum over an interval would be to:

(1) find all points such that $\frac{df}{dx} = 0$.

(2) Identify those points for which $\frac{d^2f}{dx^2} < 0$ (these are local maxima).

(3) Substitute these values as well as the end points a and b in to f(x). Select the point which gives the largest value of f(x) for the global maximum.

For global minima, change the inequality sign in step 2, and select the smallest value in step 3.

2. <u>Unconstrained Optimization in More Than Variable</u>

For a problem which can be reduced to two decision variables, x_1 and x_2 but not to one it is necessary to employ the use of partial derivatives (denoted, $\frac{\partial f}{\partial x_1}$ and $\frac{\partial f}{\partial x_2}$). To take a partial derivative with respect to x_1, one simply lets x_2 play the role of a constant and the derivative is taken as if x_1 were the only variable. Similarly x_1 plays the role of a constant when taking a partial derivative with respect to x_2.

The necessary condition for a point to be a local maximum or minimum is that $\frac{\partial f}{\partial x_1} = 0$ and $\frac{\partial f}{\partial x_2} = 0$ at that point.

The sufficient conditions for a local optimum at a point are that at that point.

(1) $\frac{\partial f}{\partial x_1} = 0$ and $\frac{\partial f}{\partial x_2} = 0$.

(2) $\frac{\partial^2 f}{\partial x_1^2} < 0$ (for a local maximum); $\frac{\partial^2 f}{\partial x_1^2} > 0$ (for a local minimum).

(3) $\left(\frac{\partial^2 f}{\partial x_1^2}\right)\left(\frac{\partial^2 f}{\partial x_2^2}\right) - \left(\frac{\partial^2 f}{\partial x_1 \, x_2}\right)^2 > 0$.

532

(If one takes the partial derivative of $\frac{\partial f}{\partial x_1}$ with respect to x_1 it is written as $\frac{\partial^2 f}{\partial x_1^2}$. If one takes the partial derivative of $\frac{\partial f}{\partial x_1}$ with respect to x_2 it is written as $\frac{\partial^2 f}{\partial x_1 \partial x_2}$). If the inequality sign in condition (3) is reversed, the point is said to be a <u>saddle point</u> which is neither a local maximum or a local minimum.

The extension of the necessary conditions for optimality to problems with more than two variables is straightforward: the partial derivative of the function with respect to any variables must be zero. However extension of the sufficient conditions is not straightforward and is beyond the scope of this text.

3. Constrained Optimization and Lagrange Multipliers

A problem which seeks to maximize or minimize a function which may be linear or nonlinear subject to linear or nonlinear constraints is called a nonlinear programming problem. This is a complex subject which in general is beyond the scope of this text.

However, if a problem in two variables can be formulated with a maximization (or minimization) objective function, $f(x_1, x_2)$ subject to an equality constraint, $g(x_1, x_2) - b = 0$, the problem can be solved by using a <u>Lagrange multiplier</u> λ. This is done by forming a Lagrangian function, $L(x_1, x_2, \lambda) = f(x_1, x_2) + \lambda(g(x_1, x_2) - b)$. Necessary conditions for a point (x_1^*, x_2^*) to be a local maximum or minimum are that there is a value of $\lambda = \lambda^*$ such that

(1) $\quad \frac{\partial L}{\partial x_1} = 0$

(2) $\quad \frac{\partial L}{\partial x_2} = 0$

(3) $\quad \frac{\partial L}{\partial \lambda} = 0$

Sufficient conditions for the point to be a local optimum for a particular $\lambda = \lambda^*$ are that at this point:

(1) $\quad \frac{\partial L}{\partial x_1} = 0$

(2) $\dfrac{\partial L}{\partial x_2} = 0$

(3) $\dfrac{\partial L}{\partial \lambda} = 0$

(4) $\dfrac{\partial^2 L}{\partial x_1^2} < 0$ (for a maximum); $\dfrac{\partial^2 L}{\partial x_1^2} > 0$ (for a minimum)

(5) $\left(\dfrac{\partial^2 L}{\partial x_1^2}\right)\left(\dfrac{\partial^2 L}{\partial x_2^2}\right) - \left(\dfrac{\partial^2 L}{\partial x_1 \partial x_2}\right)^2 > 0$

(Note (4) and (5) are evaluated at $\lambda = \lambda^*$)

For a problem in n variables with m equality constraints the Lagrangian is formed by introducing m Lagrange multipliers $\lambda_1,\ldots,\lambda_m$. Then $L(x_1,\ldots,x_n,\lambda_1,\ldots,\lambda_m) = f(x_1,\ldots,x_n) + \lambda_1(g_1(x_1,\ldots,x_n) - b_1) + \ldots + \lambda_m(g_m(x_1,\ldots,x_n) - b_m)$. Necessary conditions for a local maximum or minimum are that the partial derivatives with respect to all decision variables as well as with respect to all Lagrange multipliers must be zero. The negative value of a Lagrange multiplier can be interpreted as the instantaneous change in the objective function per unit change in the value of the right hand side of its corresponding constraint. Its role is similar to that played by dual variables in linear programming.

Another extension is the case of a nonlinear model with one inequality. The solution procedure in this case is:

(1) Solve for all local maxima of the unconstrained problem. If the best local maxima satisfies the constraint and the function does not go to infinity, STOP.

(2) Note all local maxima that satisfy the inequality constraint.

(3) Solve the problem again with the constraint holding as an equality and identify all local maxima for this problem.

(4) The global maximum is the best solution found in steps (2) and (3) above.

DERIVATIVE - A calculus tool which among other things aids in determining
local maxima and minima.   (684)

GLOBAL MAXIMUM (MINIMUM) - The maximum (minimum) value solution to a
problem.   (685)

LAGRANGE MULTIPLIER - A variable added to a problem to multiply a constraint so that the problem can be transformed into an unconstrained Lagrangian problem.   (700)

LAGRANGIAN FUNCTION - A function obtained by adding to the objective
function λ_i times constraint i (for all i).   (700)

LOCAL MAXIMUM (MINIMUM) - A point such that any very small change causes
the corresponding value of the objective function to be lower
(higher).   (682)

NONLINEAR FUNCTION - Any function which is not of the form
$a_1x_1 + a_2x_2 + \cdots + a_nx_n + b$.   (679)

PARTIAL DERIVATIVE - A calculus tool which allows a derivative to be
taken with respect to one variable while treating all other
variables as constants.   (692)

SADDLE POINT - A point where all partial derivatives are zero and yet a
local maximum or minimum has not been reached.   (695)

UNCONSTRAINED PROBLEM - A problem with an objective function but no
constraints.   (690)

Chapter 18 Check List

536

W 1) Given the function $f(x) = 3x^4 - 4x^3 - 12x^2$

a) Find all local maxima and minima for the problem.

b) What is the global minimum for the function?

c) What is the global maximum for the problem?

d) What is the global maximum if x is constrained in the interval $-2 \le x \le 4$?

SOLUTION:

a) A necessary condition for a point to be a local maximum or minimum is that $\frac{df}{dx} = 0$.

Now $\frac{df}{dx} = 12x^3 - 12x^2 - 24x$.

Setting this to zero and factoring out 12x we have
$12x(x^2 - x - 2) = 0$ or $12x(x - 2)(x + 1) = 0$.

Thus x = -1, x = 0, and x = 2 are local optima. To see which are local maxima and which are local minima determine the second derivative at these values.

$$\frac{d^2f}{dx^2} = 36x^2 - 24x - 24$$

Then, $$\frac{d^2f(-1)}{dx^2} = 36(-1)^2 - 24(-1) - 24 = 36;$$

$$\frac{d^2f(0)}{dx^2} = 36(0)^2 - 24(0) - 24 = -24$$

$$\frac{d^2f(2)}{dx^2} = 36(2)^2 - 24(2) - 24 = 72$$

Therefore x = -1 is a local minimum

x = 0 is a local maximum

x = 2 is a local minimum

b) Note the global minimum can occur at a local minimum or at $x = -\infty$ or $x = +\infty$. But $f(-\infty) = \infty$ and $f(\infty) = \infty$. Thus either $x = -1$ or $x = 2$ is the global minimum. Substituting these values into the original function we have

$$f(-1) = 3(-1)^4 - 4(-1)^3 - 12(-1)^2 = -5$$

$$f(2) = 3(2)^4 - 4(2)^3 - 12(2)^2 = -32$$

Therefore $x = 2$ is the global minimum.

c) The global maximum can occur at a local maximum or $x = -\infty$ or $x = +\infty$. Since $f(-\infty) = \infty$ and $f(\infty) = +\infty$, $-\infty$ and ∞ are global maxima for this problem.

d) The global maximum of a function over an interval can either occur at a local maximum in the interval or at an end point. Note $x = 0$ is a local maximum in the interval. Evaluating the function at $x = -2$, $x = 0$, and $x = 4$ gives

$$f(-2) = 3(-2)^4 - 4(-2)^3 - 12(-2)^2 = 32$$

$$f(0) = 3(0)^4 - 4(0)^3 - 12(0)^2 = 0$$

$$f(4) = 3(4)^4 - 4(4)^3 - 12(4)^2 = 320$$

Thus $x = 4$ provides the global maximum over this interval.

O 2)   Solve the following problem

$$\text{Min} \quad 2x^3 - 33x^2 + 144x + 50$$

$$\text{s.t.} \quad 0 \leq x \leq 10$$

Outline of Solution:

1. Take the derivative of the objective function and set it equal to zero.

2. Solve for the two roots of this equation either by factoring or by the quadratic formula. Result: $x = 3$ and $x = 8$.

3. Take the second derivative of the objective function. Then, substitute $x = 3$ and $x = 8$ to see which is a local maximum (second derivative negative) and which is a local minimum (second derivative positive). $x = 8$ is the local minimum.

4. The global minimum can occur at the local minimum ($x = 8$) or at either of the end points of the interval ($x = 0$, $x = 10$). Substitute each of these three values into the objective function and choose the minimum.

Answer:

Global minimum occurs at $x = 0$ and gives an objective function value of 50.

* 3) Given the following function $f(x) = 3x^3 - 6x^2 + 3x + 4$

    a) Solve for the local minimum and maximum for this problem.

    b) What are the global minimum and maximum if $0 \leq x \leq 2$?

4) Suppose a profit function is given by:

$$P(x) = x^4 - 8x^3 + 22x^2 - 24x + 15$$

    a) Show that $x = 1$, $x = 2$, and $x = 3$ give the local maxima and minima for this problem and identify which are local maxima and which are local minima.

    b) What is the global minimum for this function with no constraints?

    c) Find the global maximum for each of the three following cases:

        (i) $0 \leq x \leq 5$

        (ii) $0 \leq x \leq 3.4$

        (iii) $.7 \leq x \leq 3.4$

W 5) Given the following problem

$$\text{MIN } 12x_1^2 + 3x_2^2 + 4x_1x_2 - 20x_1 - 14x_2$$

a) Write the necessary conditions that the optimal solution must satisfy.

b) Solve for the optimal solution.

c) Verify that it is a minimum.

Suppose the constraint $4x_1 + x_2 = 16$ were added.

d) Write the Lagrangian for the problem.

e) Solve for the optimal solution to this constrained problem.

SOLUTION:

a) $\dfrac{\partial f}{\partial x_1} = 24x_1 + 4x_2 - 20 = 0$

$\dfrac{\partial f}{\partial x_2} = 6x_2 + 4x_1 - 14 = 0$

b) Rewriting the above gives

$$24x_1 + 4x_2 = 20 \qquad (1)$$

$$4x_1 + 6x_2 = 14 \qquad (2)$$

Solving these simultaneous equations gives

$$24x_1 + 4x_2 = 20 \qquad (1)$$

$$\underline{24x_1 + 36x_2 = 84} \qquad (2)$$

$$-32x_2 = -64$$

$$x_2 = 2$$

and (by substituting) $x_1 = \tfrac{1}{2}$

c) $\dfrac{\partial^2 f}{\partial x_1^2} = 24 > 0$

$$\left(\dfrac{\partial^2 f}{\partial x_1^2}\right)\left(\dfrac{\partial^2 f}{\partial x_2^2}\right) - \left(\dfrac{\partial^2 f}{\partial x_1 \partial x_2}\right)^2 = (24)(6) - (4)^2 = 128$$

Therefore this is a minimum.

d) $L(x_1, x_2, \lambda) = 12x_1^2 + 3x_2^2 + 4x_1 x_2 - 20x_1 - 14x_2 + \lambda(4x_1 + x_2 - 16)$

e) $\dfrac{\partial L}{\partial x_1} = 24x_1 + 4x_2 - 20 + 4\lambda = 0$ $\qquad\qquad$ (1)

$\dfrac{\partial L}{\partial x_2} = 4x_1 + 6x_2 - 16 + 2\lambda = 0$ $\qquad\qquad$ (2)

$\dfrac{\partial L}{\partial \lambda} = 4x_1 + x_2 - 16 = 0$ $\qquad\qquad$ (3)

From (2) $\lambda = -2x_1 - 3x_2 + 8$ $\qquad\qquad$ (4)

Substituting this in (1) we have

$\qquad\qquad 24x_1 + 4x_2 - 20 + 4(-2x_1 - 3x_2 + 8) = 0$ $\qquad\qquad$ (5)

From (3) $x_2 = 16 - 4x_1$; Substituting this into (5) gives

$\qquad\qquad 24x_1 + 4(16 - 4x_1) - 20 - 8x_1 - 12(16 - 4x_1) + 32 = 0$

Thus

$\qquad\qquad 48x_1 - 116 = 0$

or $\qquad\qquad x_1 = \underline{2\ 5/12}$

Substituting into (3) we have, $x_2 = 16 - 4x_1 = \underline{6\ 1/3}$

Substituting x_1 and x_2 into (4) gives $\underline{\lambda} = -2x_1 - 3x_2 + 8 = \underline{-15\ 5/6}$

Thus $x_1 = 2\ 5/12$, $x_2 = 6\ 1/3$ is the optimal solution.

To verify that this gives a minimum, note that

$$L(x_1,\ x_2,\ -15\ 5/6) = 12x_1^2 + 3x_2^2 + 4x_1x_2 - 20x_1 - 14x_2$$

$$- 15\ 5/6(4x_1 + x_2 - 16)$$

$$\frac{\partial^2 L}{\partial x_1^2} = 24 > 0$$

$$\left(\frac{\partial^2 L}{\partial x_1^2}\right)\left(\frac{\partial^2 L}{\partial x_2^2}\right) - \left(\frac{\partial^2 L}{\partial x_1 \partial x_2}\right)^2 = (24)(6) - (4)(4) = 128 > 0$$

Therefore this is a minimum.

0 6) Given the following problem

$$\text{MAX} \quad -x_1^2 - 2x_2^2 - x_1 x_2 + 8x_1 + 10x_2$$

$$\text{s.t.} \quad x_1 + 2x_2 = 4$$

a) Solve for the optimal solution.

b) Using your result to (a) determine the value of an extra unit of the resource.

c) Solve for the optimal solution if the constraint were $x_1 + 2x_2 \geq 4$.

d) Solve for the optimal solution if the constraint were $x_1 + 2x_2 \leq 4$.

Outline of Solution:

a) 1) Rewrite the constraint as $x_1 + 2x_2 - 4 = 0$. Then form the Lagrangian by multiplying the left side by λ and add it to the objective function.

   2) Take the partial derivatives with respect to x_1, x_2 and λ respectively and set them equal to 0. Solve the resulting three equations in three unknowns.

   3) Show $\dfrac{\partial^2 L}{\partial x_1^2} < 0$ and $\left(\dfrac{\partial^2 L}{\partial x_1^2}\right)\left(\dfrac{\partial^2 L}{\partial x_2^2}\right) - \left(\dfrac{\partial^2 L}{\partial x_1 \partial x_2}\right)^2 > 0$ to verify it is

      maximum.

b) The value is equal to the negative of the value of the Langrange multiplier.

c) 1) Referring to the original objective function find the partial derivatives with respect to x_1 and x_2. Set them equal to zero and solve for x_1 and x_2. Use the second partial derivative test to verify this is a local maximum.

   2) Note that this does satisfy the constraint. Thus it is the global maximum.

d) 1) Repeat 1 of part (c).

2) Note the constraint is not satisfied.

3) Form the Lagrangian treating the constraint as an equality and solve for the local maximum of the constrained problem (part (a)).

4) Since there are no other local maxima, the solution found in step 3 is the global maximum.

Answers:

a) $x_1 = 2\ 1/2$, $x_2 = 3/4$ $(\lambda = -2\ 1/4)$; $z = 18\ 1/4$

b) $2\ 1/4$

c) $x_1 = 3\ 1/7$, $x_2 = 1\ 5/7$

d) $x_1 = 2\ 1/2$, $x_2 = 3/4$

* 7) Solve the following problem

$$\text{MAX} \quad -5x_1^2 - x_2^2 - 2x_1x_2 + 80x_1 + 20x_2$$

$$\text{s.t.} \quad 2x_1 + x_2 = 10$$

* 8) Boxco, Inc. is designing a new 24 cubic foot box requested by a customer. The box is to have a rectangular base in which the width, x, is to be half as long as its length, 2x. The base and the four sides are to be made of wood, the top to be made of chicken wire. The wood costs .20 per square foot, the chicken wire .10 per square foot. What is the best design to minimize total costs? What is the minimum cost of this box?

9) Columbia Mopeds has ascertained that monthly demand for its new moped will vary with the price charged. The best estimate is that Columbia Mopeds can sell x mopeds at a price of ($1,110 - .10x). Fixed monthly costs are $100,000 per month and production costs are $110 per moped.

a) Determine the optimum production and pricing policy for Columbia Mopeds.

b) What is the optimal monthly profit?

c) Suppose a tax of $10 per moped is imposed on the manufacturer. How much of this tax should be passed along to the customer if Columbia wants to continue to maximize profits?

* 10) Halgreen, Inc. manufactures two styles of lawn mowers, the Z-model
and the W-model. Halgreen had a study performed concerning price-
sales ratios. The study shows that z model Z lawn mowers per week
can be sold at a price of ($200 - .01z) per lawn mower, and that w
model lawn mowers can be sold at a price of ($300 - .02w). Fixed
costs are $40,000 per week. Manufacturing costs are $50 per unit
for model Z and $80 per unit for model W. If both items are
produced there is an intermix cost of .025wz. What is the optimal
product mix and what would be the expected weekly profit? What are
the optimal selling prices for both models?

W 11) A crude mathematical model for return on two types of investments of under $25,000 each is:

$$r(x_1, x_2) = -.00008x_1^2 - .00012x_2^2 + .00016x_1x_2 + .4x_1 + .8x_2$$

where x_1 and x_2 are the sums invested in investment 1 and investment 2 respectively. How would you advise an investor wishing to invest $10,000$? What would be the return on an extra investment dollar?

SOLUTION:

The problem is

$$\text{MAX} \quad r(x_1, x_2) = -.00008x_1^2 - .00012x_2^2 + .00016x_1x_2 + .4x_1 + .8x_2$$

$$\text{s.t.} \quad x_1 + x_2 = 10,000$$

Form the Lagrangian,

$$L(x_1, x_2, \lambda) = -.00008x_1^2 - .00012x_2^2 + .00016x_1x_2 + .4x_1 + .8x_2$$

$$+ \lambda x_1 + \lambda x_2 - 10,000\lambda$$

$$\frac{\partial L}{\partial x_1} = -.00016x_1 + .00016x_2 + .4 + \lambda = 0 \tag{1}$$

$$\frac{\partial L}{\partial x_2} = -.00024x_2 + .00016x_1 + .8 + \lambda = 0 \tag{2}$$

$$\frac{\partial L}{\partial \lambda} = x_1 + x_2 - 10,000 \qquad\qquad = 0 \tag{3}$$

Solving, from (1) and (2) we can write

$$\lambda = .00016x_1 - .00016x_2 - .4 = -.00016x_1 + .00024x_2 - .8$$

Rearranging the above and rewriting (3) we have

$$-.00032x_1 + .00040x_2 = .4$$

$$x_1 + x_2 = 10,000$$

549

Solving for x_1 and x_2 we get $x_1 = 5,000$, $x_2 = 5,000$ and by substituting we get $= -.4$.

To show this is a maximum, consider $\lambda = -.4$

Now $\dfrac{\partial^2 L}{\partial x_1^2} = -.00016 < 0$

and $\left(\dfrac{\partial^2 L}{\partial x_1^2}\right)\left(\dfrac{\partial^2 L}{\partial x^2}\right) - \left(\dfrac{\partial^2 L}{\partial x_1 \partial x_2}\right)^2 = (-.00016)(-.00024) - (.00016)^2$

$$= .0000000128 > 0$$

Thus this is a maximum.

The optimal solution is to invest $5,000 in investment 1 and $5,000 in investment 2. The return of investing an extra dollar is $= -\lambda = .40$.

*12) Consider the Halgreen, Inc. (problem 10). Suppose that manufacturing times for both model Z and model W lawn mowers are 1 hour each. What would be the optimal production schedule if 5,000 hours were to be used weekly for production? What would be the (marginal) value of an extra production hour?

13) Togan Company manufactures two styles of toy wagons. The weekly profit function which takes into account all revenues and costs including changing production from one style to the next is given by

$$P(x_1, x_2) = -.01x_1^2 - .02x_2^2 - .01x_1x_2 + 30x_1 + 50x_2$$

The number of production hours required per wagon are:

Wagon	Production Hours
x_1	.20
x_2	.25

a) Given no restriction on the number of production hours Togan uses weekly, determine the optimal weekly product mix. What is the optimal weekly profit?

b) Suppose Togan has 400 man-hours available weekly. What is the optimal product mix and the optimal profit if all 400 hours are to be used weekly?

c) What is the optimal product mix and weekly profit if no more than 400 hours are to be used weekly?

* 14)   Island Cruises and Friendly Ferry are the two cruise lines that have
        been granted licenses to operate between Los Angeles and a small
        island off the coast. Market surveys have estimated 90,000 potential
        customers yearly will make the trip from Los Angeles.

        The proportion of the market that Island Cruises can expect to
        capture is proportional to the percentage of advertising it under-
        takes as compared to the total advertising for the island trip.
        Friendly Ferry is known to be spending $200,000 on advertising.
        Therefore if Island Cruises also spends $200,000 it will capture
        200,000/(200,000 + 200,000) = 1/2 the market. If it spends $600,000
        it will capture 600,000/(600,000 + 200,000) = 3/4 the market, etc.

        If there are fixed yearly costs of $100,000 and variable costs of
        $30 per passenger and a ticket sells for $50, what is the amount
        Island Cruises should spend for advertising? (Be sure to consider
        the revenue from ticket sales and all costs--fixed, variable, and
        advertising.)

*15)   A car dealership handles a demand of 1,600 cars per year and demand
        is constant throughout the year. A shipment (order) of cars costs
        $840 to process regardless of the number of cars shipped. Holding
        costs are figured at $400 per car per year. This is exclusive of
        the rent paid by the dealership. Rent can be figured at $10 per
        space per year. The number of spaces required is the size of the
        maximum inventory. Assuming instantaneous delivery, what is the
        optimal order quantity for this dealership?

16) As every business student knows, profit = revenue - cost. In economics, the derivative of a function (which gives the instantaneous rate of change of the function) defines what is called the marginal value of the function. Thus the derivative of the profit is called marginal profit, the derivative of revenue is called marginal revenue, etc.

a) Show that a necessary condition for a point x to be optimal is that marginal revenue = marginal cost.

Given the following revenue function $r(x) = 100x$ and cost function, $c(x) = x^2 + 10x + 100$,

b) Determine the profit function.

c) Determine the optimum profit.

d) Verify by calculus arguments that this is a maximum, not a minimum.

e) Verify that at the optimal point the marginal revenue equals the marginal cost.

17) The Van Version (VV) Company converts ordinary vans and trucks into mini-motorhomes and has no trouble selling all of its conversions subject to dealer requests. If x_1 = the number (in thousands) of vans converted yearly and x_2 = the number (in thousands) of trucks converted yearly, the profit has been estimated at

$$P(x_1, x_2) = 10000x_1^2 + 20000x_1 - 50000x_1x_2 + 10000x_2^2 - 10000x_2 .$$

Dealers are requesting three times as many vans as trucks.

a) Set up the problem as a maximization problem subject to one constraint.

b) Use the constraint to define one variable in terms of the other and solve by optimizing a function in one variable.

c) Verify that it is a maximum.

d) Solve again for the optimal solution by setting up a Lagrangian and using partial derivatives.

e) Use the second partial derivative test to show that the sufficient conditions are not satisfied although this is the optimal solution as verified in (b) and (c).

18) Plush Aircraft builds three luxury aircraft, the PL1, the PL2, and the PL3. Letting x_1, x_2, and x_3 denote the number of these planes to produce annually, the profit function (in thousands of dollars) has been determined to be:

$$P(x_1, x_2, x_3) = -2x_1^2 - 3x_2^2 - 4x_3^2 + 22x_1 + 40x_2 + 50x_3$$

$$- x_1x_2 - x_2x_3 - x_1x_3$$

The number of production hours required to produce each plane are 150, 200, and 225 hours respectively for PL1, PL2, and PL3 type planes. Each aircraft must also go through 30 hours of test flights before they can be delivered to their customers. If 10,000 production hours and 1,500 test flight hours are to be used yearly, write a set of necessary conditions that the optimal solution must satisfy. DO NOT ATTEMPT TO SOLVE.

19 QUANTITATIVE DECISION MAKING AND MANAGEMENT INFORMATION SYSTEMS

<u>KEY CONCEPTS</u>

1. Definition and classification of Management Information Systems

2. The two-way interaction between Management Information Systems and Management Science

<u>REVIEW</u>

1. <u>Classification of Management Information Systems</u>

In the development of management science in this text, models were built under the assumption that the problems were clearly stated and that up-to-date relevant data was readily available. This pertinent data for decision making is called <u>management information</u> and a system for collecting, analyzing, and reporting such information is called a <u>management information system</u> (MIS). Any firm or business may have a large volume of various information available. This is called a <u>data base</u> which is most often stored on the computer. It is the function of MIS to translate and transmit this data to the decision maker.

There are three general types of management information systems: (1) report-generator MIS; (2) "what-if" MIS; and, (3) management information-decision systems (MIDS). The function of the <u>report generator MIS</u> is to transform raw data in the data base into summary reports such as balance sheets, inventory status reports, vehicle status reports, etc. <u>"What-if" MIS</u> evaluates the consequences of various courses of action as well as possible changes in uncontrollable variables, and generates reports to convey this information. Mathematical models are an inherent part of this type of MIS. <u>MIDS</u> encompasses all the components of the "what-if" MIS plus it also has the capability of recommending the apparent best courses of action. Thus, model solving techniques are incorporated into a MIDS. For maximum effectiveness, MIDS should have on-line interaction capabilities.

2. <u>Management Information Systems and Management Science</u>

Management Information Systems play a key role in the data gathering step of the quantitative approach to decision making providing the necessary current data for the mathematical models. Conversely, mathematical models are utilized both in the "what-if" MIS and the MIDS. Additionally, management science tools such as PERT/CPM and simulation can be used to effectively design a large scale MIS. Hence Management Systems and Management Science are complementary disciplines which are essential parts of the quantitative decision making process.

DATA BASE - An organized collection of data.   (721)

HARDWARE - The physical equipment used in the processing of data, such as the computer and the peripheral equipment such as card readers, tape drives, disk drives, and so on.   (722)

MANAGEMENT INFORMATION-DECISION SYSTEM (MIDS) - Transforms "what-if" MIS information into recommended decisions.   (726)

MANAGEMENT INFORMATION SYSTEM (MIS) - A system intended to provide the information management needs to make decisions.   (720)

ON-LINE - A component of a computer system is said to be on-line if it is under the direct control of the computer. When the user has the ability to directly interact with the computer, we say the user is on-line.   (727)

REAL-TIME SYSTEM - A computer system is said to operate in a real-time mode if the results of the processing are immediately available to the user.   (729)

REMOTE TERMINAL - A device that allows the user to enter data, or receive output at a location that is remote from the computer.   (729)

REPORT-GENERATOR MIS - Creates historical or current status reports on business activities.   (722)

SOFTWARE - The computer programs, procedures, and documentation used in the processing of data.   (722)

TIME-SHARING - The utilization of the computer by a number of different users. The term usually implies that the user communicates with the computer through a remote terminal.   (727)

"WHAT-IF" MIS - Creates reports of the projected consequences of possible decisions or what-if questions.   (723)

Chapter 19 Check List

ANSWERS TO "*" PROBLEMS

## Chapter 1

3) Simplified model – reduce costs and time, but still an approximate solution is attained.

5) (1) Problem definition; (2) model formulation; (3) data gathering; (4) model solution; (5) report generation.

9) (a) Uncontrollable inputs – selling prices, costs, restrictions on percentage of crude in each grade; Controllable inputs – the amount of each crude oil to be blended into each grade of gasoline.

   (b) $P = (S_R - C_1)X_{1R} + (S_R - C_2)X_{2R} + (S_R - C_3)X_{3R} + (S_P - C_1)X_{1P}$

   $+ (S_P - C_2)X_{2P} + (S_P - C_3)X_{3P}.$

Chapter 2

5) $x_1 = 12/5$, $x_2 = 12/5$, $z = 216/5$

8) (a) $(0,0)$, $(5,0)$, $(5,1.5)$, $(4,3)$, $(0,7)$ (b) numerous answers

11) (a) MIN $3x_1 + x_2$

   s.t. $x_1 + x_2 - s_1 \qquad\qquad = 40$

   $2x_1 + 4x_2 \qquad - s_2 \qquad = 60$

   $x_2 \qquad\qquad + s_3 = 12$

   $x_1, x_2, s_1, s_2, s_3 \geq 0$

   (b) $x_1 = 28$, $x_2 = 12$, $s_1 = 0$, $s_2 = 44$, $s_3 = 0$, $z = 96$

16) Lease 48 machines, buy none – annual cost $334,720.

18) Spend $5 million on new products, $5 million on traditional products; realize a profit of $25 million.

20) Produce 14,285 5/7 small toys; 14,285 5/7 medium toys; and 0 large toys. Profit = $57,142.86 per day.

Chapter 3

3) (a) MAX $\quad 3x_1 + 4x_2 + 2x_3$

$\quad$ s.t. $\quad x_1 + x_2 + x_3 + s_1 \qquad\qquad = 50$

$\qquad\qquad 2x_1 + 3x_2 - x_3 \qquad + s_2 = 30$

$\qquad\qquad x_1, x_2, x_3, s_1, s_2 \geq 0$

$\quad$ (b) Yes $\quad$ (c) $x_1 = 0$, $x_2 = 20$, $x_3 = 30$, $s_1 = 0$, $s_2 = 0$; $z = 140$

5) (a) after adding s_1 and s_2 - tableau form-basic variables x_1 and s_2

$\quad$ (b) $x_1 = 0$, $x_2 = 0$, $x_3 = 6$, $s_1 = 1$, $s_2 = 0$; $z = -24$

7) (a) $x_1 = 6$, $x_2 = 2$. $z = 30$

$\quad$ (b) Tableau I $-$ $x_1 = 0$, $x_2 = 0$ $\quad$ Tableau II $-$ $x_1 = 6$, $x_2 = 0$

$\qquad$ Tableau III $-$ $x_1 = 6$, $x_2 = 2$

$\quad$ (c) This variable increases the objective function the most <u>per unit</u> increase in the variable.

$\quad$ (d) Any variable with a positive $c_j - z_j$ will increase the value of the objective function.

$\quad$ (e) $(0,0)$, $(0,4)$, $(6/5, 26/5)$, $(6, 2)$

12) $x_1 = 5$, $x_2 = 3/2$, $x_3 = 0$, $s_1 = 0$, $s_2 = 19/2$; $z = 8$

16) Produce 25 moderate systems, 5 expensive systems; Profit = $100,000; Note: alternate optimal basic solution - produce 75 cheap systems, 5 expensive systems.

18) Hire 6 experts only; Minimum cost = $1,800 per week.

21) Hire 12 for 7 AM, 8 for 11 AM, and 22 for 3 PM (Note: There are other optimal solutions.)

Chapter 4

5) (a) $z = 48$; all points on line $2x_1 + 3x_2 = 24$ between $(39/5, 14/5)$ and $(12, 0)$.

$\quad$ (b) Tableau III gives $(39/5, 14/5)$; $c_3 - z_3 = 0$. Thus, alternative optimal derived from Tableau IV, $(12, 0)$.

$\quad$ (c) Increasing x_2 while keeping $x_1 = 5 + x_2$, the objective function will decrease (both coefficients of x_2 are now negative).

$\quad$ (d) Tableau II gives $c_2 - z_2 = 10$, but entire x_2 column is non-positive

7) The fourth tableau is:

Basis	c_j	x_1 4	x_2 5	x_3 1	s_1 0	s_2 0	a_2 -M	
x_3	1	-1	0	1	-1	-2	0	10
x_2	5	2	1	0	0	1	0	4
a_2	-M	-2	0	0	-1	-3	1	11
	z_j	9+2M	5	1	-1+M	3+3M	-M	30-11M
	$c_j - z_j$	-5-2M	0	0	1-M	-3-3M	0	

There is an artificial variable still positive in this "optimal" solution.

14) (a) $x_1 = 10$, $x_2 = 0$, $x_3 = 0$, $s_1 = 0$, $s_2 = 4$; $z = 50$

(b) $-1 \leq \Delta c_5 \leq 5/2$ or $-1 \leq c_5' \leq 5/2$ (c) Yes (d) No

17) 35¢

20) (a) $x_1 = 4$, $x_2 = 6$, $x_3 = 0$, $s_1 = 0$, $s_2 = 0$, $s_3 = 8$, $s_4 = 12$; $z = 32$

(b) $x_1 = 7$, $x_2 = 0$, $x_3 = 3$, $s_1 = 0$, $s_2 = 0$, $s_3 = 2$, $s_4 = 9$; $z = 32$

(c) $x_1 = 0$, $x_2 = 8$, $x_3 = 0$, $s_1 = 0$, $s_2 = 2$, $s_3 = 12$, $s_4 = 8$; $z = 32$

(d) Yes

(e) With weights of 1/3 each on solutions to (a), (b), and (c) $x_1 = 11/3$, $x_2 = 14/3$, $x_3 = 1$, $s_1 = 0$, $s_2 = 2/3$, $s_3 = 22/3$, $s_4 = 29/3$; $z = 32$

22) (b) Extreme points - (0,4) , (1,2) , (3,1)

(c) (i) terminates optimally at (3,1) (iii) terminates optimally in the line segment of $x_1 - 2x_2 = 1$ from (3,1) to (∞,∞) (iii) unbounded.

26) (a) MIN $15u_1 + 16u_2$

s.t. $u_1 + 4u_2 \geq 10$

$3u_1 + u_2 \geq 8$

$u_1, u_2 \geq 0$

(b) Primal $x_1 = 3$, $x_2 = 4$, $z = 62$

Dual $u_1 = 2$, $u_2 = 2$, $z = 62$

(c) The dual variables are negative of $c_j - z_j$ values for s_1 and s_2 in final tableau.

563

28) (a) MIN $15u_1 + 10u_2 + 24u_3$

s.t. $2u_1 + u_2 + 4u_3 \geq 5$

$2u_1 - u_2 + 3u_3 \geq 2$

$u_1 + u_2 + u_3 \geq 7$

$u_1, u_2, u_3 \geq 0$

(b) $x_1 = 0$, $x_2 = 5/3$, $x_3 = 35/3$, $z = 85$.

(c) From negative of $c_j - z_j$ values of s_1, s_2, s_3,

$u_1 = 3$, $u_2 = 4$, $u_3 = 0$

(d) These values are ≥ 0. Substituting in the left side of the constraints in (a) gives 10, 2, 7, respectively, thus satisfying the constraints.

(e) $15(3) + 10(4) + 24(0) = 38 = z$.

Chapter 5

3) x_{ij} = the number of units of type i of cost type j
$i = 1(H), 2(T), 3(C)$, $j = 1(L), 2(S), 3(1)$

MAX $5x_{11} + 12x_{12} + 25x_{13} + 4x_{21} + 10x_{22} + 18x_{23} + 9x_{32}$
$+ 16x_{33}$

s.t. $1800x_{11} + 2200x_{12} + 3000x_{13} + 740x_{21} + 1600x_{22} + 2230x_{23} + 1000x_{32}$
$+ 1500x_{33} \leq 300,000$

$1800x_{11} + 2200x_{12} + 3000x_{13} \qquad \geq 75,000$
$1800x_{11} + 2200x_{12} + 3000x_{13} \qquad \leq 120,000$

$740x_{21} + 1600x_{22} + 2230x_{23} \qquad \geq 75,000$
$740x_{21} + 1600x_{22} + 2230x_{23} \qquad \leq 120,000$

$1000x_{32}$
$+ 1500x_{33} \geq 30,000$
$1000x_{32}$
$+ 1500x_{33} \leq 75,000$

$.75x_{11} - .25x_{12} - .25x_{13} + .75x_{21} - .25x_{22} - .25x_{23} - .25x_{32} - .25x_{33} \geq 0$
$x_{ij} \geq 0 \qquad j = 1,2,3 \qquad j = 1,2,3$

6) x_{ij} = the number of yards of fabric i used in making shirt j
$i = 1(X), 2(Y), 3(Z); \quad j = 1(C), 2(T), 3(E), 4(F)$

MAX $9.50x_{11} + 5.50x_{12} + 13.50x_{13} + 7.50x_{14} + 8.75x_{21} + 3.75x_{22} + 12.75x_{23}$
$\qquad + 6.75x_{24} + 8.00x_{31} + 4.00x_{32} + 12.00x_{33} + 6.00x_{34}$

s.t. $\quad .2x_{11} - \quad .8x_{21} - \quad .8x_{31} \geq 0$

$\qquad .5x_{12} - \quad .5x_{22} - \quad .5x_{32} \geq 0$

$\quad -.4x_{12} - \quad .4x_{22} + \quad .6x_{32} \leq 0$

$\quad -.5x_{13} + \quad .5x_{23} - \quad .5x_{33} \geq 0$

$\quad -.2x_{13} - \quad .2x_{23} + \quad .8x_{33} \leq 0$

$\quad -.3x_{14} - \quad .3x_{24} + \quad .7x_{34} \geq 0$

$\qquad x_{11} + \qquad x_{12} + \qquad x_{13} + \qquad x_{14} \leq 4000$

$\qquad x_{21} + \qquad x_{22} + \qquad x_{23} + \qquad x_{24} \leq 2000$

$\qquad x_{31} + \qquad x_{32} + \qquad x_{33} + \qquad x_{34} \leq 3000$

$\qquad x_{11} + \qquad x_{21} + \qquad x_{31} \geq 450$

$\qquad x_{11} + \qquad x_{21} + \qquad x_{31} \leq 540$

$\qquad x_{12} + \qquad x_{22} + \qquad x_{32} \geq 625$

$\qquad x_{12} + \qquad x_{22} + \qquad x_{32} \leq 800$

$\qquad x_{13} + \qquad x_{23} + \qquad x_{33} \geq 266$

$\qquad x_{13} + \qquad x_{23} + \qquad x_{33} \leq 475$

$\qquad x_{14} + \qquad x_{24} + \qquad x_{34} \geq 180$

$\qquad x_{14} + \qquad x_{24} + \qquad x_{34} \leq 360$

$\qquad x_{ij} \geq 0 \quad i = 1,2,3 \quad j = 1,2,3,4$

12) x_{ij} = flow from node i to node j along the arc between i and j.

MAX $\quad\quad\quad\quad x_{3t} + x_{4t}$

s.t. $\quad x_{s1} \quad\quad\quad\quad\quad\quad\quad\quad\quad\quad\quad \le 8$

$\quad\quad\quad x_{s2} \quad\quad\quad\quad\quad\quad\quad\quad\quad \le 10$

$\quad\quad\quad\quad x_{12} \quad\quad\quad\quad\quad\quad\quad\quad \le 4$

$\quad\quad\quad\quad\quad x_{13} \quad\quad\quad\quad\quad\quad \le 2$

$\quad\quad\quad\quad\quad\quad x_{14} \quad\quad\quad\quad\quad \le 6$

$\quad\quad\quad\quad\quad\quad\quad x_{23} \quad\quad\quad\quad \le 5$

$\quad\quad\quad\quad\quad\quad\quad\quad x_{24} \quad\quad\quad \le 3$

$\quad\quad\quad\quad\quad\quad\quad\quad\quad x_{34} \quad\quad \le 6$

$\quad\quad\quad\quad\quad\quad\quad\quad\quad\quad x_{3t} \quad \le 7$

$\quad\quad\quad\quad\quad\quad\quad\quad\quad\quad\quad x_{4t} \le 12$

$\left. \right\}$ capacities

$$x_{s1} \quad\quad\quad = x_{12} + x_{13} + x_{14}$$

$$x_{s2} + x_{12} \quad = x_{23} + x_{24}$$

$$x_{13} + x_{23} \quad = x_{34} + x_{3t}$$

$$x_{14} + x_{24} + x_{34} = x_{4t}$$

$\left. \right\}$ flow through nodes

$$x_{ij} \ge 0 \quad i = s,1,2,3,4 \quad j = 1,2,3,4,t$$

14) x_1 = # new non-minority hires

$\quad\quad x_2$ = # new minority hires

$\quad\quad x_3$ = # non-minority management promotions

$\quad\quad x_4$ = # minority management promotions

MIN $\quad\quad\quad\quad\quad\quad 3d_1^- \quad\quad + d_2^- + d_3^+ \quad\quad + d_4^+$

s.t. $\quad x_1 \quad\quad\quad -d_1^+ + d_1^- \quad\quad\quad\quad\quad\quad\quad = 19{,}680$ (Goal 1)

$\quad\quad\quad\quad x_3 \quad\quad\quad\quad - d_2^+ + d_2^- \quad\quad\quad\quad = 472$ (Goal 2)

$\quad\quad x_1 \quad\quad\quad\quad\quad\quad\quad - d_3^+ + d_3^- \quad\quad = 11{,}680$ (Goal 3)

$\quad\quad\quad\quad x_3 \quad\quad\quad\quad\quad\quad\quad - d_4^+ + d_4^- = 375$ (Goal 4)

$\quad x_1 + x_2 \quad\quad\quad\quad\quad\quad\quad\quad\quad\quad = 16{,}560$

$\quad\quad\quad x_3 + x_4 \quad\quad\quad\quad\quad\quad\quad\quad\quad = 562$ (Promoting)

$$x_j, \ d_j^+, \ d_j^- \ge 0 \quad j = 1,2,3,4$$

## Chapter 6

4) (a) Rebuild Playground - Quillstone
        Build Roads - Holmes
        Construct Office Building - Mitchell Brothers
        Modernize Courthouse - Fitzpatrick Company
        Total Cost = $272,000

   (b) Rebuild Playground - Quillstone
        Build Roads - Mitchell Brothers
        Construct Office Building - Holmes
        Modernize Courthouse - Fitzpatrick
        Total Cost = $278,000

9) | Pilot | Assignment |
    |-------|------------|
    | F | S |
    | K | N |
    | M | H |
    | O | L |
    | Y | T |

    Total Points = 205

10) | Site Selection | Responsibility |
    |----------------|----------------|
    | 1 | B |
    | 4 | C |
    | 5 | A |

15) Two optimal sequences giving 17:

    1-2-6-5-4-3-1 and 1-6-2-4-5-3-1

Chapter 7

5) (a) VAM   Truck - SD = 30
                Train - N = 5
                Train - P = 25
                Air   - SD = 10
                Air   - N = 20

   (b) Optimal   Truck - SD = 10
                   Truck - N = 20
                   Train - N = 5
                   Train - P = 25
                   Air   - SD = 30

                   Total Cost = $142,000

7) (a-b)

	D1	D2	D3	D4
01	6 (+2)	4 10	3 2	7 (+3)
02	6 1	8 (+2)	5 13	8 (+2)
03	2 4	3 (+1)	3 (+2)	2 20

(c) Add dummy column, D5, with allocation of 1 from 02-D5. Same solution optimal.

(d) Add dummy column, D5, with allocation of 1 from 01-D5. New optimal solution.

01 – D2 = 10	02 – D1 = 1	03 – D1 = 4
01 – D3 = 3	02 – D3 = 12	03 – D4 = 20

(e) $c_{24} \geq 6$

(f) $c_{12} \leq 5$

9) (b)

P1 – Dayton 400	P2 – Omaha 100	P3 – Jackson 100
P1 – Jackson 400	P2 – Phoenix 700	P3 – Omaha 700

Total Cost – $15,000

13) (a)

Newspaper – MR1	15
Newspaper – MR2	5
Newspaper – MR3	10
TV – MR2	15
Radio – MR2	5
Radio – MR4	20

Total Cost = $106,500

(b)

Newspaper – MR2	20
Newspaper – MR3	10
TV – MR1	15
Radio – MR2	5
Radio – MR4	20

Total Cost = $106,500

(c) Many solutions; in (b) any number between 0 and 15 could be shipped around loop into TV–MR1 cell.

Chapter 8

3) (a) $x_1 = 2.8$, $x_2 = 3.4$, $z = 48.8$

(b) $x_1 = 3$, $x_2 = 3$ is infeasible

(c) $x_1 = 2$, $x_2 = 3$ $z = 36$ is not optimal $x_1 = 2$, $x_2 = 9$ is optimal

(d) Integer program more constrained than linear program.

5) (a) $x_1 = 7/3$, $x_2 = 1/3$, $z = 31/3$

(b) $x_1 = 2$, $x_2 = 0$ $z = 6$

(c) (i) $x_1 = 2.37$ $x_2 = .27$ $z = 9.81$

(ii) Problem infeasible.

10) Optimal solution $x_1 = 2$ $x_2 = 2$; $z = 14$

12) (a) 4/5 containers grain A, 2 containers grain B; Profit = $3960

(b) 2 containers grain A, 1 container grain B; Profit = $3900

14) $x_1 = 0$, $x_2 = 1$, $x_3 = 4$, $z = 22$ is optimal.

Chapter 9

5) Critical path A, C, D, I, L; Completion Time = 15

7)

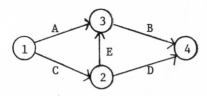

(a)

Activity	Description	t	σ^2
A	Floor Sanding	4	1/9
B	Floor Buffing	2	1/9
C	Paint Mixing	1	1/36
D	Wall Painting	3	16/9
E	Ceiling Painting	5	1

(b)

Activity	ES	EF	LS	LF	Slack
A	0	4	2	6	2
B	6	8	6	8	0
C	0	1	0	1	0
D	1	4	5	8	4
E	1	6	1	6	0

Completion Time = 8 hrs.; Critical Path - C,E,B

(c) .8264

11)

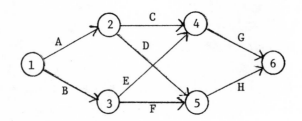

x_i = time represented by node i.

y_j = amount of time crashing activity j.

MIN $1250y_A + 0y_B + 2000y_C + 500y_D + 500y_E + 2000y_F + 5000y_G + 6000y_H$

s.t. $x_6 \leq 16$

$y_A \leq 4$

$y_B \leq 0$

$y_C \leq 4$

$y_D \leq 2$

$y_E \leq 1$

$y_F \leq 2$

$y_G \leq 1$

$y_H \leq 2$

$x_6 \geq x_5 + (7 - y_H)$

$x_6 \geq x_4 + (5 - y_G)$

$x_5 \geq x_3 + (3 - y_F)$

$x_5 \geq x_2 + (4 - y_D)$

$x_4 \geq x_3 + (2 - y_E)$

$x_4 \geq x_2 + (10 - y_C)$

$x_3 \geq x_1 + (3 - y_B)$

$x_2 \geq x_1 + (6 - y_A)$

$x_i \geq 0 \quad i = 1,\ldots,6$

$y_j \geq 0 \quad j = A,\ldots,H$

15) (b)

Activity	AC	V	D
A	5400	5000	400
B	3900	4000	−100
C	2000	1600	400
D	1000	750	250
E	400	750	−350
F	400	400	0
G	0	0	0
H	0	0	0
	13,000	12,500	600

Cost overrun = $600. Suggest transferring some funds slated for E and H to activities C and D. This could affect the completion times of E and H, but there is slack time on E and H.

17) Do not hire the firm.

Chapter 10

5) City 6.

7) (B-2), (R-0), (P-0), (F-5), (D-0). Profit = 53¢ per gallon or $5300.

11) 18.

14) 792,000 cups per hour.

17)

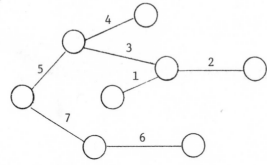

19)

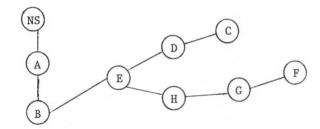

## Chapter 11

4) (a) Stock C – It dominates Stock B.
   (b) (1) Stock A (2) Stock C (3) Stock D
   (c) Stock D

5) (a)

Sales (in millions)

	100	50	1
Introduce	1000	200	−2000
Do not Introduce	−400	−400	−400

(in thousand $)

   (b)

Sales (in millions)

	100	50	1
Introduce	0	0	1600
Do not Introduce	1400	600	0

(in thousand $)

   (c) (1) Do not introduce.
       (2) Introduce.
       (3) Do not introduce.
   (d) Yes
   (e) No.

9) (a)

# of Subscribers

Plan		10K	20K	30K	40K	50K	60K
	I	−550	−400	−250	−100	+50	+200
	II	−520	−340	−160	+20	+200	+380
	III	−500	−300	−100	+100	+300	+500
	IV	−460	−220	+20	+260	+500	+740

in thousand dollars

   (b) Maximax – Plan IV
       Maximin – Plan IV
       Minimax Regret – Plan IV

   (c) Plan II – expected value = $11,000

13) (a) Choose d_2 if the outcome is J_1. Choose d_4 if the outcome is J_2.
    (b) EVSI = .78
    (c) EVPI = 1.3
        efficiency of J = .60   efficiency of I = .01

15) (a) $P(I_1) = .42$ $P(I_2) = .34$ $P(I_3) = .24$

(b) $P(S_1|I_1) = .71$ $P(S_1|I_2) = .53$ $P(S_1|I_3) = .50$

$P(S_2|I_1) = .29$ $P(S_2|I_2) = .47$ $P(S_2|I_3) = .50$

(c) I_1 - choose d_2 I_2 - choose d_1 I_3 - choose d_1

Expected value - 14.12

19) (a) Introduce the root beer.
(b) EVPI = $112,000
(c) EVSI for Stanton = $11,862
(d) EVSI for New World = $6,424
(e) Hire Stanton
(f) Hire New World - the expected net gain is greater

20) If I_1 choose Stock D. If I_2 choose Stock A. If I_3 choose Stock E.

22) (a) Build Shopping Center
(b) EVPI = $10,000
(c) If I_1 choose d_2. If I_2 choose d_3. If I_3 choose d_3.

If I_4 choose d_1.

(d) Yes

23) (a)

PAYOFF TABLE IN $1,000

# of clients purchasing
a computer

		0	1	2	3	4
# of	1	-40	50	30	10	-10
computers	2	-70	20	110	90	70
manufactured	3	-80	10	100	190	170
	4	-70	20	110	200	290
Probability		.13	.35	.35	.15	.03

(b) Build 4 computers.

(c) Nothing.

573

Chapter 12

3) Q* = 20; so reorder 50 times per year; total cost = $14,800;
   reorder when supply = 273.

5) $600 - $200 = $400 per year.

8) (a) Q* = 109,544

   (b) 9.13 production runs per year.

   (c) 13.3 days per run.

   (d) 116 vacation days per year.

12) Order 2000 every week.

15) Choose Option III - order 100 once a week.

19) 25 weeks.

Chapter 13

4) (a) Order 648 every 3.08 weeks when supply hits 42.

   (b) 12

   (c) $6.60

11) 5 salads.

16) 196 donuts.

Chapter 14

5) (a) Critical Paths

        (1) B-C-F-G-H
        (2) B-D-G-H   17 weeks to complete project.
        (3) A-F-G-H

   (b) Assume the following random numbers correspond to the different
        job completion times.

Job Completed	Random Numbers
1 week early	00-24
On time	25-74
1 week late	75-99

Using the last two digits of column 6 and working down the column we have the following simulation.

	TRIAL 1		TRIAL 2		TRIAL 3		TRIAL 4		TRIAL 5	
Job	Random #	Comple-tion Time	Random #	Comple-tion Time	Random #	Comple-tion Time	Random #	Comple-tion Time	Random #	Comple-tion Time
A	14	6	20	6	38	7	3	6	41	7
B	41	4	21	3	73	4	14	3	10	3
C	35	3	40	3	92	4	26	3	27	3
D	38	6	88	7	10	5	26	6	05	5
E	91	6	51	5	69	5	12	4	91	6
F	78	4	62	3	35	3	93	4	66	3
G	90	4	84	4	62	3	82	4	07	2
H	18	3	17	3	24	3	11	3	47	4

Answer:

Trial 1 - Critical Path B-C-F-G-H time = 18
Trial 2 - Critical Path B-D-G-H time = 17
Trial 3 - Critical Path B-C-F-G-H time = 17
Trial 4 - Critical Paths A-F-G-H, B-C-F-G-H time = 17
Trial 5 - Critical Path A-E-H time = 17

Average completion time = 17.2 days

10)

Time On Freeway 5	Random #	Time On Freeway 57	Random #	Time On Freeway 55	Random #	Time On Freeway 91	Random #
5	0,1.2	4	00-09	6	0,1	3	00-29
6	3,4	5	10-29	7	2,3	4	30-64
7	5,6,7,8	6	30-64	8	4,5,6,7	5	65-84
8	9	7	65-84	9	8,9	6	85-99
		8	85-94				

Route 5 - 57   Route 55 - 91

Random #*	Time on 5	Random #**	Time on 57	Total Time	Random #+	Time on 55	Random #++	Time on 91	Total Time
6	7	59	6	13	7	8	51	4	12
8	7	09	4	11	9	9	79	5	14
5	7	57	6	13	8	9	09	3	12
4	6	87	8	14	4	8	67	5	13
5	7	07	4	11	3	7	15	3	10
			Total	62				Total	61

```
 * column 1 of Appendix B
** column 2 of Appendix B
 + column 3 of Appendix B
++ column 4 of Appendix B
```

Answer: Take route 55 - 91 on the basis of this simulation.

13) (i) Determine a random number policy for weekly demand.

Weekly Demand	Random #
0	00–09
1	10–29
2	30–49
3	50–69
4	70–89
5	90–99

(ii) Determine a random number policy for lead time.

# Weeks	Random #
1	00–39
2	40–89
3	90–99

Week	Beginning Inventory	Random* #	Weekly Demand	Ending Inventory	Holding+ Costs	Reorder Costs	Random** #	Time to Deliver	Stockout Costs
1	5	51	3	2	7	40	80	2	–
2	2	79	4	0	2	–	–	–	1	20
3	0	09	0	0	0	–	–	–	0	–
4	8	67	3	5	13	–	–	–	–	–
5	5	15	1	4	9	40	01	1	–
6	4	58	3	1	5	–	–	–	0	–
7	9	04	0	9	18	–	–	–	–	–
8	9	78	4	5	14	–	–	–	–	–
			Total Costs		68	80			20

Total Cost = $168

*First two numbers of column 4

**First two numbers of column 6

+(Beginning Inventory) + (Ending Inventory) x (Holding Cost Per Item)

15) (a) Q* = 40   Total weekly cost = $161

(b) Using the following random number policy

Weekly Demand	Random #
19	0-2
20	3-7
21	8
22	9

gives the simulation below:

Week	Reorder Cost	Begin-ning Inven-tory	Random* #	Demand	Ending Inven-tory	Holding	Costs Shortage	Excess
1	160	40	9	22	18	58		
2		18	6	20	0	16.2	10	
3	160	40	2	19	21	61		
4		21	1	19	2	23		
5	160	41	2	19	22	63		10
6		22	2	19	3	25		
7	160	41	7	20	21	62		20
8		21	5	20	1	22		
9	160	41	7	20	21	62		
10		21	8	21	0	21		
Total	800					413.20	10	30

Average total weekly cost = $166.32

This is fairly close to the estimated model cost of $181. The difference is due to the random fluctuations in demand.

## Chapter 15

4) (a) $P(x = 0) = .135$

    (b) $P(t \leq 45 \text{ minutes}) = .6321$

    (c) $W_q = 2\frac{1}{4}$ hours

    (d) $P_3 = 27/256$

7) (a) $\lambda/\mu = 11/12$

    (b) $W = 4$ hours

    (c) P (at least 3 letters) = .77

    (d) $L_q = 10.08$

8) 97.2 per hour

12) (a) $L_q = 25/24$

    (b) $P_0 = 9/64$

    (c) $W = 20$ minutes

    (d) P (both order clerks are busy) = 25/64

15) $49.20 - No System Installed
     $50.00 - System A
     $47.20 - System B
     Install System B

17) Hire Kenneth Weeks.

Chapter 16

4) Shortest Path.

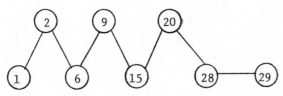

Total Cost = $1,400,000. The optimal policy is to trade in the machine
for a new machine when it gets to be two years old.

9) There are two optimal solutions which give a total value of 4.80. These are (1) make one package of 6' wire, one package of 16' wire, and one package of 8' wire, or (2) make two packages of 11' wire and one package of 8' wire. The profit from either solution is $1.80 per spool of wire.

15) Make 0 batches in February, 4 batches in March, 3 batches in April, and 2 batches in June. Total Cost = $53,000.

16) Year 1 install S1240
Year 3 install S1240
Year 5 install VF78
Year 6 install VF78
Year 7 install VF78
Year 8 install VF78
Year 9 install SS13
Year 10 install VF78

Total Cost = $16,500,000

Chapter 17

4) Burger Prince market share will decline by .196.
Feisty Fowl market share will decline by .054.

8) (a) .85

(b) .86

(c) .856

12) (a) $\Pi_1 = .291$, $\Pi_2 = .373$, $\Pi_3 = .336$

(b) .14

(c) .085

(d) .135

(e) $42,333 per week

14) (a) The states – increase, unchanged, decrease – do not form the states of a Markov chain because the transition probabilities are not only a function of today's stock market performance, but also of yesterday's performance.

(b) We must define our states to account for the market performance for today and yesterday.

Define state (i,j) as market performance of i one day and j the next day.

Let I = DJIA increased   U = DJIA unchanged   D = DJIA decreased
We have a 9 by 9 transition matrix.

	(I,I)	(I,U)	(I,D)	(U,I)	(U,U)	(U,D)	(D,I)	(D,U)	(D,D)
(I,I)	.4	.3	.3	0	0	0	0	0	0
(I,U)	0	0	0	.2	.4	.4	0	0	0
(I,D)	0	0	0	0	0	0	.2	.5	.3
(U,I)	.3	.4	.3	0	0	0	0	0	0
(U,U)	0	0	0	.2	.4	.4	0	0	0
(U,D)	0	0	0	0	0	0	.2	.5	.3
(D,I)	.3	.4	.3	0	0	0	0	0	0
(D,U)	0	0	0	.2	.4	.4	0	0	0
(D,D)	0	0	0	0	0	0	.1	.2	.7

Chapter 18

3) (a) $x = 1/3$ is a local maximum; $x = 1$ is a local minimum

(b) $x = 0$ and $x = 1$ are global minima; $x = 2$ is the global maximum

7) $x_1 = 6$, $x_2 = -2$, $\lambda = -24$

8) Width = 2 feet; length = 4 feet; height = 3 feet.
Total Cost = $7.20

10) Manufacture 3714 2/7 Model W lawnmowers per week to sell for $225.71 each; and 2857 1/7 Model Z lawnmowers per week to sell for $171.43 each; Total Profit = $591,845.33

12) Manufacture 4500 Model W lawnmowers and 500 Model Z lawnmowers per week. Value of extra hour = $22.50

14) $400,000

15) Order 80 cars at a time.

APPENDICES

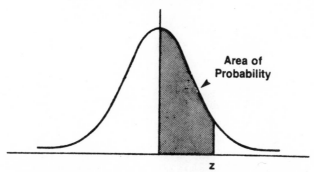

Entries in the table give the area under the curve between the mean and z standard deviations above the mean. For example, for $z=1.25$ the area under the curve between the mean and z is 0.3944.

z	0.00	0.01	0.02	0.03	0.04	0.05	0.06	0.07	0.08	0.09
0.0	0.0000	0.0040	0.0080	0.0120	0.0160	0.0199	0.0239	0.0279	0.0319	0.0359
0.1	0.0398	0.0438	0.0478	0.0517	0.0557	0.0596	0.0636	0.0675	0.0714	0.0753
0.2	0.0793	0.0832	0.0871	0.0910	0.0948	0.0987	0.1026	0.1064	0.1103	0.1141
0.3	0.1179	0.1217	0.1255	0.1293	0.1331	0.1368	0.1406	0.1443	0.1480	0.1517
0.4	0.1554	0.1591	0.1628	0.1664	0.1700	0.1736	0.1772	0.1808	0.1844	0.1879
0.5	0.1915	0.1950	0.1985	0.2019	0.2054	0.2088	0.2123	0.2157	0.2190	0.2224
0.6	0.2257	0.2291	0.2324	0.2357	0.2389	0.2422	0.2454	0.2486	0.2518	0.2549
0.7	0.2580	0.2612	0.2642	0.2673	0.2704	0.2734	0.2764	0.2794	0.2823	0.2852
0.8	0.2881	0.2910	0.2939	0.2967	0.2995	0.3023	0.3051	0.3078	0.3106	0.3133
0.9	0.3159	0.3186	0.3212	0.3238	0.3264	0.3289	0.3315	0.3340	0.3365	0.3389
1.0	0.3413	0.3438	0.3461	0.3485	0.3508	0.3531	0.3554	0.3577	0.3599	0.3621
1.1	0.3643	0.3665	0.3686	0.3708	0.3729	0.3749	0.3770	0.3790	0.3810	0.3830
1.2	0.3849	0.3869	0.3888	0.3907	0.3925	0.3944	0.3962	0.3980	0.3997	0.4015
1.3	0.4032	0.4049	0.4066	0.4082	0.4099	0.4115	0.4131	0.4147	0.4162	0.4177
1.4	0.4192	0.4207	0.4222	0.4236	0.4251	0.4265	0.4279	0.4292	0.4306	0.4319
1.5	0.4332	0.4345	0.4357	0.4370	0.4382	0.4394	0.4406	0.4418	0.4429	0.4441
1.6	0.4452	0.4463	0.4474	0.4484	0.4495	0.4505	0.4515	0.4525	0.4535	0.4545
1.7	0.4554	0.4564	0.4573	0.4582	0.4591	0.4599	0.4608	0.4616	0.4625	0.4633
1.8	0.4641	0.4649	0.4656	0.4664	0.4671	0.4678	0.4686	0.4693	0.4699	0.4706
1.9	0.4713	0.4719	0.4726	0.4732	0.4738	0.4744	0.4750	0.4756	0.4761	0.4767
2.0	0.4772	0.4778	0.4783	0.4788	0.4793	0.4798	0.4803	0.4808	0.4812	0.4817
2.1	0.4821	0.4826	0.4830	0.4834	0.4838	0.4842	0.4846	0.4850	0.4854	0.4857
2.2	0.4861	0.4864	0.4868	0.4871	0.4875	0.4878	0.4881	0.4884	0.4887	0.4890
2.3	0.4893	0.4896	0.4898	0.4901	0.4904	0.4906	0.4909	0.4911	0.4913	0.4916
2.4	0.4918	0.4920	0.4922	0.4925	0.4927	0.4929	0.4931	0.4932	0.4934	0.4936
2.5	0.4938	0.4940	0.4941	0.4943	0.4945	0.4946	0.4948	0.4949	0.4951	0.4952
2.6	0.4953	0.4955	0.4956	0.4957	0.4959	0.4960	0.4961	0.4962	0.4963	0.4964
2.7	0.4965	0.4966	0.4967	0.4968	0.4969	0.4970	0.4971	0.4972	0.4973	0.4974
2.8	0.4974	0.4975	0.4976	0.4977	0.4977	0.4978	0.4979	0.4979	0.4980	0.4981
2.9	0.4981	0.4982	0.4982	0.4983	0.4884	0.4984	0.4985	0.4985	0.4986	0.4986
3.0	0.4986	0.4987	0.4987	0.4988	0.4988	0.4989	0.4989	0.4989	0.4990	0.4990

APPENDIX B.   RANDOM DIGITS

63271	59986	71744	51102	15141	80714	58683	93108	13554	79945
88547	09896	95436	79115	08303	01041	20030	63754	08459	28364
55957	57243	83865	09911	19761	66535	40102	26646	60147	15702
46276	87453	44790	67122	45573	84358	21625	16999	13385	22782
55363	07449	34835	15290	76616	67191	12777	21861	68689	03263
69393	92785	49902	58447	42048	30378	87618	26933	40640	16281
13186	29431	88190	04588	38733	81290	89541	70290	40113	08243
17726	28652	56836	78351	47327	18518	92222	55201	27340	10493
36520	64465	05550	30157	82242	29520	69753	72602	23756	54935
81628	36100	39254	56835	37636	02421	98063	89641	64953	99337
84649	48968	75215	75498	49539	74240	03466	49292	36401	45525
63291	11618	12613	75055	43915	26488	41116	64531	56827	30825
70502	53225	03655	05915	37140	57051	48393	91322	25653	06543
06426	24771	59935	49801	11082	66762	94477	02494	88215	27191
20711	55609	29430	70165	45406	78484	31639	52009	18873	96927
41990	70538	77191	25860	55204	73417	83920	69468	74972	38712
72452	36618	76298	26678	89334	33938	95567	29380	75906	91807
37042	40318	57099	10528	09925	89773	41335	96244	29002	46453
53766	52875	15987	46962	67342	77592	57651	95508	80033	69828
90585	58955	53122	16025	84299	53310	67380	84249	25348	04332
32001	96293	37203	64516	51530	37069	40261	61374	05815	06714
62606	64324	46354	72157	67248	20135	49804	09226	64419	29457
10078	28073	85389	50324	14500	15562	64165	06125	71353	77669
91561	46145	24177	15294	10061	98124	75732	00815	83452	97355
13091	98112	53959	79607	52244	63303	10413	63839	74762	50289
73864	83014	72457	22682	03033	61714	88173	90835	00634	85169
66668	25467	48894	51043	02365	91726	09365	63167	95264	45643
84745	41042	29493	01836	09044	51926	43630	63470	76508	14194
48068	26805	94595	47907	13357	38412	33318	26098	82782	42851
54310	96175	97594	88616	42035	38093	36745	56702	40644	83514
14877	33095	10924	58013	61439	21882	42059	24177	58739	60170
78295	23179	02771	43464	59061	71411	05697	67194	30495	21157
67524	02865	39593	54278	04237	92441	26602	63835	38032	94770
58268	57219	68124	73455	83236	08710	04284	55005	84171	42596
97158	28672	50685	01181	24262	19427	52106	34308	73685	74246
04230	16831	69085	30802	65559	09205	71829	06489	85650	38707
94879	56606	30401	02602	57658	70091	54986	41394	60437	03195
71446	15232	66715	26385	91518	70566	02888	79941	39684	54315
32886	05644	79316	09819	00813	88407	17461	73925	53037	91904
62048	33711	25290	21526	02223	75947	66466	06232	10913	75336
84534	42351	21628	53669	81352	95152	08107	98814	72743	12849
84707	15885	84710	35866	06446	86311	32648	88141	73902	69981
19409	40868	64220	80861	13860	68493	52908	26374	63297	45052
57978	48015	25973	66777	45924	56144	24742	96702	88200	66162
57295	98298	11199	96510	75228	41600	47192	43267	35973	23152
94044	83785	93388	07833	38216	31413	70555	03023	54147	06647
30014	25879	71763	96679	90603	99396	74557	74224	18211	91637
07265	69563	64268	88802	72264	66540	01782	08396	19251	83613
84404	88642	30263	80310	11522	57810	27627	78376	36240	48952
21778	02085	27762	46097	43324	34354	09369	14966	10158	76089

Used by permission from *A Million Random Digits with 100,000 Normal Deviates*, The Rand Corporation, 1955.

APPENDIX C.   VALUES OF $e^{-\lambda}$

λ	$e^{-\lambda}$	λ	$e^{-\lambda}$
0.0	1.0000	3.1	0.0450
0.1	0.9048	3.2	0.0408
0.2	0.8187	3.3	0.0369
0.3	0.7408	3.4	0.0334
0.4	0.6703	3.5	0.0302
0.5	0.6065	3.6	0.0273
0.6	0.5488	3.7	0.0247
0.7	0.4966	3.8	0.0224
0.8	0.4493	3.9	0.0202
0.9	0.4066	4.0	0.0183
1.0	0.3679	4.1	0.0166
1.1	0.3329	4.2	0.0150
1.2	0.3012	4.3	0.0136
1.3	0.2725	4.4	0.0123
1.4	0.2466	4.5	0.0111
1.5	0.2231	4.6	0.0101
1.6	0.2019	4.7	0.0091
1.7	0.1827	4.8	0.0082
1.8	0.1653	4.9	0.0074
1.9	0.1496	5.0	0.0067
2.0	0.1353	5.1	0.0061
2.1	0.1225	5.2	0.0055
2.2	0.1108	5.3	0.0050
2.3	0.1003	5.4	0.0045
2.4	0.0907	5.5	0.0041
2.5	0.0821	5.6	0.0037
2.6	0.0743	5.7	0.0033
2.7	0.0672	5.8	0.0030
2.8	0.0608	5.9	0.0027
2.9	0.0550	6.0	0.0025
3.0	0.0498		

APPENDIX D. A SHORT TABLE OF DERIVATIVES

1. $\dfrac{d(c)}{dx} = 0$ (where c is a constant).

2. $\dfrac{d(x^n)}{dx} = nx^{n-1}$.

3. $\dfrac{d(cu)}{dx} = c\dfrac{du}{dx}$.

4. $\dfrac{d(u+v)}{dx} = \dfrac{du}{dx} + \dfrac{dv}{dx}$.

5. $\dfrac{d(uv)}{dx} = u\dfrac{dv}{dx} + v\dfrac{du}{dx}$.

6. $\dfrac{d(u^n)}{dx} = nu^{n-1}\dfrac{du}{dx}$.

7. $\dfrac{d\left(\dfrac{u}{v}\right)}{dx} = \dfrac{v\dfrac{du}{dx} - u\dfrac{dv}{dx}}{v^2}$.

8. $\dfrac{d(\ln x)}{dx} = \dfrac{1}{x}$.

9. $\dfrac{d(e^x)}{dx} = e^x$.

10. $\dfrac{d(\ln u)}{dx} = \dfrac{1}{u}\dfrac{du}{dx}$.

11. $\dfrac{d(e^u)}{dx} = e^u\dfrac{du}{dx}$.